grasping for the wind

wind

the search for meaning in the 20th century

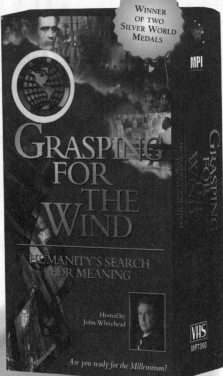

grasping for the wind

wind

the search for meaning in the 20th century

john w. whitehead

ZondervanPublishingHouse
Grand Rapids, Michigan

A Division of HarperCollinsPublishers

Grasping for the Wind
Copyright © 2001 by Glass Onion Productions, Inc.™

Requests for information should be addressed to:

☖ZondervanPublishingHouse
Grand Rapids, Michigan 49530

Library of Congress Cataloging-in-Publication Data

Whitehead, John W., 1946-
    Grasping for the wind : the search for meaning in the 20th century / John W. Whitehead.
       p. cm.
    Includes bibliographical references.
    ISBN 0-310-23274-0
    1. Civilization, Western—20th century. 2. Civilization, Modern—20th century 3. Twenty-first century—Forecasts. Philosophy, Modern. 5. Christianity and culture. I. Title.
CB245.W515 2001
909.82—dc21

                                           00-051292
                                             CIP

Interior design by Laura Blost
Composition by Todd Sprague and Rob Monacelli
Graphic Design by Curt Diepenhorst
Edited by Robert Hudson
Assistant Editors: Angela Scheff and Hannah Mylander

Printed in the United States of America

01 02 03 04 05 06 07 /❖ DC/ 10 9 8 7 6 5 4 3 2 1

TABLE OF CONTENTS

List of Illustrations 7

Credits 9

Introduction 11

1. Breaking with the Past 15

2. Where Are We Going? 47

3. Children of the Machine 73

4. The Lost Generation 113

5. The Fat Dream 149

6. The Winds of Revolution 185

7. The Narcissistic Culture 227

Afterword: Into the New Millennium 273

Bibliography 277

Notes 303

Index 312

LIST OF ILLUSTRATIONS IN THE TEXT

1. François Voltaire 17
2. Jean-Jacques Rousseau 20
3. Ludwig van Beethoven 25
4. Lord Byron 27
5. William Blake 30
6. William Blake, *The Body of Abel Found by Adam and Eve (c. 1826–27)* 31
7. Oscar Wilde 33
8. Francisco Goya, *Sueño 1 (First Dream)* 35
9. French poet Arthur Rimbaud 43
10. Charles Darwin 48
11. Karl Marx 51
12. Arthur Schopenhauer 60
13. Richard Wagner 60
14. Friedrich Nietzsche 64
15. Jim Morrison 67
16. A scene from *Blade Runner* 70
17. An advertising poster of the 1889 Paris World Exposition 74
18. The Eiffel Tower 75
19. Kurt Schwitters, *The Cathedral of Erotic Misery* 90
20. A scene from *The Cabinet of Dr. Caligari* 94
21. Scenes from F. W. Murnau's *Nosferatu* and Tim Burton's *Batman Returns* 96
22. Sigmund Freud 98
23. A scene from Buñuel's *Un Chien Andalou* 106
24. A scene from Hitchcock's *Vertigo* 108
25. T. S. Eliot 110
26. Albert Einstein 118
27. Margaret Sanger 119
28. Jazz innovator Louis Armstrong 123
29. Pablo Picasso, *Guernica* 132
30. The Pan Am Building, New York City 136
31. Orson Welles in *Citizen Kane* 142
32. Jean-Paul Sartre 150
33. *Dr. Strangelove* (played by Peter Sellers) 153
34. A scene from *Invasion of the Body Snatchers* 156
35. Allen Ginsberg 160
36. Jack Kerouac 163
37. Dr. Martin Luther King Jr. at the Lincoln Memorial in Washington, D.C. 179
38. Tom Hayden 186
39. Chicago street fighting during the 1968 Democratic Convention 193
40. Warren Beatty and Faye Dunaway in *Bonnie and Clyde* 203
41. John Cage 209
42. Jerry Garcia and Phil Lesh of the Grateful Dead 220
43. The Rolling Stones 222

44. John Lennon and Yoko Ono   223
45. A scene from *The Big Chill*   228
46. Joseph Beuys, *Coyote: I Like America and America Likes Me*   230
47. A scene from *A Clockwork Orange*   240
48. Frank Zappa and the Mothers of Invention   243
49. The Sex Pistols   244
50. Nirvana band leader Kurt Cobain   246
51. Madonna on MTV   250
52. Robert Crumb   253

LIST OF COLOR ILLUSTRATIONS

1. Rembrandt van Rijn, *The Adoration of the Shepherds*
2. Morton Schamberg, *God*
3. Francis Bacon, *Three Studies for Figures at the Base of a Crucifixion*
4. Jacques-Louis David, *The Oath of the Horatii*
5. Francisco de Goya y Lucientes, *The Third of May, 1808, at Madrid*
6. Francisco de Goya y Lucientes, *A Tribunal of the Inquisition*
7. Gustave Courbet, *A Burial at Ornans*
8. Georges Seurat, *A Sunday Afternoon on the Island of La Grande Jatte*
9. Paul Gauguin, *Where Do We Come From? What Are We? Where Are We Going?*
10. Pablo Picasso, *Les Demoiselles d'Avignon*
11. Jacob Epstein, *Torso in Metal from "The Rock Drill"*
12. Marcel Duchamp, *The Bride Stripped Bare by Her Bachelors, Even (The Large Glass)*
13. Giorgio de Chirico, *The Nostalgia of the Infinite*
14. Hans Bellmer, *The Doll*
15. Chuck Berry
16. Edward Hopper, *Nighthawks*
17. Mark Rothko, *The Rothko Chapel North Wall Paintings*
18. James Dean
19. Willem de Kooning, *Woman and Bicycle*
20. John F. Kennedy and Jackie Kennedy in Dallas motorcade
21. Bob Dylan and Bruce Springsteen
22. A scene from *Apocalypse Now*
23. Robert Rauschenberg, *Bed*
24. Andy Warhol, *Two Hundred Campbell's Soup Cans*
25. Edward Kienholz, *The Future as an Afterthought*
26. The Beatles
27, The original Woodstock Festival
28. Jeff Koons, *Saint John the Baptist*
29. Judy Chicago, *The Dinner Party*
30. Philip Guston, *The Street*
31. A scene from *Fight Club*
32. A scene from *The Last Temptation of Christ*

Credits

The author and publisher of *Grasping for the Wind* would like to thank these people and organizations for their kind permission in allowing us to use the following graphic images from among their holdings. It is with much gratitude that we acknowledge:

Stephen Aiken

Coyote: I Like America and America Likes Me by Joseph Beuys (photo © 1989 Stephen Aiken)

AP/Wide World Photos

Chicago Street Fighting, 1968 Democratic Convention (© AP/Wide World Photos); Bob Dylan (© AP/Wide World Photos); Frank Zappa and the Mothers of Invention (© AP/Wide World Photos); Nirvana—Kurt Cobain (© AP/Wide World Photos)

Archives/Shooting Star

Dr. Strangelove, played by Peter Sellers (© S.S. Archives/Shooting Star)

The Art Institute of Chicago

A Sunday Afternoon on the Island of La Grande Jatte by Georges Seurat (Helen Birch Bartlett Memorial Collection, 1926.224. Photograph © 1999, The Art Institute of Chicago. All Rights Reserved); *Nighthawks* by Edward Hopper (Friends of American Art Collection, 1942.51. Photograph © 1999, The Art Institute of Chicago. All Rights Reserved)

Art Resource, N.Y.

Adoration of the Shepherds by Rembrandt van Rijn (Giraudon/Art Resource, N.Y.); *Burial at Ornans, 1849–50* by Gustave Courbet (Giraudon/Art Resource, N.Y.); *The Third of May* by Francisco de Goya y Lucientes (Erich Lessing/Art Resource, N.Y.); *The Oath of the Horatii* by Jacques-Louis David (Erich Lessing/Art Resource, N.Y.); *Sueño 1 (First Dream)* by Francisco de Goya y Lucientes; *The Tribunal of the Inquisition* by Francisco de Goya y Lucientes (Scala/Art Resource, N.Y.); *God* by Morton Schamberg (Philadelphia Museum of Art: The Louise and Walter Arensberg Collection); *Three Studies for Figures at the Base of a Crucifixion,* c. 1944 by Francis Bacon (Tate Gallery, London/Art Resource, N.Y. © 2000 Estate of Francis Bacon/Artists Rights Society [ARS], N.Y.); *The Rock Drill* by Jacob Epstein (Tate Gallery, London/Art Resource, N.Y.)

Artists Rights Society (ARS), N.Y.

Les Demoiselles d'Avignon by Pablo Picasso (acquired through the Lillie P. Bliss Bequest. Photograph © 2000 The Museum of Modern Art, N.Y. © 2000 Estate of Pablo Picasso/Artists Rights Society [ARS], N.Y.); *The Bride Stripped Bare by Her Bachelors, Even (The Large Glass)* by Marcel Duchamp (Philadelphia Museum of Art: Bequest of Katherine S. Dreier. © 2000 Artists Rights Society (ARS), N.Y./ADAGP, Paris / Estate of Marcel Duchamp); *The Nostalgia of the Infinite* by Giorgio de Chirico (© 2000 Artists Rights Society [ARS], N.Y. / SIAE, Rome); *The Doll (1936)* by Hans Bellmer (© 2000 Artists Rights Society [ARS], N.Y. / ADAGP, Paris); *Guernica* by Pablo Picasso (Giraudon/Art Resource, N.Y. © 2000 Estate of Pablo Picasso/Artists Rights Society [ARS], N.Y.); *The Rothko Chapel North Wall Paintings* by Mark Rothko (photo by Hickey-Robertson); *Woman and Bicycle* by Willem de Kooning (© 2000 Willem de Kooning Revocable Trust/Artists Rights

INTRODUCTION

Clearly, disciplines do not operate in vacuums. Rather, they intertwine and interact. Music, art, film, politics, literature, and other artifacts of human culture affect one another and the people who create them. These truths became increasingly obvious to me as I was working on *Grasping for the Wind* and the video series which was adapted from it—work that has been ongoing since the mid-1980s.

Many important individuals and movements could not be adequately covered in the video series due to lack of time, and many could not be discussed at all. Thus the book is more complete and detailed, although even this book is condensed from a manuscript that was nearly thrice again as long.

Grasping for the Wind is not intended to be a scholarly text, nor is it exhaustive on the subjects discussed. Instead it is, in many instances, an interpretive view of various people and events, intended for the reader who wishes to better understand modern Western culture in the past century. My hope is that the book, as well as the video series, will serve as an introduction to many subjects about which the reader is unfamiliar.

No person is an island. The Japanese phrase *naijo no ko* ("success from inside help") is particularly relevant to this project. My first and foremost gratitude is to my wife, Carol, who performed many duties on the book and video series. The following individuals helped in both the video and book process, and to them I offer a sincere thank you: Alexis Crow, Nisha Mohammed, and Jill Smith. I am also grateful to the following researchers, who played various roles in the final published book: Jayson Whitehead, David Reynaud, Bobby Maddox, Johan Conrod, and Jonathan Whitehead. Finally, I am appreciative of Robert Hudson, my editor, for his assistance in putting the final touches on the book. Without these people, this book would not have been possible.

John W. Whitehead
Spring 2001

I have seen all the works that are done under the sun; and indeed, all is vanity and grasping for the wind.

Ecclesiastes 1:14 NKJV

Still from the video series *Grasping for the Wind*. John Whitehead discusses four icons of the Enlightenment: Descartes, Voltaire, Rousseau, and Kant.

CHAPTER 1
Breaking with the Past

Life imitates Art far more than Art imitates Life.

OSCAR WILDE[1]

We live in a time of great fragmentation, a time of rapid change, protest, revolution, terrorism, governmental instability, inhumanity, and tribalization. Aware that something troubling is happening around us and to us, we sense that our foundations are continuously moving and appear to be crumbling. Yet we are often unsure why. The only thing that is certain is that the changes are dramatic—even cataclysmic.

Increasingly, modern life is characterized by a dehumanized view of people and a bewildering acceptance of conflict and persecution around the world. The carnage caused by wars in the twentieth century and the continuing oppression of people worldwide are clear examples of this dehumanization. Furthermore, extreme cruelty, such as that faced by Jews in the 1930s and '40s, became the hallmark of the twentieth century. For many, modern society has been reduced to a struggle for survival and an attempt to overpower the forces of nature and other human beings. Despite this, even as we begin a new decade, century, and millennium, people still yearn for a sense of worth, dignity, and meaning.

What is it that gives us this sense of worth? Throughout the twentieth century, it was widely believed that men, women, and children possessed an inherent value that could not be taken away or destroyed by other human beings or governments. An individual's right to that sense of worth and dignity was virtually unquestioned. Today, however, increasing numbers of people despair of discovering meaning in their lives.

Where do we come from? Who are we? Where are we going? And how did we get here—to this point where meaning and the very essence of what it is to be human are questioned? We will explore these issues as we look at Western humanity's search for meaning during the past few centuries, especially the last one hundred years.

STARTING WITH SIGHT

In this modern age of mass communication, we are constantly inundated with information: magazines, newspapers, books, television, movies, cyberspace, and so on. A single *New York Times* contains the same amount of information as a bound volume from an earlier century. For example, people of the fifteenth, sixteenth, or seventeenth century did not have such a vast array of media, and only a few (mostly the upper class) could both read books and afford to own them. Public discourse, therefore, was the primary mode of exchanging information, and people communicated largely through the spoken word.

But another important form of communication should not be ignored: the visual image. To ask "Where do we come from?" and "What is our future?" we need to begin with a look at these ideas, as depicted in the visual arts.

SHEPHERD, GOD, AND CRUCIFIXION

Three works of art succinctly symbolize humanity's search for meaning since the seventeenth century.

The first, Dutch painter Rembrandt van Rijn's (1606–69) *Adoration of the Shepherds* (1646), is a painting that depicts the biblical story of Jesus Christ's birth in a concrete, historical way. (See color plate 1.) Christ, while divine, is presented as an actual person who existed in a clear historical context. Rembrandt painted for a society that shared his Judeo-Christian view of the world, and as a result his audience would have understood and agreed with the painting's message.

The second work is Morton Schamberg's (1881–1918) sculpture *God*, created in 1917, during the First World War. (See color plate 2.) Represented by a twisted, disconnected piece of plumber's pipe, Schamberg's "god" is removed from and unrelated to humanity, and the God Rembrandt's society worshiped is replaced by an impersonal "concept" with little influence over people's lives.

The third artwork, painted by Francis Bacon (1902–92) in 1944 during World War II, is entitled *Three Studies for Figures at the Base of a Crucifixion*. (See color plate 3.) In this triptych of anguished figures, Bacon portrays the final deconstruction of God and the complete dehumanization and isolation of humankind. Bacon's *Crucifixion* evokes a world without hope, where people are destined only to be carcasses.

So how did Western society move from Rembrandt's reverent portrayal of God to Bacon's hopeless cry? This dramatic change began to occur during the critical transition period known as the Age of Reason or the Enlightenment.

THE ENLIGHTENMENT

The first principles of the Enlightenment were developed in France and England by such philosophers as François Voltaire, René Descartes, Thomas Hobbes, John Locke, David Hume, and Jean-Jacques Rousseau, among others. Descartes' famous

1. FRANÇOIS VOLTAIRE, as pictured in a carved medallion. Two catastrophes threw Voltaire into the public arena: his imprisonment in the Bastille (and subsequent two and a half years of exile in England) and his failure as a courtier—first at Versailles and then at the court of Frederick the Great. While in England, Voltaire was influenced by the English "Bloodless Revolution" of 1688, when sweeping reforms limited the power of the English monarchy and made Parliament coequal with the Crown. Voltaire returned to France with a new determination toward free thought for his country. Although the leading playwright in Europe and a popular personality, Voltaire was unsuccessful in currying the favor of the ruling class. Forced to flee the Prussian court and unwelcome in France, Voltaire finally settled in Switzerland, from which he inundated Europe with political pamphlets, novels, poems, and letters. Voltaire encouraged Europeans to emulate England's peaceful revolution.

phrase "I think, therefore I am" sums up Enlightenment philosophy, according to which people must rely only on their own reason to understand life and the natural order—and everything must be judged by asking what is humanly *reasonable*.

According to Enlightenment philosophy, as people learn to apply their reason to more and more situations, they need the Creator's written revelation less and less. God might be useful in one's personal life, but for science, politics, and government, human reason alone will suffice. Enlightenment philosophy, as it was interpreted by successive generations, eventually eliminated the need for supernatural beings and divine commands while at the same time implicitly eliminating clear distinctions between humans and other living organisms. Albeit unknowingly, Enlightenment philosophers took the first significant steps toward the dehumanization of people.

VOLTAIRE

French philosopher François Voltaire (1694–1778) is often called the father of the Enlightenment. Until age fifty-six, he believed that God was a conscious intelligence who designed and ruled the world, but when the Catholic Church censored some of his work for heresy, his views changed dramatically. A few years later, when the Catholic hierarchy deemed a horrendous earthquake in 1755 to be God's judgment on the French people, Voltaire became more radical.

Finally, Voltaire's anti-Catholicism reached its inevitable extreme as a result of the torture and execution of Huguenot Jean Calas in 1762, an event that incited Voltaire to a vehement public attack on Christianity. Calas, falsely convicted of having killed his son to prevent him from converting to Catholicism, was tortured by the Catholic authorities in the hopes that he would confess. He was subjected to what was called the *question ordinaire:* his arms and legs were stretched until they were pulled from their sockets. When he did not confess to murdering his son (who had actually committed suicide), Calas faced the *question extraordinaire:* fifteen pints of water poured down his throat. When he continued to protest his innocence, fifteen more pints were forced into him, swelling his body to twice its normal size. An executioner then broke each of his limbs in two places and finally strangled him to death. Calas' corpse was burned at the stake.

Voltaire believed passionately in the need to reform society and the church, but when he found it impossible to influence both the monarchs and the Catholic leaders, he turned instead to the common people, becoming the leading defender of human rights and social reform, and flooding Europe with his incisive political pamphlets, novels, poems, and letters. He sharply criticized the Bible and organized religion, which he believed were used to propagate superstition and crush dissent. He questioned how anyone could believe in the Bible, which revealed an Old Testament God he saw as boastful, jealous, angry, cruel, and homicidal.

Although it now seems easy to criticize Voltaire's passionate embrace of the rule of reason, we must remember that his society imposed arrest and torture upon its citizens simply for expressing opinions that stood in opposition to the prevailing views on religious, social, or political issues.

HOBBES

While early Enlightenment thinkers like Voltaire began the dismantling of the supernatural basis for society, that society still needed an organizing principle. Consequently, theories such as the "social contract," developed a hundred years earlier by British philosopher Thomas Hobbes (1588–1679), began to gain popular currency in the eighteenth century. Under the social contract, individual members of a society relinquish some of their liberties in exchange for the protection and benefits of the group. This social contract was a crucial development in humanity's search for meaning because, according to its tenets, good and evil were no longer considered in absolute terms; right and wrong were now determined simply by the collective decision of the group.

ROUSSEAU

Another important Enlightenment thinker was Jean-Jacques Rousseau (1712–78), a French-speaking Swiss from Geneva and a contemporary of Voltaire. Rousseau argued that the Enlightenment's emphasis on reason and science had caused people to lose more freedom than they had gained. He believed people should have absolute freedom—freedom not only from culture but from authority of any kind. For Rousseau, then, the individual became the center of the universe.

Rousseau rejected the Judeo-Christian concept of original sin and argued that humans are born innocent and pure and remain so until society corrupts them. Therefore, he argued, those societies that lived closest to nature, that is, aboriginal peoples around the world, were in fact more civilized than the so-called civilized people. This concept of the "noble savage" had a great impact in its time and still does today.

Even Rousseau, however, had to devise a way for his noble savages to organize their societies. He hypothesized that social order could only be maintained and

2. JEAN-JACQUES ROUSSEAU. Rousseau believed that what he called "sentiments of sociability" could be promulgated and enforced by the government. Rousseau proposes that the state establish a "purely civil profession of faith ... not exactly religious dogmas, but ... social sentiments without which a man cannot be a good citizen or faithful subject." He further writes: "While it can compel no one to believe them, it can banish from the State whoever does not believe them—it can banish him, not for impiety, but as an anti-social being, incapable of truly loving the laws and justice, and of sacrificing, at need, his life to his duty. If anyone, after publicly recognizing these dogmas, behaves as if he does not believe them, let him be punished by death: he has committed the worst of all crimes, that of lying before the law."

In apparent contradiction of this, Rousseau also asserts that religious toleration is necessary for the state to function properly, contending that "tolerance should be given to all religions that tolerate others, so long as their dogmas contain nothing contrary to the duties of citizenship."

individual freedom preserved through what he called the "general will." Obedience to the general will was supposed to become instinctive through a process of cultural engineering and indoctrination. "Sentiments of sociability," as he called them, would be compulsory, with the government promulgating and enforcing them. This way, there would be no social, political, economic, or moral inequality among people. Thus Rousseau took the "social contract" a step further: the contract was no longer voluntary—no one would be allowed to "opt out."

THE FRENCH REVOLUTION

The theories of Voltaire and Rousseau, though seemingly abstract and largely benign, would prove to have tragic consequences during the French Revolution and the Reign of Terror, times when the "general will" came to mean not only the loss of individual freedoms but also the reign of the guillotine.

THE ART OF DAVID AND REVOLUTIONARY FERVOR

The French government, both the monarchy and later the revolutionaries, used artists to promulgate their views and reform ideas. One such artist was the revolutionary painter Jacques-Louis David (1748–1825), who used his works to undermine faith in the established government. David's 1784 painting *Oath of the Horatii* illustrates the moral earnestness and stoicism that preceded the French Revolution. (See color plate 4.) King Louis XVI (1754–93) actually commissioned the painting, but what David painted was soon viewed more as a piece of reform, if not outright antimonarchal propaganda.

When the *Horatii* was first exhibited in 1785 in David's studio in Rome's Piazza del Popoto, enthusiastic viewers strewed a carpet of flowers in front of the painting. The *Horatii* was next shown in Paris where, in spite of growing official opposition, it again enjoyed wide praise from the public. The painting represents a heroic episode from early Roman history in which the three Horatii brothers had sworn to die, if necessary, for their nation by fighting three brothers from the rival city of Alba. The Horatii women witness the oath and then collapse in their secret knowledge that one of them is betrothed to a member of the enemy camp.

The *Horatii* made such an impact because many in the general public saw the French hierarchy, both secular and religious, as lacking any true moral strength or authority. It was a time of great political and social upheaval in France, and the *Horatii*, by presenting the three Horatii brothers as having great moral strength, subtly undermined the French hierarchy. Moreover, David painted in a day when the average schoolboy was generally familiar with classic subjects. Thus the intent of his message was generally understood.

The painting's attack on members of the French establishment and its Catholic support electrified Paris just as would the political and social upheaval following the storming of the Bastille four years later. The painting established David as one of the leaders of French national life, and his works were thereafter treated as political manifestoes. The public read them as tracts for the times—comments on the failure of the civil will and on the refusal of the king and his ministers to subordinate their well-being to the common good.

Yet David's *Horatii* attacked more than the French establishment and its morality. By arranging his figures in the style of a classical frieze, David helped initiate a compositional trend that would become a key feature of modernist painting: the abandonment of the illusionism that Renaissance painters had invented to deal with the three-dimensional world. Not only did David compromise the grand unity of vision of Raphael and other Renaissance painters, he also broke with the past by dramatizing an event for political import instead of its moral conflict. Soon the search for moral truth would no longer be the central element of Western art, as it had been in the Renaissance.

Five years after *Horatii,* the first phase of the French Revolution was at its height. In *The Oath of the Tennis Court,* David depicted the French National Assembly swearing to establish a constitution based on a humanistic theory of human rights. In 1789, the Assembly issued its Declaration of the Rights of Man, proclaiming that the sovereignty of the nation—or the general will of the people—was now supreme. Although Rousseau had died a decade before the Revolution, his theories were immortalized in the Declaration.

David's finest hour came in 1793 when Revolutionary authorities commissioned him to paint commemorative pictures of two revolutionaries assassinated at the Assembly Halls. One of these revolutionaries is depicted in *The Death of Marat,* a fine piece of propaganda. Instead of showing the assassinated revolutionary writer and leader Jean-Paul Marat (1743–93) as he really was—putrefied with sores, soaking in a bathtub of medicine, and stabbed to death—David depicted him with noble simplicity and silent grandeur. Against the gray-green walls of a room, white sheets establish a funereal note and provide a subtle transition between the body subsiding in death and the simple geometry of an inkpot, wooden block, and papers, meant to symbolize Marat's dedication to the welfare of the people.

THE RESULTS OF REVOLUTION

As David and others fed the flames, revolutionary fever swept through the French National Assembly and culminated in the Feast of Reason in Paris. Congregating in what had been the Cathedral of Notre Dame, dignitaries of the Assembly, dressed in medals and plumes, cheered as the symbolic Goddess of Reason sat grandly on the high altar. In their rebellion against the centralization of authority in the government and Catholic Church, the revolutionaries had managed, both literally and figuratively, to elevate individualism to a religious concept.

The French revolutionaries made their position unmistakably clear by even altering the calendar so that 1792 became "year one," symbolically destroying the Judeo-Christian past and its traditional chronology. In various parts of the country, revolutionary tribunals forbade, under pain of death, the practice of any form of the Jewish or Christian religions. One government official, growing impatient with the guillotine—because it could only kill one person at a time—loaded some barges with priests and had them towed to the middle of the Loire River and then scuttled. The priests sank with what were described as "satisfying gurgles."

The two years that the French National Assembly devoted to drafting the new constitution were therefore wasted. By the time the Revolution was fully underway, violence was the only law of the land. Before the trauma ended, the revolutionary government and its agents had killed forty thousand people, including many peasants and even one of its own most fervent revolutionary leaders, François-Maximilien-Joseph de Robespierre (1758–94). As one historian records some of the nightmare: "Watchers told of women and men alike falling on the bodies of those executed and hacking off their heads, separating torsos, waving genitals aloft, and pinning limbs to their pikes." An observer wrote, "A woman appeared, white as a sheet . . . a killer grabbed her, tore off her dress, and slit her belly open." One man, who joined in a dismemberment with a crowd and carried a woman's head into a wine shop and placed it on the counter while drinks were ordered, was accused of roasting and eating her heart before the others and of carrying her genitals around on his sword.[2] The French Revolution marked a crucial turning point in the history of dissent in general and religious dissent in particular. Resistance through force and overt violence, the hallmark of this bloody era of upheaval, would eventually become the most common form of mass protest against government. In addition, the French had developed a new understanding of human rights that, with lasting consequences, replaced the worth and dignity of human beings with faith in reason and the collective will.

ROMANTICISM

Many of the ideas that took root during the French Revolution did not die at the end of the reign of terror; rather they blossomed a few years later into another important movement: Romanticism. The Romantics saw intuition rather than reason as the way to truth and thus are often placed in contrast to the thinkers of the Enlightenment. Despite this important difference between the two eras, however, there was much continuity of thought between the two movements. In fact, the Romantic movement, which lasted from approximately 1774 to 1859, carried over Enlightenment ideas about traditional religion and people that had given impetus to the fervor of the French Revolution. Like the Enlightenment thinkers, Romantic poets and philosophers, taking their cue from Rousseau, believed that people are born pure and good and remain so until society corrupts them. They rejected the Judeo-Christian view of nature that had once prevailed, that of the natural world as spoiled by the Fall. For them, nature became instead a symbol of innocence, a contrast to the corruption of society. The Romantics' ideal of the noble savage, an offshoot of their Enlightenment predecessors, celebrated the person who denounced the poisonous influence of both the Industrial Revolution and the rising middle class, one who remained untainted by materialism.

Three defining figures of the Romantic era are the philosopher Immanuel Kant, the composer Ludwig van Beethoven, and the writer George Gordon, better known as Lord Byron.

KANT

The German philosopher Immanuel Kant (1724–1804) is an appropriate figure with whom to begin a discussion of Romanticism, for he exhibits well the continuity between the schools of Enlightenment and Romantic thought. Kant began with Enlightenment ideas but took them one step further; while Voltaire had seriously questioned traditional religion, Kant believed that nature itself was nothing more than a biological machine and that God was, at most, simply a cosmic plumber responsible for keeping the system in order, a being beyond the ken of science or philosophy. For Kant, therefore, there were no overriding moral laws beyond human beings themselves, and the only realities were experience and reason. Tellingly, although Kant held a uni-

3. LUDWIG VAN BEETHOVEN, captured in all his furious Romanticism in an oil painting by Josef Carl Stieler (1819–20). Beethoven also shared the Romantics' idealization of the common people and faith in the brotherhood of man. In addition to his aversion toward the middle class and his strong individualism, Beethoven held the Romantics' love of nature, which is reflected in his *Pastorale Symphony* (1807–8). Liberty, equality, brotherhood: the watchwords of the French Revolution were also Beethoven's. For him, all men were brothers under God. The great musician particularly disliked all class-related pretensions. Goethe recounted Beethoven's reaction to a group of aristocrats on horseback who approached them on a country road. While Goethe moved to the side of the road and respectfully greeted them, Beethoven refused, passing through the middle of them, barely acknowledging the aristocrats' existence.

versity teaching position, he lived in a small apartment with only a single decoration: a silhouette portrait of Jean-Jacques Rousseau.

BEETHOVEN

Ludwig van Beethoven (1770–1827), intriguingly portrayed in the 1995 film *Immortal Beloved,* claimed to be not merely a composer but also a philosopher and poet, seeing his art (as the Romantics tended to do) as far more than entertainment. Beethoven even invoked supernatural language to express his role, writing,

> When I open my eyes I must sigh, for what I see is contrary to my religion, and I must despise the world which does not know that music is a higher revelation than wisdom and philosophy, the wine which inspires one to new generative processes. . . . Music is the one incorporeal entrance into the higher world of knowledge.[3]

26

Beethoven's Ninth Symphony (and last), completed in 1824, best reflects one of his most salient romantic characteristics: his deep reverence for the common people. In the symphony's famous finale, Beethoven borrows themes from the three preceding movements and then begins the stirring "Ode to Joy," based on a poem by Romantic poet Johann Schiller (1758–1805). Its rousing theme, beginning with the cellos and basses, is gradually taken up by the entire orchestra, building until the progress is interrupted by "the loudest dissonance."

Next a chorus sings, "O friends, let us not have this kind of sound but rather let us strike up more pleasant, more joyful music." The chorus then cries out, "Follow your path with joy, Brothers, like a hero marching to victory," and the text climaxes with a triumphant concluding stanza: "Be embraced, ye millions! This kiss to the whole world! Brothers, above the starry canopy [a] loving Father must dwell." Beethoven's lyrics thus imply that the generous sentiments of ordinary people offer the best hope for humankind.

Because Beethoven concluded his Ninth Symphony with a solo vocal and the choral setting of Schiller's "Ode to Joy," he revolutionized the conception of symphonic music, which was before then conceived of as strictly an instrumental form. Because he was willing to defy established boundaries, some music historians have said that no composer in history has exercised greater influence on Western music than Ludwig van Beethoven. As historian Gerald Abraham writes, "The choral finale of the Ninth smashes the old instrumental conception of symphony to smithereens. After that anything could be done."[4]

BYRON

Throughout much of the nineteenth century, Lord George Gordon Byron (1788–1824) was viewed as one of the greatest English poets and the prototype of literary Romanticism. His reputation in Europe was based not only on his poetry but also on his lifestyle, for in both he defined the Romantic hero.

"I want a hero," Byron wrote in his epic poem *Don Juan* (1819–24), in which, in its two thousand stanzas, he critiques Western culture through the comic misadventures of the legendary amorist Don Juan. Even some of Byron's most trusted literary advisers called the poem disgracefully immoral, primarily because it made a mockery of religion, was full of "indecent allusions," and (as other critics complained) "recommended" the crime of adultery and incited the passions of young minds.

4. LORD BYRON. While his great English contemporaries were admired only by small coteries in England and America, Byron achieved an immense European reputation during his lifetime. Through much of the nineteenth century, he continued to be rated as one of the greatest English poets and "the very prototype of literary Romanticism."

Byron's style and subject matter, however, were in part the result of an unstable and often traumatic childhood. Raised by an erratic, moody, and sternly Calvinistic mother who alternately spoiled and scolded him, Byron was also subjected to the unloving attentions of a nurse who may have sexually abused and beaten him. Although born with a club foot, Byron constantly strove to compensate for his deformity by excelling in athletics, including boxing, fencing, horseback riding, cricket, and swimming.

Famously handsome, Byron was also sexually precocious. He fell in love with his cousin at the age of seven and later developed an incestuous relationship with his half-sister, Augusta Leigh, who reportedly gave birth to a daughter presumed to be Byron's. Separated from his wife in 1814 after the birth of this child, ostracized and deeply embittered, Byron left England, never to return. Byron traveled to Italy, where in 1817 he commenced various love affairs, culminating in a period of frenzied debauchery that by Byron's own estimate involved more than two hundred women.

Despite this lifestyle, or perhaps because of it, Byron invented a kind of literary hero that his contemporaries could both sympathize with and admire. His "Byronic hero"—a saturnine, passionate, moody, and remorse-torn but unrepentant sinner who is outside all institutions and morals and relies on himself alone—became a common figure in his romances, dramas, and poetry and was soon imitated by others, both in fiction and in life.

In Byron's poem *Cain* (1821), a drama in verse based loosely on the Bible, the title character exemplifies the Byronic hero. Cain, the tragic, unrepentant sinner who kills his own brother, refuses to pray with the others, telling Adam:

> *The snake spoke truth: it was the tree of knowledge;*
> *It was the tree of life: knowledge is good,*
> *And life is good; and how can both be evil?*

Cain passionately continues to question God's dealings with men and finally champions Lucifer's opinion of God:

> *Indefinite, indissoluble tyrant;*
> *Could he but crush himself, 't were the best boon*
> *He ever granted: but let him reign on,*
> *And multiply himself in misery!*[5]

Thus Byron's Cain, though a tragic hero, is also the noblest of Adam's family because he questions God so boldly.

Byron not only wrote about Byronic heroes but, to some extent, lived the life of one. After the death of his friend Percy Bysshe Shelley (1792–1822), Byron devoted himself to the cause of Greek independence from the Turks. Having helped to kindle European enthusiasm for the Greek cause through his writings, Byron felt honor-bound to aid the Greek cause and in 1823 set out for Greece carrying weapons, medical supplies, and impressive red-and-gold uniforms with elaborate helmets. Byron died for his cause, contracting malaria at Missolonghi in 1824, just after his thirty-sixth birthday. Thereafter his death became the rallying point for the Greek revolution. The temporary Greek government issued a proclamation making the anniversary of Byron's death an official day of mourning, and even today the Greek people revere Byron as a national hero.

A Romantic to the end, Byron said of himself, "There are but two sentiments to which I am constant—a strong love of liberty, and a detestation of cant."[6] Although his love of striking a pose has caused some over the years to question his sincerity, Byron's influence on literature was pervasive. Even Byron himself jokingly asserted that the three most influential figures of his time were Beau Brummel (the "inventor" of long pants), Napoleon, and himself. English philosopher Bertrand Russell wrote in his *History of Western Philosophy* (1945) that "Byronism"—the attitude of "Titanic cosmic self-assertion"—established a worldview important to nineteenth century philosophy, and there is no doubt that Byron helped shape the intellectual and cultural history of all that followed him.

Byron's influence can be seen everywhere. The German writer John Wolfgang von Goethe (1749–1832) memorialized Byron in his two-part masterpiece *Faust* by patterning Euphorion, son of Faust and Helena, after him. Euphorion dies when his own wings will not keep him in flight. Later, Friedrich Nietzsche's concept of the Superman, the great hero who stands outside the jurisdiction of ordinary good and evil, owes a debt to Byron as well.

Still, while Byron's influence on the Romantic movement was far-reaching, the ideas of the Romantics, as we shall see, would not remain unaffected by other forces.

OUTGROWTHS OF ROMANTICISM: MYSTICISM AND BLAKE

In their preoccupation with nature, the Romantics eventually linked the natural world to humanity's spirituality and introduced mysticism as a spiritual option. The English Romantic writer William Blake (1757–1827) was one of the first poets to contrast the innate goodness of people with society's inherent evils. His well-known volumes of poems, *Songs of Innocence* (1789) and *Songs of Experience* (1794), deal largely with the beauty of childhood and the evils of poverty and child labor in England.

Blake's works, however, also exhibit the mystical side of Romanticism. In his tract *All Religions Are One* (c. 1788), Blake set forth certain "principles," including the idea that the "poetic genius" is the most powerful force in the universe and that angels, spirits, and demons are all simply forms of this genius. In other words, he used fictional characters, in much the way Byron used biblical characters in *Cain,* to represent psychological or spiritual forces.

Blake's mystical tendencies were eventually accompanied by a revolutionary and political interpretation of Judeo-Christian theology. Although Blake was deeply religious,

30

5. WILLIAM BLAKE, as painted by portraitist Thomas Phillips. According to Blake, all writers could potentially produce inspired works—a theory highly attractive to any artist. Blake believed that an artist disqualified himself from creating inspired material only when he embraced the philosophies of reason and failed to seek truth introspectively—a concept prevalent throughout modern artistic endeavors.

he was convinced that organized Christian religion was a limitation people imposed on themselves. Among his many so-called prophetic poems, *The French Revolution* (1791), *America* (1793), and *Visions of the Daughters of Albion* (1793) show Blake's view of the American and French Revolutions as attempts to overthrow not only the repression of absolutism and sexual inhibition but also that of institutionalized religion. Blake rejected traditional religion and created his own mythology, in which man was a part of God until he separated himself from God.

In his long and perhaps most profound prophetic epic, *Jerusalem* (1804), Blake wrote about Judaism, Deism, and Christianity, expressing the belief that religion imprisons both nature and human beings with its laws. Blake, however, carefully excluded Jesus Christ as an imprisoning element of religion, though Blake presented Christ as standing in opposition to traditional faith in his poem *The Everlasting Gospel* (c. 1818).

The Marriage of Heaven and Hell, written in 1793, directly challenges popular views of good and evil. In this poem, Blake characterizes God as the truth that flows through all life, and in a passage in *Marriage,* Blake presents himself as the spiritual equal of the Old Testament prophets. Blake believed that God speaks to everyone but that most refuse to listen. He also believed that no one has an excuse for failing to transcend the physical and experience the spiritual and that all writers can potentially produce divinely inspired works—a theory that is still highly attractive to modern artists, including such writers as Irish poet William Butler Yeats and American Beat poet Allen Ginsberg.

6. WILLIAM BLAKE, *The Body of Abel Found by Adam and Eve (c. 1826–27).* Cain, who was about to bury the body of Abel, flees from the faces of his parents. Blake, a gifted artist, anticipated art movements that did not develop until the early twentieth century. For example, this illustration is almost Expressionist in style.

Although best known as a poet, Blake was also a gifted artist and illustrated most of his own volumes in hand-printed editions. His illustrations, which are now widely recognized, served as visual metaphors for his mystical ideas and proved that Neoclassical forms could accommodate profoundly subjective, even idiosyncratic, feelings. Blake's art reflected the expressive, inventive nature of Michelangelo's elongations and figural distortions, such as that found in the Sistine Chapel, instead of the traditional study of antique sculpture. Blake's illustrations for *The Marriage of Heaven and Hell,* for example, unify the physical and spiritual and the good and evil, suggesting that "everything that lives is Holy."

Blake's spirituality and mysticism were perhaps his most profound contributions to his art. Believing that life is holy but that reason violates the natural instinct, Blake exemplified the Romantic desire to escape materialism and embrace spirituality. Although Blake passed his last years in obscurity without wealth or material comfort, he directly influenced both his and subsequent cultures. The Beat and Rock generations would be only two of the many modern movements to revere Blake.

OSCAR WILDE: "ART FOR ART'S SAKE"

The Romantic notion that the artist's only responsibility was to his art inevitably brought about the concept of art as a form of self-expression. The artist *was* his art. Oscar Wilde (1854–1900) took the Romantic conception of art into the twentieth century. In his 1891 essay "The Decay of Lying," Wilde outlined his four principles of "art for art's sake": (1) that art never expresses anything but itself; (2) that bad art comes from elevating life and nature to the status of ideals; and (3) that life imitates art far more than art imitates life. Wilde also argued (4) that lying—which he defined as the telling of beautiful untrue things—is the proper aim of art.

In 1892 Wilde published *The Picture of Dorian Gray,* in which he wrote, "There is only one thing in the world worse than being talked about, and that is not being talked about."[7] This novel ended that worry for Wilde. The book's depiction of a world where homosexuality was accepted, though not explicit, shocked critics.

Wilde's greatest play, *The Importance of Being Earnest,* opened on February 14, 1895. Four days later the Marquess of Queensberry, the father of a young man with whom Wilde spent much of his time, accused Wilde of homosexuality. Wilde's subsequent libel lawsuit resulted in the Marquess being found not guilty. Soon after, however, Wilde himself was found guilty of homosexuality and sentenced to two years in prison with hard labor. His time in prison forced Wilde to examine his life, and he wrote, "I was no longer captain of my soul, and did not know it. I allowed pleasure to dominate me. I ended in horrible disgrace. There is only one thing for me now, absolute humility."[8] After his release, Wilde settled in France under an assumed name and resumed his artistic and gay lifestyle.

Wilde's idea of living life as if it were one's art later deeply affected the artists of the mid-twentieth century. The Beat poets, student revolutionaries, and artists of the 1950s and 1960s took this concept to its ultimate conclusion.

7. OSCAR WILDE, photographed in Spain in June 1882, self-consciously posing, tongue-in-cheek, in the garb of an aesthete. Frivolity was Wilde's trademark. He lived his artistic ideals dressing and decorating extravagantly. Wilde was well-known for his artsy and artificial lifestyle long before he became a literary success. His love for striking a pose made him reminiscent of Lord Byron. He was, according to his son Vyvyan Holland, recognized as "an eccentric, a wit, and the great apostle of Aestheticism."

GOTHIC NOVELS: THE DARK SIDE OF HUMANITY

By emphasizing the primacy of the individual and nature, Romanticism identified both as basically good and as sources of redemption from evil. Still, since the early Romantics' theories had failed to fully explain humanity's apparent propensity toward evil, the later Romantics began to explore humanity's darker side.

Horace Walpole (1717–97), an esteemed member of the English Parliament, wrote the first highly successful Gothic novel, *The Castle of Otranto* (1764), which he initially published as a supposed translation of a sixteenth century Italian romance. In the preface, using the pseudonym William Marshall, the imaginary translator of the work, Walpole apologizes for the excess of dreams, visions, and miracles in the book, citing the ignorance of the times. The book, however, was an instant success; the public, largely urbanites starved for entertainment and excitement, welcomed the superstition and mystery of the medieval period, though in subsequent editions Walpole admitted the work to be his own. Readers eagerly read the new Gothic and horror novels as escapist literature and craved the transcendence and mystery they evoked, without the trappings of traditional religion.

Walpole's novel gave the Gothic genre the respectability it would enjoy for the rest of the century, and it inspired other authors to work in the Gothic genre. Walpole even turned his house, Strawberry Hill, into a Gothic castle and filled it with the medieval relics he collected.

Lord Byron especially was attracted to Gothic scenes of Walpole's work; that is, those that most suggested mystery, horror, and the dark side of human nature. Byron's *The Prisoner of Chillon* (1816) tells the story of a man wasting away in a dungeon, and his *Giaour* (1813) features a vampire.

The influence of the Gothic genre, moreover, is by no means dead today. Mary Wollstonecraft Shelley's famous novel *Frankenstein, or the Modern Prometheus* (1818), itself written in a deeply Gothic vein, demonstrates the evolution of the genre into a phenomenon that is still with us. Contemporary horror novels and movies draw heavily on Gothic works such as Shelley's and Walpole's, one example being director Kenneth Branagh's 1994 *Frankenstein* film, which is closely based on Shelley's novel. Starring Robert DeNiro, the film perpetuates the Romantic theme that man's interference with nature eventually brings down upon him a curse.

The phenomenal success of novelist Stephen King (b. 1947) demonstrates the public's current appetite for the bizarre. Slasher movies such as *Halloween* (1978), *The*

Texas Chainsaw Massacre (1974), the more serious *Silence of the Lambs* (1991), and the *Scream* films (1996, 1997, and 2000) incorporate elements of horror. They also draw on the older Romantic idea of the victim-hero, the figure who suffers pain and fright to vanquish the forces of oppression. Since the late 1970s, the victim-hero has often been a female. Actress Sigourney Weaver's triumph over the hideous and terrifying villain-creature in director Ridley Scott's *Alien,* released in 1979, is a poignant example of the rise of the female as protagonist in the horror genre.

GOYA: "THE SLEEP OF REASON PRODUCES MONSTERS"

The great painter Francisco Goya y Lucientes (1746–1828) shared many of the ideas and concerns of both the Enlightenment philosophers as well as the Romantics—especially the Romantics' beliefs in nature and mysticism. Although the

8. FRANCISCO GOYA, *Sueño 1 (First Dream).* This introductory illustration for *Los Caprichos* shows the artist asleep at a table, covered with idle drawing instruments. It served as a preliminary sketch to Goya's famous etching *The Sleep of Reason Produces Monsters* where, in front of the table, a tablet reads, "El sueno de la razon produce monstrous" ("The sleep of reason produces monsters"). Goya seems to suggest that reason, to whom the Cathedral of Notre Dame in Paris had been temporarily rededicated during the French Revolution, had been put to sleep, allowing monsters to arise from the inner darkness of the mind. Goya's menacing cat and the rising clouds of owls and bats glowing in light and dark are lineal descendants of the beasts of medieval art and the monsters of Hieronymus Bosch (c. 1450–1516).

early Romantics did not know of his works, Goya, like many of them, rebelled against artistic and intellectual straitjackets virtually all his life.

Goya's early works, such as *Adoration of the Name of God,* painted in 1772, presented a theistic view of the universe. His royal appointment in 1775, however, began a change that became even more acute when he contracted an illness, probably syphilis, that he believed he had brought on himself. Thereafter his work took on a decidedly bleak character.

Goya's *Los Caprichos,* a collection of prints completed in two sections from 1796 to 1798, is a starkly pessimistic piece. It satirizes daily life and depicts fantastic events enacted by monsters, witches, and malevolent nocturnal beasts from the demonic tradition of Spanish folklore. Goya's monsters possess a Gothic quality and illustrate the artist's belief in the dark side of human nature.

In 1814 Goya created the earliest explicit example of social protest art. At the beginning of 1808, factionalism and discord permeated Spanish society. Napoleon took advantage of the opportunity offered by a government in crisis. Of course, there was resistance by the Spanish, and the French soldiers put down the rebellion. In his masterpiece *The Third of May, 1808, at Madrid: The Shootings on Principe Pio Mountain,* Goya depicts the shooting of thousands of Spaniards by the French in response to a final weak resistance by several old-fashioned Spanish loyalists. (See color plate 5.) Goya depicts the French firing squad as a dehumanized, many-legged, faceless monster raising bayoneted guns to its helpless victims. The first group of victims has already been shattered by bullets and is streaming with blood, while the next victims are waving their arms wildly in the last seconds of life. A lantern illuminates the execution while a man, arms lifted in Christian symbolism, awaits crucifixion by gunfire. The victims in the third group hide the horror from their eyes with their hands. In the dimness of evening, the nearest houses and a church tower blend into the night sky.

Even in his final years, Goya seemed obsessed with the cruelty he witnessed. In his paintings of madhouses and the Catholic Church, Goya expressed his deep anger toward an authority that showed no pity for its subject-victims. Goya's *Procession of Flagellants* (1816), for example, depicts the Catholic Church's judges and priests in terrifying masks and grotesque headdresses. *A Tribunal of the Inquisition* (1816) shows a nightmare travesty of justice, with people condemned for opinions they may not even have known they held. (See color plate 6.)

1848: REVOLUTION REDUX

As the Romantic era drew to a close, it became clear that neither the Enlightenment concept of reason nor a Romantic view of humankind had filled the void once occupied by traditional religion. Only one hope, it seemed, remained for Europe—a final wave of revolutions. The Romantics themselves were clearly divided in their attitudes toward political revolutions. Such early Romantic English poets as William Wordsworth (1770–1850), Samuel Taylor Coleridge (1772–1834), and Robert Southey (1774–1843), although they initially supported the French Revolution and anti-state philosophies, later rejected the excesses of the French Revolution and accepted and even welcomed the English government. The second generation of Romantics, on the other hand, condemned the earlier Romantics' respect for the state. Both Byron and Shelley enthusiastically supported the idea of revolution. Shelley hoped revolution would create a perfect human society, while Byron simply hated all existing forms of government. John Keats (1795–1821) alone remained above the political turmoil of his day, refusing to engage his art in the social debate.

Despite the revolutionary sympathies of the Romantic artists, the common people from virtually all classes were inclined toward peace and conservatism, a result of the nightmare produced by the French Revolution of 1789. European leaders widely distrusted reformers, fearing radicalism and violent change. In fact, they resisted most social reforms and refused to accept the more radical attitudes of a growing number of intellectuals who were calling for change.

Finally, however, the forces of change won out, erupting first in France. French dissidents seeking more reforms ignited a new revolution in 1848. The French revolutionaries consisted of two main groups: republicans who desired moderate political reform, and socialists who demanded radical change and a proletariat empowerment. In 1847 the revolutionaries held meetings and circulated petitions regarding the country's economic depression and the rising cost of bread. Government officials in turn, increasingly fearing these agitators, banned a public meeting to be held on February 22, 1848. When the dissidents protested, the national guard joined the chorus, demanding reform. The protest was only a small riot until an unknown individual fired a shot on February 23. The government troops panicked and killed sixteen people, and suddenly the riot turned into a revolution. Inspired by the French dissidents, other European revolutionaries sought reform in 1849 in Prussia, Austria, and the Italian states. In Great Britain, the Chartist Movement advocated better social and industrial conditions for the working classes.

This new revolutionary fever, however, dissipated almost as swiftly as it had erupted. The agitators were generally young and politically naive. Their efforts were poorly organized, and few of the reforms for which they pushed had been well thought out. The agitators tended to be overly idealistic, believing they could cure social wrongs they did not wholly understand. In addition, their success was impeded by their conflicts among themselves and lack of unity.

Although the revolutionaries achieved no substantial or lasting victories, their effect on the decades that followed cannot be overstated. These were the first truly modern revolutions in the sense that they provided the urban working class with a dissenting voice and fomented change in virtually every area of life. The effect of their revolutions on art and literature was immense, in many cases bringing more realism and social awareness in its content. Before this final wave of mid-century revolutions, the Romantic, utopian dream of a better world excited the minds of reformers and visionaries and led to an extravagance in art and literature. After the monumental facelift given to Europe by the 1848 revolution, however, art, philosophy, and literature became less romantic and speculative and more realistic, pragmatic, and scientific. These middle years of the century formed a dividing line, a watershed, separating two recognizably different periods.

Perhaps the most lasting impact of the revolutions of 1848 was the gradual emergence and popularity of socialism and communism. The French, though initially unprepared for a republican democracy, socialism, or communism, eventually showed signs of sympathy for such political theories. This post-revolutionary period marked the dawn of socialism and the new struggle between worker and bourgeois. Ultimately, it foreshadowed the Russian Revolution of 1917, an event that has cast its shadow over the entire twentieth century.

COURBET'S REALISM

If the years before the French Revolution of 1848 were marked by Romanticism, the years following it were marked just as noticeably by Realism, a change that surfaced quickly in the art of painting. Just as the French revolutionaries had changed the nature of dissent and political thought, the French artist Gustave Courbet (1819–77) revolutionized painting.

Courbet was deeply affected by David's *Oath of the Horatii,* impressed by both its technical clarity and its direct moral message. And yet Courbet did not merely imitate David or the painting's classical subject matter but moved beyond him to something completely new. Before Courbet and his contemporaries, painters depicted historical events not for their own sake or for their special historical interest but as examples to illustrate human truths. For instance, an artist might paint Hercules as an allegory of the human soul or the mighty deeds of Alexander the Great as an illustration of the greatness of humanity. Biblical scenes were often chosen to teach spiritual concepts.

Courbet's canvases, by contrast, were an assault on the prevailing canons of taste. Instead of clinging to what he saw as dead tradition, Courbet wanted to paint only what he could see. Since he had never seen an angel, he would not paint one; since he was familiar with village life, he painted peasant girls at work and people coming from the market. Courbet's "Realism" was a radical departure from allegorical treatments of subjects and ultimately threatened the self-image of all of Western culture. Sarah Faunce, an art historian, has written that Courbet's work "had the effect of cutting off the possibility of a certain kind of historically reassuring self-identity and bringing in its place something that appeared alien and disturbing."[9] The old principles were gone. Enlightenment views had triumphed in the arts. Now, in a rationalistic, scientific age, there seemed to be no laws or norms exterior to man himself. Instead, there were only human-made values, and a more closed view of the universe began to prevail. Many people, not unlike Courbet, now believed that meaning and value should be based entirely on empirical observation alone.

Courbet disdained officially constituted authority in art, as in politics. Thus he declared his independence by setting up his own pavilion at the 1855 Universal Exposition in Paris. The paintings Courbet exhibited there proved even more monumental than those the academic masters hung.

Courbet's first showing of his groundbreaking *A Burial at Ornans* in 1850 shocked the public and generated strong criticism. (See color plate 7.) In this painting, he gathers what appears to be the whole of his village birthplace—the mayor, clergy, farmers, laborers—in a dense frieze that, even more than David's *Horatii,* blocks the traditional Renaissance recession of depth. Perspective—the Renaissance illusion of depth—is almost lost, and the painting possesses a flatness uncannily similar to what would emerge with the art of the modernists of the next century. Courbet's democratically monochrome palette and artless crowd had none of the compositional or gestural climaxes still present in David's work.

Courbet was accused of painting ugliness in *Ornans*. One common criticism was that all the people in the painting wear stiff, black clothing. Courbet's Symbolist poet friend Charles Baudelaire (1821–67), however, had earlier called for an end to historical scenes full of flowing, colorful costumes, and he saw great significance in Courbet's depiction of the stiff, black clothing of French rural life. Baudelaire acknowledged the heroism of modern life, which, he said, consisted of recognizing that all people are victims of life. "We are all celebrating some burial," wrote Baudelaire.[10]

Courbet became even more radical in a series of erotic paintings such as *The Sleepers* (1866). In this painting, two women lie together in a provocative pose on a bed. Broken pearls and other items indicate that the women are not merely sleeping but that they have just finished a lesbian encounter. Such a frank depiction of erotic connection between women had not occurred in the tradition of high art before Courbet completed this painting. He deliberately challenged cultural taboos by transforming a subject once confined to covert or vulgar imagery into a splendid work of art.

In *The Origin of the World* (1866), Courbet depicts, in photographic detail, a woman's midsection with her legs spread apart for the viewer's inspection. The mere title of the work sums up Courbet's anti-tradition philosophy: the origin of the world is not an act of God but only a natural expulsion from the female midsection. When the Musee d'Orsay exhibited the painting in 1995, it caused an uproar, even in modern Paris.

Courbet believed that art is essential to the development of humankind, and he was convinced that his new perspectives and philosophies would prevail. He wrote to a friend: "Never fear! Even if I have to go all over the world, I am sure to find men who will understand me; even if I should find only five or six, they will make me live, they will save me. I am right! I am right!"

COURBET'S LEGACY

Courbet's art and philosophy revolutionized his culture, and his work influenced subsequent painters, such as Édouard Manet (1832–83). When Manet's *Luncheon on the Grass* was first exhibited at the Salon des Refuses in 1863, it generated a notorious scandal. *Luncheon* depicted an unmistakably modern naked woman, along with a pair of fully-clothed gentlemen and a second scantily-clad female, picnicking on the banks of the Seine. Manet left little room for subterfuge, since his principal nymph stares down and fixes the viewer with the brazen directness of one prepared to hold her own in any game of sexual exploitation. In much the same way, Picasso would fix the stares of his prostitutes in *Les Demoiselles d'Avignon* some forty years later.

Instead of softening and distancing his principal trio of figures by immersing them in a romantically suffused atmosphere, Manet pressed them forward near the front of the picture and illuminated the nude with a blaze of light. It was as if the party had been caught in the flash of a tabloid camera so that, as art historians Sam Hunter and John Jacobus note, "The image struck contemporaries as shockingly flat, like the Queen of Spades on a playing card."[11]

Like David's *Horatii,* Manet's *Luncheon on the Grass* does not have the unity of Renaissance art, since the rearground bather is disproportionately large. Therefore the Renaissance technique of receding toward a single vanishing point is undermined and yet again abandoned. This was a significant step toward what many at first considered ugly about the modern art to follow—that is, the flatness and one-dimensional character of the art of Picasso and others.

Courbet's influence extended not only to Manet but also to artists of the modern era as well. For example, the photographic detail of Philip Pearlstein's *Female Nude on a Platform Rocker* (painted from 1977 to 1978) is reminiscent of Courbet. And the debt of Eric Fischl's *Bad Boy* (1981), which depicts a young boy gazing at a female prostitute who lies on a bed with her legs spread, to Courbet is obvious. Lucian Freud's *Naked Portrait with Reflection* (1980), an excruciatingly detailed painting of a nude woman lying on a couch, is yet another example of a work influenced by Courbet. The gaze of Freud's nude is infamous for its supposed detachment—portraying every burst vein, inch of sagging flesh, and tuft of body hair. Freud dehumanizes the body by removing its majesty and mystery. Even today Courbet's provocative paintings seem to be reflected, for example, in Hugh Hefner's nude centerfolds in *Playboy* magazine. What was taboo in the 1800s has become a form of modern entertainment.

The unfortunate and final message of the work of artists like Courbet, Manet, and their successors is that human beings are nothing more than flesh. Increasingly, people came to be seen as mere parts of nature, nothing more.

A NEW APPROACH: RIMBAUD, THE "SEER"

Where earlier poets and artists aspired to communicate a philosophy and perhaps even change the course of history, the new nineteenth century artists saw art as an end in itself. In this way, the new artists would change the world. To them, art was essen-

42

tially amoral, and there was no beauty higher than physical beauty. The great spiritual truths of the past began to fade.

French poet Arthur Rimbaud (1854–91) had an even more ambitious course. He hoped to change life through a superior reality and metaphysical knowledge. Rimbaud exhorted the artist to be a "seer"—someone who could plumb the depths of the unknown and attain a hallucinatory state of clairvoyance.

Though an obscure poet in his own time, Rimbaud powerfully influenced future generations. Part of this influence came through his lifestyle, which he saw as inseparable from his writing, a lifestyle that so many of the Beatniks, hippies, and revolutionaries imitated in the 1950s and 1960s. The changes of these decades in turn led to the punk, new wave, and nihilistic tendencies of modern art, music, and literature.

At age seventeen Rimbaud traveled to Paris, where the charged atmosphere indelibly marked him, initiating a five-year period of rebellion as well as his years as a poet. During this rebellion, Rimbaud grew cantankerous, wore dirty clothes, and refused to bathe or cut his hair. He came to believe a poet could only become a seer through a "rational disordering of *all the senses*" and that a poet should know every form of love, suffering, and madness.[12] Therefore only through an unspeakable and tortuous path could the poet arrive at these new visions. Rimbaud felt that even if he ended up crazed and unable to understand the visions, at least he would have seen them!

Rimbaud called for a new language not bound by logic, grammar, or syntax. He wrote poems like *Drunks* (1871) that consisted of one-word lines, a new form that the Beat poets would copy decades later in America. By rejecting the past, Rimbaud believed he would become free to experiment and cross literary and moral boundaries.

Viciously anti-clerical, Rimbaud used every opportunity to express his hatred of religion. Writing "Death to God" on park benches and hurling torrential insults to priests were not enough—he even threw lice, which he had especially cultivated in his hair, at priests who passed by. Nothing about Christianity (particularly Catholicism) escaped Rimbaud's wrath. Consider, for example, his 1871 poem, "The Savior Bumped Upon His Heavy Butt":

> *Behold the son of God! And if the cold*
> > *Heels of the divine feet trampled on my shoulders,*
> *I'd call you coward still! That fly-specked forehead!*
> > *Socrates, Jesus: righteous both! Stupid Saviors!*
> *Respect me, Accursed forever in nights of blood!*[13]

Besides attacking God, the church, and the family, Rimbaud's poems describe bodily functions, diseased flesh, filth, and the clutter of old age and poverty. His disgust for women, whom he referred to generically as the "monstrous whore," was perpetuated later by an entire class of intelligentsia, including artists such as Edvard Munch, Pablo Picasso, and later the Surrealists.

Rimbaud became friends with French poet Paul Verlaine (1844–96), who eventually left his wife and infant son to live with Rimbaud in Paris in May of 1872. The relationship between Rimbaud and Verlaine was tumultuous and violent. For example, prior to Verlaine's final abandonment of his wife and child, he and his wife were to have dinner with renowned writer Victor Hugo. When Hugo expressed surprise at seeing Verlaine walk with a limp, Verlaine explained that he had boils on his legs—he could hardly reveal that Rimbaud had amused himself carving up Verlaine's thighs.

Upon completion and publication of *A Season in Hell* in 1873, a nineteen-year-old Rimbaud ended his career as a poet. Eighteen months later Verlaine left prison—where he had been sent for shooting Rimbaud—a changed and deeply religious man. Failing to convert Rimbaud to Catholicism, Verlaine abandoned their relationship in 1875.

THE GHOST OF RIMBAUD

At the age of twenty Rimbaud entered the world of business, eventually serving as an illegal gunrunner. Although he died

9. FRENCH POET ARTHUR RIMBAUD, as photographed in 1870, at sixteen years of age. A letter to a teacher in May 1871 reveals Rimbaud's new outlook regarding his vocation as a poet: "Now, I am degrading myself as much as possible. Why? I want to be a poet, and I am working to make myself a seer: you will not understand this, and I don't know how to explain it to you. It is a question of reaching the unknown by the derangement of *all the senses*. The sufferings are enormous, but one has to be strong, one has to be born a poet, and I know I am a poet."[14]

seventeen years later, his philosophy of no boundaries, absolutes, or moral restraints lived on. He passed on his conception of the poet as seer who achieved the visionary state through the complete disorientation of the senses, as well as his antagonism toward Christianity, to subsequent generations. Even today his influence can be seen in the physical sufferings and death of many in the art and entertainment world who achieve this disordering of the senses through a lifestyle filled with alcohol, drugs, and violence.

Rimbaud's influence was particularly strong among the Cubists and Surrealists of the early twentieth century and in the Beat poetry and rock music that came later. The Surrealist writer and artist André Breton (1896–1966), for example, wrote that "Rimbaud has done no more than express, with amazing vigor, a confusion encountered, no doubt, by many thousands of generations."[15]

Beat Generation poet and writer Allen Ginsberg, who influenced fellow Beat writer Jack Kerouac and musician/writer Bob Dylan, among others, considered Rimbaud an icon, almost a god. A picture of Rimbaud hung in at least two of Ginsberg's apartments, and Ginsberg taught Rimbaud's poetry in a college literature class and introduced his work to Dylan.

Rimbaud's influence on modern music, especially rock, is evident both in the music and the often chaotic lifestyles of the musicians. Some music critics and commentators have called Bob Dylan the "rock-n-roll Rimbaud," and punk rocker Patti Smith has closely identified herself with Rimbaud. A poignant example of Rimbaud's lasting influence on the arts is the British punk rock group the Sex Pistols, who burst onto the music scene in the late 1970s. Although their career lasted less than three years, some claim the Sex Pistols had a greater impact on British rock music than any group since the Beatles. Among the first recorded words of lead vocalist John Lydon were, "I am an anti-Christ. I am an anarchist."[16] Even Lydon's stage name, Johnny Rotten, reflected a Rimbaudian influence—a faithful lack of toothbrushing had produced rotten green teeth. Sex Pistols bassist Sid Vicious, who died of a heroin overdose in 1979, is a further example. His destructive lifestyle is chillingly depicted in the 1986 film biography *Sid and Nancy*.

Rimbaud also affected the development of the novel through his influence on writers such as Henry Miller (1891–1980). Miller's *Tropic of Cancer,* published in Paris in 1934, was praised by such literary elites as Aldous Huxley, Ezra Pound, and T. S. Eliot, and his book sales increased dramatically when *Tropic of Cancer* was banned in the United States and Great Britain because of its graphic sex scenes. The legal battle that followed the 1961 publication of *Tropic of Cancer* in the United States made Miller's name synonymous with the fight against censorship. The furor resulted in the sale of more than 1.1 million copies of the book in one year. Praise for Miller's artistic achievement, however, declined significantly after the Supreme Court decided in favor of *Tropic of Cancer* in 1963.

Miller claimed to be deeply religious, though he believed Christianity made too great a distinction between the soul and the body. Miller also considered sex to be a spiritual as well as a physical experience—an experience that leads a person to God. To Miller, any intense physical experience, whether positive or negative, had spiritual value.

Miller in turn influenced American writers like William Burroughs (1914–97), the author of the notorious novel *Naked Lunch,* which director David Cronenberg brought to the screen in 1991. Burroughs admitted that he had drawn on Rimbaud for his description of the derangement of the senses.

SUCCESSIVE REVOLUTIONS

The lesson from history is clear: when a culture abandons its religious traditions, it needs to find something strong enough to replace them to give people a sense of meaning and purpose in their lives. What we have seen and will continue to see, however, is that humanity has not succeeded in its attempt to fill this gap and that each successive revolution against tradition has led not to a new moral order but only to more revolution and dehumanization. The Enlightenment's faith in Reason led to the Romantic movement's rejection of Reason and its deification of nature and primitive humanity. This movement in turn led only to a stark realism and then a deep pessimism—not to a new moral order. Just as Enlightenment ideals spawned the violence of the French Revolution, the failure of the Romantic movement paved the way for the more dehumanized society of the late twentieth century.

Western culture has moved a long way since Rembrandt's *Adoration of the Shepherds.* Once content to be defined by traditional religious precepts, modern society now provides its own concept of humanity. The results have been catastrophic.

CHAPTER 2
Where Are We Going?

The human being who has become free—and how much more the spirit who has become free—spits on the contemptible type of well-being dreamed of by shopkeepers, Christians, cows, females, Englishmen, and other democrats. The free man is a warrior.

FRIEDRICH NIETZSCHE

After the French Revolution of 1848, the mid-nineteenth century produced numerous new scientific theories and ideas. In particular, the rise of biology and the doctrine of evolution gave science an unprecedented position of authority. Geological theories that had circulated since the end of the eighteenth century received notoriety in the 1830s when Scottish scientist Charles Lyell's *Principles of Geology* was published. Lyell explained landscape and geological structure in terms of ongoing forces, rather than as the result of a single completed act of creation. Geology was thus the first scientific field to undermine traditional religious belief in a special creation—a belief that had been a foundational concept of Western culture.

EVOLUTION, DARWIN, AND DARWINISM

As early as the 1850s, Herbert Spencer had discussed biological evolution. Nevertheless, Charles Darwin (1809–82) came to symbolize the nineteenth century's fascination with science, despite the fact that he was connected closely to the Romantic movement.

Initially, as exemplified in his *Journal of Researches* (1839), Darwin believed that nature was glorious and redemptive. As he studied nature, however, he began to see the world differently. Darwin noted that in our desire to see the "face of nature bright

48

with gladness," we often forget "that the birds which are idly singing round us mostly live on insects or seeds, and are thus constantly destroying life."[1]

In 1858 Darwin and Alfred Russel Wallace (1823–1913), a British naturalist, read their famous papers before the Linnaean Society. It was not until the publication of Darwin's *The Origin of Species* in 1859, however, that the old world of ideas was crashed to pieces, for it was in that book that Darwin theorized that plants and animals develop through a process of natural selection, which ensures the survival of the fittest. His work firmly dislodged people from the traditional notion that they possessed an exalted position as special creations in God's image.

Darwin expanded his theories in *Descent of Man,* published in 1871. In this work, Darwin applied evolutionary concepts specifically to the human race:

> He who wishes to decide whether man is the modified descendant of some preexisting form, would probably first enquire whether man varies, however slightly, in bodily structure and in mental faculties; and if so, whether the variations are transmitted to his offspring in accordance with the laws which prevail with the lower animals.[2]

Darwin insisted on the rigorous governance of natural laws, but there was no agreement among scientists and scholars about how the evolutionary process actually occurred. Darwin himself was particularly impressed by Englishman Thomas Malthus's (1766–1834) vision of humankind's murderous competition for food. In 1798 Malthus published *An Essay on the Principle of Population as It Affects the Future Improvement of Society,* which predicted that people would eventually overpopu-

10. CHARLES DARWIN, though credited with developing the theory of evolution, was in part refining the ideas of others. In the writings of Marquis Jean Baptiste de Lamarck (1744–1829) and Erasmus Darwin (1731–1802), the grandfather of Charles who acquired the label "atheist" because of his enthusiasm for pagan folklore and his acceptance of evolutionary ideas, there are other early presentations of the theory of biological evolution. Moreover, simultaneous with Charles Darwin, there were still others working on a theory of evolution of the species. Indeed, there is evidence indicating that Darwin may have based parts of his theory of evolution on the work of Alfred Russel Wallace, another British naturalist.

late the world. Thus any increases in the food supply would lead to equal increases in the population, and in the long run people would be condemned to a life of bare subsistence. This is known as Malthus's "dismal theorem." Today similar theories are perpetuated through the population control movement.

Although Darwin confined his ideas to biology, others adapted them to nearly all aspects of intellectual life. Darwin eventually became a hero to the international academic community and received honorary doctorates from three foreign universities and honorary memberships in fifty-seven foreign learned societies.

Science by now had in essence become the new religion. It would be recognized as such by notable individuals like British playwright George Bernard Shaw, who observed that "the world jumped at Darwin,"[3] and J. D. Rockefeller, who used Darwinian thought to justify industrial monopoly without restraint: "The growth of a large business is merely a survival of the fittest."[4] Andrew Carnegie expressed his conversion to Darwinism by saying, "Light came in as a flood and all was clear. Not only had I got rid of theology and the supernatural, but I found the truth of evolution."[5]

Although Darwin never fully abandoned his conviction of God's existence, he forever altered people's comprehension of their standing in what they had previously believed to be the "created" order. The effects of evolutionary thinking and its application to various facets of life would later be played out in the fascist and totalitarian regimes of the twentieth century.

EVOLUTION: HUMANS AND MACHINERY

The intellectual groundwork for the theory of evolution had already been laid in European thought. Nineteenth century humanity, as noted, had long been prepared for the acceptance of a comprehensive biological theory because society had been exposed to a philosophy of evolution by various theorists. Thus Darwin's idea did not occur in a vacuum. Yet, unlike his predecessors, Darwin succeeded in spreading his theory throughout Europe and America.

While the intellectual climate provided the setting for Darwin's warm reception into circles of higher learning, the Industrial Revolution functioned as a catalyst to popularize the theory of evolution among the masses. Society quickly drew connections between Darwinian thought and the Industrial Revolution. In fact, Darwin's description of the evolution of species bears a remarkable resemblance to the workings of the industrial production process in which machines were assembled from their individual parts. People thus could now be spoken of in the terms one might use to speak of a mechanical apparatus.

Indeed, the ominous presence of the machine was even reflected in the arts. For example, paintings of the period, such as the 1863 *Work* by Ford Madox Brown (1821–93), dramatized the woes of manual labor and the convenience of the machine. In 1844 English painter Joseph Turner (1775–1851) created the extraordinary painting *Rain, Steam, Speed,* one of the first depictions of the train in a Romantic light. At the time, many people detested the railways, but Turner depicted them as a symbol of progress through which men were conquering the earth by using its natural forces. The depiction of the train's lighted carriages (supposedly preceded by a speeding rabbit) moving across a high bridge makes the train an almost mystical subject.

Turner went to great lengths to experience his subject matter. On one occasion, for example, he had himself tied to a mast during a storm at sea so that he could understand the full force of the wind, waves, and clouds swirling about him.

MARX: MAN AS THE REFLECTION OF HIS POSSESSIONS

The period after the French Revolution of 1848 also marked the dawn of socialism and a new struggle between the working class and the bourgeoisie. This era foreshadowed the Russian Revolution of 1917 for, as historian Geoffrey Bruun recognizes, "1848 was a turning point where history failed to turn.... The revolution of 1848 came before its time."[6]

Karl Marx (1818–83) was intimately involved in the 1848 revolutions, and the impact of his political and social ideas on subsequent generations may be unsurpassed in history. Before Marx can be fully appreciated, however, one must first understand the theories of German philosopher Georg Wilhelm Friedrich Hegel (1770–1831). Before the time of Hegel, the Judeo-Christian concept of "antithesis"—the idea that a thing cannot be its opposite, that "A" cannot be "non-A," that evil cannot be good—was the generally accepted foundation of philosophy. Hegel, however, rejected the notion of "antithesis" and adopted instead the idea of "synthesis," theorizing that every idea or statement fundamentally contains its opposite. History, he believed, is driven by a perpetual process of "dialectical materialism," in which an idea develops, struggles against its opposite, and finally unites with it to take another form. According to Hegel's view, facts—and even life—are pure potentiality. Nothing is ever *being* or *existing* but is instead always *becoming.* Nietzsche would later translate these concepts into the philosophy that people are mere bridges to becoming a race of "Supermen."

Hegel's logic obliterated the older ideas of an objective God, absolute truth, and moral absolutes, since for him all values were relative. He believed that the things of this world were merely partial aspects of a single all-consuming whole that he called the "Absolute" and that the Absolute was best represented here on earth by the government, to which all individuals were subordinate.

"[All] worth which the human being possesses," Hegel wrote, "all spiritual reality, he possesses only through the State."[7] The state, then, becomes in effect God walking on earth, and the individual's supreme duty is to become a member of the state. Modern totalitarians later embraced Hegelian thought to justify their rule.

Marx partially inverted Hegel's dialectic. He believed that the theory should apply to perfection here on earth rather than to a higher "spiritual" perfection. Unlike Hegel, who claimed that consciousness determines the existence of people, Marx argued that people's social existence determines their consciousness, thus legitimizing the view of people as products of their environment. According to Marx, people's ideas are formed by their physical existence. Nevertheless, Marx regarded the dialectic as the one infallible method of scientific thinking to which all empirical knowledge of facts is subordinate.

Although Marx applied the theory of the dialectic in a practical manner to economic, social, and political issues, he also perpetuated the theory in a philosophical manner by popularizing Hegel's belief in the real as rational and the dialectic of "becoming." In addition, Marx popularized Hegel's views of reality as a process and life as an inherent contradiction that expires when the contradiction is resolved.

Marx's reputation as a radical made an academic career under the Prussian government impossible.

11. KARL MARX. After 1849, when Marx was arrested, tried for sedition, acquitted, and expelled from France, he lived the rest of his life in London, supported financially by Friedrich Engels (1820–95), who in the 1850s and '60s owned a prosperous textile business. Marx, however, eventually led a life of poverty that was complicated by his own notions of respectability, worsened by chronic illness, and saddened by the deaths of his three children.

Most of those years were spent in the British Museum, gathering material for his historical analysis of capitalism, *Das Kapital* (1867 and later), of which he was able to publish only one volume. Engels later constructed the other two volumes from posthumous papers.

Instead he became the editor of a leftist businessmen's newspaper. After the newspaper was finally suppressed, Marx began a lifelong exile, first moving to Paris, where he met Friedrich Engels (1820–95), with whom he shared perhaps the most momentous literary partnership in history.

In 1847 the London-based Communist League commissioned Marx and Engels to write the *Communist Manifesto,* which was completed one year later. The *Manifesto* suggested that people are only a reflection of their material possessions and economic status. Thus capitalism (a word never used in the *Manifesto*) produces two opposite classes—those who own (the bourgeoisie) and those who work (the proletariat).

Since the owner-class constantly consumes and thus cannot exist without continually revolutionizing the instruments of production, it is forced to expand its markets constantly. The owners might conquer the world economically with their cheaply priced commodities, but because the markets are often limited, overproduction will inevitably occur. The workers will then bear the brunt of economic depression caused by overproduction. Eventually, as Marx theorized, instead of competing with each other for low-wage jobs, they will unite against the owner-class. In order to prevent this problem from recurring, Marx argues that the instruments of the owning class—private property, the traditional family, and organized religion—must be abolished. Only one thousand copies of the *Communist Manifesto* were initially printed, and it was not immediately influential. Marx's works, however, achieved a wide and influential readership in the 1880s and 1890s.

Marx continued to apply his theories to modern life. He attempted to demonstrate through historical analysis that the owner-class could not adapt to modernity and must inevitably give rise to the working class. He believed that change was the only immutable quality of life.

Marx wrote that Darwin's *Origin of Species* served as "a basis in natural science for the class struggle in history." In fact, Marx was so enthusiastic about the evolutionary implications for socialism that he tried to dedicate his book *Das Kapital* to Darwin. Darwin, however, rejected the offer, fearing that an association with Marx might undermine his credibility among his peers.

Marx's impact as a philosopher was significant. He directly affected the minds of the mass of humanity, not only appealing to their material interests but also giving them an unshakable confidence in the truth of his predictions. Many modern belief systems have been influenced by Marx; for example, his materialistic view of history produced a psychological-sociological theory of people as not completely responsible for their actions. Marx's influence on Western thought is almost universally acknowl-edged. As Oxford historian J. M. Roberts notes, "The last non-European whose words had any comparable authority in Europe was Jesus Christ."[8]

IMPRESSIONISM: THE SHOCK OF THE NEW

A similar questioning of the nature of humanity was also occurring in the arts. Like their predecessors, Impressionist artists struggled with the question of whether there was any reality outside of human beings, though unlike their predecessors, the Impressionists rebelled against the extreme realism in technique that had preceded them. Some artists viewed Impressionism as the dictatorship of the eye over the mind. In describing Claude Monet, for example, painter Paul Cézanne said, "He's only an eye, but my God, what an eye!"[9] According to the art movement known as Impressionism, only sensations could be known with certainty to be real, as Immanuel Kant had written earlier. Therefore the Impressionists—Monet, Renoir, and others—painted their perceptions of reality, their *impressions,* rather than reality itself.

Auguste Renoir's (1841–1919) *Le Moulin de la Galette* (1876), for example, is a painting of an open-air dance, with the painter's friends sitting in the foreground. The painting is striking because of its blurred vision, unclear structure, and spots of color. In fact, the painting's first viewers thought Renoir's "spots" of dappled sunlight were mistakes.

Claude Monet (1840–1926) also painted his own perceptions of what he saw. For example, in *Haystack at Sunset Near Giverny,* painted in 1891, Monet simply recorded the sensation that the light beams made on his retinas.

The obvious question is whether there is anything behind the light beams—that is, an objective reality. This is unanswered by the Impressionists themselves, and their work ultimately suggested that no one can know whether there is an objective reality outside of humankind. The Impressionists called even the physical world into ques-tion, leaving, where reality had once been, only "impressions." The Impressionists therefore could not provide a definitive answer for the questions they raised. Ultimately they themselves knew their theories could not provide the answers they sought. As Renoir put it, "In a word, Impressionism was a blind alley."[10]

THE CRISIS: SEURAT AND CÉZANNE

As the nineteenth century neared its close, a generation of revolutionary and cre-ative individuals blossomed in virtually every area of human endeavor, from art to politics to economics to philosophy to fiction. These individuals, including the post-Impressionists, brought a new tension to art by acknowledging and attempting to counterbalance the supposed dualities of mind and spirit.

Painters Georges Seurat and Paul Cézanne tried to resolve this duality mainly through the intellect, while others, such as Paul Gauguin and Vincent van Gogh, looked primarily to intuition.

Georges Seurat (1859–91) believed he could resolve the tension by painting the artist's impression—the "view"—so that it reflected order and structure. He went beyond the Impressionists by attempting to provide structure to the artist's perception. As such, Seurat applied scientific theories to his work. For example, he sought to portray all the individual components of the whole by composing a painting entirely of dots in a technique known as "pointillism." He first exhibited this new technique at the newly formed Independents Salon in 1884 with his painting *Bathers*.

Unlike the Impressionists, who preferred scenes of pre-industrial innocence, Seurat, a passionate socialist, chose his subjects from the urban and suburban working class. Although he died at thirty-one, he left behind six major paintings. His masterpiece, *A Sunday Afternoon on the Island of La Grande Jatte,* was painted from 1884 to 1886. (See color plate 8.) The huge painting—ten feet by nearly seven feet—granted middle-class recreation the ceremonious treatment once reserved only for gods and kings, thus making a social statement by portraying pleasure with the gravity of earlier historical paintings.

Spellbinding, the painting derives much of its fascination from the subtlety with which Seurat energized a monumental calm on a Sunday outing. The optical dazzle of the painting is stimulated by countless points of color and three isolated instances of action (the charging terrier, the skipping girl, and the wind-filled sails), as well as a slightly off-center perspective that places the figures somewhat at variance with the space they inhabit.

Unlike the classical artists before him, Seurat never painted gods or other themes from the past. Like Courbet, he merely depicted the world around him as he understood it. One of his contemporaries, a critic, wrote, "Strip his figures of the colored fleas that cover them; underneath you will find nothing, no thought, no soul."[11] Seurat said, "They see poetry in what I have done. No, I apply my method, and that is all there is to it."[12]

Paul Cézanne (1839–1906), often called the father of abstract art, doubted that an artist could ever approximate reality in his work. As he wrote to his son just weeks before his death in 1906, "I cannot attain the intensity that is unfolded before my senses. I do not have the magnificent richness of colouring that animates Nature."[13]

Cézanne's painting *Mont Ste-Victoire* (1904–6) shows his unsuccessful attempt truly to "see" the motif. No previous painter, some say, had taken his viewers through the process of painting reality so frankly. While Renaissance viewers had admired an artist's certainty about what he saw, with Cézanne the statement "This is what I see" became "Is this what I see?" For Cézanne, everything was relative, and doubt became part of his subject matter. The idea that doubt is heroic, if locked in a structure as grand as a late Cézanne painting, is one of the touchstones of twentieth century modernism.

Cézanne's premeditated structures and Seurat's science-oriented paintings left a spiritual and emotional void in art. Painters such as van Gogh (1853–90) and Gauguin would respond to the call for a less calculated approach to painting. Their inspiration, however, would come not from traditional religion but from non-traditional faiths and psychology.

SYMBOLISM

In the 1800s a small group of relatively unknown figures, including Gustave Moreau (1826–98), pioneered the use of literary subject matter and fantasy in their art. Moreau's 1876 painting *The Apparition,* for example, portrayed a severed human head suspended in midair. Charles Baudelaire reflects the same philosophy in his collection of poems *The Flowers of Evil* when he writes, "To keep thy fangs fit in the curious sport, / Each day thou need'st a man's heart freshly caught." Baudelaire believed that all human experience and communication were simply fact and felt it was the poet's task to interpret the so-called "hieroglyphic" meanings of sensation. This philosophy of uncertainty, relativism, and doubt was later manifested in the Symbolist movement. Painters van Gogh, Gauguin, and their contemporaries applied the concepts of Symbolism to the visual arts. In the process, they converted art into a vehicle for emotions, fantasy, reverie, and dreams.

The Symbolist movement was officially born in 1886 when Jean Moréas (1856–1910) wrote the *Symbolist Manifesto.* Moréas singled out three poets as fathers of the movement: Baudelaire, Stéphane Mallarmé (1842–98), and Paul Verlaine (Rimbaud's companion). Symbolism combined the Romantic preoccupation with emotion with an emphasis on sensory perception. Although the Symbolists filled their poetry with great physical detail, they were not interested in painting beautiful pictures in the mind. On the contrary, Baudelaire and Rimbaud specialized in describing the ugly, in an attempt to symbolize a broader range of human experience. The more intense the experience, the more worthy it was for the Symbolists to record. In order to reach a level of higher meaning, Symbolists such as Baudelaire, Verlaine, and Rimbaud used alcohol, drugs, and sex to expand their experience.

The Symbolists inherited the Romantics' hatred of the middle class and detested the materialism of society. In turn, the middle class disliked the Symbolists. The Symbolists also rebelled against the influence of science, believing it rationalized human experience and stripped it of its deeper meaning. Though the Symbolists sought a truth beyond the physical, most rejected traditional religion. They instead sought redemption through their art and poetry.

GAUGUIN: THE SEARCH FOR MEANING

French Symbolist painter Paul Gauguin (1848–1903) believed that art was an abstraction to be inspired by nature and considered technology and other modern developments to be enemies of art and pure living. Gauguin, a frequent attendee of the literary soirees of his friend Mallarmé, epitomized the philosophical problems facing thinkers at the end of the nineteenth century. He understood the ramifications of a mechanistic view of the universe and recognized that the so-called "facts" of reality were eating away at the mystery and enigma of the world.

Searching for natural expressions of experience untainted by modern thinking, Gauguin turned to the primitive art of Central and South America. The Parisian display of the same Peruvian mummy that Edvard Munch used as the subject of his famous 1893 painting *The Scream,* for example, attracted him. Eventually Gauguin concluded that the sources of art lie deep within human consciousness. Painting, for this reason, should return to its original purpose—the examination of the interior life of people. Gauguin believed he could rediscover this purpose in what he saw as the primitive paradise of the South Seas. Although the South Seas paradise had been a staple of Western art for more than a century, Gauguin was one of the first French artists to seek this earthly paradise.

After resigning from his profitable position on the stock exchange to become a painter, Gauguin set out for the South Seas in 1891, leaving his family behind. In search of blissful innocence among the bounties of nature, Gauguin wanted to observe the scene Mallarmé had described in his poem *The Afternoon of a Faun* (1876), a piece that also had inspired Debussy's musical prelude of the same name. The poem began, "I would perpetuate these nymphs."

Arriving in Tahiti, Gauguin wrote ecstatically, "These nymphs, I want to perpetuate them, with their golden skins, their searching animal odour, their tropical savours." Gauguin quickly realized, however, that he had not found Paradise or an island of Noble Savages. Instead he saw prostitutes and a culture turned on its head by missionaries, alcohol, exploitation, and gonorrhea—its rituals dead, its memory lost, and its population diminished from forty thousand to six thousand.

Gauguin next turned to diabolism, attempting to challenge the existing system of good and evil. He presented himself as a messiah figure—the prophet of a new morality and art. His 1890 painting *Nirvana,* a portrait of his friend and fellow artist Jacob Meyer de Haan, reflects this attempt. It transforms de Haan into a primitive idol, a model for the "dark gods" that Gauguin admired as a lifegiving force. In *Nirvana's* Eden, two languid, Western Eves wail and avert their eyes in shame of their nudity. These are guilt-ridden civilized Eves whom Gauguin later compared scornfully with the Tahitian females he found sensual and those he perceived to be unashamed in their nakedness.

In 1889–90, Gauguin produced what he called his best and strangest work, *Be in Love and You Will Be Happy.* The subject of the painting is the artist himself, "like a monster, seizing the hand of a woman who resists him, and telling her, 'Be in love and you will be happy.'"

By this time, however, Gauguin had reached an impasse. Like Courbet and Rimbaud before him, he had searched in vain for the absolute, discovering instead only flawed human nature. Despondent, Gauguin left his defiled Eden and returned to Paris in 1893. A couple of years later, however, fed up with civilization once again, he returned to Tahiti, where, haunted by mounting debts and deteriorating health, he contemplated suicide. Before attempting to take his life, however, he completed, in one month, a huge five-by-twelve-foot canvas entitled *Where Do We Come From? What Are We? Where Are We Going?* These questions were the very ones Voltaire had raised a century earlier. While Voltaire had concluded that the answer could not be known, Gauguin believed his painting provided an answer on a level comparable to the Christian Gospels. (See color plate 9.)

In the painting, we see the Tahitian Eve in the center plucking fruit from a tropical Tree of Paradise. In the background, an idol glows with an eerie bluish light as two rosy phantom-like figures glide by. Before them, in the words of Gauguin, "an enormous crouching figure, out of all proportion, and intentionally so, raises its arms and stares in astonishment upon these two who dare to think of their destiny." The imagery suggests that life and the supernatural confront each other and merge imperceptibly in a primeval setting. The painting is a cyclical allegory of life and a philosophical meditation played out on a darkening stage.

Thus Gauguin poses his questions, to which he never gives a definitive answer. Interpretations of the painting, however, abound. Where do we come from? *A source, a child.* What are we? *Man stands questioning.* Where are we going? *An old woman, a bird of death.* What seems to be referenced in the painting is the cycle of human life—birth, conscious existence, and death. But the painting cannot be deduced by reason alone. It must be experienced, both intellectually and sensually.

As the nineteenth century belief in progress, as expressed in science and industry, began to fracture, Gauguin looked for another philosophy of life that would provide some type of fulfillment. Until his death, he hoped there might be a different direction for civilization to take from the commercial squalor and the spiritual emptiness that "progress" left in its wake.

Where are we going? is the final question for all. The answer that Gauguin may have offered is that of eternal renewal, rebirth, and continuity. This seems to be his hope, but it was ultimately unfulfilled. Thus Gauguin died in a small hut in Tahiti, isolated, embittered by financial problems, and unable to satisfactorily answer the three great questions he had raised. These questions still haunt us today.

EVOLUTION IN PRACTICE

These questions about the nature of people and their environment were ones Darwin had initially tried to answer, and the far-reaching effects of Darwin's theories were by now becoming apparent. The reductionary and evolutionary view of people begun by Darwin was in fact beginning to rear its ugly head in the forms of racism, fascism, and totalitarianism.

Social evolution clearly formed a basis for fascism and its oppressive, racist actions. Italian fascist Benito Mussolini (1883–1945), who watched the killing of nearly half a million persons at the Caporetto battle front, justified war as a means of evolutionary progress. In public, he repeatedly used Darwinian catch words while mocking perpetual peace, lest it hinder evolution. Adolf Hitler (1889–1945) wrote *Mein Kampf* in 1923 and expressed in it his adherence to evolution in justifying genocide. As anthropologist Arthur Keith has said, "The German Fuhrer . . . consciously sought to make the practice of Germany conform to the theory of evolution."[14] Evolutionary ideas can also be seen in Hitler's wish to develop a master race and in his human breeding experiments.

Racism therefore is also a sequel to evolutionary thinking, and Darwin himself may have provided the racist element of the theory. Though the title of his book is often cited as *The Origin of Species,* the complete title is *The Origin of Species of Means of Natural Selection, or the Preservation of Favoured Races in the Struggle for Life.* The probable implication in Darwin's title is that the favored race is the white race.

Esteemed Harvard biologist Stephen Jay Gould, an evolutionist himself, has documented the racism of evolutionary thinking. Concerning Darwin and "non-Western people," Gould has written that "his basic belief in a hierarchy of cultural advance, with white Europeans on top and natives of different colors on the bottom, did not change."[15]

Darwin also taught that women were biologically inferior to men and that human sex differences were due in part to natural selection. He theorized that men must prove themselves physically and intellectually superior to other men in order to compete for women. Therefore they attain a higher eminence than women. As Darwin concluded in his autobiography, a man attains "a higher eminence, in whatever he takes up, than can women—whatever requiring deep thought, reason, or imagination, or merely the use of the senses and hands.... [T]he average of mental power in man must be above that of women."[16]

Despite its flaws, the theory of evolution captured the public. Even today Steven Spielberg's blockbuster 1993 film *Jurassic Park* has attracted millions of viewers with its evolutionary premise. This popular film is an example of how the modern entertainment media presents evolutionary theory as fact. The danger raised in Spielberg's film (and in the book of the same title by Michael Crichton), however, is that biotechnology is out of control. Crichton laments that "most disturbing is the fact that no watchdogs are found among scientists themselves to monitor the development of new and possibly frightening forms of life."[17] The film depicts dinosaurs as genetically resurrected beasts chaotically destroying the world, including their human progenitors. These "superbeasts" are not saviors, but neither are the "supermen" who manipulate technology to bring them to life.

THE ALL-PERVADING WILL

Philosopher Arthur Schopenhauer (1788–1860), one of Nietzsche's strongest influences, has not been taken as seriously as other philosophers by various modern

60

thinkers because of some obvious shortcomings in his thought—such as his view that marriage conferred upon women an "unnatural position of privilege, by considering her throughout as the full equivalent of the man, which is by no means the case."[18] Nevertheless, his belief that an indifferent force, the "all-pervading will," lay behind all existence has been extremely influential. According to Schopenhauer, this force, although incomprehensible to people, rules them completely. Schopenhauer thus rejected the concept of autonomous freedom. For humans, the will shows itself in desires, especially sexual drives and unconscious behaviors, and thus, Sigmund Freud later acknowledged Schopenhauer as his intellectual predecessor.

The concept of the all-pervading force or will was popularized through director George Lucas's *Star Wars* film series of the late 1970s and early 1980s and resurrected with his *The Phantom Menace* in 1999. Lucas has said that he believes in "the Force": "If you use [The Force] well, you can see the future and the past. You can sort of read minds and you can levitate and use that whole netherworld of psychic energy."[19] These films seem little more than Schopenhauer resurrected in popular culture.

12. ARTHUR SCHOPENHAUER, who found his own ideas reflected in the writings of Buddhists, other Eastern mystics, and the Hindu concept of Nirvana. Schopenhauer wrote that religion, like art, was a form of escape from life, but this form was only for the undiscriminating and unlearned.

13. RICHARD WAGNER believed that true art is revolutionary and sought to implement his philosophy through music.

Unlike Lucas's films, however, Schopenhauer's actual philosophy was extremely pessimistic: Life is and will always be more painful than pleasurable, and all human efforts are doomed to fail. Even if their endeavors succeed, people cannot take credit for them since it is the universal will that ultimately determines everything. Thus Schopenhauer recommends an escape into art—a recommendation that becomes an extreme version of "art for art's sake." When people participate in pure art, especially music, they become part of the greater arbitrary will. Schopenhauer's goal of escape into art resembles the Hindu Nirvana and the beliefs of Buddhists and other Eastern mystics.

Schopenhauer believed that traditional religion was an escape from life, one reserved for the undiscriminating and unlearned. It offered an escape from life's ugliness at all social levels. Schopenhauer's attitude toward religion resembled that of Marx, who believed the common people accepted religion as an escape from the reality of material oppression.

RICHARD WAGNER

The German composer Richard Wagner (1813–83) is another artist whose art and thought have influenced succeeding generations. Wagner's anti-semitism, for example, is well known, and it left a legacy for future generations of Germans. Wagner firmly believed that Jewish and German people could not co-exist and talked time after time about the invasion of the "German nation by an utterly alien element." He fretted over what he saw as the capacity of Jews to exploit the German character financially and artistically.

Adolf Hitler was an ardent admirer of Wagner and perverted Wagner's epic cycle of operas, *Ring of the Nibelungen,* into a paranoid gospel of violence. Moreover, *Mein Kampf* was littered with phraseology from the *Nibelungen.* Hitler often attended performances of Wagner at Bayrenth, Germany, and in fact made the Bayrenth Festival a ward of the German state, thus guaranteeing its survival during the Nazi era.

THE LUST OF HELL: WAGNER AND NIETZSCHE

Wagner also influenced another famous thinker, Friedrich Nietzsche (1844–1900), who as a young man idolized the great composer. While Nietzsche, who became one of the most influential thinkers in Western history, was the intellectual child of Darwin, he also closely identified with Wagner, as both came from Germany (the birthplace of Lutheranism), both rejected Christianity, and both viewed reason and the will in a sexual context. Wagner said that music was a woman, by which he meant some formless matrix upon which the poet could impose his meanings. Nietzsche also called truth a woman. For both men, the will simply imposed its own desires on an ever-compliant, therefore female, reality.

Wagner's principal complaint against Christianity arose from his view of Christian teachings about sexual love. He felt that abstinence from sexual love was held up as a Christian virtue and that following Christianity would thus sweep the human race from the earth. Love in its true sense, Wagner believed, was possible only in a sexual context; all other forms of love were merely variants, derivatives, or counterfeit copies. This view seemed to dominate Wagner's relationship with women, and both he and his first wife had numerous affairs.

By Wagner's time, melody had become the primary means of expression in music. While acknowledging the necessity of melody, Wagner wanted to limit its importance because he believed it had taken over the dominant role in music to the exclusion of emotion. Instead Wagner wanted to emphasize the importance of the text, which would allow music to cultivate emotion unrestrained by melodic structure.

Wagner attempted to revolutionize music by using chromaticism instead of the seven-note diatonic scale. The twelve half-tones of the chromatic scale attracted him because their indeterminence represented freedom not only from musical order but from sexual and political order as well. Music, for Wagner, was a revolution, a sexual liberation combined in one overly emotional, overly long, endless melody. Wagner's music thus encapsulated his obsession with sexual freedom. To modulate the notes continually from one key to another, as Wagner did, was tantamount to slanting their emotional focus. To bend them away, never returning to the dominant note, gave the feeling of tumultuous, unsatisfied passion, a passion that was never resolved.

Although Wagner was initially ambivalent about traditional Judeo-Christian values, by the time of his opera *Tristan und Isolde* in 1863, chromaticism and sex had won. Tristan exhibits no tension between "free sex" and purity, for he succumbs to sexual desire during the first act. The opera is, in fact, primarily about adultery. And Wagner asserts his role as a musical revolutionary in act 2 when Tristan and Isolde celebrate sexual gratification. Wagner himself fathered a child out of wedlock (although he did later marry the child's mother). Nietzsche, present at the birth, used this as an example of Wagner's living out *Tristan* in his own life.

Nietzsche first read a score of Wagner's *Tristan und Isolde* at age seventeen and claimed he was a "Wagnerian." He said, "All of the strangeness of Leonardo da Vinci is made mundane by the sounding of the first note of *Tristan*." When Nietzsche initially heard the opera played by an orchestra, he declared that it sent a "thrill through every fibre, every nerve." He believed the opera aroused "the lust of hell."

Nietzsche became disillusioned with Wagner in later years, however, when Wagner entertained Judeo-Christian beliefs. In his 1882 opera *Parsifal*, Wagner's theme was an exaltation of some elements of Christianity—pity, fleshless love, and a world redeemed by a pure fool, termed the "fool in Christ." Nietzsche could not forgive Wagner for acknowledging Christianity's moral values and beauty. In *The Case of Wagner*, published in 1888, Nietzsche writes, "Richard Wagner is a decrepit and desperate romantic, collapsed suddenly before the Holy Cross. Was there no German then with eyes to see, with pity in his conscience to bewail, this horrible spectacle?"

Nevertheless, Nietzsche believed the musical invention in *Tristan* was so powerful that it could overturn the hegemony of Christian culture in the West, leading to a new age of sexual excess and unfettered will. The new age would center around a rebirth of sexual license so strong that it would overwhelm the order of every family. It would unleash the wildest bestiality of nature in a mixture of lust and cruelty.

NIETZSCHE: "GOD IS DEAD"

Nietzsche eventually left art. His refuge became science and philosophy, which he believed offered "an asylum where no tyranny can penetrate." After several illnesses and a failed love affair, Nietzsche sought solitude in his depression. He retreated to the Alps and prayed that "Man" might be surpassed. On the lonely heights came the inspiration for his most renowned work, *Thus Spake Zarathustra* (1883). The book expounds his concept of the Superman, an idea which apparently evolved from his study of mythology—particularly from the myth of Prometheus, the titan chained to a rock by Zeus for stealing fire from heaven and giving it to humanity. Nietzsche had found a new teacher (Zoroaster), a new god (the Superman), and a new religion (eternal recurrence). *Zarathustra* was Nietzsche's masterpiece, and he knew it. "This work stands alone," he said.

At age thirty Zarathustra, the novel's main character, comes down from his meditative mountain to preach, like his Persian prototype Zoroaster, of the sixth century B.C. The crowd, however, turns from him to see a rope walker perform. When the rope walker falls to his death, Zarathustra lifts him upon his shoulders and carries him away, saying, "Because thou hast made danger thy calling, therefore shall I bury thee with

64

my own hands." Zarathustra then preaches, "live dangerously. Erect your cities beside Vesuvius. Send out your ships to unexplored seas. Live in a state of war."

Zarathustra then meets an old hermit who talks to him about God. When alone again, Zarathustra asks, "Can it actually be possible? This old saint in his forest hath yet heard ought of God being dead?" Nietzsche's atheism unfolds as the "higher men" gather in Zarathustra's cave to prepare themselves to preach his doctrine. He leaves them and later returns to find them offering incense to a donkey who has "created the world in his own image, i.e., as stupid as possible." He goes on to say, "He who hath to be a creator in good and evil—verily, he hath first be a destroyer, and break values into pieces." The old God is dead, and the new god is the Superman. What is great in man, Nietzsche believed, is that he is a *bridge* and not a goal. What can be loved in man is that he is a transition and a destruction. Eternal Recurrence follows the stage of Superman.

Nietzsche's philosophy of Eternal Recurrence posits that since we live in a universe with infinite time and finite space, all combinations of matter and all events in our lives will happen again and again for eternity. For the weak, the idea that one will have to live one's life over and over again, with every pain and regret intact, for eternity is a frightening thought. Not so for Nietzsche's Superman. Because he has cast aside the morality of the weak, he can affirm every moment of his life and celebrate the fact that he will live his life again and again. There is some debate as to whether Nietzsche means this to be a theory about the universe or if it is merely a psychological doctrine, as in we should live our lives as if we will have to live them exactly the same way for eternity.

14. FRIEDRICH NIETZSCHE (here photographed in 1882), whose admiration for Schopenhauer and Wagner finally coalesced into his concept of the Superman.

Nietzsche's works present two contrasting views of human behavior, the morality of the masters and the morality of mass humanity. The teaching of Christ and the prophets before him had assigned to every person equal worth and equal rights, the basic principles of democracy and Western society. According to Nietzsche, however, assigning worth to mass humanity would reduce the importance of the leaders. Instead he believed that moral systems must first bow before the gradations of rank. It therefore became immoral to say that what is right for one is right for all.

Nietzsche considered severity, violence, danger, and war as valuable as kindness and peace because great individuals—Supermen—appear only in dangerous times. Man's greatest qualities are thus strength and a passion for power. Greed, envy, and hatred are indispensable in the struggle for survival, and the Superman personifies the man who is both good and evil. Nietzsche, uninterested in the development of all humanity, expressed an exclusive interest in creating a class of finer and stronger individuals. The Superman, he believed, can survive only by human selection—through eugenic foresight and an ennobling education. Natural selection would be too haphazard.

While many of Nietzsche's contemporaries rejected Judeo-Christian theology, they did not cease to revere Christian ideals altogether. As Nietzsche said: "The secret stimulus of the French free-thinkers from Voltaire to August Comte was not to remain behind the Christian ideal...but to outbid it if possible."[20] But Nietzsche went a step further by formulating a philosophy devoid of traditional religion altogether. He called Christianity the "negation of life" and created a new ethical system based on the premise that the battle of life required not goodness but *strength,* not humility but *pride,* not altruism but *resolute intelligence.*

Nietzsche eventually faced his own mortality. Plagued by disease and increasing blindness, he fell into paranoid delusions of grandeur, persecution, and hysterical laughter. His insanity may have been the result of syphilis. In his biographical novel, *Doktor Faustus* (1890), German novelist Thomas Mann suggests that Nietzsche may have deliberately infected himself with the disease. In the book, Nietzsche's character is forewarned by a prostitute of her disease, yet he chooses to have intercourse with her anyway. In reality Nietzsche was eventually taken to an asylum, where he died in 1900.

Nietzsche once prophesied, "One day my name will be associated with the memory of something tremendous—a crisis without equal on earth, the most profound collision of conscience, a decision that was conjured up against everything that had been believed, demanded, hallowed so far."[21] His rebellion—an abrupt break with the past far more drastic than would have occurred in a gradual process of development— did make him a perfect model for many modernists, and his ideas had a strong influence on political thought. While modern scholars believe that the fascists who drew on Nietzsche misunderstood his work, the Nazis found much in Nietzsche to fit their schemes.

JIM MORRISON: THE END

Nietzsche's ambiguous legacy has lived on. Although his influence on twentieth century culture has been ubiquitous, one of the most visible examples can be found in Jim Morrison (1943–71), the poet and influential singer of the rock group the Doors. Morrison, who saw more than a mere literary or political symbol in Nietzsche, began reading his works at age sixteen and idolized the German philosopher. After reading *Beyond Good and Evil* (1886) and *The Genealogy of Morals* (1887), Morrison deeply incorporated Nietzsche's views on aesthetics and morality into his poetry, music, and life.

Morrison was especially interested in Nietzsche's view of the relationship young people have with their families and with culture. In *Beyond Good and Evil* Nietzsche writes, "Involuntarily parents turn children into something similar to themselves— they call that 'education'...and like the father, teachers, classes, priests and princes still see, even today, in every new human being an unproblematic opportunity for possession." These subversive themes fascinated Morrison. James Riordan and Jerry Prochnicky, two of Morrison's biographers, wrote,

> Jim ate this kind of stuff up and it fueled the fires of rebellion already burning within him, for Nietzsche too was controversial to the bone. He preached a message that was in direct conflict with the Bible and the Judeo-Christian ethic of Jim's parents.[22]

Morrison was also interested in Nietzsche's concepts of freedom. Nietzsche's statements that "we are born, worn, jealous friends of solitude: that is the type of man we are, free spirits" and "one has to do everything oneself in order to know a few things oneself" captured young Morrison's mind. Nietzsche may have most strongly shaped Morrison, however, through his concept of the Superman. "He shall be greatest who can be loneliest, the most concealed, the most defiant, the human being beyond good and evil.... Like a rider on a steed that flies forward, we drop the reins before the infi-

15. JIM MORRISON. By the end of 1967, the Doors were regarded as the leading exponents of acid rock, and Jim Morrison was "acid evangelist to a musical cult that numbered in the hundreds of thousands."

nite, we modern men, like semi-barbarians—and reach our bliss only where we are most in danger."[23] Such statements seem like a roadmap for Morrison's life. Nietzsche prophesied that someday a great redeemer would come who would "liberate the will and restore its goal to the earth." He called this redeemer the "Antichrist...the victor over God and nothingness." Whether he realized it or not, Morrison tried in vain to be that person.

As a student at UCLA, Morrison considered writing a film on Nietzsche's life but eventually found expression for Nietzsche's philosophies through his rock group, the Doors. The name of the group was most likely derived from *The Doors of Perception* (1954) by Aldous Huxley, who had in turn taken the title from a line in a William

68 Blake poem. By the end of 1967 the Doors were the leading exponents of acid rock, and Morrison was "acid evangelist to a musical cult that numbered in the hundreds of thousands." Film director Oliver Stone examined the group's cult status in *The Doors,* his 1991 film about Morrison's life.

The Doors dedicated their music to the release of neurotic energy, breaking barriers, and thrusting listeners into another physical and emotional place. They accomplished this for their audiences—but also for Morrison himself. "There's this theory about the nature of tragedy and comedy," Morrison said, "that Aristotle didn't mean catharsis for the audience but a purgation of emotions for the actors themselves. The audience is just a witness to what's taking place on the stage."

In the late 1960s the Doors created the sound of contemporary tragedy. Through his music and live performances, Morrison tried to show his young audiences that "the spirit of tragedy is right beneath the surface of America." The times were characterized with social turmoil and upheaval as the young questioned the "artificial" values of the prior generation. As singer-poet Bob Dylan would proclaim during this period, "All is phony." Therefore in the 1960s Morrison's Dionysian lifestyle, to many of the young, seemed a viable alternative to the rigid, plastic mold the Establishment presented as the "American Dream."

Like Rimbaud, Morrison reflected his philosophy in his lifestyle. He consumed large amounts of alcohol and drugs and lived out his ideas of rebellion. Considering himself an erotic politician, Morrison was arrested some ten times between 1963 and 1969, several times for lewd conduct onstage. One of his most prominent arrests was for his conduct at a Miami concert before nearly thirteen thousand people. Arriving drunk, Morrison sang only five or six songs. He then shouted obscenities and encouraged the audience to strip and have sexual intercourse. Many did take off their clothes. One of his bandmates commented that "Jim's audiences were always a major part of his performance, his 'theater,' and he instinctively sensed that these exploding young bodies were clamoring for more. So he pushed them and lured them into pushing him."[24]

Morrison's most explicit expression of Nietzsche probably came in his poem set to music, *The End.* Nietzsche's *Birth of Tragedy* inspired references to Oedipus at the end of the song, where Morrison writes that he wanders into his sister's room and then his brother's, then tells his father that he wants to kill him and expresses the need to have sex with his mother. When Morrison sang the song in 1967 at a concert that his mother attended, she was stunned and embarrassed. After screaming obscenities at her, he gave her a vacant stare and screamed the obscenities again, this time showing his teeth. It was probably the last time he saw his mother alive.

The song provided a fitting soundtrack for Francis Ford Coppola's 1979 film *Apocalypse Now,* and maybe the perfect song for the horrors of the Vietnam War. Indeed, the Doors were a favorite band among the armed forces stationed in Vietnam. Coppola opened and closed the film with *The End.* He had the song remixed to bring up the guitar and Morrison chanting, "Kill, kill, kill" along with several obscenities—vocal parts that had been mixed down in the original recording.

On July 3, 1971, Morrison was found dead in his bathtub in Paris, where he had been living in virtual exile. One explanation is that an errant blood clot triggered by a respiratory ailment caused his heart to stop, but contrary information indicates he may have died of a heroin overdose. The official French death certificate lists him as "James Morrison, Poet." Several days after his death, Morrison was buried at Père-Lachaise, one of the oldest and most prestigious cemeteries in Paris. It is also the final resting place of numerous celebrated artists including Chopin, Molière, and Oscar Wilde. Morrison was buried in the section known as the "Poet's Corner" near the grave of Molière. Today Morrison's grave is a popular spot for young people, who cover the tomb with graffiti and sometimes sleep there.

Although Morrison has been dead for three decades now, more than a million albums by the Doors are still sold nearly every year. Morrison's early death testifies to the fallacies of Nietzsche's philosophy, and his search for the Superman ended at the young age of twenty-seven the truth that no man can transcend his own mortality. Instead of casting doubt on his and Nietzsche's philosophy, however, Morrison's sudden death made it even more attractive. Morrison, Nietzsche, and their philosophies live on.

THE QUESTIONS REMAIN

Although hundreds or even thousands of people may see a painting, millions will see a film. Even an unsuccessful film will attract a greater audience than paintings of the late nineteenth and early twentieth centuries. Today the power to communicate through films and other mass media such as television is awesome. While the same questions Voltaire and Gauguin asked continue to be raised in films, they are asked on a much larger scale than those earlier thinkers and artists could have dreamed.

16. SCENE FROM *BLADE RUNNER*. The replicants have a mission. With his three partners now destroyed by explosive bullets, Batty succeeds in finding his way to Tyrell, the genetic engineering genius who designed him. Batty wants his genetic code altered to extend his assigned four-year life span. He simply wants to live, but when he discovers he cannot, Batty kills Tyrell in a despairing rage, calling him (as Zeus to Cronos) "Father." At one point Batty remarks, "It's a hard thing to meet your maker."

For example, film director Ridley Scott's (b. 1939) widely influential 1982 film *Blade Runner* posed these classic questions some eighty years after Gauguin. Scott, who also directed the 1979 classic film *Alien* and the epic *Gladiator* (2000), in *Blade Runner* depicts a bleak and energy-starved futurescape of the year 2019. Genetic engineering has become one of the earth's major industries, and scientists have now assumed the "creator" role. Artificial animals (to replace the original ones that became extinct) and artificial people called "replicants" have been created to do the difficult, hazardous, and often tedious work necessary in the colonies on other planets. Yet occasionally a repli-cant finds its way back to earth, and specially trained detectives, called "blade run-ners," hunt and exterminate such replicants. The film's central encounter is between blade runner Deckard and Batty, the leader of a group of warrior replicants who have returned to earth.

In the film's final scene, Deckard combats Batty on the rooftops of Los Angeles. When Batty feels the life force draining from his body, he drives a nail through his hand in a Christlike gesture. Batty overcomes Deckard and leaves him hanging from a ledge by his fingertips, ready to drop hundreds of feet onto the street below. But Batty spares him by pulling him onto the rooftop, saying, "Now you know what it's like to live in fear." The film ends with Deckard asking, "Where do we come from? Where are we going? How much time have we got?"

QUESTIONS AND ANSWERS

The twentieth century has been a period of social experimentation based on eigh-teenth and nineteenth century ideas. The theorists and artists of the nineteenth and early twentieth centuries might be shocked to find their ideas taken so seriously. Would Darwin have expected Hitler to build on his ideas of the survival of the fittest? Would Gauguin have expected a powerful film to ask his questions in a popular medium a century after he lived? Could Marx have foreseen the rise and fall of communism? Would the Impressionists have understood a world in which the idea of reality is so uncertain that entertainment has replaced religion as the central facet of our existence?

Perhaps not. Their ideas had significant consequences. And as humanity surges into the twenty-first century, the desperate questions of the nineteenth and twentieth centuries remain unanswered: *Where do we come from? What are we? Where are we going?*

CHAPTER 3
Children of the Machine

We are at the dead season of our fortunes. . . . We have been moved beyond endurance, and need rest. Never in the lifetime of men now living has the universal element in the soul of man burnt so dimly.

JOHN MAYNARD KEYNES

We think of the twentieth century as the "machine age" and largely take machines for granted. But the birthing of the machine age, which was by no means easy, took place more than two centuries ago. For much of that time, humankind's relationship with machines has been difficult and painful.

In the early eighteenth century, during the advent of the Industrial Revolution, the peasants bore unimaginable hardships. Working in extremely hazardous workplaces for employers who had no concept of worker safety, the people labored long hours, with little or no compensation if they grew sick from the fumes or were injured by the machinery. Despite their efforts, workers did not share in the triumphs of industry. Their standard of living, by and large, remained low, and they experienced all too clearly the metaphorical link between the industrial furnaces and the fires of hell. Poet William Blake blatantly referred to the factories as "dark Satanic mills."

The machine was blamed for taking man's place and denying his livelihood. Thus, many opposed the new technology. At times this opposition took a violent form, as in the Luddite Revolution (1811–16), which culminated in angry attacks against the textile machines that had replaced human weavers. While such protests created a fervent defense of the common laborer by such contemporary celebrities as Lord Byron, their efforts were futile. The machine became a permanent fixture on the economic landscape.

74

By the middle of the nineteenth century, the working class began to discover that it could, to a degree, take technology's power and potential into its own hands. The great proponent of this new perspective was, of course, Karl Marx, who went so far as to preach universal liberation through the control of technology itself, while at the same time attacking those who enslaved workers through its use.

By century's end, a mere hundred years after the French Revolution, the Paris World's Fair of 1889 heralded a new revolution—a revolution that did not overthrow political structures but altered people's very concept of themselves. Machines had become so sophisticated that they no longer required highly trained operators to run them—any person could do it. In other words, people were becoming mere adjuncts to the mechanical. Humans were becoming faceless.

17. AN ADVERTISING POSTER of the 1889 Paris World Exposition. The Eiffel Tower can be seen through the background mist. The Eiffel Tower was built for the International Exhibition of Paris of 1889 commemorating the centenary of the French Revolution. The Prince of Wales, later King Edward VII of England, opened the tower. Of the 700 proposals submitted in a design composition, Gustave Eiffel's was unanimously chosen.

THE APOTHEOSIS OF TECHNOLOGY

The main attraction at the 1889 Paris World's Fair was the Eiffel Tower, at the time the tallest human-made structure in the world. To the ruling classes of Europe, the tower represented the promise of technology: the accumulation of unlimited wealth and power. But for French poet Guillaume Apollinaire (1880–1918), the tower was a universal symbol of the human condition. In one of his poems, he imagined the second coming of Christ taking place in the new Paris, but this Christ was not the God of traditional religion. It was the new Messiah of mass technology—represented by the tower itself. Apollinaire, who coined the term *surrealist,* also was apparently the first to describe humankind as "faceless" against the onslaught of the new era of the machine.

In the 1880s technology exploded. That decade saw the invention of the recoil-operated machine gun, the first synthetic fiber, the Parsons steam turbine, coated photographic paper, the Tesla electric motor, the Kodak box camera, the Dunlap pneumatic tire, cordite, the diesel engine, the Ford motor car, the cinematograph, and the gramophone. In the following decade came X-rays, radio telegraphy, and the first movie camera. The principle of rocket propulsion was enunciated, and Sigmund Freud published his fundamental studies on hysteria. Then came the discovery of radium, the magnetic recording of sound, the first voice transmissions, and the Wright brothers' first powered flight in 1903. In 1905 Albert Einstein formulated his "Special Theory of Relativity" and single-handedly ushered in the nuclear age.

Almost everyone could sense the magnitude of these changes. As the age of steam faded into the age of electricity, the sense of accelerating change intensified. The new religion of technology was born. Every new technological breakthrough almost came to be perceived as a sacred event. After French aviator Louis Blériot (1872–1936) became the first person to fly across the English Channel in 1909, Parisians carried his small plane through the streets and installed it in a deconsecrated church—now part of the Musée des Arts et Métiers (the Museum of Art and Industry). There it still hangs under blue shafts of light from stained windows, looking for all the world like the relic of an archangel. Blériot and the technology that put him aloft were immortalized by Robert Delaunay in his 1914 painting *Homage to Blériot*.

WILD BEASTS — THE FAUVES

But in this new religion of technology, what became of the soul? What role would it play? That is the question that was left for the artists to wrestle with.

In response to the new machine age, whose shadow seemed to obscure humankind, the Fauve ("wild beasts") movement startled the art world in 1905 with its explosions of brilliant color, rough brushstrokes, and anti-naturalistic perspectives. Fauvist paintings were seen as violent and bestial—especially in contrast to the subtle tones and intimate subject matter of the late Impressionist painters.

Although Henri Matisse (1869–1954), the acknowledged "King of the Fauves," began as a competent painter in a modified Impressionist style, he soon began to apply masses of brilliant color with broad brushstrokes and to juxtapose them in large, flat areas—with jarring results. His 1905

18. THE EIFFEL TOWER, in an old photo with the Wright brothers' airplane flying past it. "The important thing," wrote art historian Robert Hughes, "was that the Tower had a mass audience; millions of people, not the thousands who went to the salons and galleries to look at works of art, were touched by the feeling of a new age that the Eiffel Tower made concrete."[1]

painting *The Green Stripe* was a blazing bouquet of colors applied not only to the arbitrarily divided background and the figure's dress and collar but also to the face. In this painting, the woman's face is dominated by a vivid green stripe through the center of the forehead and down her nose.

One of Matisse's greatest pieces is *Joy of Life* (1905–6), an eight-foot-long painting depicting a forest glade. An open space is pushed back into depth by a series of one-dimensional trees and abruptly diminishing figures, distorting the perspective. One can see Gauguin's influence through Matisse's representation of a hypothetically calm society, distant in time but not geography. Art historian Frederick Hartt suggests that Matisse had in mind "the mythical golden age of the Greek gods, known to Europeans of the Christian era through Greek and Latin and known to Matisse particularly through visual interpretations of ancient stories in Italian Renaissance painting."[2]

In 1943 Matisse moved to the Riviera, where Dominican nuns cared for him during a serious illness. In gratitude, he created a chapel for them. Matisse drew the chapel's murals in blank brushstrokes on glazed white ceramic tile with a spareness that reflects the Dominican way of life. The murals of the fourteen Stations of the Cross are so powerful that it seems as if Matisse himself were experiencing the exhaustion and pain of the Cross. Although he professed no formal religion, Matisse's mural is one of the few great works of religious art created in the twentieth century.

CUBISM AND LES DEMOISELLES D'AVIGNON

Another important group of artists, the Cubists, arose and offered the first real attempt to find humanity's place in a world dominated by machines. For the Cubists, reality was the interaction between the viewer and the object being viewed. As scientists like Albert Einstein were developing a more subjective view of life, a more relativistic one, the Cubists reflected this shift in their paintings. Instead of presenting a unified focus, as in Renaissance perspective painting, the Cubists offered multiple perspectives within a single work.

Pablo Picasso (1881–1973) quickly became the most important Cubist, influencing nearly every phase of artistic activity throughout Europe and the Americas. His importance can be compared with that of Michelangelo and Titian in their times.

Picasso drew from many sources. Gauguin's primitivism, as in *Where Do We Come From? What Are We? Where Are We Going?* along with Iberian sculpture, Greek classical art, and African masks and sculptures all strongly influenced Picasso. For example, he became enamored with an African statuette that Matisse had given to American writer and entrepreneur Gertrude Stein (1874–1940), who helped support and motivate the new emerging artists in Paris. Picasso saw the mask and other African art as mediators against unknown, threatening spirits. He identified with them, saying that he too was against everything—that he believed everything is unknown, everything is an enemy. For Picasso, the established order—in fact, all of creation—could be manipulated through art.

Picasso's 1907 masterpiece *Les Demoiselles d'Avignon* ("the women of Avignon") is a landmark in modern art. (See color plate 10.) While it undoubtedly took its general inspiration from Cézanne's *The Great Bathers* (1898–1905), Picasso chose to emphasize the architectural development of five huge female nudes whose anatomies form the ribs of a vault-like space. Their faces are masks, entirely freed from humanity. Although Picasso denied any influence other than Iberian sculpture, the two heads at the far right seem inspired by French African Congolese art. The painting's violent dissonances make it far uglier and less accessible than Cézanne's. Although the pink and ocher of the grotesque figures reflect the colors of Roman fresco painting, their dark, synthetically colored, scarified faces introduced a new element—they ushered a new psychological content into modern art, as well as new criteria for pictorial consistency.

The painting did not acquire its title from Picasso but originated with one of his poet friends—either André Salmon or Max Jacob. It is a jesting reference to a particularly lower-class brothel in the Calle d'Avignon in Barcelona, which the impoverished Picasso frequented as a young artist. The suggested title was a swipe at what seemed like the extreme ugliness of the female figures in the work. The painting, however, is completely amoral. It is neither propaganda for sexual activity nor a statement against it. Originally entitled *The Wages of Sin,* the painting was meant to be an allegory of venereal disease. One of the original studies showed a sailor carousing in the brothel, but by omitting the sailor, Picasso forces the viewer to receive the stares of the five women themselves. The stares are not forms of welcome; rather than appearing seductive, the prostitutes appear cruelly judging.

PICASSO'S WOMEN

In *Les Demoiselles* Picasso announced a recurrent subtheme—his fear of women, which often expressed itself as outright misogyny. As art critic Robert Hughes writes, "No painter ever put his anxiety about impotence and castration more plainly than Picasso did in *Les Demoiselles,* or projected it through a more violent dislocation of form. Even the melon, that sweet and pulpy fruit, looks like a weapon."[3] Paradoxically, no artist since Rubens was more entranced by women than Picasso, whose rapturous sexuality and sexual hostility are both evident. Picasso left psychological scars on virtually every woman with whom he was intimate, yet it did not seem to trouble him terribly. Among the seven women with whom Picasso had serious relationships, two committed suicide, and one, Dora Maar, suffered a nervous breakdown during their years together. Although Maar underwent shock therapy, she never fully recovered.

Picasso admitted the often merciless message of his art: "It must be painful for a girl to see in a painting that she's on the way out."[4] This cold-bloodedness is evident in works such as *Head of a Woman* (1927) and *Head on a Red Background* (1928). The head of a woman—presumably his wife, Olga Koklova—is shown as nothing more than a bean-shaped armature supporting a voracious mouth. The 1931 canvas *The Kiss* acutely captures failed love by showing a pair of heads devouring one another.

Picasso's 1930 *Seated Bather* depicts woman as a monster constructed from bone and stone with the imagery of genital warfare. And his 1937 portrait of Maar, *The Weeping Woman,* portrays utter panic and despair as warplanes hover where the irises of her eyes should be—eyes that also read as suspended teacups spitting tears. Finally, *The Peeing Woman,* the 1965 painting of his wife Jacqueline, documents Picasso's disgust and loathing for the female body.

Later in life, in his eighties, Picasso focused on sexual violence, voyeurism, and sexual impotence, all of which can be seen in a series of 347 prints he produced in a burst of creative energy between May 16 and October 5, 1968. A frequently repeated subject is an erotic scene where a young artist (distinguished by a beret, palette, and brushes) copulates with a young woman and is spied upon by an old man, sometimes wearing a fool's cap.

It is unfortunate that the depersonalization of people—particularly women—has been evidenced in the work of many recent artists. Picasso's legacy lives on, for example, in the work of British artist Allen Jones, whose most notorious creations include a series of sculptures that transform women dressed in scanty leather costumes into items of furniture—a chair, a table, even a hat stand—as in his 1969 *Table Sculpture.* Not surprisingly, feminists have protested against Jones's work.

Or consider Robert Mapplethorpe (1946–89). While he is known for raising photography to the status of fine art, he also typically objectified the human body. In his *Black Males* portfolio of the early 1980s, he concentrates on parts of the body, rather than the whole person, reducing the individual to an object, as Courbet had in *Origin of the World.* The 1980 *Man in Polyester Suit,* part of the *Black Males* portfolio, depicts disproportionately large genitals protruding from the pants of a man who remains anonymous because the photograph is cropped across the torso and at mid-thigh. In the 1979 *Phillip Prideau,* a black man crouches on top of a tall pedestal, as if his body were a rare art object such as a precious Chinese vase.

PICASSO RECONSIDERED

Picasso had no final answers, but his work suggested that a painting or sculpture could be as real as (or more real than) the object it portrayed. Picasso and others came to believe that pictorial reality was something other than physical reality. To modern artists, the laws of art were no longer subject to the laws of life. The artist was his own legislator once he determined which laws he would obey.

Picasso also created the concept of *objet trouvé,* or "found object." He first added a found object to a series of wooden wall reliefs of still-life subjects and later to a cast bronze sculpture entitled *Glass of Absinthe,* which he created in 1914. A silver strainer, used in Paris cafés to sweeten absinthe, served as *Absinthe*'s commonplace or ordinary element. The sculpture *Head of a Woman,* created fifteen years after *Glass of Absinthe,* also incorporated found objects. The head is formed with vegetable colanders welded into a hollow sphere. The hair is made from coiled springs and curves of welded iron. Stick-like features—eye, nose, and lips—protrude from a dehumanized concave sheet-metal face.

One particular anecdote tellingly describes Picasso's influence. American writer Ernest Hemingway, who recognized Picasso's revolutionary importance, attempted to visit his old acquaintance in Paris shortly after World War II. Learning that Picasso was out, Hemingway decided to leave him a present. He went to his car and returned with a case of grenades on which he wrote, "To Picasso from Hemingway."

THE RITE OF SPRING

Once established, Cubism remained prominent for many years, affecting not only painting and sculpture but also architecture and commercial and industrial design. Especially after *Les Demoiselles,* artists mixed primitive forms with classical or traditional art.

For example, Russian composer Igor Stravinsky (1882–1971) incorporated primitivism into his musical works. His first success, the 1910 ballet *The Firebird,* was based on a fairy tale. It opened in Paris and brought Stravinsky instant international fame. Then, inspired by a dream of pagan rituals with virgin dancers sacrificed to the god of

Spring, Stravinsky wrote *The Rite of Spring* in 1913, a composition of various folk melodies centering around a dissonant chord, now known as the *sacre* chord. Although he knew he was creating something strikingly new, Stravinsky was unprepared for the hostility of the usually sympathetic Paris audience. The first performance created an uproar in the theatre, with the music's disturbing dissonance and the unnatural movements of Russian ballet dancer Vaslav Nijinsky's unconventional choreography.

Although Stravinsky had not yet met Picasso, Cubism and primitivism clearly influenced *The Rite of Spring*. The two artists finally met in 1920 when Stravinsky began work on a new ballet for which Picasso designed the scenery. Stravinsky unreservedly praised Picasso, paying tribute to the "amazing inventiveness of this remarkable man." That year, Stravinsky moved to Paris where he and Picasso, only a year apart in age, paralleled each other's careers closely.

THE FUTURISTS

While the Cubists wrestled with the implications of the machine age, many people still lived in rural areas and remained largely insulated from modern machine technology. A movement called Futurism accelerated the general public's understanding of the issues, however, particularly in France and Italy.

In 1909 the Belgian Symbolist poet Emile Verhaeren (1855–1916) wrote a prophetic declaration: "Future, you exalt me as once my God exalted me."[5] The artists of the Futurist movement saw themselves as children of the machine, the "primitives of a new and transformed sensibility." They exalted change and identified with the machine almost mystically. The Futurists launched an ideological program that raised machine-Romanticism to the status of a religion. Futurism attacked anything old and advocated the destruction of academies, museums, and monumental cities, which they saw as barriers to progress. They extolled the glories of industrial achievement and even modern war—all of which led precariously in the direction of Italian fascism. The Futurists promoted their cause through advertising. They devised a variety of new geometric typefaces and labored over their titles to make them interesting.

Between 1909 and 1915 a major new art form arose—the Manifesto, about fifty of which were published in Italy alone during that period. Filippo Tommaso Marinetti (1876–1944), Italian poet and ideological father of the Futurist movement, composed the first Futurist Manifesto in Paris. Henceforth, he declared, poets should "sing only of revolution and the glorification of the machine." His ideas affected the entire

European, American, and Russian avant-garde, and his techniques were later incorporated into the innovative Dada art movement during World War I and eventually into 1960s art and literature.

Marinetti attracted a group of gifted artists who loved nothing more than to outrage the public with their manifestoes and demonstrations. In July 1910, for example, Futurists dropped copies of Marinetti's pamphlet "Against Past-Loving Venice" from the top of Venice's clock tower while Marinetti gave an impromptu speech to the crowd. Marinetti and other Futurists were particularly fascinated by a relatively new art form, the cinema, which they believed embodied the future of art. Primitive cinematography proved useful to them.

Umberto Boccioni (1882–1916) was one of the most expressive and artistically powerful Futurists. His painting *The City Rises* (1910–11) depicts a muscular red horse dissolving under the power of its own energy and every animal and human figure fading under the speed of change. The only permanent object in the painting is the new construction in the background. Upon seeing new construction underway on the outskirts of Milan, Boccioni proclaimed, "I am nauseated by old walls and old palaces. I want the new, the expressive, the formidable."[6] The Futurists' "mechandolatry," or idolatry of mechanization, translated such images as Boccioni's speeding figure in his 1913 sculpture *Unique Forms of Continuity in Space* into a kind of superman.

THE ROCK DRILL

A fundamental concept of artists during the Industrial Revolution was the concern that the creations of humans could rise against them and eventually destroy them—the same notion that underlies Mary Shelley's classic novel *Frankenstein* (1818). Jacob Epstein's (1880–1959) startling sculpture *The Rock Drill* (1913–14) takes this concept a step further by portraying the Futurist vision of man literally being eaten by a machine. (See color plate 11.) *Frankenstein* may have indeed fueled Epstein's sculpture, as the drill, with its marked head and machine-like appendages, is a fusion of human and machine.

Epstein understood the implications of Futurism and its glorification of the machine. He said, "This is the sinister armored figure of today and tomorrow. Nothing human, only the terrible Frankenstein's monster into which we have transformed ourselves."[7]

MECHANO-SEXUAL MAN

While Epstein did not deeply explore the mechano-sexual metaphor, *The Rock Drill* introduced a powerful image of castration by discarding the drill's machine section (leg, genitalia, and mechanical torso) and keeping only its thorax and masked head. Artists such as Francis Picabia (1879–1953) and Marcel Duchamp further developed the analogy between machine action and sexuality. They suggested that the machine had become a perverse but substantially accurate self-portrait of humanity.

Picabia expressed this view in the title of one of his works, *La Fille Née Sans Mère* ("The Daughter Born without a Mother"), painted in 1916–17. Picabia saw the machine as a modern counterpart to the Virgin Birth because Christ, like the machine, was born without an earthly father. Machinery parodied not only the Virgin Birth but other attributes of Catholicism. Parallels were drawn between attending to a machine and attending Mass.

One of the most influential artist/philosophers of the twentieth century, Marcel Duchamp (1887–1968), refined and championed the mechano-sexual metaphor. Duchamp's initial mechano-sexual work was the 1912 *Nude Descending a Staircase No. 2,* which outraged the orthodox Cubists at a 1912 Paris exhibition. It also scandalized American audiences at the 1913 New York Armory Show. *Nude Descending a Staircase* rejected the decorative values of Cubism and suggested the conquest of people by the "Infernal Machine." The painting suggests that all human movements are programmed and circumscribed—that people are nothing more than absurd machines in an absurd world.

Nude, however, was but a precursor to Duchamp's landmark work, *The Bride Stripped Bare by Her Bachelors, Even (The Large Glass)* (1915–23). (See color plate 12.) Although widely debated and analyzed, the artistry in *The Large Glass* is deliberate. Nothing in it is accidental apart from the dust that Duchamp allowed to accumulate and then preserved with a fixative and the cracks that appeared in the twin panes after a trucking accident. Outlined in lead wire in transparent panes, *The Large Glass* spawned numerous conflicting interpretations. Duchamp describes the machine as running on a mythical fuel he invented called "Love Gasoline," which passed through "filters" into "feeble cylinders" and activated "a desire motor." In the top half of *The Large Glass,* the naked bride perpetually disrobes. In the bottom pane, the bachelors, depicted by jackets and uniforms, grind away at a chocolate grinder, signaling to the girl their sexual frustration. Separated by the prophylactic bar that divides the panes, the bride is condemned forever to tease and the bachelors to suffer frustration.

Some see the perpetual separation of the bride and bachelors as a metaphor for narcissism and sublimation. Others view the painting as a declaration of freedom in its portrayal of masturbation, a symbol of the revolt against the institution of the traditional family and its authority. The work's sterile and gratuitous functioning made it a key image for an avant-garde that tended increasingly toward narcissism. Whatever the interpretation, *The Large Glass* is a glimpse into a peculiarly modern hell of repetition, frustration, and loneliness.

The Large Glass is also a tragic machine, a testament to indifference and defiance, a state of mind suggested by Duchamp in his so-called "Readymades." This was a style of sculpture that took Picasso's concept of found art a step further and gave rise to memorable public scandals in Duchamp's day. Readymades are commonly manufactured products that Duchamp elevated to the level of art objects, such as his 1916 *Comb.* Readymades included everything from a snow shovel Duchamp titled *In Advance of the Broken Arm* (1915) to a white urinal he called *Fountain* (1917) and signed with the pseudonym "R. Mutt." By associating art with non-art, Duchamp challenged the traditional hierarchy of artistic values and helped to undermine the privileged status of fine art.

In the early 1940s Duchamp announced he was abandoning art for chess. In reality, between 1946 and 1966 he was producing a secret elaborate peep show of a nude woman in a vegetation-lined box entitled *Given: 1. The Waterfall, 2. The Illuminating Gas.* The work was revealed after Duchamp's death in a permanent installation at the Philadelphia Museum of Art.

ART IN AMERICA

During the nineteenth and early twentieth centuries, Europe, especially France and Germany, was widely exposed to this new art. The United States, on the other hand, remained virtually untouched by the innovations. The 1913 New York Armory Show, officially called the International Exhibition of Modern Art, ended this isolation. The month-long show, held at the New York National Guard's 69th Regiment Armory, displayed a wide collection of some two thousand pieces of modern European art. Painter and show representative Walter Kuhn wrote, "We want this old show of ours to mark the starting point of a new spirit in art, at least as far as America is concerned."[8] Mable Dodge (1879–1962), a leading Greenwich Village activist, called the Armory Show "the most significant American event since 1776."[9]

The show had a great cultural impact because it introduced the leading examples of European modern art to an artistically naïve American public. Scarcely aware of anything beyond America's Ash Can School, which had focused on the grimy urbanscapes of New York or the traditional portraiture of John Singer Sargent, Americans saw for the first time the works of Courbet, Monet, Gauguin, van Gogh, Cézanne, Seurat, Rousseau, the Fauves, Matisse, the Cubists, Picasso, Braque, Leger, Picabia, and Duchamp.

Duchamp's *Nude Descending a Staircase* became a cause célèbre and inspired shameless and frequent mockery by cartoonists and others. Even the liberal-minded Teddy Roosevelt confessed that the painting reminded him of a Navajo blanket, while others called it "an explosion in a shingle factory" or a "staircase descending a nude."[10]

The New York Times, after describing the show as "pathological," called the Armory modernists "cousins to the anarchists." *Art and Progress,* the official magazine of the American Federation of Arts, compared the European artists to anarchists: "bomb throwers, lunatics, depravers." America of 1913 found the European art radical and revolutionary.

Still, the controversial show attracted nearly three hundred thousand spectators and lifted its audience out of the narrowness of a complacent provincial taste, compelling them to judge American painting and sculpture by a more exacting and ambitious world standard. As a consequence of the show, when Duchamp arrived in New York in 1915, he was greeted as an international celebrity and emerged as the leader of a new breed of iconoclasts.

The Armory Show stimulated the American art world. Artists such as Arthur Dove and Georgia O'Keefe pursued new modernist ground. Modern art galleries soon began appearing in many American cities, including New York. American photographer Alfred Stieglitz's influential gallery at 291 Fifth Avenue in New York, known simply as 291, pioneered exhibitions of the new American painting and sculpture. In 1920 Katherine Dreier, one of the first American abstract painters and a foresighted collector of modern art, founded the Museum of Modern Art along with Marcel Duchamp and Man Ray, using rented quarters. Since then, museums have replaced the church as the center of civic pride in cities and communities.

THE WAR: MOVED BEYOND ENDURANCE

Meanwhile back in Europe, the Futurists, led by Marinetti, became obsessed with technology as the most sublime experience of modern life. Futurism contained an element of irrational worship, and its stridency foretold fascism. Marinetti was an early supporter of Italian dictator Benito Mussolini, and the Futurists endorsed Italy's entrance into the First World War in 1915. Gino Severini's propagandist painting *Armored Train* (1915) epitomizes the Futurists' glorification of war. Its blasting cannons, shooting soldiers, clouds, and rays of light merge to create a blazing portrait of deadly conflict.

Even on the verge of war, a stubborn hope for a Futurist utopia remained. Gertrude Stein proclaimed: "[A]s everything destroys itself in the twentieth century and nothing continues, so then the twentieth century has a splendor which is its own."[11] This splendor of the new age soon faded into the Frankenstein of 1914 and the worst war in history.

Although the carnage of World War I cast a shadow over millions and extinguished Futurism's appeal, the movement's influence on modern aesthetics remained central. By calling attention to the specific character of modern life, Futurism forced the public to accept the artist as interpreter of life, even in its rawest and most immediate forms.

Simply put, World War I was the beginning of the destruction of traditional Western culture. Although the warring countries had fought colonial wars with professional soldiers and mercenaries before, no one could dream of the horrors of fully mechanized trench warfare. The Futurists' concept that war is the "world's only hygiene" was unmercifully unmasked by the machines of war. As Ernest Hemingway wrote, World War I was "the most colossal, murderous, mismanaged butchery that has ever taken place on earth."[12]

Ten million soldiers and millions of civilians died. Thousands of others were maimed. The lost fathers, brothers, and husbands left an unredeemable spiritual vacuum and a near total destruction of ideals, confidence, and goodwill. Standing in their huge cemeteries, Europeans were appalled at what had been done to their fellow human beings and to their countries that now lay in ruins. John Maynard Keynes, then a young British economist, wrote, "We have been moved beyond endurance, and need rest. Never in the lifetime of men now living has the universal element in the soul of man burnt so dimly."[13]

Language too was broken. World War I changed the life of words and images radically and forever as the age of mass-produced, industrialized death was ushered in.

THE RISE OF THE MODERN STATE

The primary concern of the postwar Peace Conference and the 1919 Treaty of Versailles was to punish Germany, which lay exhausted at the center of the chaos. Economic reparations made Germany's defeat even harder to bear and provided Germany with some self-justification for the Second Great War that would follow two decades later.

The war also destroyed the Russian state. German armies had broken the hearts of even the long-enduring Russian soldiers. Russian cities were starving because the transport system had broken down and the government was full of incompetent, corrupt men who feared constitutionalism and liberalism as much as defeat. When mutiny followed the 1917 food riots in Russia, the autocracy suddenly seemed powerless. The Tsar abdicated, and a provisional government of liberals and socialists took his place. This government was in turn swept away in a coup called the October Revolution, which was led by Vladimir Ilich Lenin (1870–1924), who simply understood that the Russians wanted peace and bread. This Bolshevik Revolution, together with the American entry into the war, marked 1917 as a break between two eras of European history.

But the Russian dominoes continued to fall: first Lenin, then Stalin with his "Five Year Plan," which led to a civil war and the deaths or exile of millions of peasants. The Union of Soviet Socialist Republics (USSR) came into being, with its founders committed to destroying the entire pre-war European order.

Halfway around the world, the echoes were heard in China, as Mao Tse-tung came to power and initiated a social cleansing that continues even today.

THE AMERICANS

Because of its late entry into World War I, the United States suffered the least in terms of death and psychological damage. But the war irrevocably changed American culture by triggering the beginning of the manipulation of public opinion through an official media machine. President Woodrow Wilson believed that a united American opinion about the war was critical to victory and regarded any dissent as "intolerable after April 1917." Although the era was known as "Progressive," the manipulation of public opinion for political purposes became a highly refined art. The government and civic organizations fought the battle for America's minds primarily in the public schools and universities. These efforts became a grassroots crusade, and some states even forbade the teaching of German.

Bowing to pressure from patriotic groups, the federal Bureau of Education cooperated with the National Board of Historical Service and the Committee on Public Information, which was a government propaganda agency. These groups distributed various "war study courses," which promulgated the government's views of the war to the nation's schools. Colleges and universities served as "pre-induction centers where young men could be temporarily held prior to call-up for active military duty."[14] "War Issues Courses" presented the war as a life or death struggle between democracy and autocracy, upon whose outcome the future of civilization depended.

As a result of the widespread availability of prostitutes in war-torn Europe, the U.S. government conducted frank discussions about sex in the armed forces, all of which had far-reaching effects in postwar America. Determined to keep its troops healthy for battle, the army instituted a massive effort to fight venereal disease, with little concern for modesty. Posters such as "A German Bullet is Cleaner than a Whore" and "How could you look at the flag in the face, if you were dirty with gonorrhea?" proclaimed the government's views to its soldiers. Many of them still lived in the glow of Victorian culture and were thus receiving their very first sex education. These programs contributed to the demythologizing of erotic life by bringing sexual matters into public discourse. This would become a characteristic feature of twentieth century American culture.

All the government's propaganda efforts succeeded, but at the cost of the very social philosophy the Progressives had championed. Their various campaigns struck down their most cherished assumptions about the reasonableness of humankind, the malleability of society, and the value of education and publicity as tools of progress. Notions of "the people" as good and educable gave way to concepts of "the masses" as brutish and volatile. And of course, once large corporations realized the potential for manipulating public opinion by such means, they initiated another great shift brought about by the Great War: the evolution of America into a consumer society.

THE GENERATION GAP IN EUROPE

Perhaps the least understood effect of the war was its creation of a "generation gap." Because the horrors of the war were impossible to communicate to noncombatants, a vast gulf developed between the soldiers and their civilian counterparts.

World War I's effect on Europe, and especially Germany, in dividing the young from the old was similar to Vietnam's impact on America half a century later. The crimes of the elders seemed boundless to the young: they had not only started a war but had also lost it. The only institution that seemed intact in postwar Germany was its military machine. This generational divide became a permanent cultural feature in those societies, and for us it remains an accepted fact to this day.

A similar chasm also developed between the people and their leaders. Those who fought in the trenches knew that their respective governments had lied to their civilian populations—not one photograph of a corpse, for example, ever found its way into French, German, or British newspapers. Never had there been a wider gap between official language and perceived reality.

CLEAN SLATE: DADA

A hatred of authority and tradition developed among certain artists, writers, and entertainers. Some, disdainful of the past, wanted a clean slate, a new beginning. Others sought utopias through art and literature, while some simply sought escape from the madness.

Zurich, Switzerland, became a haven for the new avant-garde. The refugees consisted of every kind of intellectual, including writers and painters—Lenin and James Joyce among them. The common meeting ground in Zurich was the Café Odeon, or "café intellectual." Other cafés across Europe—from Berlin to Barcelona to Paris—became a home for exiles and natural theaters for the new and bizarre. As such, they represented a threat to the established culture.

Zurich intellectual Hugo Ball (1886–1927), who had lived in Berlin in the early 1900s, had tried to enlist in the army when war broke out but was rejected because of his weak heart. Nonetheless, he made his way to the front lines and returned with a respect for the horrors of the war. After Ball met actress and singer Emmy Hennings at a Berlin café, the two moved to Switzerland in 1915. They founded the Cabaret Voltaire (in the Zurich neighborhood where Lenin lived) and provided musical entertainment. Ball played the piano and composed "sound poems," such as "zimzim urullala zimzim urullala zimzim zanzibar zimzalla zam," which became popular with the young artists. They mixed the bizarre and archaic. Ball, for example, would dress as a Cubist bishop in cardboard "robes" and utter long mock-sacerdotal chants in gibberish. More than just entertainment, these chants were an assault on traditional language. Ball said, "In these phonetic poems we totally renounce the language that journalism has abused and corrupted. We must return to the innermost alchemy of the word, we must even give up the word too, to keep for poetry its last and holiest refuge."[15]

Ball took much of his inspiration from his predecessor, Frank Wedekind (1864–1918), who, according to Ball, "was struggling to eliminate both himself and the last remains of a once firmly established civilization."[16] Wedekind specialized in extemporaneous performances where he excoriated the Kaiser, spewed profanity, masturbated, and even went into onstage convulsions. If Wedekind had been an isolated eccentric, his cynical spectacles would not be worth remembering. But he was one of the fathers of Expressionism and influenced the Dada movement.

Such stage happenings, simultaneous poems, and mock rituals as these that occurred at the Cabaret Voltaire again came into vogue in the 1960s. In fact, the influence of Ball and Wedekind still is felt today in modern performance art. For example, 1990s performer Tim Miller stripped to the nude, groped the audience in the dark, and sexually stimulated himself onstage in his one-man performance *My Queer Body*. After his show received a grant from the National Endowment for the Arts, a reviewer for the *Village Voice* noted, "You don't have to agree with Jesse Helms to understand that some things are inappropriate."[17] Another controversial present-day performance artist, Annie Sprinkle, performed nude and invited the audience to examine her genitals with a flashlight at the Kitchen Theatre in New York in her 1990 work *Post-Porn Modernist*. Robert Mapplethorpe's *The Perfect Moment* is performance art constructed through photography. The work is a series of photographs that include men performing various homosexual acts and children with exposed genitals. One photograph, the *1977 X Portfolio, Jim and Tom, Sausalito,* depicts a man holding his genitals and urinating into another man's open mouth.

ELEMENTARY ART

The Dada movement sprang from the Zurich café scene in Zurich in 1916, although similar activities were already underway elsewhere. It took the brilliance of Ball and the energy of Tristan Tzara (1896–1963) to pull the anti-art movements together under the name *Dada*. In keeping with the spirit of opposition to the world of grown-ups, the nonsense title of the movement, *Dada,* which means simply a "child's hobbyhorse," was selected from the dictionary, probably by Ball and fellow Dadaist Richard Huelsenbeck. The movement symbolized the release of new psychic energies based on instinct, which the Zurich group celebrated.

90

Dada, however, was never an art style in the sense that Cubism was; nor did it begin with a sociopolitical program as had Futurism. Instead it stood for a wholly eclectic freedom to experiment and enshrined play as the highest human activity, rejecting everything that seemed false or hypocritical. Jean Arp (1887–1966), one of the most gifted of the Zurich Dadaists, explained the impetus of Dadaism: "Repelled by the slaughterhouses of the world war, we turned to art. We searched for an elementary art that would, we thought, save mankind from the furious madness of these times."[18]

19. *The Cathedral of Erotic Misery,* in Jean Arp's words, was "pierced from top to bottom with passages like mineshafts, crevasses artificially created through the storeys and spiral tunnels connecting the cellar with the roof."[19] It was a veritable city of Surrealistic overtones within a larger city.

CATHEDRAL OF EROTIC MISERY

The great lyric artist of Dadaism was Kurt Schwitters (1887–1948), who made art from odds and ends he found on the street. His acclaimed 1923 work *Cathedral of Erotic Misery,* known as *K.d.e.E.* for short, was destroyed in 1943 during World War II air raids, but photographs taken by Schwitters remain.

The first *Cathedral,* which was eleven-and-a-half feet high, stood in Schwitters' house in Hanover. It was a column that ran two stories of the building and was pierced from top to bottom. Spiral tunnels and passages like mineshafts connected the cellar with the roof. Schwitters placed light bulbs in its grottoes to illuminate the whole. After the bulbs short-circuited, he replaced them with candles which made it look like a Christmas tree. Visitors could wind up an organ that played "Silent Night, Holy Night."

In the "sadistic grotto" reposed the mutilated body of a young girl. In another corner stood the ten-percent disabled war veteran with his headless daughter. There were also a Goethean grotto with one of Goethe's legs as a relic, a corner devoted to Luther, and a brothel with a three-legged lady. In front of a visitor, Schwitters once took a box containing a doll from a niche and presented it as a tomb of St. Cecilia. From another recess, he took a closed jar containing what he called the "master's urine" in which everlasting flowers were dissolved.

CHANCE

Dada incorporated all art forms and tried to break all taboos, all norms of art, all sacred or nonsacred traditions. The past was its enemy. The Dada technique was spontaneity, and its two main sources of inspiration were childhood and chance. For example, Jean Arp's jigsawed wooden reliefs of 1916 through 1920 and his 1920 *Birds in an Aquarium* are like children's toys, simple and direct. Chance became the byword. Arp tore out scraps of papers and let them drop on a sheet, fixing them where they fell, making collages wholly by chance. Dadaist poets wrote by arbitrarily scrambling sentences and drawing words at random from a bag.

Although Futurism exerted an influence on Dada, Dadaism did not worship the machine. Marinetti and the Futurists wanted to destroy culture in the name of the Future, but Ball and the Dadaists wanted to destroy it in the name of Destruction. "We should burn all of the libraries and allow to remain only that which everyone knows by heart. A beautiful age of the legend would then begin."[20] The Dadaist hope lay in a fresh start, in cultural infancy.

Although its influence remains, Dadaism finally ran its course. Tzara left the Dadaists and joined André Breton's Surrealists. And Hugo and Emmy Ball converted to Catholicism.

EXPRESSIONISM: SCREAMS INTO THE DARKNESS

A fierce and respectable antiwar movement in Germany, called Expressionism, pessimistically mourned the loss of moral structures. While the Expressionist artists turned inward to examine humans' most intimate passions, their object was not a Romantic interest in the private soul; the Expressionists were searching for something universal. German Expressionist drama was particularly concerned with relationships between the sexes, and Expressionist plays usually used archetypal characters. Family relationships were a favorite subject, especially conflicts between father and son. Nietzsche's worship of creativity and the life force was a major influence on the early

Expressionists, as were Fyodor Dostoyevski's psychological novels and Walt Whitman's energetic poetry. German Expressionism poetry took on an especially apocalyptic tone.

Expressionist author Jakob von Hoddis (1887–1942) attempted to define Expressionism in 1914: "Man screams from the depths of his soul, the whole age becomes one single, piercing shriek. Art screams too, into the deep darkness, screams for help, for the spirit. That is expressionism."[21] This statement made Edvard Munch's 1899 painting *The Scream* a permanent symbol of the entire movement.

The Expressionist painters tried to capture the meaning behind the oppressive appearance of reality. For example, Franz Marc's (1880–1916) 1913 painting *The Fate of Animals* is a vision of apocalypse overwhelming innocent life. Marc saw himself as emotionally and physically inseparable from the animals he portrayed: "I try to feel myself pantheistically into the trembling and flow of the blood of nature—in trees, in animals, in the air.... I can see no happier means to the 'animalizing' of art, as I call it, than the animal picture."[22]

The original title of *The Fate of Animals,* written on the back of the painting, was *All being is flaming suffering.* The painting depicts an apocalyptic holocaust: a blue deer lifts its head to a falling tree; red foxes on the right, green horses at the top left. Colors have symbolic value: blue, for example, represents hope, but it is in the process of being extinguished. The fate of the animals is, ultimately, that they are bound to rigid cosmic laws that leave no room for freedom. Man is different from the animals, as he knows he has to die. But like the animals, he too is bound to die.

This tragic vision now seems prophetic. Shortly before his death in action on the Western Front in World War I, Marc sent a postcard of *Fate* to his wife on which he had written, "It is like a premonition of this war, horrible and shattering. I can hardly conceive that I painted it. It is artistically logical to paint such pictures before the war—but not as stupid reminiscences afterwards, for we must paint constructive pictures denoting the future."[23]

Another important Expressionist painter, Max Beckmann (1884–1950), created an indictment of official cruelty in *Night* (1919). The powerful jagged forms and almost monochromatic coloring tell of horror and disillusionment. The painting seems to prophesy the rise of Nazism, which would later designate Beckmann, like most German artists, "degenerate."

CARDPLAYING CRIPPLES

Both German Dadaists and postwar Expressionists became obsessed by "wretched half-men"—the people whom the war had crippled and whose bodies had been re-formed by politics: part flesh and part machine. Otto Dix (1891–1961) played out this theme in his 1920 painting *Cardplaying War-Cripples*. Raoul Hausmann produced one of the most memorable of all Dada sculptures in 1921, *The Spirit of Our Time,* in which a coiffeur's dummy carries an array of knobs and numbers and even a tape measure for making judgments.

Berliner George Grosz (1893–1959) became the most savage critic of the bourgeois-dominated, demoralized Germany. His 1920 *Republican Automatons* depicts a scene from the "new" Berlin recovering from the war. Two war cripples, one dressed in a black tie and white shirt, wearing an Iron Cross, and the other in the stiff collar and bowler hat of the capitalist bourgeoisie, occupy the foreground. The peg-legged one waves a German flag, and as machine cogs turn, a reflexive cheer issues from the empty egg-cup of a skull. The message is clear: in Grosz's Germany, everything and everyone are for sale. The world is owned by four breeds of pig: the capitalist, the officer, the priest, and the hooker, whose other form is the socialite wife.

Some of the Berlin Dadaists believed the photo montage—created from photo-reproduced images clipped from newspapers and magazines—could give art the necessary urgency. Max Ernst (1891–1976) produced one of the first genuinely interesting works of this kind. His 1920 *Murdering Airplane* is half machine, half woman. The female arms give the work a monstrous coquettishness, and the three tiny soldiers are powerless against its visitation.

John Heartfield (1891–1968) used photo montages as an effective protest against German militarism, Nazism, and Hitler himself, as can be seen in his 1932 caricature *Adolf Hitler as Superman ("He Swallows Gold and Spits Out Tin-Plate")*. If Heartfield's scenes of brute power and social anarchy had been painted or drawn, they would have seemed overwrought. But the realism of the photograph made them credible.

THE CABINET OF DR. CALIGARI

The Italian Futurists had called films "living paintings." Soon Expressionist ideas too were applied to film. In the 1919 film *The Cabinet of Dr. Caligari,* audiences

20. A SCENE FROM *THE CABINET OF DR. CALIGARI*. Eric Pommer, the film's producer, was intrigued by the novelty of applying Expressionism to film to create what the Italian Futurists had called "living paintings." In fact, Expressionist artists were commissioned to paint the sets before it was decided that the narrator of the story would be portrayed as insane.

experienced psychological terror on the screen. The film caught the public's imagination, for it was the first to portray an unreal environment in what was perceived as a nightmare existence. Its serious narrative focused on the inner psychological nature of real characters engaged in unusual but not impossible activities. Hans Janowitz and Carl Mayer, writers of *Dr. Caligari,* probably did not realize at the time that they were creating a film that symbolized Germany between the World Wars.

Some critics interpret *Dr. Caligari* as significant for all of Western culture, as it caught the alienation, frustration, tension, and horror of existence. What only a few European intellectuals of the time perceived has now filtered down into popular culture so that *Caligari* is not just a freakish artwork but is closer to the Kafkaesque reality of our era.

The Cabinet of Dr. Caligari has become a landmark in film history and is regularly studied in introductory film courses, film societies, and museums. As the quintessential Expressionist film, it helped solidify the place of cinema in the arts and paved the way for Surrealism.

METROPOLIS

Many Expressionist filmmakers and producers emigrated to the United States. Filmmaker Fritz Lang (1890–1976), who made the influential 1926 film *Metropolis,* believed that films should turn and twist, following the patterns of society and indicating contemporary social ailments and their possible cures. His early German movies often revolved around a struggle between the individual and Fate, with Fate represented by some power, dictatorship, or specific law—anything that tries to suppress or destroy the individual.

Lang's films reflected the world's fears of the rising Nazis. In *Metropolis* Fate is represented by a group of future industrialists who enslave an entire city through technology. The head industrialist's son acts as mediator and brings the autocrats and workers into intimate contact with one another, which ironically creates an even greater opportunity for the industrialists to manipulate the workers.

Joseph Goebbels, who was Adolf Hitler's director of propaganda, once asked Lang if he was interested in making Nazi propaganda films. Lang gave no answer but packed his things that night, leaving Germany and his wife behind. Thereafter he settled in Hollywood.

In 1931 Lang made the classic thriller *M,* starring actor Peter Lorre, who plays a child serial murderer directed by an uncontrollable psychological force. Lang's symbolism for the internal struggles of his characters is heightened by violence and hallucinations. This can be seen in his 1936 film *Fury,* in which the character portrayed by actor Spencer Tracy sees the ghosts of twenty-two people he has condemned to die.

EXPRESSIONISM IN FILM

Expressionism emerged strongly in the black-and-white films that made up film noir in the 1940s. Expressionism is even evident in such popular films as Frank Capra's 1946 *It's a Wonderful Life,* especially in its shadowy nightmare sequence.

The Cabinet of Dr. Caligari specifically influenced countless films and many of the great directors, including Orson Welles, Alfred Hitchcock, and John Huston. Most recently, its influence can be seen in the neo-noir work of such directors as Tim Burton (b. 1960). There are clear similarities between sequences from *The Cabinet of Dr. Caligari* and *Metropolis* and Burton's *Batman, Batman Returns, Edward Scissorhands,* and *Ed Wood.*

21. SCENES FROM F. W. MURNAU'S *NOSFERATU* and Tim Burton's *Batman Returns*. Expressionism has always maintained a strain through cinema, most recently in the work of director Tim Burton.

Burton apparently has made a conscious choice to insert psychological nuances into his films, which can be seen in *Batman Returns,* in which the director pays tribute to another classic German film, F. W. Murnau's 1922 *Nosferatu,* a startling and visually remarkable adaptation of the Dracula legend. In *Batman Returns* the Penguin character closely resembles Murnau's Dracula. Moreover, one of the main characters in *Batman Returns*, Max Schreck, is the actor who played Dracula in the original *Nosferatu.*

SIGMUND FREUD: CAUSE, EFFECT, AND PSYCHE

For all its power, Expressionism faced a dilemma. On one hand, it was idealistic and celebrated the need for love and brotherhood in a bewildering world. On the other, it stridently encouraged the grotesque dramatization of virtually every form of brutality, cruelty, bestiality, and sensuality. Expressionist philosophy helped set the stage for the big questions about why humanity seems to float as a ship with no mooring. What is it that drives many people and certain cultures to destruction? For instance, Expressionist films like *Dr. Caligari* usually presented characters with whom the audience was not meant to identify—that is, they showed not only the alienated self but also an alienated humanity. Expressionism ultimately centered around the question of why humanity appears driven to self-destruction. Psychologists Sigmund Freud and later Carl Jung would try to supply the answer.

Sigmund Freud (1856–1939) first achieved recognition outside of Vienna in the early 1900s. At the first International Psycho-analytical Congress, held in Salzburg in 1908, psychoanalysis went beyond theory and therapy to become an intellectual movement as well—even though Freud's ideas would not circulate widely until after World War I.

During the war, prolonged trench fighting caused a stress-induced mental disturbance then referred to as "shell shock." Well-born scions of military families, who had volunteered for service, fought with conspicuous gallantry, and were repeatedly decorated, were now suddenly suffering from emotional breakdowns. Postwar fury at the cruelties that occurred in military hospitals, especially the psychiatric division of the Vienna General Hospital, led the Austrian government to establish a commission of inquiry in 1920. The commission called in Freud, whose psychoanalytic techniques were believed to provide a sophisticated alternative to current methods of treating mental illness, which included drugs, bullying, and electric-shock treatment. The controversy, though inconclusive, gave Freud the international publicity he needed. The year 1920 proved to be a breakthrough year for Freud in other ways. In that same year, the first psychiatric polyclinic opened in Berlin, and Freud's pupil and future biographer, Ernest Jones, launched the *International Journal of Psycho-Analysis*.

Even more important, however, was the discovery of Freud's work by intellectuals and artists in the early '20s. Described by some as not a scientist but a great artist, Freud became a household name in Europe and the United States. He was also popularized through literature and art, especially Surrealism. Freud's appeal was strong among the novelists, ranging from Aldous Huxley to Thomas Mann.

Freud seemed to offer a new and exciting explanation for human thoughts and behavior and became the voice of the new age. He understood the implications of his work and wrote in 1938 that three great challenges had been leveled at humanity's "naïve self-love": Copernicus, Darwin, and Freud. Freud saw himself as the bitterest blow because his research proved to each of us that we are not in control. We must be

22. SIGMUND FREUD (front, left) with his pupil and future biographer Ernest Jones (back, center), Carl Jung (front, right), and colleagues. Even more important in terms of enduring impact was the sudden discovery of Freud's work and ideas by intellectuals and artists. In a very short time, Freud was not only a household name in Europe and the United States, but he was popularized generally in literature and art, especially through Surrealism, discussed later. As Havelock Ellis (1859–1939), a physician and author who was an advocate of the sex education movement, said at the time, Freud was not a scientist but a great artist.

content with only scraps of information about what is happening in our own minds, with most of what Freud considered relevant information being hoarded in our subconscious minds.

Freud was deeply influenced by Jean Lamarck (1744–1829), the French naturalist and precursor of Darwinism who had coined the word *biology*. Lamarck believed in "biological predestination," the idea that past experiences constitute a vital part of people's heredity. Freud adapted this concept of acquired characteristics to psychology, formulated his theories through self-analysis, and confirmed them, he believed, in the psychoanalysis of others. The central problem Freud dealt with was guilt, which he believed is an acquired characteristic. He thought guilt originated in humanity's primitive past with three violent acts—incest, parricide, and cannibalism.

Freud also developed the well-known concept that the human personality consists of three parts: the *id, ego,* and *super-ego.* The id, present at birth, is instinct, fearless and amoral, driven to seek pleasure and self-gratification. The ego is the "I" of the human being, determined by the person's own experiences and responsible for self-preservation, repressing the id's incessant demands. The super-ego is the "conscience," the source of our moral attitudes and guilt, the internalization of society's rules and parental commands.

One of Freud's most controversial theories was his description of the *libido,* the sex drive that he believed came from primitive biological urges. Freud theorized that all neuroses originate in the sexual life. The sexual life is driven by strong impulses for sex but is also burdened by guilt. This conflict inevitably leads to anxiety and sexual repression. The solution, according to Freud, is to alleviate repression concerning the sex drive.

RELIGION AND FREUD

His own "depth-psychology," Freud believed, was a science ready and able to satisfy people's need to understand the world around them. He also believed that religion posed the only real threat to science because religion teaches people about the source and origin of the universe. It assures them of protection and final happiness and guides their thoughts and actions through precepts backed up by the whole force of religion's authority. However, to Freud, religion was only people's attempt to control the sensory world through a wish-world they had developed. From here, Freud argues that religion is a result of man's need for a father figure. Like a father, God provides identity, security, and rules to live by.

Freud not only asserts that religion is a useless fantasy, but he goes on to say that religious thought is actually dangerous to the future of humanity. Thus, Freud showed no deference toward religion. As he wrote,

> I stand in no awe whatever of the Almighty. If we were ever to meet I should have more reproaches to make to Him than He could make to me. I would ask why He hadn't endowed me with a better intellectual equipment, and He couldn't complain that I have failed to make the best use of my so-called freedom.[24]

Freud's theories and practices have not gone unchallenged, as is discussed in biographer Paul Ferris's *Dr. Freud* (1997). Many people are now at least suspicious of Freud's theories or have revised his thinking to fit more postmodern preconceptions of human personality. For many of us, Freudianism has thus been discredited as a sort of arcane astrology, fairly adept at providing some explanations after the fact but almost useless in predicting behavior. After ninety years of experience with his methods of therapy, there have been some costly failures but also a stunning impact on Western culture.

JUNG: THE COLLECTIVE UNCONSCIOUS AND MYTH

Carl Jung (1875–1961) collaborated with Freud but took a different approach to religion, which, among other things, led to a decisive break in their relationship. Influenced by Schopenhauer, Kant, and Nietzsche, Jung was particularly impressed with Freud's use of dreams as guides through the unconscious depths of the psyche. Jung, however, extended his psychological approach, basing it on symbol and myth. He believed that people need religion's symbolic language since there are innumerable things human beings cannot define or understand.

Jung's studies repeatedly led him back to religious symbols, or "archetypes," as the manifestations of the "collective unconscious," which represent the place where the mind and nature are one. These archetypes are common to people everywhere, regardless of their cultural background, Jung believed. His theory of the unconscious placed religion in a manageable position for modern humanity since, to Jung, religion could be assimilated as part of the collective unconscious.

Jung's psychology of myth and archetype is a human-made salvation. It tells people that all the answers they need are within themselves. Jung recognized that religion is the expression of a deep and common need in the human psyche. To Jung, this did not mean religion was invalid or that there was no God. Jung, in fact, believed in God and respected religion as the highest expression of the collective unconscious. Yet he believed one religion should not be considered more valid than another; they are all only varying symbolisms, pointing back to the same basic human psychological needs.

The symbol, according to Jung, has the power to change history because it has power over the mind. For example, Hitler's regime deceived the German nation with a highly visible army and propaganda. The Nazi swastika resembles the mandala, Jung's ultimate symbol of wholeness.

Jung's view of human nature has become pervasive. He did not see people as essentially good but believed evil was a necessary part of existence. Repression of the "shadow," present in each one of us, is as dangerous as allowing it to take over the mind. This duality is a familiar aspect of contemporary cartoon characters, with good and evil advisors on either shoulder. It can also be seen in the double-sided "Force" in George Lucas's four *Star Wars* films of 1977, 1980, 1983, and 1999.

Some Jung-influenced scholars find popular culture to be largely a reflection of the shadow side of the human psyche. Consider, for instance, horror films like 1974's *The Texas Chainsaw Massacre* and books such as Stephen King's *The Dark Half* (1989). Some scholars conclude that horror movies are necessary for the psychic health of the community since they offer us ways to release the repressed and vent taboo fantasies.

THE SURREALIST SOLUTION: A NEW REALITY

By the early 1920s utopianism seemed outdated. The First World War had convinced many people that humankind, contrary to the beliefs of certain artists and intellectuals, is not essentially good. The problem was how to reconcile the older notion of sin with Western culture's unwillingness to take responsibility for it. Freud and Jung spoke to this question by theorizing that all people have a dark side; the trick is to find acceptable outlets for it. Sin, they argued, is only a mismanagement of the dark side of the mind. But this argument eventually leads to the notion that all criminal acts are a result of mental imbalance.

The Surrealists searched for a way to allow the dark side to prevail. This philosophy was a fertile breeding ground for the likes of André Breton (1896–1966), who believed in the supremacy of poetry and loathed the generation whose values had led to the slaughters of the war. He thus became a natural leader for the Surrealists.

While Breton did not fight in World War I, he did work as an intern at a psychiatric center that treated shell-shock victims—an experience that deeply marked him. Helping patients analyze their dreams laid the groundwork for Surrealism. Above all, Surrealism meant liberation from logic and morality, with the aim of recovering what the Surrealists believed to be the original power of spirit.

One patient particularly impressed Breton—a young man who had experienced trench warfare and been driven to the illusion of invulnerability. The young man lived in parallel worlds. He would stand on the parapet of a trench during a bombardment, pointing to explosions with his finger, believing that the corpses were dummies, the wounds greasepaint, the shells blanks, and the whole war a sham played out by actors. No bullet ever touched him, and no argument could convince him that the war was real. To Breton, this man epitomized the relationship between an artist and his chosen reality. Chance, memory, desire, and coincidence would meet in a new reality—a "sur-reality," a word borrowed from French poet Guillaume Apollinaire—and the dream was the gate to art.

To the Surrealists, religion was corrupt and false. In fact, they published a blurred photograph of one of their own, poet Benjamin Peret, insulting a priest on the street (in the tradition of Arthur Rimbaud). They believed they were commemorating the liberation of humanity from superstition. As a "performance piece," this was the forerunner to a thousand equally trivial actions that would be recorded on Polaroid or videotape by and for American audiences from the 1960s onward.

As the movement developed, Surrealists became strongly Marxist, though they opposed capitalism from the beginning. The emergence of Hitler's highly organized state particularly threatened them. Breton admired Leon Trotsky (1879–1940) and once gave a speech that saluted him as the victor and great survivor of the October Revolution. Breton and many of the Surrealists believed a communist revolution was the only hope to overthrow the existing order—and, moreover, true art had to be revolutionary.

THE REALITY BENEATH REALITY

Artist Giorgio de Chirico (1888–1978), an Italian born in Munich and educated in Athens, succeeded in linking Romantic art and Surrealism. His paintings directly addressed Rimbaud's exhortation that the artist make himself a "seer" by attaining a hallucinatory state in order to plumb the depths of the unknown.

In a brief four years in Paris, de Chirico created a body of work that fulfilled the Surrealist poet's programme and found a fantastic world "supplementary" to our own. He created an authentic and troubling dream world of great power and intensity— the first in the twentieth century—and discovered, true to the spirit of the age, "irremediable anxiety." To de Chirico, there was a reality underneath the reality in which we live and have our being, a reality that could only be found in the mysterious relationships between ordinary objects when released from commonsense causality.

Many of the images in de Chirico's work are real and came from actual places, especially Turin, Italy. In one of the most haunting of his compositions, *The Nostalgia of the Infinite* (1913–14), a tower becomes a desolate and forlorn image; the townscape is emptied; human society has ceased to exist or has been shrunken to tiny, faraway figures that cannot communicate with the human occupant of the townscape, who is de Chirico himself, the Onlooker, whose eye is the root of all perspectives. (See color plate 13.)

THE UNCONSCIOUS MIND ON CANVAS

Salvador Dalí (1904–89) first encountered Sigmund Freud's influential book *The Interpretation of Dreams* when he was an art student and, thereafter, spoke of Freud as a devout Christian would speak of the Gospels. Dalí's paintings reflect the unconscious mind and Dalí's own personal dream world. His 1937 *Metamorphosis of Narcissus* shows direct Freudian influence. In this dreamscape, a hand sprouting from the ground and holding an enormous egg—from whose cracked shell a narcissus flower sprouts—turns into the figure of Narcissus in the background, gazing into a pool.

Dalí's 1929 *Lugubrious Game* is replete with Freudian symbols—the figure of the plinth, averting its head in shame, with its enormously enlarged hand—and coprophilia. The minutely-painted smudge of excrement on the shorts of the gibbering man in the foreground, which Dalí labored to perfect, greatly troubled a segment of the Surrealists at the time. Dalí pointed out, however, that a censored dream was no dream at all but a conscious construction.

Dalí, more than anyone, would popularize Surrealism and thereby affect other media. Soon Surrealist images began to appear in American films and in the television series of the 1950s—the influential television series *The Twilight Zone* (which aired from 1959 to 1964), for instance, and the BBC's *The Prisoner* series of the late 1960s, which also aired in the United States. The most recent example is the popular 1990s television show *The X-Files,* in which two FBI agents become involved in a bizarre assortment of cases ranging from encounters with aliens to possession by spirits.

A TRIBUTE TO THE MARQUIS

The Surrealists' ultimate goal was freedom, no matter how extreme. Thus they admired the eighteenth century French writer Donatien Alphonse François de Sade (1740–1814), known as the "Divine Marquis." De Sade never submitted, in life or writing, to any morality, and his erotic fantasies, half dream and half reality, were considered a major part of the Surrealist heritage. De Sade's castle at La Coste in the South of France was a sacred spot for Breton and his friends, who devoutly visited its ruins, carved their initials in the crumbling plasterwork of its roofless salon, and had their photographs taken.

Composing most of his works in prison (to which he was sentenced for "criminal debauchery"), de Sade argued the supremacy of "Desire" over all moral contracts—as in his novels *Justine* (1791) and *Juliette* (1797). He was the first writer to describe the fundamental relationship between sex and politics, anticipating Nietzsche and Freud by more than a hundred years. De Sade became the unthinkable answer to Rousseau's milky belief that man, left in a state of nature, is good. Instead de Sade argued that man is a monster from the beginning and that only by following our desires to the end can we discover who we really are, no matter how appalling.

Surrealist tributes to de Sade were frequent and had anti-religious overtones, as seen in Man Ray's 1933 *Monument to D.A.F. de Sade,* a work that consisted of a girl's buttocks montaged onto an upside-down crucifix—a daring attack on Catholic taboos.

Extreme Sadist imagery in Surrealist art may be seen in the work of Hans Bellmer (1902–75), whose obsession with a young girl caused him to make an erotic dummy, articulated with ball-and-socket joints, which he called *The Doll* (1935). The doll's links could be splayed, bent, and combined at will, producing a potent vehicle for images of sexual fantasy centered on rape and violence. Bellmer took photographs of the doll in different settings, which looked like police evidence shots taken after a crime. *The Doll* was the image of woman as beautiful victim.

Then in 1936 Bellmer created a sculpture, now at the Museum of Modern Art in New York City, which he also entitled *The Doll.* (See color plate 14.) Here he combined the vaginal areas of two women—one as the head positioned on a female's midsection. Protruding spheres where there should be leg gives the overall feeling that women are something less than human. They are instead entities to be manipulated as the male would see fit.

A main Surrealist theme therefore was to break social taboos concerning sex, but only with respect to male sexual freedom. For example, in René Magritte's (1898–1967) 1934 painting *The Rape,* a woman's face becomes a "genital face"—blind, mute, and pathetic. The females depicted in Surrealist art generally had no real faces. The preferred female form was a mannequin. Kurt Seligmann's (1900–62) 1938 *Ultra-Furniture* is a stool supported on the legs of three mannequins. It is a direct transcription from the fantasies within the mad ogre Minski's castle that de Sade described in his novel *Juliette,* in which visiting orgiasts eat a dinner of roast boy while sitting on chairs "constructed" of live interlocked slaves.

Allen Jones's (b. 1937) woman-furniture, such as the 1969 *Table Sculpture,* would keep this tradition alive. This type of furniture is also featured in director Stanley Kubrick's (1928–99) landmark Futurist 1971 film *A Clockwork Orange,* in which Sadeian appetite reigns among the young underworld.

Today the mythology of sexual violence is an important legacy of Surrealism. For example, the treatment of women's bodies as objects for men's use or targets for male hostility is a staple of pornography. The negative feminist reaction to sexual violence is understandable. Photographer Cindy Sherman (b. 1954), for example, used prosthetic body parts ordered from medical catalogues in her 1992 *Untitled (No. 264— Woman with Mask)* to express her anger at physical violence against women.

UN CHIEN ANDALOU

Surrealism attempted to take people out of their conscious minds and into the subconscious. One way to accomplish this was by shocking or startling the viewer, something that Luis Buñuel (1900–83), a schoolmate and friend of Dalí, understood and used in his 1930 film *L'Age d'Or.* In a love-death scene, as a man passionately cries out for his lover, his mouth and face are streaming with blood. For that time in history, the moment, for many, was too intense to take consciously. Of course, in our overstimulated culture of today, *L'Age d'Or* would hardly cause a ripple.

The Marquis de Sade was perhaps the most influential figure in Buñuel's own life, for he found immense freedom in de Sade's belief that imagination should not be censored and the mind should have total freedom. Believing, however, that the fantasies of the imagination should not be played out in real life, Buñuel saw film as a way to visualize the imagination and the subconscious, with all the evil that lurked therein.

Buñuel's first film, the innovative and influential 1928 *Un Chien Andalou* ("An Andalusian Dog"), is an excellent example of Surrealist attempts to shock and subvert the conscience. Routinely studied by students and scholars, the film is now considered a classic for its use of a method called "paranoia criticism," which Dalí described as being "based on the critical and systematic objectivisation of delirious associations and interpretations."[25]

The film begins in ghastly fashion as an apparently passive woman has her eyeball sliced with a razor. Buñuel believed that in order to produce a state permitting the free association of ideas, it was necessary to produce a near traumatic shock at the start of the film. Continuing with ant-infested sores, dismembered hands, sexual assaults, live human burials, and murder, Buñuel suggested that the script should be taken as a desperate, impassioned call for murder. Although Buñuel eschewed any meaning to the film, *Un Chien Andalou* seems to describe the collision between desire and the object of desire in a context reeling with danger. It challenges the conventions of a society that Buñuel believed had set a curse on love and thwarted and racked human sexual desire.

In the savagely anti-clerical satire *L'Age d'Or,* Buñuel mocked bourgeois social conventions and celebrated the Surrealist notion of mad love. Scorpions come and go in front of the camera and attack a rat or fight each other to death. The *intertille* that follows ("A few hours later …") introduces a group of bishops celebrating mass among some rocks. In one scene, the lovers identify so closely that they attempt to devour each other by sucking on fingers and biting lips—they are, in a sense, cannibals.

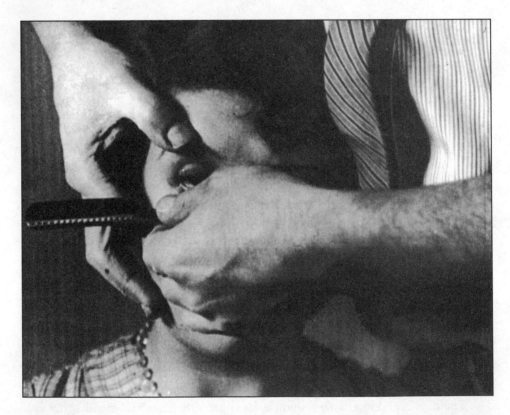

23. Scene from Buñuel's *Un Chien Andalou.* The film is routinely studied at the university level and is considered a classic. During the script writing and initial filming, Dalí and Buñuel worked closely together.

The film was seen as so blatantly anti-Catholic that riots broke out in Paris when it was shown. A Catholic youth group damaged the screen at one theatre, tore up the seats, and destroyed an exhibition of Surrealist paintings in the foyer. Censors and the press around the world condemned the film, and all copies of *L'Age d'Or* were seized. While Buñuel clearly intended to destroy the kind of conformism that wants everyone to think they are living in the best of all possible worlds, he declared thirty years later that the film was now a harmless work. In fact, in 1965 an audience at the Lincoln Center in New York applauded after it was shown.

THE SURREALIST LEGACY: HITCHCOCK TO LYNCH

In addition to shock, Surrealism also used surprise to reveal the previously unknown or inexperienced. The merging of truth and the marvelous is a Surrealist influence that can be seen in one of Hollywood's grandest films, Cecil B. DeMille's (1881–1959) *The Ten Commandments* (1956). DeMille depicts the marvelous throughout the film—the miracles of the ten plagues, the parting of the Red Sea, the voice of God talking to Moses, and the burning bush—all of which DeMille believed to be historical facts.

Surrealist filmmakers relished carrying things to their extremes while maintaining some foothold in the "real" world (whether by use of plot, character, location, and so on). Walt Disney's (1901–66) *Snow White and the Seven Dwarfs* (1938) and *Pinocchio* (1940) contain unexpected elements of the ideal exaggerated to the surreal. For instance, in *Snow White,* the witch's poison apple is so perfectly formed and so startlingly red that it is an ideal, the very archetype of the word *apple.* In *Pinocchio* the Blue Fairy radiates a golden-blue glow and has the most delicately white complexion that ever existed on screen. Although Disney may have only intended to conjure images of childhood fantasy with the utmost precision, one can still experience these images as surreal.

Two film styles that are employed to exaggerate the ideal are "clutter," which exemplifies life, and "sparsity," which illustrates a more pessimistic view, possibly even death. The sparsity concept is exemplified by Alfred Hitchcock's (1899–1980) thriller *The Birds* (1963), a film in which throngs of birds arrive and attack, mutilate, and kill people in a seaside village. Every image in the film is captured with crystal-clear vision but a minimum number of elements.

Hitchcock, who had many connections to Surrealism, hired Dalí to create a surreal dream sequence for his film about psychoanalysis, *Spellbound* (1945). Dalí's sequence is full of sinuous lines, eye imagery, long shadows, and a feeling for heightened perspective—all observed with great clarity.

Hitchcock also incorporated Surrealism into many of his other films. De Chirico-like images, reminiscent of his painting *The Nostalgia of the Infinite,* find their way into Hitchcock's *Vertigo* (1958), in which Scottie (played by James Stewart) follows Madeleine (Kim Novak) around San Francisco. De Chirico's surreal landscapes give the film an otherworldliness. The exteriors were shot late in the day; a low sun casts long shadows and a golden glow, giving the scenes their feeling of deep perspective. Every location is empty and hushed. Madeleine drifts through the landscapes like a dream—which she is, in fact, to Scottie.

In *The Birds,* by contrast, the central theme is human complacency, which is an immediate concern of Surrealism, and the viewer is attacked constantly by every visual image. People are shown as puppets, as Hitchcock attempts to intensify the shocking hopelessness of the characters' lives. The heroine, Melanie, is filmed with occasional back projections that underline her complacent qualities, her petty whims and mannequin-like nature.

Psycho (1960), arguably the first slasher film, initially shocked audiences and set the tone for audience manipulation in films. Through the slow build-up of suspense, the audience is carefully conditioned for the coming shocks. This method of

24. Scene from Hitchcock's *Vertigo.* Hitchcock's surreal vision finds an ideal representation in *Vertigo*. Images of Giorgio de Chirico, such as his painting *The Nostalgia of the Infinite,* seem to pervade the film. In a long, wordless sequence (accompanied only by the haunting score), Scottie (actor James Stewart) follows Madeleine (actress Kim Novak) around the city of San Francisco.

building suspense was consciously copied later by William Friedkin in his 1973 film *The Exorcist,* and it has become a standard for suspense and horror films.

Artists like Andy Warhol took things a step further and filmed movies in real time, as opposed to fictional movie time, which showed that observing life in real time is an intolerable thing to watch. His six-hour 1963 film *Sleep* consists of half a dozen shots of a man asleep in the nude. Warhol's subsequent movies stuck to the theme of ordinary events recorded meticulously and extended over extraordinary lengths of time. His shorter compositions included 1963's *Haircut,* which featured thirty-three minutes of a man receiving a haircut. Warhol began to work with more explicitly sexual themes in 1964 with *Blow Job,* a thirty-minute film of a young man's face as he experiences oral sex.

Surrealism's influence on film continues. An example is the work of David Lynch (b. 1946). His first feature film, *Eraserhead* (1977), took six years to make and is a nightmare that explores the relationship between man and monster. After his acclaimed and dreamlike *The Elephant Man* (1980), Lynch made *Blue Velvet* in 1986, which shows the influence of *Un Chien Andalou.* His later films—such as *Wild at Heart* (1990), *Twin Peaks: Fire Walk with Me* (1992), and *Lost Highway* (1996)— would continue in this vein. Lynch later had television success with the weird and influential dream-trance show *Twin Peaks.* He clearly influenced other directors, such as Oliver Stone in his 1994 *Natural Born Killers* and 1997 *U Turn.* Darren Aronofsky's 1998 π (Pi) and Vincent Gallo's 1998 *Buffalo 66* both continued the Lynchian style.

The horror genre perpetuates the Surrealist mode as well. For example, in the film series *A Nightmare on Elm Street* (the first one appeared in 1984), waking and dreaming are often indistinguishable.

THE WASTE LAND

The art experiments of Dada, Expressionism, and Surrealism and the lingering effects of World War I coalesced into the pessimism that became the hallmark of the twentieth century. By the 1920s the foundations of the past were shaken, and intellectuals like Buñuel, who wanted to destroy the rules of any kind of conformism, were beginning to have their way.

Yet in the midst of this pessimism, T. S. Eliot (1888–1965), for one, believed that the roads of modern culture led nowhere. In his long 1922 poem *The Waste Land,*

110

25. T. S. ELIOT. In *The Waste Land,* Eliot employs the anthropocentric philosophy of Kant and his successors. Reality is completely dependent on human perception. We think of the key, locking the door that separates us from others, and so we are separated. Eliot dramatizes the modern preoccupation with self. Individualism has led us to a place where we dwell on our differences and idiosyncrasies rather than what we have in common. In this way, we lock ourselves away from each other.

Eliot introduces a variety of characters in a number of settings, but they are all somehow related (even if we are not sure exactly how).

Eliot's documented allusions come from sources as unrelated to one another as the Bible, Baudelaire, and Hindu sacred texts—a combination that gives a feeling of many traditions merging into one conclusion. Eliot also varies his style. Cadences and rhyme schemes vary. A line may be ten words or two words long. Sometime the "I" in the poem is a specific character, sometimes it is the poet, and sometimes it is some sort of "everyman."

All this gives one the impression that Eliot has taken *everything* and synthesized it into one long poem. In this way, the poem is reminiscent of the biblical book of Ecclesiastes (which Eliot even alludes to early in the poem), in which the writer says he has seen everything and pronounces it all to be meaningless. Eliot gives the impression of a sage who has seen it all.

Leading American critic and essayist Edmund Wilson's influential essay on *The Waste Land* summarizes the poet's theme: "Not only is life sterile and futile, but men have tasted its sterility and futility a thousand times before."[26]

For many, the poem became a symbol of the plight of the modern mind. Others go so far as to blame Eliot himself for the state of culture today. Literary critic Van Wyck Brooks was convinced that the poem's publication was the worst thing to happen to American literature. Poet and writer William Carlos Williams later described the poem as having wiped out our world, as if an atom bomb had been dropped. But Eliot, far from being responsible for culture's collapse, seems to be saying that modern thought has destroyed modern humanity. It has robbed man of his past, his future, his fellowman, and finally himself. The poem expresses the frustration of the modern mind, which even as it denies that any structure exists still searches for a frame of reference. In parts I through IV of the poem, the reader encounters images of dryness, sterility, and death. Part V takes up the theme again where a dead mouth cannot spit and the cacophony of thunderclaps without rain is all there is.

Just as Eliot's *The Waste Land* illustrates the hopelessness of a culture, his 1925 poem *The Hollow Men* expresses the hopelessness of the human race. To Eliot, part of the problem was Romanticism, which he saw as the most destructive force in the history of literature. He even considered the Romantic movement responsible for the state of modern culture. To Eliot, Romanticism stands for excess in any direction. It splits in two directions: escape from the world of fact and devotion to brute fact. Even before his conversion to Christianity, Eliot believed that human beings are not good in themselves. Therefore he was completely against an individualism, Romantic or otherwise, that tried to free people from all authority.

While Eliot finally found the structure he sought in the traditions of religion, history, and literature, Irish writer James Joyce worked under the assumption that a structure does not have to be completely valid in order to be useful. For instance, Joyce regularly attended Mass, even though he was not professedly a Christian. Eliot found this double standard unsatisfactory and searched for the proper outside force to which he could give his allegiance. As literary analyst John Middleton Murry wrote in 1926, Eliot had only two choices: He could make a blind act of faith and join the Catholic Church, where he would find authority and tradition. Or he could trust himself and see what happened; a principle of authority may come to birth. Contrary to Murry's prediction, Eliot took the way of the Anglican Church in 1926. Many of his admirers were disillusioned, and most considered the poetry he wrote after his conversion to be inferior.

Eliot, however, saw himself as having transcended the wasteland of modern existence and as awaiting the awakening of the rest of humanity. In the meantime, Eliot would preserve, as he said, the Judeo-Christian faith in the hope of someday helping to "renew and rebuild civilization, and save the World from suicide."[27]

CHAPTER 4
The Lost Generation

Those who have crossed
    With direct eyes, to death's other kingdom
Remember us—if at all—not as lost
    Violent souls, but only
As the hollow men
    The stuffed men.

T. S. ELIOT[1]

By breaking with the past and discarding their connections to traditional religion, many people turned to the machine for meaning— perhaps as a substitute for religion. But technology could not provide true meaning, nor could it answer the questions the great artists such as Gauguin posed: Where do we come from? What are we? Where are we going? The hollow men of the twentieth century—or as Gertrude Stein called them, "the lost generation"—seemed even more lonely, perplexed, and threatened, sometimes driven primarily by guilt.

THE TRUTH BEYOND APPEARANCE

Franz Kafka (1883–1924), perhaps the most self-conscious literary representative of the modern age, wrote Surrealistic novels about the absurdity of modern life. Kafka was born in Prague to Jewish parents and had, by his own account, an unhappy childhood. When he was thirty-six, Kafka, who worked professionally as a lawyer, wrote a fifty-page letter to his father detailing the grievances of his childhood. *Dearest Father,* like most of Kafka's other works, was only published after the author's death.

Kafka was a master of psychological drama. He lived in the time of Freud, an age that was becoming increasingly self-conscious. Kafka's self-consciousness and obsession with his childhood exhibit definite Freudian overtones, and Kafka considered Freud's influence on his work obvious. While composing his 1913 story "The Judgment," Kafka says he had "thoughts of Freud, of course." Kafka's work thus is characterized by a portrayal of an enigmatic reality, in which the individual is seen as lonely, perplexed, and threatened. Guilt is one of his major themes.

Although Kafka had Freudian explanations for his psychological ill health, they did not provide a cure. He battled depression, headaches, physical ailments, and insomnia throughout his life and blamed all his problems, physical and emotional, on his psychological state, which he in turn blamed on his circumstances—including his family, his job, and Prague itself. Everyone and everything, it seemed to Kafka, was against him. It was Kafka's agitated state of mind, though, that provided the material for his stories.

In a sense, Kafka was primarily concerned with the state of his own mind and wrote about himself. Every Kafka story contains a Kafka character, and it's usually the main character. He even gives anagrams of his own name or simply the initial "K" to some of his protagonists. Multiple characters are often patterned after various aspects of the author's mind. Kafka's works are dreamlike, often placing an absurd unreality in a realistic environment. In this respect, they resemble the visual art of Surrealism. For instance, in "The Judgment" Georg Bendemann succeeds in his father's business and is on the threshold of marrying a suitably well-off girl until his father's senile ravings reverse the image Georg has of himself. When his father says that he is sentencing him to death by drowning, Georg immediately carries out the sentence by jumping off a bridge.

In Kafka's famous 1915 novella "The Metamorphosis," Gregor Samsa awakens one morning to find himself changed into a giant beetle that eventually dies because his family fails to take care of him. And his novel *The Trial,* published in 1925, is the tale of a man named Joseph K. who, after being accused of some unknown crime, is sent through the court bureaucracy, only to eventually see his own unjust execution as a relief. Orson Welles brought *The Trial* to screen in 1963 in an effective Expressionistic adaptation, and the story was again filmed in 1993 by director David Jones.

Nearly all of Kafka's protagonists are condemned to die senseless deaths, each being defeated by an absurd situation. His readers are thereby compelled to look intently into the chaos of existence. This theme has been taken up by many modern filmmakers who can be described as nothing else but Kafkaesque. A casual look at their films—for instance, *Dark City* (1999), *Eyes Wide Shut* (1999), *Fight Club* (1999), *The Matrix* (1999), and others—shows Kafka's far-reaching influence.

French Existentialist philosopher Jean-Paul Sartre (1905–80) later found encouragement in Kafka's writings. Sartre believed that Kafka had found a way to show the truth beyond appearance—the fact that humans will always be denied. In his 1938 novel *Nausea,* Sartre also tried to communicate the metaphysical sickness that comes from realizing that one has known and experienced more than can be understood.

Author and playwright Samuel Beckett (1906–89) carried the absurdity of existence even further in his play *Waiting for Godot,* which was first produced in Paris in 1951. The main characters, Didi and Gogo, seldom say anything memorable while they wait for Godot, who never arrives. Godot may never come, yet they wait until the end of each day and then return the next day to wait again. Kafkaesque life thus is boring, repetitive, sad, unjust, and painful. Nothing meaningful ever happens. Even in death, Beckett seems to epitomize the Kafkaesque ending—as mirrored by his unmarked grave in Paris.

CASTING OFF THE VICTORIAN SHACKLES

The absurd, hopeless life Kafka portrayed could not have been imagined before the twentieth century. The United States, for example, experienced dramatic changes from 1880 to 1920. Big-city industrial economies smothered the rural, agrarian systems that had been built around independent farm families, and the shift from a country to a city population meant more than urbanization. It symbolized a shift in American values as morality shifted from the changeless principles of things such as *The McGuffey Readers* to the spontaneity and open expression called for by the artists, writers, philosophers, and intellectuals of the time. City life encouraged anti-Victorianism—in which the neighbors across the hall are viewed as strangers and where people are freer to do what they want than in a village or small town where everyone knows them.

Victorian notions of abstinence from alcohol, nonmarital sex, dancing, swearing, nudity, prize-fighting, and uncleanliness were more or less reflected in the European and American paintings of women—idealized, unearthly, and like no woman who ever lived. Untouchable, they were revered by Victorian men who would never use words like trousers, leg, or pregnant in mixed company.

Thus it was not surprising that Édouard Manet's *Olympia,* painted in 1863, created a furor when it was exhibited. Though modeled on Titian's *Venus of Urbino,* it was nevertheless an attack on classical style—and classical morality. The genuinely

116

sexual creature looked her viewer in the eye. Like his contemporary Courbet (and later Picasso), Manet exposed the fraud of the Victorian nudes: Olympia ripped the skin from Victorian prurience. When the painting was exhibited at the 1865 Paris salon, two guards were required to protect it from the walking sticks of indignant visitors. Even that was not enough. The painting, now located in the Musee D'Orsay in Paris, was then placed so high that the "offending nakedness" was beyond the demonstrations of anger, as well as beyond the eye.

THE PRAGMATISTS: SOCIAL AND PSYCHOLOGICAL EVOLUTION

Explicit anti-Victorian thought appeared early in the ideas of the pragmatist philosophers. The most renowned American pragmatists were William James of Harvard University and John Dewey of Columbia.

William James (1842–1910) called his approach "Pragmatism" or "Radical Empiricism" because he believed that experience—not immutable laws—should be the guide to truth. If hard facts are not available, projected consequences should determine the answer. For James, the truth of religion, for example, lay in its usefulness. Any religion that provides a practical benefit to humanity is true: polytheism is just as good as monotheism if it produces "good" results.

Like James, John Dewey (1859–1952) significantly affected Americans' view of reality, especially since he was deeply involved in the philosophy of education. While a professor at the University of Chicago, Dewey worked in the city at the Hull House with Jane Addams (1860–1935) and became involved with an experimental elementary school based on his theories. Believing that concepts should not be ends in themselves but instruments to achieve practical results, Dewey called his brand of pragmatism "instrumentalism." He argued in *The Quest for Certainty* (1929) that philosophy and religion encouraged a reverence for the unseen, perhaps because of the unpredictability of our physical lives. Thus religion and philosophy should make themselves useful by bettering the physical world. Dewey believed that education should be directed toward the child's interests, not necessarily those of society. The purpose of education was not to impart a body of knowledge but to help individuals be happy and productive. Dewey's ideas led to the notion of "life adjustment" as the goal of education, an idea that has now come to dominate American public schools.

John Watson (1878–1958), another pragmatist, did graduate work at the University of Chicago in the psychology department, which John Dewey chaired and ruled ideologically. Watson captured the attention of young intellectuals in the early decades of the century with his Freudian view that people's upbringing often caused them to repress their emotions. He argued that repressed emotions were likely to surface as anxiety, depression, or actual illness.

Considered the founder of the behaviorist school of psychology, Watson put his skills to work at the J. Walter Thompson Advertising Agency after being exiled from academia for what was viewed as personal and professional misconduct. The hope of Watson's behaviorism was

> to reach such proficiency in our science that we can build any man, starting at birth, into any kind of social or a-social being upon order. On the other hand, we hope some day to attain such proficiency that we can take the worst adult social failure . . . pull him apart, psychologically speaking, and give him a new set of works.[2]

Influential psychologist B. F. Skinner (1904–90) later carried behaviorist theories even further. He opposed Watson's insistence that mind and consciousness do not exist, arguing instead that they simply do not matter. Skinner's theory of learning, called "operant conditioning," focused on the intangible. He argued that human behavior could be greatly improved by using incentives or "reinforcers." Skinner's work raised questions about people's dignity or worth. If a person is responsible for his behavior, then he may be blamed for his misdeeds, but he may also take responsibility for his achievements. A behaviorist's analysis shifts the credit as well as the blame exclusively to one's environment.

The ideas of the pragmatists made good press copy and soon became widespread as they were popularized through the media. Through the mass media, middle-class people began to believe it was dangerous, especially for children, to repress feelings. Self-fulfillment became a birthright. This shift away from the traditional religious belief in a flawed, or "sinful," human nature to a view of people as blank slates to be molded was perhaps one of the most important changes in modern times. Today most Americans believe that people can be shaped, not only as they grow but later in life by their environment.

EINSTEIN'S RELATIVITY AND RELATIVISM

Twentieth century science would give the concepts of absurdity, futility, and malleability yet another significant twist. It happened on May 29, 1919, when Albert Einstein (1879–1955) reduced the concept of the absolute to irrelevance.

Photographs of a solar eclipse, taken on the Island of Principe off West Africa and at Sobral in Brazil on that fateful day in May, confirmed the theories of the twenty-

118

26. ALBERT EINSTEIN. Innumerable books have sought to explain how Einstein's theory had altered Newtonian concepts, which, for ordinary men and women, formed their understanding of the world about them and how it worked. Einstein summarized his own theory: "The 'Principle of Relativity' in its widest sense is contained in the statement: The totality of physical phenomena is of such a character that it gives no basis for the introduction of the concept of 'absolute motion'; or, shorter but less precise: There is no absolute motion."[3]

six-year-old German Jew that the totality of physical phenomena gives no basis for absolute motion. Known as the "Special Theory of Relativity," Einstein's ideas aroused worldwide interest and demolished the theories of Isaac Newton (1642–1727) and others who had provided the framework for the European Enlightenment and the Industrial Revolution.

Einstein's effect on scientific thought was cataclysmic. His impact on society, however, may have been even greater. Ordinary men and women had previously formed their understandings of the world based on Newton's ideas. Although Einstein did not intend it, many people mistakenly believed he had proved there were no absolutes, even in the moral realm. Relativity became confused with relativism, and the knife of relativity would eventually cut society adrift from the traditional Judeo-Christian concept of absolute truths.

The theory of relativity was a formative influence on the twentieth century, especially as it coincided with the rise of pseudo-sciences such as Freudianism and the general flow of the arts and literature away from tradition and history.

SANGER AND THE SEXUAL REVOLUTION

Like Einstein, Margaret Sanger (1879–1966) was also a powerful influence in the shaping of the twentieth century mind. A nurse from White Plains, New York, Sanger was determined that women should not suffer the death and ill health that followed unplanned or unwanted pregnancies and the self-inflicted abortions that attempted to end them. Her mother had died at the age of forty-nine from tuberculosis, a disease Sanger believed resulted from her eighteen pregnancies.

Yet Sanger championed more than the cause of contraceptive information for women. She propagandized for "sex knowledge" and asserted that sexual activity was both pleasurable and important. She believed sexual freedom should be available to women as well as men.

Sanger's speeches and distribution of contraceptive information through the United States mail system resulted in many legal skirmishes, the most publicized involving anti-vice crusader Anthony Comstock. The Comstock Law, passed in 1873, was intended to prevent obscene material from being sent through the mail, and Comstock successfully included contraceptive information in this category.

When Sanger and her sister, Ethel, opened a birth control information clinic in New York—where they received an overwhelming response—both were arrested after only ten days. Ethel was tried first and sentenced to thirty days in jail, where she

27. MARGARET SANGER. Mabel Dodge (1879–1962), who ran one of the great radical New York City salons of the period, wrote of Sanger: "It was she who introduced us all to the idea of Birth Control and it, along with other related ideas about Sex, became her passion. It was as if she had been more or less chosen by the powers that be to voice a new gospel of not only sex knowledge in regard to contraception, but sex knowledge about copulation and its intrinsic importance."[4]

went on a hunger strike. She was eventually granted a pardon, on the condition that she not break the law again (Margaret made the promise on her behalf). When Margaret's turn came, she refused to make such a promise and was sentenced to thirty days in a workhouse. After serving her sentence, she emerged a national heroine. Thereafter Sanger's lecture tours, publications, and frequent arrests kept the birth control issue controversial.

Sanger managed to turn each attack aimed at her into a victory and eventually expanded her support from lower-class women and radicals to "society wives" who were generally college-educated women with an interest in social causes. She used all of this to shift the focus from herself to those who were threatening what were increasingly seen as basic civil liberties. Finally, in January 1918, the New York Court of Appeals held that contraceptive information could be legally distributed to men and women for prevention or cure of disease, thereby legalizing clinics like the one Sanger and her sister had opened.

Following this court victory, Sanger and her second husband, J. Noah Slee, funded and directed efforts to smuggle diaphragms into New York. When these efforts proved unsuccessful, the determined Sanger used the mails to bring the diaphragms into the United States. A legal attempt to stop her resulted in a court victory that opened the mails to contraceptive devices. Thereafter contraceptive sales reached $250 million annually by 1937.

Sanger's purpose was always clear: "If you like my religion—birth control," she said, "we shall be friends."[5] She disliked euphemisms such as "Planned Parenthood," believing them to be terms of appeasement. Although she began her crusade as a radical defender of the rights of women and lower classes, Sanger began to understand that she could strike a more sympathetic chord with lawmakers on the theme of eugenics. "More children from the fit, less from the unfit," she said.[6] Although she tried to avoid racism, her propaganda attracted a new audience of mostly white American workers. Combined with overt racists, this group provided Sanger with a powerful bloc of the United States population.

Her agenda moved from a radical program of social disruption to a more conservative one of social control. As a result, the Birth Control Federation changed its name to Planned Parenthood Federation of America. From there, the organization expanded its work from merely distributing contraceptive information to seeing itself as a major influence on population trends in the United States.

Sanger did not support abortion as an acceptable alternative to the consequences of the free love she advocated. She believed that contraception would eliminate the need for abortion, although she also believed there were instances when abortion was justifiable. Sanger said,

> To each group we explained simply what contraception was; that abortion was the wrong way—no matter how early it was performed it was taking life; that contraception was the better way, the safer way—it took a little time, a little trouble, but was well worthwhile in the long run, because life had not yet begun.[7]

Concerned that contraception remained primitive, Sanger teamed up with Katharine Dexter McCormick, a wealthy woman who married into the McCormicks of International Harvester fame, to fund the development of a birth control pill by the brilliant geneticist, Gregory Goodwin Pincus (1903–67). In May 1960 the Food and Drug Administration approved oral contraceptives. At the dawn of the 1960s, some 2.3 million women were using "the pill." Articulating Sanger's dream, writer and political figure Claire Booth Luce said, "Modern woman is at last free as a man is free, to dispose of her own body, to earn her living, to pursue the improvement of her mind, to try a successful career."[8]

The consequences of the pill have been far-reaching. The concept that women are as free as men to indulge in sex altered the basic structure of traditional male-female relationships. The older religious view that women were somehow different from men and were to be "protected" by them became passé. Now the male was no longer the sole sexual aggressor. The female could also pursue and stake out her own territory. In fact, in the end men may not be necessary at all for sex, as test-tube technology, genetic tinkering, cloning, and the growing lesbian movement seem to say.

COMING OF AGE

The work of anthropologist Margaret Mead (1901–78) paralleled Sanger's sexual liberation crusade. Mead's 1928 book *Coming of Age in Samoa* was based on nine months of graduate fieldwork studying adolescence in Samoa. Like Paul Gauguin, Mead traveled to the South Seas to see what paradise had to say about modern people.

Mead's work confirmed the theories of her instructor, Dr. Franz Boas, who believed that environmental forces were a primary influence on a person's behavior and personality. In her straightforward and accessible style, Mead emphasized the casualness of the Samoan lifestyle, relationships, sexual behaviors, and achievements. In particular, Mead wrote that Samoans were well adjusted because they had an early and complete knowledge of sex, which they viewed as natural and pleasurable. Sexual freedom was limited only by social status, and marriage was only a matter of convenience. Communal responsibility alleviated much of the burden associated with marriage, divorce, and illegitimacy.

Mead applied her data to the American adolescent. She theorized that American teenagers should be educated for "choice," a system of tolerance in which the young person is not pressured toward any particular ideology. She believed that utopia would be a culture that had universal tolerance for all ways of life and beliefs.

Mead, whom *Time* magazine named "Mother of the World" in 1969, was both a mother and grandmother and had been married and divorced three times. By advocating a casual attitude toward sex and the loosening of family ties, Mead anticipated an era when sexual experimentation, including homosexuality and bisexuality, would be considered normal and natural.

Although they disagreed on whether the birth control pill would be a panacea, Mead and Sanger both agreed on the need for contraception and population control. As a result, they engendered animosity from many in the religious and conservative communities. Mead once wrote, "Young people have begun to advocate frankness and honesty, rebelling against the extreme hypocrisy of the 1950s, when religious and educational institutions alike connived to produce pregnancies that would lead to marriage."[9]

THE NEW MUSIC: JAZZ

Like the ideas of Mead and Sanger, jazz was part of the spirit of the age. First emerging around 1913, jazz was spontaneous and free of the demands of tradition. Jazz challenged the high music that preceded it and had a mysterious power to strike at the heart. It moved the body and was seen by many at the time as guttural, sexual, and racial.

Rhythmically, its opponents originally believed that jazz seemed to originate in the groin, hips, and sexual organs—not from the belly, interior organs, arms, and legs as in Hindu, Japanese, and Chinese music; or from the breast, brain, ears, and eyes of the music of the European tradition. Jazz was offensive to many, including some African-American religious leaders, because of its sexual implications.

Despite opposition, by 1923 jazz had established itself in mainstream entertainment, and its acceptance among white middle-class listeners was growing. The emergence of the radio, the phonograph, and the record industry made the new form available to millions.

The vice districts, which were centered around brothels and saloons, were also key to jazz's development. Known as the "black and tan," saloons and cabarets ostensibly operating for a black clientele were actually intended to draw a substantial white patronage. These clubs featured black entertainment, waiters, and bartenders in response to white Americans' growing interest in the African-American subculture. These clubs were an early sign that segregation would eventually fail and that music itself would help lead the way to integration.

Jazz also began to spread as social dancing became the new American craze. Illegal sales of alcohol stemming from Prohibition inflated the profit in bootleg liquor and supported nearly all the famous early jazz venues—the Cotton Club (where the legendary Duke Ellington was often featured), Connie's Inn, the Sunset Café, and the Plantation.

Emerging feminism was also important to the acceptance of jazz. Until middle-class women could go out drinking and dancing, their boyfriends and husbands did not, either. By 1920 women were frequenting speakeasies, cabarets, and dance halls where the new music—jazz—was played.

28. JAZZ INNOVATOR LOUIS ARMSTRONG. No one disputes Armstrong's greatness as an instrumentalist. This has been borne out even by classical musicians. On one occasion, the brass section of the Boston Symphony went backstage after hearing Armstrong and asked him to repeat a certain part of his performance. The group was awestruck. As one said: "I watched his fingers and I still don't know how he does it. . .playing there all by himself, he sounded as if a whole orchestra were behind him. I never heard a musician like this, and I thought he was just a colored entertainer."[10]

THE SOLO

Jazz began as improvised ensemble music, with virtually no solo work. Later, clarinetist and saxophonist Sidney Bechet (1897–1959) introduced the solo to jazz. The legendary Duke Ellington (1899–1974) considered Bechet the foundation: "His things were all soul, all from inside."

But it was not Bechet alone that caused jazz to change from ensemble music to a soloist's art. By the mid-1920s, the spirit of modernism, with its crying-up of freedom, emotionalism, and personal expression, had escaped bohemian and artistic circles and was rushing into the mainstream. The call had changed from "community" to "individualism" and "self-expression." Society was no longer the structure within which the individual worked out his fate. Rather, society was increasingly being viewed as that which inhibited the individual.

Jazz soloists were quite explicit about what they were doing through their art. Spontaneously throwing off music from the heart was a key attraction of jazz, and the musicians admitted they were not only hearing a new form of music but experiencing a new way of life.

Louis Armstrong (1900–71) is considered the greatest of the jazz revolutionaries. Between 1925 and 1929 he recorded music that redirected the course of jazz and music in general. The Hot Five series (the Hot Five being the members of Armstrong's band) recorded two instant classics: "Heebie Jeebies" and "Cornet Chop Suey." "Heebie Jeebies" was the first recorded improvised vocal—improvised because Armstrong supposedly dropped the sheet music just as he started to sing.

Jazz analyst Nat Hentoff described Armstrong's famous grin as "the broadest and seemingly most durable grin in the history of Western man."[11] After he moved into the entertainment mainstream, many jazz critics saw that grin as the mark of a sell-out, while others recognized Armstrong's ability to balance the emotional gravity of the artist with the communal good cheer of the entertainer as a force that helped him demolish the "Jim Crow/Zip Coon/Ol' Dan Tucker stereotypes." In their place, Armstrong installed the liberated black man, the pop performer as world-renowned artist who dressed stylishly, lived high, and slapped palms with the Pope. Thus Armstrong regularly passed through white-only portals, leaving the doors open behind him for others of his race to follow.

Armstrong's musical greatness is undisputed. The brass section of the Boston Symphony, for example, once asked him to repeat a certain part of his performance backstage. The musicians were awestruck by Armstrong's innovative playing and sound, even while performing by himself offstage. Composer Virgil Thomson noted that Armstrong combined "the highest reaches of instrumental virtuosity with the most tensely disciplined melodic structure and the most spontaneous emotional expression, all of which in one man you must admit is pretty rare."[12] All this was from a man who could not read music.

THE CUBIST CONNECTION

Armstrong developed his music through chord progressions that generated a maximum of creative originality. Each preceding chorus and combined variation technique dissolved into splinter subdivisions of the original sixteen-bar structures. The technique recalls the Cubist process of breaking and dissolving previously solid forms.

One of the first true American Cubists, the painter Stuart Davis (1894–1964), sought to inject the brisk new jazz rhythms and mildly irreverent gaiety into his abstract painting. His art reflected his concern with ordering the "frenzy" he found in the American scene, which undoubtedly included jazz. His painting *Hot Still-Scape for Six Colors—7th Avenue Style* (1940) contains an astonishing variety of lively, dancing shapes, sharply contoured and smoothly fitted together in a sequence of syncopated rhythms.

Matisse's first major cutout project was *Jazz,* begun in 1943 at the height of World War II. The book's twenty color plates seemed an apt description of the musical theory of jazz applied to painting—the shapes appear to float in space, unconnected to any location by perspective or rigid compositional lines.

Cubism was a radical way of ordering space and time, and the brevity of a jazz solo parallels the shallowness of Cubist space. Within each circumscribed arena, the artist carries out a finely modulated work of dissection. The objects dissected are humble: a bottle, a newspaper, a guitar in the case of Cubism; a blues, a rag, or a popular song in the case of jazz. The interest lies in the process of dissection, which tests the artist's powers of formal analysis and his aesthetic sense.

BEBOP

Bebop is the jazz equivalent of analytic Cubism. With bebop, jazz improvisation shifted from simply ornamenting an original melody to organizing new patterns of fast, active melody lines. The patterns often ended with an abrupt two-note figure that suggested the word "be-bop" or "re-bop."

The supreme example of bebop can be heard in saxophonist Charlie "Bird" Parker (1920–55), perhaps the only jazz musician to rival Louis Armstrong in influence. Film director Clint Eastwood brought Parker's tragic life to the screen in the 1988 film *Bird*.

Bebop developed its own improvisational freedom partly through the influence of drugs, as was later to occur in rock music. Bebop influenced other artists, particularly the Beats, a 1950s group of writers and poets that included Jack Kerouac and Allen Ginsberg. To the Beats, Charlie Parker was a living justification of their philosophy—amoral, anarchistic, gentle, and over-civilized to the point of decadence.

RHYTHM AND BLUES

Swing music and the Big Band sounds of such white performers as Tommy Dorsey, Harry James, Benny Goodman, and others rest solidly on a jazz foundation, making the music palatable and more widely accessible to white audiences. Many of the singers who took over popular music for the decade after 1945, such as Frank Sinatra, started as Big Band singers. But when the Big Band era came to an end after World War II, postwar optimism left people ready for innovation—and for a good time.

At first, the music that began to capture urban black ears and feet had no name, but by the end of the war, it came to be known as rhythm and blues—R&B. Drawing together elements of both jazz and blues, as it did, it was a music perfectly suited to the heady new era—and ideal for dancing.

Jazz and blues are two distinct streams from the same musical source: both derived from the unique mix of West African and European music that fermented in the slave states of America. In fact, the blues emerged as a distinct musical form only after the American Civil War. In their new "leisure" time, former slaves gave birth to a hybrid form of music that joined the old "field holler" with white ballads. The field holler, the basic ingredient of the blues, was a plaintive West African–derived chant used while picking cotton or working on a levee. It softened the pain of work and did battle with the enervating, lonesome existence of a field hand.

Few popular forms of music are more important to the twentieth century than the blues. Dozens of types of folk music, skiffle, gospel, soul, rhythm and blues, and rock 'n' roll have all claimed the blues as a common ancestor. Elvis Presley, Bob Dylan, and the Rolling Stones all drew on the blues. One of the most direct influences on rock music came from the Mississippi Delta and was called "Delta blues," created by such seminal perfomers of the twenties and thirties as Charlie Patton and the influential Robert Johnson (1914–38).

THE EMERGENCE OF ROCK

Giving a kind of musical continuity to the twentieth century, jazz formed a bridge between the classical music of the nineteenth century and the rock 'n' roll of the 1950s—a form of music that arrived with a speed that shocked older Big Band fans and the music industry alike.

Though the term was not coined until later, rock 'n' roll can arguably be traced to a 1936 creation by a Chicago group called the Harlem Hamfats, whose combined music had a strong blues character with simple, rhythmically direct melodies. The Hamfats' songs frequently contained humorous and erotic lyrics, as in their "Let's Get Drunk and Truck," which was a popular dance of the time.

Then Louis Jordan (1908–75), an alto saxophonist, added his unique vocals to an original style he called the "blues jump." By the mid-1940s his group, the Tympany Five, was one of the most popular black bands in America and had five million-selling singles, such as "Is You Is or Is You Ain't My Baby."

During the late 1940s a disc jockey named Bill Haley (1925–81) began to include Jordan and other rhythm and blues musicians on his radio program. A man with deep country roots, Haley formed the Four Aces of Western Swing to blend rhythm and blues with slick western swing. But by 1951 Haley began to forsake country music to become a "hepcat"—wearing a dinner jacket and sporting a spit curl on his forehead. In 1952 he and his group were called "Bill Haley and His Comets." When they recorded "(We're Gonna) Rock Around the Clock" in 1954, it went largely unnoticed. But then a 1955 film called *Blackboard Jungle* lifted Haley and his songs from obscurity. *Blackboard* featured "Rock Around the Clock," which subsequently became the theme song for Haley's highly successful rock film *Rock Around the Clock*.

More than any other song, "Rock Around the Clock" gave birth to modern rock. It sold more copies—over 25 million, according to the *Guinness Book of World Records*—and became the most popular anthem to come out of the 1950s for more than a quarter of a century.

Haley's debt to jazz and the blues is clear. Jordan, however, later had strong views on the success of Haley and other white performers: "There is nothing that the white artist has invented or come along within the form of jazz or entertainment. . . . Rock and roll was not a marriage of rhythm and blues and country and western. Rock and roll was just a white imitation, a white adaptation of negro rhythm and blues."[13]

THE COUNTRY INTERPLAY

Rock music, however, could never have exerted the great influence it has had on Western culture without the underlying strength of what came to be called country music, which had subsumed black music as well. As such, it would be performers from the southern United States—such as Bill Haley, Elvis Presley, Buddy Holly, and others—whose recorded songs would infiltrate the rest of the country with rock 'n' roll.

The seminal influence on rock music was thus so-called "hillbilly music." One form of this music was the "Mountain" music of the Appalachians, which consisted primarily of the older traditional songs and ballads. The other form of "hillbilly music" was country music. Jimmie Rodgers (1897–1933) was the first country star to attract a national audience, and he successfully integrated black and white influences into his music. Most country singers of the 1930s or later owe a debt to Rodgers. His influence can be heard in such diverse country performers as Gene Autry, Bill Cox, Cliff Carlisle, Daddy John Love, Hank Williams (1923–53), Ernest Tubb (1914–84), Hank Snow, Bill Haley, Elvis Presley, and others.

Rodgers was known as the "Blue Yodeler." His famous trademark was simply a yodeling section tacked onto an approximation of the old "Negro blues form." Indeed, many of Rodgers' "Blue Yodels" contained stanzas borrowed from earlier blues singers.

Some argue, in fact, that much of Rodgers' success lay in his ability to popularize and "whiten" traditional black music, to make the ever-popular blues acceptable to a white audience. Carrie Rodgers, in her biography of her husband, describes how Rodgers as a boy would carry water to Negro section hands in Mississippi. As music analyst Patrick Carr wrote,

> During the noon dinner-rests, they taught him to plunk melody from banjo and guitar. They taught him darkey songs; moaning chants and crooning lullabies. . . . Perhaps that is where he learned that peculiar caressing slurring of such simple words as "snow". . . ."go" . . . [In fact,] songs like "In the Jailhouse Now" [recorded by blues singer Blind Blake before Rodgers recorded his version] gave Rodgers a black element in his repertoire. He recorded with a number of black sidemen, including, on one auspicious occasion, jazz great Louis Armstrong.[14]

Although Rodgers' influence on what would later herald rock music was deep and wide, the performer who achieved the most fabulous success by intermingling country and rhythm and blues was Elvis Presley. His first single, recorded in 1954, was "Blue Moon of Kentucky," which was originally a composition by Bill Monroe (1911–97), a Kentucky bluegrass singer and mandolin player. But the single's B-side featured "That's All Right, Mama," an old rhythm and blues tune first recorded by black bluesman Arthur Crudup (1905–74). The success of this combination helped spawn a new style called "rockabilly"—the blues with a country beat.

Carl Perkins (1932–98) and Jerry Lee Lewis (b. 1935) were two of rockabilly's biggest stars. This was accentuated by African-American Chuck Berry (b. 1926), sometimes referred to as the "Father of Rock Guitar", who combined a rockabilly sound with a strong rhythm and blues beat. (See color plate 15.)

Texan Buddy Holly (1936–59), who was influenced by rockabilly, recorded a score of classic songs in the last two years of his short twenty-two-year life. Holly and his band, the Crickets, used the standard rockabilly instrumentation of two guitars (one for lead, one for rhythm), bass, and drums. However, both of their guitars were electric, and the drummer played a more prominent role than other rockabilly drummers. The Beatles later used Holly's instrumentation, hand-clapped rhythms, and simple backups in early songs like "I'll Follow the Sun" and "One After 909." Holly had toured in Great Britain and influenced many blossoming young rock musicians. In this respect, Holly may have been the all-important bridge to the British rock invasion of the 1960s.

Holly and other country musicians placed an indelible stamp on the Beatles. In fact, the Beatles' 1964 *Beatles for Sale* album included two songs by country singer-songwriter Carl Perkins and one by Holly. This Beatles collection, known as their country album, is most likely the first popular fusion of modern rock and country forms.

Rock 'n' roll, even in our own time, however, could not have developed without Presley, who built on the foundation laid by jazz and R&B. On that combination, the enormous international rock industry was built.

FITZGERALD'S GENERATION

The work of F. Scott Fitzgerald (1896–1940) paralleled the rise of the "Jazz Age." His 1919 novel *This Side of Paradise* haunted the decade of the twenties like a song—popular but not perfect. Shortly after its publication, Fitzgerald wrote, "My idea is always to reach my generation. The wise writer, I think, writes for the youth of his own generation, the critic of the next and the schoolmasters of ever afterward."[15]

Like Lord Byron a hundred years earlier, Fitzgerald embodied the personality of his times. Also like Byron, he based his work on incidents and conversations from his own life, as he and his wife Zelda, along with their friends, lived the Roaring Twenties to the extreme. The restlessness of the age can be seen in the loosening of traditional moral standards, for as Fitzgerald noted, "by 1926, the universal preoccupation with sex had become a nuisance."[16] The advent of the automobile meant that everyone was more mobile and independent. This meant that sex as well was now mobile and independent. Prohibition also contributed to the trend toward the disregard of authority. America tasted the addictive excitement of breaking the law and getting away with it, and the rise of Freudian psychology made Americans even more self-absorbed, especially when they turned their attention to sex.

Like many authors of the time, Fitzgerald lived in self-imposed "exile" in Paris. Although he met many other expatriate Americans there, including Ernest Hemingway and Gertrude Stein, he was never a true member of the expatriate community. Spending much of his time drunk while there or in adventure seeking, he referred to the months of June and July 1925 as "1000 parties and no work."[17]

However, while Fitzgerald was partying, the times changed. His 1934 novel *Tender Is the Night,* with its Riviera setting and cast of predominantly idle, wealthy expatriates, was not well received in Depression-era America. Then Zelda failed to recover from a mental breakdown, and Fitzgerald died in Hollywood after an unsuccessful attempt to become a screenwriter. Nonetheless, Fitzgerald left his imprint on history. After his death, the *New York Times* wrote that he "invented a 'generation' and did as much as any writer to form as well as record its habits." A 1920 *Atlantic Monthly* article entitled "'These Wild Young People' by One of Them" spoke of "that immodest, unchivalrous set of ne'er-do-wells, so delightfully portrayed by…the amazing young Fitzgerald."[18]

DEHUMANIZING ART

The "lost generation" chronicled by F. Scott Fitzgerald had fought one world war, was en route to another, and would soon face a devastating economic depression. Albert Einstein had dismissed the fixedness of the physical world with his theory of relativity. Sigmund Freud was recreating the human mind. Picasso and the post-Impressionist painters were redefining visual art. And T. S. Eliot and other writers were pronouncing the death of hope.

Then in 1925, Spanish philosopher José Ortega y Gasset (1883–1955) announced the "dehumanization of art" in his book of the same name. Ortega argued that the old forms had been exhausted and that rebellion was the only way to create anything new. He theorized that since traditional art had made life its main subject, modern artists must do the opposite and dehumanize their work. This suicidal gesture, Gasset argued, would bring about art's preservation and triumph. The artist, he claimed, hostile toward life and tradition, must also hate art, science, the state, and civilization as a whole.

The "dehumanization" movement championed a new art that most people initially would not understand and many would even despise. The new art would separate society into two ranks: one class that understands it and one that does not. The group that understands, in Ortega's way of thinking, "possesses an organ of comprehension denied to the other; they are two variations of human species."

In his 1929 *The Revolt of the Masses,* Ortega recorded the European power shift resulting from political and technological changes and called for the masses to cede social control to the cultivated minority—a new elite. Many intellectuals on both sides of the Atlantic generally agreed with his thesis.

ECONOMIC COLLAPSE: THE CRASH OF '29

Around the same time, Russian economist N. D. Kondratieu (1892–c. 1931), (his date of death is uncertain because he disappeared under the dictatorship of Joseph Stalin) discerned an economic pattern of fifty- to sixty-year "long wave" periods, which he used to predict the economic downturn that culminated in the United States Stock Market crash on October 29, 1929. Others, including economist John Maynard Keynes, had earlier warned that the Allies' harsh treatment of Germany after World War I would cripple the European economy.

"Black Tuesday" signaled the beginning of an economic depression that altered cultures and political structures worldwide. Within a mere decade after World War I, the Great Depression reduced millions of people in the Western world to the poverty levels of twentieth century Asians, South Americans, and Africans.

COMMUNISM, SOCIALISM, AND FASCISM

Some believe that without the stock market crash and depression in the United States, the Soviet system would never have been regarded as a serious alternative to

132 capitalism. At the time, only the Soviet Union seemed immune to economic disaster. Many came to believe that communism was the only solution to the periodic booms and depressions that bedevil the trade cycle. Many Westerners embraced communism and came to view the Soviet Union as the ideal state. But Joseph Stalin's (1879–1953) state planning from 1929 to 1934 created extreme hardships for the Soviet people. Stalin instituted terrorist policies to stifle opposition which ultimately cost some 20 million people their lives. As Stalin's death-grip tightened, the years from 1936 to 1938 became known as the Great Terror.

Significantly, within two decades—from the beginning of World War I to the beginning of World War II—the communist and fascist states, the Japanese dictatorship, and the Nazi state were erected.

GUERNICA

Post–World War I cultures were heading toward destruction. Picasso's 1937 painting *Guernica* captured the political climate in the sole humane political work of art in the last seventy years to achieve any lasting fame. *Guernica* depicts the bombing by

29. PABLO PICASSO, *Guernica*. After the Republican government of Spain had granted autonomy to the Basques, the city of Guernica became the capital of the independent republic. German aircraft, manned by German pilots, destroyed Guernica at the request of the Spanish Nationalist commander, General Emilio Mola. Guernica's razing soon symbolized fascist dehumanization and barbarity to the world.

German aircraft of a Basque town during the Spanish Civil War, a raid made at the request of the Spanish Nationalist commander, General Emilio Mola.

The painting's images have become universal symbols of bitter wartime affliction: broken warriors, a woman with a dead child, a disemboweled horse with a spear-point tongue, a crazed and cross-eyed woman whose nipples have become bolts, the fearful face of a woman, and a long arm holding a lamp over the scene jut out of a window—symbols of the conscience of a horrified humanity. The gored and speared horse represents the Spanish Republic. The bull symbolizes the brutality and darkness of General Francisco Franco. Along with a broken sword, a surviving flower, and a dove, all the images have the impact of a nightmare and the bold schematic presentation of a comic strip.

COMMUNISM AND THE EMERGING LEFT IN AMERICA

The period between 1929 and 1933 made a return to pre–World War I conditions impossible. By the mid-1930s, most governments had changed dramatically, as most European governments, with the exception of Scandinavia, moved to the political right. Spain experienced an almost simultaneous victory of nationalist, warlike, and actively aggressive regimes. Japan and Germany became major military powers. By the end of this period, only three remaining options competed for intellectual-political hegemony: Marxism, limited capitalism, and fascism.

Marxism gained popularity as Karl Marx's predictions about capitalism appeared to many to be materializing. Liberal American intellectuals flocked to the Communist Party, hoping for a peaceful revolution, and they pointed to the Soviet government's apparent success.

Although the Party gained a significant following, most Americans balked at supporting outright revolution. Instead the majority of voters chose a "New Deal" within the old system offered to them by President Franklin D. Roosevelt (1882–1945), who quickly pushed economy-boosting legislation through Congress. This move on Roosevelt's part forced the Communist Party to abandon many of its criticisms of American capitalism.

After losing the 1932 presidential election, the Communist Party USA de-emphasized Party membership and encouraged involvement with sympathetic nonmember organizations and individuals, so-called "fellow travelers." "Front" organizations promoted communist ideals while avoiding direct anti-communism encounters. The Party's on-again, off-again support of Stalin and the Soviet Union became a liability after World War II. Moreover, the discovery of Soviet spy rings in the United States led to the investigation of communist activities in America. In 1947 even the American movie industry was investigated, and in 1950 Joseph R. McCarthy, then the junior senator from Wisconsin, burst onto the national scene.

Alleging that 205 communists were employed at the State Department, the Republican Party and conservative Democrats used the ensuing "Red Scare" to discredit liberals and pass anti-communist legislation. By the mid-1950s, McCarthyism had ensured the demise of the Communist Party in America. Although Stalin's death made the Soviet Union seem less threatening, a new generation saw that anti-communism propagandizing could be an effective political posture.

GUTHRIE AND SEEGER: SONGS FOR THE PEOPLE

One of the many Americans who looked to communism to solve America's problems was folksinger Woody Guthrie (1912–67). Seeing the plight of California migrant workers firsthand, Guthrie performed at union gatherings and became involved with the Communist Party. After several years of performing and writing for left-wing groups and publications and a stint in the Merchant Marines, Guthrie learned about People's Songs, a group of folk singers who agreed to provide material to unions.

Guthrie's songs spoke intelligently or ironically of the hardships of the common people in a unique mixture of protest and patriotism. Because of its ties to communism, the folk protest movement dwindled during the "Red Scare." However, it was later to directly influence American popular music, particularly Bob Dylan, Joan Baez, Phil Ochs, Tom Paxton, and other "protest singers" of the 1960s.

According to one historian, Woody Guthrie and singer Pete Seeger first met at a union rally in New York City, an event that marked the beginning of a new era in American music. Seeger and Guthrie tried to help people understand their troubles and encouraged them to take action to improve their nation.

In 1941 Pete Seeger (b. 1919) formed the Almanac Singers, one of whose goals was to promote Stalin's nonaggression treaty with Hitler by espousing nonintervention ideals. Later, in 1949, Seeger and former members of People's Songs formed the Weavers, a group that sang about peace and civil rights. Although the Weavers became the first commercially successful folk group—selling four million records in two years—the House Un-American Activities Committee blacklisted them in 1952. As a result, they could no longer record or appear on radio or television.

Refusing to implicate his friends or fellow artists during the "Red Scare," Seeger began touring on his own and developed a new generation of folk singers who looked to him as their mentor. Seeger primarily extended existing materials to create several of the most popular folk revival songs of the 1960s, including "If I Had a Hammer," "Guantanamara," and "Where Have All the Flowers Gone?" He used references from the Old Testament and Welsh poet Idris Davies for lyrics in songs such as "Turn, Turn, Turn" and "The Bells of Rhymney."

When a 1994 article in the *Washington Post*, reporting on his receipt of the prestigious 1994 Kennedy Center Honors, referred to Seeger as a "life-long socialist," Seeger did not object. He said of his politics, "I learned that trying to stay away from an argument is not necessarily a good idea. People are out there being killed, and if you say, 'Oh, no, I am going to remain neutral' and take the safer stand, that to me is rather immoral."

AGITPROP: PHILOSOPHIES OF ART AND ARCHITECTURE

The influence of Marxist-communist ideologies was certainly not limited to the United States. Marxism influenced virtually every form of government and cultural figure of the time. It had an impact on art as well. In the Soviet Union, *agitprop,* or "agitation and propaganda," promoted the new Soviet ideals through posters, street-theater floats, and even parade decorations. Curiously, the Soviet poster art of the early 1920s inspired propaganda posters in the West during World War II.

A movement called Soviet Constructivism perhaps best reflected the ideals of Lenin and the Revolution: art—expressed through architecture—merged distinctions between artist and artisan, architect and engineer. A man named Vladimir Tatlin (1885–1953), trained as an icon painter, was one of the most influential Constructivists. He believed that art was a product of society and that it must directly express society's needs. Believing that still-life art was the chief image of private property, Tatlin advocated "socialist," abstract art that did not depict ownable items.

Tatlin's 1919 *Model for the Monument to the Third International* was to be the symbol of twentieth century skill and the world's highest building. The tower was never built, but it may well be the most influential nonexistent object of the twentieth century—and one of the most paradoxical in that it is an unworkable, probably unbuildable, metaphor of practicality.

136

THE BAUHAUS

Germany, not the Soviet Union, provided the emerging international style of architecture in Europe during the 1920s. Architect Walter Gropius (1883–1969) inaugurated the Bauhaus, which means "House for Building," in 1919. The Bauhaus was reminiscent of the Bauhutten, the lodges that housed masons and designers of medieval cathedrals during the Middle Ages. It also suggested a close society of crafts-men devoted to a heroic project. Gropius believed that only traditional crafts could renew unity in the spiritual confusion of the lost war. The Bauhaus thus presented art as a quasi-religious activity.

In his desire to create a new guild of craftsmen without class distinctions, Gropius wanted to construct a new structure that would "one day rise toward heaven from the hands of a million workers like the crystal symbol of a new faith." The Bauhaus would address practical questions such as mass housing, industrial design, layout, photography, and the development of prototypes. The students and staff designed household items such as lamps, kitchenware, pottery, and furniture.

In April 1933, less than three months after Adolf Hitler became chancellor of Germany, the National Socialist Police raided and closed the Bauhaus. The government proclaimed it "one of the most obvious refuges of the Jewish-Marxist conception of 'art.'"[19] Still, intellectuals in England and America heralded the Bauhaus as a mecca of modern art and avidly sought to preserve the Bauhaus legacy.

Harvard University secured Gropius to chair the Harvard Department of Architecture, where he also designed houses for himself and other Harvard faculty members. Gropius also obtained federal government work for a low-income hous-

30. THE PAN AM BUILDING, New York City. Architect Walter Gropius collaborated on prominent Bauhaus projects such as the Pan Am Building in New York City (1958), shown here, and later the John F. Kennedy Federal Building in Boston (1961–66).

ing project and planned affordable postwar housing using prefabricated structures. In addition, he worked on designs for Chicago's South Side renewal project and various buildings on the Harvard campus. Gropius also collaborated on projects such as the Pan Am Building in New York City and the John F. Kennedy Federal Building in Boston.

Gropius' student László Moholy-Nagy (1895–1946) founded the School of Design in Chicago in 1939. This school eventually became the Chicago Institute of Design and part of the Illinois Institute of Technology.

In 1933 painter Josef Albers (1888–1976), who once taught the Basic Course at the Bauhaus, accepted a post at North Carolina's Black Mountain College. This was an experimental school based in part on John Dewey's theories. Black Mountain students, including musician John Cage, designer R. Buckminster Fuller, and painters Robert Motherwell and Robert Rauschenberg, among others, would later make their own unique, influential contributions to promoting freedom in modern art and anticipating the '60s counterculture.

Former Bauhaus students and instructors in America maintained an artistic network, calling on each other for advice and recommending one another for commissions, projects, and teaching positions. As a result, the Bauhaus style dominated American art and architecture during the 1930s, '40s, and early '50s. Dissenters claim that American architecture has never recovered from the seemingly dehumanized Gropius glass and steel box.

THE ARCHITECTURE OF STATE POWER

The Bauhaus refugees deeply understood the link between architecture and politics. Every effort was made by the Bauhaus leaders to depoliticize their art and architecture. Architecture to the Bauhaus designer was to be functional for easy use by the people. A good architect, Gropius believed, constructed buildings first to be useful, then to be admired. As Bauhaus artists witnessed the rise of the powerful European states and their use of architecture primarily for aesthetics, they believed it could only lead to one thing— war. The reason was that tyrants such as Hitler used architectural aesthetics to manipulate and control the masses in order to enhance their power in preparation for war.

In 1925, a decade before his rise to power, Hitler was already sketching giant domes and arches for a rebuilt Berlin, which he intended to be the capital of the world. Albert Speer (1905–81) designed the Berlin Dome ("The Empire of Light") for Hitler. Meant to accommodate 130,000 Nazi Party members, the Dome would have been more than

250 meters high and seven times the diameter of Michelangelo's dome for St. Peter's. But it was never built. Speer, ironically, could not have anticipated the possibilities of mass media technology. If Speer could not bring all the people to the Fuhrer, perhaps the alternative would have been to bring the leader to the people. But that technology had to wait another twenty-five years—for television.

Italian dictator Benito Mussolini (1883–1945) clearly understood the power of architecture as a tool of manipulation and control. He hoped to surpass the Rome of the Caesars and the Popes with his Tezra Roma, the Rome of fascism, set halfway between St. Peter's and the mouth of the Tiber. Mussolini expected to finish the project by 1942, his planned date for Rome's World Fair. However, Mussolini's Palace of Italian Civilization did in fact reflect Speer's belief that authoritarian architecture must be clear and regular on the outside and "let the passing eye deduce nothing of what goes on inside. . . . The mask must not slip."

Twenty-five years later, most new American university campuses, particularly southern California schools, included at least one building like the Palace of Italian Civilization. Indeed, as Robert Hughes astutely notes in *The Shock of the New* (1993), the style of Mussolini and Speer became the reigning one for cultural centers and civic buildings in America—but it became known as the "Architecture of Democracy" in the America of the 1950s.

Perhaps the most disturbing example is the intimidating and impersonal Albany Mall, a group of buildings that make up the seat of New York's state government. The Mall illustrates corporate and bureaucratic states of mind, irrespective of country or ideology. It is difficult to see how human beings fit in with such authoritarian design. These buildings sum up Mussolini's philosophy that such structures should disguise what goes on inside them. Moreover, one could as easily imagine any of the buildings at the Albany Mall topped with a swastika or a hammer and sickle as with an American eagle. It makes no difference to the building.

Thus modernist culture developed its own language of power. Value free and lacking ties to any particular ideology, however, some modernist art became a tool of its patron—and thus the architecture of coercion.

MODERN ART AND THE NEW TEMPLE

In America, state patronage of the arts, particularly modern art, began to blossom soon after the 1913 Armory Show. This patronage continues today through the National Endowment for the Arts, the U.S. federal agency that funds art projects.

Franklin Roosevelt recognized the importance of the arts. His administration's assistance to artists during the Depression resulted in more than 2,500 murals; almost 18,000 sculptures and 110,000 easel paintings; about 250,000 impressions of 11,300 different prints; 2 million copies of 35,000 different posters; half a million photographs; 450 exhibitions; the production of two how-to films; and the staffing and financing of 103 community arts centers.

A few non-modernist American artists went so far as to hope that government support would break the so-called "vulgar domination" of the art market. They believed that the art market was monopolized by a small, elite class of society with large incomes and by art dealers who demanded work they could sell to the monied dilettantes and aesthetic connoisseurs. Federal funding did indeed increase art production and heightened interest in art among the broad public, especially for modern art. But it may have only traded one elite class for another.

The increasing popularization of art coincided with a boom in museum building. As gathering points and arenas for social display, museums came to be seen as depositories of culture, just as churches had in the past. As such, museums erased old boundaries; many denominations could come together under a museum's roof. Museum directors increasingly defined art and were called upon to explain it. This is much like the ministers of the Middle Ages who explained the imagery of the stained glass windows in Chartres and other cathedrals to their illiterate or semi-literate pilgrim congregations. As Ortega predicted, an elite would eventually define and explain art for the masses.

HEMINGWAY

While visual art was rapidly changing, literature also experienced a revolution. This was epitomized by the work of Ernest Hemingway (1899–1961). After a stint as a Red Cross ambulance driver in Italy during World War I and an interlude as an admired member of the American expatriate community in Paris, Hemingway, some believe, became preoccupied with death and killing. He not only wrote about violence, he participated in it, and the killing art of Spanish bullfights became one of his most ardent, lifelong passions.

Hemingway's 1929 classic *A Farewell to Arms* reflected his tragic outlook. Frederic Henry, the hero, considers the impending death of the woman he loves: "Now Catherine would die. That's what you did. You died. You did not know what it was about. You never had time to learn. They threw you in and told you the rules and the first time they caught you off base they killed you."[20] While Frederic blames vengeful gods for Catherine's mortality, his real frustration lies in the realization that there is no "they."

Like Fitzgerald, Hemingway largely wrote about himself and the people he knew, and he was probably the most popular and critically acclaimed writer of his time. Perhaps Hemingway's greatest contribution was his original, cryptic use of language, especially in dialogue, giving his readers only a hint of the story's substance and requiring them to find the larger meaning on their own.

RADIO: THE NEW AURAL CULTURE

In terms of art produced on a mass scale, the twentieth century was the era of the "common people," as witnessed by the rise of radio during the Depression. Radio audiences doubled during that decade, because even poor people could afford a radio. Although radio did not transform people's perception of reality, as film and other media had, it was a powerful tool of mass communication. It reached millions simultaneously, making each hearer feel that he or she was addressed individually. Politicians quickly recognized the power of radio for propaganda. Franklin Roosevelt was the first president to address the nation live on radio, and his fireside chats became famous. During his presidency, Bill Clinton used the same radio tactic with success.

Radio affected music more than any other art form. For the first time, music was carried (in intervals of greater than five minutes) across distances to a theoretically limitless number of listeners. Radio uniquely popularized the music of minority groups and also became the most powerful means of selling records. Radio also changed the role of music in contemporary life, not excluding its role as a kind of "aural wallpaper" for everyday living.

It's difficult to recognize the innovations of the radio culture, since so much that it pioneered has become a part of everyday life. For instance, radio transformed the life of the poor, especially housebound poor women. "Henceforth," as Eric Hobsbawm writes in *The Age of Extremes* (1994), "the loneliest need never again be entirely alone. And the entire range of what could be said, sung, played or otherwise expressed in sound, was now at their disposal."[21]

It also meant that families and individuals would gather around the radio, as if it were a shrine, to listen to their favorite game shows, sports commentary, celebrity guest shows, soap operas, news bulletins, or serial programs of every kind. As such, perhaps radio's most important influence was that it privatized and structured life according to a rigorous timetable. Thereafter it ruled not only the sphere of labor but also of leisure.

Anticipating television, the VCR, and DVD, radio created its own public sphere where, for the first time in history, complete strangers could discuss their common experience of listening to a particular program. Woody Allen's 1987 film *Radio Days* affectionately portrays that early radio culture.

CITIZEN KANE

Technological innovations and industrial forces, including the press, camera, film, radio, and recording, began to dominate the popular arts, but only two of these avant-garde arts became immediate and universally admired: jazz and especially film. Increasingly, more people viewed "reality" through the camera lens—much like television's influence today. As the Depression deepened and the world fought a war, Western cinema attendance reached an all-time peak.

When young Orson Welles (1915–85) arrived in Hollywood, he was already well-known due to the national furor over his 1938 radio dramatization of H. G. Wells' *War of the Worlds* and his production of *Macbeth* at the Negro Theater Project in Harlem, directed by John Houseman.

In 1941, at the age of 25, Welles released the now classic film *Citizen Kane*. This story of the rise and corruption of a newspaper magnate was based on the career, thinly disguised, of yellow journalism tycoon William Randolph Hearst (1863–1951), a leading isolationist and opponent of Roosevelt's New Deal. Even Hearst's visit with Hitler was included in the movie.

But the film was about much more than Hearst. It raised questions about the inner psychological nature of Welles himself, as well as the nature of American politics and its relationship to the European crisis. A swing toward isolationism in American politics would have jeopardized Europe and ensured the triumph of fascism abroad. Kane's image at the end of the film provides an allegorical warning to Europe and America about the fate of their relations; Kane is shown as an old man, lonely and alone, isolated at the enormous, claustrophobic castle (a metaphor for America), which was constructed as a fantasy world against the outside. This in part reflects how Welles himself often lived out his later years.

Citizen Kane is universally acknowledged as a turning point in motion picture history. It was an amazing triumph for Welles since Hearst and leaders in the movie industry attempted to suppress the film through intimidation, bribery, and boycotts.

142

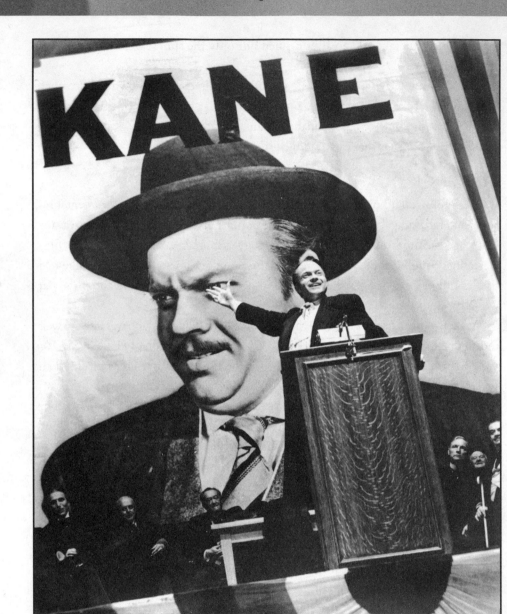

31. ORSON WELLES in *Citizen Kane*. Whether one loved or hated it, the visual extravagance of *Citizen Kane* was undeniable. John Russel Taylor notes in his study on Welles: "It is perfectly understandable that *Citizen Kane* should have had such an overwhelming influence on Hollywood films that came after. Shaw remarked of Ibsen's impact on late nineteenth-century England, 'A modern manager need not produce *The Wild Duck,* but he must be very careful not to produce a play which will seem insipid and old-fashioned to play-goers who have seen *The Wild Duck,* even though they may have hissed it.' The exact same was true of Welles and *Kane* in the Hollywood of the 1940s."[22]

Citizen Kane's influence, however, did not so much reflect new cinematic practices or technologies as it did Welles' remarkable insight into film technique and storyline.

WORLD WAR II: THE NAKED AND THE DEAD

Despite warnings from artists, philosophers, and writers, World War II roared upon humankind. It sprang from the economic, social, philosophical, cultural, and political chaos in Europe following World War I. World War II decimated Europe, just as World War I had. Capitals lay in ruins, and some 45 million people were killed. Millions of others were enslaved or died in Nazi death camps. The mechanization of warfare reached new levels. The airplane was important both on land and at sea. Moreover, the United States introduced the atomic bomb at the end of the war, thereby opening the age of nuclear warfare.

With the possible exception of violent revolution, total war is the most devastating dehumanizer and most catastrophic instigator of social change. The war forced people in the West, whether gladly or grudgingly, to adapt to new realities. However, in the shadow of war's vast impersonality, change became the daily pattern of life.

One important area of change was sexual behavior. With the groundwork laid by Margaret Sanger, Margaret Mead, and various cultural movements such as feminism, the kindling for a sexual revolution was laid. Alfred Kinsey (1894–1956) had the match to ignite it. His 1948 book *Sexual Behavior in the Human Male* and his 1953 *Sexual Behavior in the Human Female* made his name a household word. Perhaps relying on the *Human Male*'s 804 pages of data, most Americans agreed with Kinsey and believed his studies were accurate and useful. Evangelist Billy Graham, however, said, "It is impossible to estimate the damage this book will do to the already deteriorating morals of America."[23] Kinsey's work, including his 1976 *The Modernization of Sex,* greatly increased tolerance for sexual activity, particularly among unmarried young people. The basic reason for this was Kinsey's postulation that a great deal of sexual activity, among young and old alike, was occurring outside of marriage.

In addition, American writers began to detail the effect of the war on servicemen in terms of sexual metaphors. Norman Mailer (b. 1923), for example, published his first novel, *The Naked and the Dead,* in 1948 when he was twenty-eight. Reviewers called the book "virtually a Kinsey Report on the sexual behavior of the G.I.,"[24] and the book's explicitness shocked many readers. Mailer depicts combat as either the sublimation of sexual energy or direct sexual release. As he continued to explore the relationship between sex and war, Mailer concluded that any individual act of violence subtracts from society's overall propensity for violence.

The Naked and the Dead established a pattern for World War II fiction: modern warfare would no longer be romanticized, and the public was prepared for more open and explicit cultural discussions. Moreover, the confrontation between human sexuality and humanity's technological capacity for self-destruction became the focus of much contemporary literature. This can be seen in James Jones' *From Here to Eternity* (1951), which was transformed into an Academy Award–winning film in 1953.

THE BLANKNESS OF MODERNITY

Nor was sex the only area of cultural change brought about by World War II. The post–World War II world faced new levels of alienation, dehumanization, and uncertainty, as reflected in Sloan Wilson's 1955 novel *The Man in the Gray Flannel Suit*.

Tom Rath, the book's main character, tries to explain the problem to his wife: "One day a man's catching the 8:26, and the next day he's killing people, and the next he's catching the 8:26 again." Rath comes to believe that the only way to reconcile the war experience and his present life as a businessman is to "learn to believe that it's a disconnected world, a lunatic world, where what is true now was not true then. . . ."[25]

The fact that alienation had become a feature of the Western psyche can be seen in much of Edward Hopper's (1882–1967) painting, but especially in his 1942 *Nighthawks*. (See color plate 16.) The painting captures the grim loneliness of modern American life as reflected in the shadowed, hollow eyes of a customer at a diner against the backdrop of a dark and haunted city. Humanity, it seems, is being swallowed up in the blankness of modernity.

The Abstract Expressionist artists of New York, of which Jackson Pollock (1912–56) was the most prominent, dominated American artistic efforts for fifteen years after the end of World War II. These artists wanted to place their discourse beyond events—in a field not bound by historical time. Pollock, Mark Rothko, and others turned to myths and primitive art for inspiration. They also developed the technique of automatism—automatic or unconscious action—in order to recollect humanity's primordial past and reveal the archetypal symbols that "lived" in the "collective unconscious" first postulated by psychologist Carl Jung. Their work was a reaction to the alienation and complexity of the modern world.

Pollock, for example, poured, dribbled, and flung paint on oversized canvases that he placed on the floor, resulting in works such as *Autumn Rhythm (Number 30, 1950)*.

Blue Poles, painted by Pollock in 1952, was created in a drunken stupor amidst broken glass. The painting was later sold in 1972 to the Australian government for $2 million. As of that date, no American painting had ever sold for such a high figure. In the entire history of Western art, only works by Rembrandt, Velasquez, and da Vinci had commanded more respect in the marketplace.

Mark Rothko (1903–70) considered painting not merely an exercise in the reproduction of human expression but a religion. Of Russian Jewish descent, Rothko was obsessed with the moral possibility that his art could go beyond pleasure and carry the full burden of religious meaning—the patriarchal weight, in fact, of the Old Testament. Art historian Robert Rosenblum notes that a "surrogate religion" is a force in Rothko's work. Commenting on his 1954 painting *Ochre and Red on Red,* Rothko explained that the "people who weep before my pictures are having the same religious experience I had when I painted them. And if you. . .are moved only by their color relationships, then you miss the point."

Shortly before committing suicide in 1970, Rothko was commissioned to create a series of paintings as objects of contemplation in a nondenominational chapel at Rice University in Houston. (See color plate 17.) The Rothko Chapel evokes emotion with its huge obscure paintings in plum reds and stygian violets—almost monochrome in their blocks. Art historian Robert Hughes noted that the paintings

> represent an astonishing degree of self-banishment. All the world has drained out of them, leaving only a void. Whether it is The Void, as glimpsed by the mystics, or simply an impressively theatrical emptiness, is not easily determined, and one's guess depends on one's expectation. In effect, the Rothko Chapel is the last silence of Romanticism.[26]

Centre Triptych for the Rothko Chapel (1966) replaces the world with a convulsion of pessimistic inwardness. It's as if Rothko, facing his own finiteness, chose despair. He apparently found only a dead end in his mortality and could create no more. The placement of Rothko's paintings in the chapel only highlights the modern crisis in traditional religion. To the extent that it accepts form over content, religion also faces the void of modernity.

FRANCIS BACON'S CARCASSES

Irish-born artist Francis Bacon (1909–92) illustrated the dehumanization of modern culture by painting people's lonely cries for lost values and human dignity. One of the great artists of modernity, Bacon depicted a humanity robbed of its freedom, love, and rationality—of everything the great humanist painters had celebrated in the classical tradition.

Having suffered extreme sexual molestation as a boy, alienation from his family, and anxiety as an adult homosexual in London's 1930s literary and artistic circles, Bacon seemed to face constant torment, dissatisfaction, and uncertainty. An atheist, he was, ironically, one of the most deeply religious painters of the twentieth century. The agony of his unbelief became so acute that the negative in his work—pessimism, loneliness, despair, emptiness, distortion, darkness, stark mortality—became an almost religious attribute. In fact, Bacon had an acute fascination with the crucifixion of Christ. "I've always been very moved by pictures about slaughterhouses and meat, and to me they belong very much to the whole thing," Bacon once said. "I know for religious people, for Christians, the Crucifixion has a totally different signature. But as a nonbeliever, it was just an act of man's behavior, a way of behavior to another."[27]

His 1944 *Three Studies for Figures at the Base of a Crucifixion* depicts all loss of hope. (See color plate 3.) The three figures in the triptych join in the theme of the violence that people do to one another through the power of sex and hatred. The force with which the three Greek Furies hurl their misery and rage at us proves the extent of Bacon's loss of faith in humanity.

His 1953 study *After Velasquez's Portrait of Pope Innocent X* turns Diego Velasquez's powerful portrait of Pope Innocent X Pamphill into a "screaming Pope." It also introduces an element of dislocation from the primary image, a concept that greatly influenced modern art. These vivid and powerful inventions transformed the crafty and smug Prince of the Church into a monstrously depraved image—as if the Pope represented, for Bacon, the last gasping scream of the religion he despised. The Pope is held in a cube—a boxed hell without escape. The picture seems to intentionally assault the power of the Church and may represent Bacon's protest against the organized religion he had known in Ireland.

Bacon's 1946 *Painting* shows his fascination with blood and carnage; it is redolent of decay and bleeding meat under a mushroom cloud, represented by an open black umbrella. Bacon called the carcass at the back of the painting "the armchair of meat."[28] *Painting* was a gruesome replacement of the ornate throne of the traditional state portrait. Bacon thus combined three major themes of his time: war, the dictator, and dead meat. No one has better depicted the despair of the generations that lived between the

early 1900s and the late 1950s than Bacon. His art epitomized alienation, dehumanization, and pessimism. "Man now realizes that he is an accident," Bacon noted, "that
he is a completely futile being, that he has to play out the game without purpose, other
than of his own choosing." On another occasion he remarked, "We are born and we
die and there's nothing else. We're just part of animal life."[29]

The generation that lived through the first half of the twentieth century—what
I here call, in Gertrude Stein's phrase, "the lost generation"—suffered the horrible ramifications of two world wars. They had sown rebellion and reaped chaos. They produced technological wonders that often seemed to turn on their human creators.
Geniuses such as Albert Einstein introduced relativity, and the world reaped relativism.
Philosophers such as José Ortega y Gasset divided the masses from the elite and reaped
revolution.

Yet even as people tried to understand their alienation and loss of hope, they
learned that the artists and philosophers had few real and lasting answers. Bacon's
work, as such, epitomizes the spirit of twentieth century man—a grasping for dignity
within an environment of dehumanization and meaninglessness. He once said:
"Nietzsche forecast our future for us—he was the Cassandra of the nineteenth century—he told us it's all so meaningless we might as well be extraordinary."[30] Western
culture seemed lost, and Bacon provided its epitaph: "Of course we are meat," he said,
"We are potential carcasses."[31]

Still from the video series *Grasping for the Wind*. John Whitehead at the Albany Mall in Albany, New York. At the end of this scene, Whitehead asks, "Where do human beings fit in all of this?"

CHAPTER 5
The Fat Dream

They were like the man with the dungeon stone and the gloom, rising, from the underground, the sordid hipsters of America, a new beat generation that I was slowly joining.

JACK KEROUAC[1]

The changes wrought by World War II were swift—and they profoundly disturbed people's understanding of life. On August 6, 1945, the United States dropped the atom bomb on Hiroshima, Japan. Most of the city was destroyed; more than 70,000 people were killed immediately, and approximately the same number died later of the new manmade death, radiation sickness. Three days later, the United States dropped a second bomb, on Nagasaki. For decades, the atom bomb claimed victims from among the survivors and their unborn.

Before then, of course, humanity knew and accepted the inevitability of death. But the bomb made death somehow more invisible, abstract, indiscriminate—and massive. Death was no longer random; it was a calculated, mechanical weapon that dehumanized and obliterated people en masse—enough so that the superpowers contained sufficient nuclear weapons in their arsenals to destroy all life on earth many times over in a relatively short period of time. That possibility of total self-destruction changed the consciousness of mankind. Science and history had become destroyers of life to the point that even the continuation of the human race was no longer certain. What meaning could an individual life have when at any time all life might vanish?

EXISTENTIALISM AND ABSURDITY

Seeking escape, a culture faced with annihilation began to turn to the trivia of fashion, the spurious excitement of spectator sports, the false hopes of reckless

150

gambling, the diversions of profligate sensuality, and the numbing haze of alcohol and drugs.

A new kind of pessimism crept into Western literature and philosophy, which was most evident in the existentialist movement. Perhaps the most influential existentialist was French philosopher Jean-Paul Sartre (1905–80), who offered an illusive hope in a senseless world with his doctrine of autonomy and self-definition. Sartre stressed the irreducible uniqueness of each individual's subjective experience as he or she purposefully acted in a purposeless world. His radical concept of freedom was that regardless of the situation, each person is free to choose a course of action and thereby define oneself. But this also meant that, to Sartre, no choices were more moral than others.

Sartre's friend, writer Albert Camus (1913–60), believed in the meaninglessness of life but still thought life was worth living. He introduced the idea of "absurdity" into his 1942 collection of essays, *The Myth of Sisyphus:*

> [I]n a universe suddenly divested of illusions and lights, man feels an alien, a stranger. His exile is without remedy since he is deprived of the memory of a lost home or the hope of a promised land. This divorce between man and his life, the actor and his setting, is properly the feeling of absurdity.[3]

Scholars applied the term *absurd* to a group of 1950s dramatists, mostly French, who denied any distinction between the absurdity of the world and of man himself. Like the Dadaists, futurists, and surrealists whom they admired, they flouted the rules of theater, mixing tragedy and comedy while rejecting rational motivation. Absurdism

32. SARTRE'S BEST-KNOWN WORK, *Nausea* (1938), details the frustration of the individual with his fellow man. The existentialist of the novel sees others as so different from himself that they are almost not human. Sartre later regretted the novel's extremism: "What I lacked was a sense of reality. Since then I have changed. I have undergone a slow apprenticeship with the real. I have seen children die of hunger. In the face of a child who dies, *Nausea* has no weight."[2]

came to America from Europe in the late 1950s and '60s. This can be seen in Edward Albee's 1959 play, *The Sandbox,* which gives an absurdist view of human relationships.

Some seven years later, in 1966, Ronald Travel, who had worked on films with the artist Andy Warhol, helped create the Theatre of the Ridiculous, which became the successor to the Theatre of the Absurd. The Theatre of the Ridiculous exposed the excesses of pop culture, especially in relation to sex and entertainment, and often parodied popular entertainment formulas without suggesting a practical solution. These absurdist themes continue to be played out in such modern films as Oliver Stone's 1994 *Natural Born Killers,* Quentin Tarantino's 1994 *Pulp Fiction,* and Mary Harron's 2000 *American Psycho*—all of which obscure the boundaries between murder, mayhem, and comedy, leaving audiences unsure whether to laugh or recoil at their brutal, dehumanizing violence.

THE COLD PEACE HYPOCRISY

While the artists were busy exposing the excesses and parodying entertainment, post–World War II society found little solace in the endeavors of painters, philosophers, and writers. The fear of a superpower confrontation leading to a nuclear conflagration was uppermost in most people's minds.

In many ways, the Cold War was a political fabrication. The governments of both the Soviet Union and the United States accepted the global distribution of force at the end of World War II as an uneven but essentially unchallenged balance of power. Despite the Korean War and the 1962 Cuban missile crisis, the superpowers tacitly agreed to treat the Cold War as essentially a Cold Peace. Mutual threats and brinkmanship supported a relatively stable international system, as symbolized by the 1963 installation of the telephone "hotline" linking the White House to the Kremlin.

Still, the United States' failure to come to the aid of Hungarian nationalists in 1956 exposed the moral bankruptcy of this policy. On October 23, Hungarian students in Soviet-occupied Budapest demanded a democratic government and the reinstallation of Premier Imre Nagy (1896–1958). Police attacked the students, and a riot ensued. Afterwards, the Hungarian government declared martial law and called for military assistance against the Soviet Union. A day later, Nagy assumed the premiership, but unsatisfied revolutionaries led fighting between the Soviet troops and Hungarian patriots. On October 31, Nagy announced Hungary's withdrawal from the Warsaw Pact and appealed to the United Nations to support Hungary's declaration of neutrality. But on November 2, instead of evacuating their troops as promised, the Soviet Union seized the Budapest airport and other major facilities. The Soviets launched a full-scale attack on Budapest on November 4.

Hungary pleaded for help from the outside world, begging the "civilized people of the world" to help them defend against the "cruel fire of Soviet tanks and bombers." A Hungarian radio station broadcast this appeal:

> Civilized people of the world, listen and come to our aid, not with declarations, but with force, with soldiers and arms. Do not forget that there is no stopping the wild onslaught of Bolshevism. Your turn will also come, once we perish. Save our souls! Save our souls![4]

Rumors of help from the United States and the United Nations encouraged the freedom fighters, but help never arrived, and Soviet forces crushed the revolution in a single day.

On November 5, President Dwight D. Eisenhower (1890–1969) publicly condemned the Soviet Union's actions. The United Nations voted to censure the Soviets and send U.N. observers into Hungary. On November 6, Pope Pius XII published an encyclical denouncing the bloodshed in Hungary. Supporters of the revolution staged anti-Communist demonstrations across Europe and America. But all of this was too little, and it came much too late. Conservative estimates of lives lost came to 30,000. This number included Premier Imre Nagy, whom the Soviets executed.

America was ostensibly committed to keeping the world free for democracy. But all it meant in most instances was ineffectually frowning on totalitarian acts.

ORWELL AND LOVING THE BOMB

Reflecting the spirit of the times, writer George Orwell (1903–50) predicted government manipulation, posturing, and deception in his novels *Animal Farm* (1946) and *Nineteen Eighty-Four* (1949). Orwell understood that in order to succeed, totalitarian states must appeal to their subjects' emotions. He saw how truth could become whatever the government wishes to advertise—a definition prevalent today in the mass media, advertising agencies, and government bureaucracies.

Orwell's insight that people can be controlled once they are taught to ignore truth has made *Nineteen Eighty-Four* the best-known futurist novel of the twentieth century. It has become part of Western culture, and terms like *doublethink* and *Newspeak* are now in most English dictionaries.

33. *DR. STRANGELOVE* (played by Peter Sellers) with his self-propelled Nazi-saluting arm, his belief in the divinity of computers, and his gleeful plans for a post-nuclear holocaust society of subterranean polygamy (the ultimate expression of America's obsession with macho potency and power) emerges as a brilliant parody of the worst strains in American politics and culture.

Filmmaker Stanley Kubrick (1928–99) examined the same theme in his movie *Dr. Strangelove, or: How I Learned to Stop Worrying and Love the Bomb* (1964). The plot concerns a Soviet-constructed doomsday machine that is triggered accidentally when an insane American general fears America's sexual potency may be undermined by a Communist plot to fluoridate the water supply. Not only does *Dr. Strangelove* satirize the foibles of the power brokers, it also links their behavior to the primal instincts of sex and death. Kubrick questions people's ability to control their destructive urges. In Sartreian fashion, the film addresses people's impotence to cope with the forces they have unleashed.

Still, Kubrick resists posing a solution to the insane world he sees. He offers no plea for sanity or belief in social change in the film. There is only the monstrous Dr.

154

Strangelove, the personification of science gone mad. With his self-propelled Nazi-saluting arm, his belief in the divinity of computers, and his gleeful plans for a post-nuclear holocaust society of subterranean polygamy, Strangelove emerges as a brilliant parody of the worst strains in American politics and culture. The film immortalizes the anxieties about nuclear disaster haunting the times by showing that the super-powers themselves created the state of anxiety.

MCCARTHY AND THE RED SCARE

Kubrick's thesis was predated by American hysteria over the danger of Communist subversion in the United States. Suspicions began with the revelation that a British atomic scientist, Klaus Fuche, had passed atomic secrets to the Soviets. Anti-Communist sentiment escalated with the debacle surrounding Alger Hiss, who, as a State Department official, was accused of committing Soviet espionage in the 1930s by former Communist Party member Whitaker Chambers. The hysteria culminated in the hearings before the House Committee on Un-American Activities, led by the then-junior Republican senator from Wisconsin, Joseph McCarthy (1908–57).

McCarthy specialized in sensational, unsubstantiated accusations about Communist infiltration of the American government. McCarthy also implicated well-known Hollywood actors and directors, trade unionists, and teachers. The broad brush of McCarthyism appealed to envy, paranoia, and a dislike for intellectuals. His attacks on basic civil liberties have been revisited in numerous films, including director Woody Allen's 1976 *The Front* and Irwin Winkler's 1991 *Guilty by Suspicion*.

The press, particularly in Washington, D.C., acquiesced to McCarthy's tactics and seemed to delight in being part of his traveling road show. Reporters chronicled each charge and then moved on to the next town, instead of staying behind and following up. Furthermore, various liberal groups and individuals tacitly supported the anti-Communist crusade, including the American Civil Liberties Union. The ACLU refused to defend suspected Communists who were under attack or lost their jobs between 1953 and 1959.

One wonders where it would have ended had it not been for Edward R. Murrow (1908–65), the most respected television newsman at the time. On March 9, 1954, in a famous broadcast editorial on his weekly television show, *See It Now*, Murrow attacked McCarthy. By showing a series of film clips from McCarthy's speeches and inserting his own comments, Murrow reported on the concern of America's allies about McCarthyism. He said:

[W]e cannot defend freedom abroad by deserting it at home. The actions of the junior senator from Wisconsin have caused alarm and dismay amongst our allies abroad and given considerable comfort to our enemies, and whose fault is that? Not really his. He didn't create the situation of fear; he merely exploited it, and rather successfully. Cassius was right: "The fault, dear Brutus, is not in our stars but in ourselves."[5]

In December 1954, the Senate voted 67 to 22 in favor of censuring Joseph McCarthy, and a mere three years later, in 1957, McCarthy died of a liver condition resulting from alcoholism.

The paranoia, however, continued. The war in Europe had not proved to be the war that would end all wars.

CINEMATIC REFLECTIONS

In 1954, Elia Kazan (b. 1909) directed the Academy Award–winning film *On the Waterfront,* an emotional melodrama about one man's personal redemption. Kazan used the film's protagonist, Terry Malloy (played by Marlon Brando), to justify being an informer before the House Committee on Un-American Activities, as Kazan himself had been. Malloy becomes an informer in a difficult situation: if he breaks the neighborhood code of silence, he will be a traitor, but if he doesn't speak out, the audience will judge him a moral coward. Kazan said: "Terry Malloy felt as I did. He felt ashamed and proud of himself at the same time. . . . He felt it was a necessary act."[6]

Malloy represents an alienated and resentful version of the classic American hero who defends good against evil. This kind of anti-hero began to appear frequently in the films of the 1950s and was brought into the forefront in the 1960s by actors such as Dustin Hoffman (b. 1937) in films like *The Graduate* (1967) and *Midnight Cowboy* (1969).

Another film that captured the ideology and politics of the 1950s particularly well was *Invasion of the Body Snatchers* (1956). It is the story of a small California town infiltrated by pods from outer space that replicate and replace human beings. The film is a snapshot of a particular moment in history, when post-war Americans were neurotically preoccupied with international political events. The dehumanization of individuals was a sensitive subject in an age filled with talk of Korean forces brainwashing American soldiers during the Korean Conflict.

The film also presents an overt Communist metaphor: the alien pod people perfectly fit McCarthy's profile of the Soviets—ice cold, outwardly peaceful, and author-

34. THERE ARE VARIOUS interpretations of the meaning of the film *Invasion of the Body Snatchers*. While these may be compelling, they seldom mention the ideas of the book's author, Jack Finney. Finney claimed that he did not read, write, or even like science fiction. He was interested instead in the ability of technology, modernization, and fragmentation to disenfranchise people and make them lose their ability to act human.

itarian. Many Americans even considered the Soviet people a different species who, because of their atheism, were soulless and wanted to destroy Americans or make them Communist clones.

Representing a completely regimented society, the pod people were sapped of emotion and individuality. The vegetable metaphor literalized the Red Scare rhetoric of the "growth" of Communism and the idea that revolutions are made by planting seeds. One scene depicts the pod people assembled in a town square receiving the day's orders from a loudspeaker—the quintessential 1950s image of socialism. One of the film's central themes is the idea that without freedom of thought, people are vegetables.

Director Don Siegel (1912–91) admitted that his film portrayed the conflict between individuals and various forms of mindless authority. On the other hand, he denied an anti-Communist motive. Instead, he believed people had lost much of their sensitivity due to advances in military weaponry and the atrocities of modern warfare. He said:

> People are pods. Many of my associates are certainly pods. They have no feelings. They exist, breathe, sleep. To be a pod means that you have no passion, no anger, the spark has left you...of course, there's a very strong case for being a pod. These pods, who get rid of pain, ill-health and mental disturbances are, in a sense, doing good. It happens to leave you in a very dull world but that, by the way, is the world that most of us live in. It's the same as people who welcome going into the army or prison. There's regimentation, a lack of having to make up your mind, face decisions.... People are becoming vegetables. I don't know what the answer is except an awareness of it. That's what makes a picture like *Invasion of the Body Snatchers* important.[7]

Some critics argued that the pod people were not Communists, but government officials—people such as McCarthy who looked like typical, fine upstanding Americans but who searched out anyone who refused to conform to the "American" way. The mob hysteria, paranoia, and witch-hunt atmosphere of *Body Snatchers* certainly reflects the ills of McCarthy's America.

Finally, some critics have seen the film as an anti-scientific statement. During the early years of space exploration, many Americans feared that space creatures would invade the earth. Some viewed the movie as a warning about the dangers of science, including developments like the hydrogen bomb. The fear of psychiatry may also be seen in the film's psychiatrist-alien who announces the death of God by banishing the idea of the individual soul.

Body Snatchers writer Jack Finney (1911–95) claimed that he did not read, write, or even like science fiction. He indicated that he was interested in the tendency of technology, modernization, and fragmentation to disenfranchise people. Finney saw the rush to modernize, bureaucratize, streamline, and cellophane-wrap as destroying traditional values. He believed that in order to be truly human, people must express their real feelings and more strongly embrace the human values of pride, dignity, friendship, and love.

THE RISE OF TELEVISION

As we have seen, at one time painting was the primary visual method by which artists communicated with the public. As the twentieth century dawned, however, new forms of media, especially electronic ones, began to predominate. Film and later television slowly became the dominant media for public commentary on important social issues.

Although television was introduced in the 1920s, it did not become a national pastime until after World War II. The rise of television was integral to the rise and fall of the anti-Communism crusade. As previously mentioned, television ended the career of Senator Joseph McCarthy in 1954 when Edward R. Murrow's documentary show, *See It Now,* used clips from McCarthy's own speeches to discredit him. McCarthy responded on the show by saying that Murrow was "a symbol, the leader and the cleverest of the jackal pack which is always found at the throne of anyone who dares to expose individual communists and traitors."[8] Indeed, Murrow was the leader and the cleverest television reporter of the 1950s.

Television became a crucial part of the political process as politicians quickly learned to campaign before a nation of television-watching families. Today the sound bite and screen image have more or less supplanted meaningful public debate on any political issue. When combined with effective political spin, television can be used to obscure truth altogether.

Television also evolved into the leading form of American entertainment. In the late 1940s, the variety show was the most popular television format. In 1951, however, a new series emerged that would determine the shape of television for the next five decades—*I Love Lucy.* America had tired of the usual vaudeville gags and began to express an interest in more realistic comedy. As veteran television personality Jackie Gleason, creator of *The Honeymooners* sitcom, said: "Situation comedy is based on honesty. On the other hand, the monologue is predicated chiefly on a success of lies. You can bet that the 'honest' factor will win out with the audience in the long run."[9]

But perhaps honesty would not win out after all. Almost every television show was paid for by sponsors who demanded that they be portrayed in the best, least controversial light—but they also wanted the broadest possible viewing audience. Television networks pandered to both the public and the sponsors. Ultimately, commercial demands drove television's best writers back into the movies. And when a 1952 Supreme Court decision included motion pictures in the definition of "press"—and thus gave Hollywood greater editorial freedom—the pace of the exodus from television to the movies was quickened.

A notable exception was Rod Serling (1924–75), an adept, creative writer who preserved the anthology genre for television with *The Twilight Zone,* which ran from

1959 to 1964. With its bold, imaginative storytelling, the series approached issues such as racism and nuclear threat from a moral, rather than an ideological, perspective. *The Twilight Zone* was one of the first series to present an alternative to the "happy ending," foreshadowing the troubled years of the 1960s.

The quiz show scandals of the 1950s proved there were no "real" people on television. In 1959, academic Charles Van Doren admitted before a congressional committee that he had cheated while appearing on the game show *Twenty-One*. (Director Robert Redford [b. 1937] effectively captured the events surrounding this scandal in his 1994 film *Quiz Show*.) In response to the Van Doren scandal, the Chairman of the Federal Communications Commission ordered each network to air at least one hour of public affairs programming each week. This marked a turning point for television, for it necessitated an expansion of news divisions and coverage of live events. It also ensured that cameras would be ready to capture the crises in such places as Birmingham, Dallas, Washington, Saigon, Moscow, Peking, and Belgrade.

THE BEATS' NEW VISION

The poets and novelists of the Beat generation provided some of the clearest commentary on the alienation and pessimism of postwar Western culture. In 1944, the word *beat*, as used by Times Square hustler Herbert Huncke, a male prostitute and thief, attracted the attention of William Burroughs (1914–97). Burroughs was a Harvard graduate whom Huncke had introduced to heroin. Within the drug culture, the word *beat* meant "cheated, robbed or emotionally or physically exhausted." Burroughs' friend, the writer Jack Kerouac, later reinvented the term "Beat" to mean "beatific." Kerouac used it to describe anyone who rebelled against the prevailing culture of materialism and personal ambition.

The Beat writers and poets congregated in New York City's Greenwich Village and Times Square. They grappled with the historical and political changes that began with the atomic bomb and continued through the Cold War and anti-Communist hysteria of the late 1940s and 1950s.

John Clellon Holmes' (1926–88) 1952 *Go* was one of the first Beat novels published. Holmes characterized the Beat generation as a group of disaffected young people who came of age immediately after World War II. The Beats struggled with their will to believe, even though they could no longer do so in conventional terms.

GINSBERG AND HOWL

In 1948, after seeing a vision of the poet William Blake, Allen Ginsberg (1926–97) formally dedicated himself to becoming a poet. Little did Ginsberg know that he would become the poet laureate of the Beat generation and later influence a bevy of other artists and writers, including poet and singer Bob Dylan, who emerged in the 1960s. Ginsberg especially admired the French poet Arthur Rimbaud (discussed in Chapter One) for breaking conventional rules of all kinds and approving madness and an unconventional lifestyle. In like style, Ginsberg embraced bohemianism, a decision that he believed helped him accept his mother's mental illness and deal with his confusion about his homosexuality.

35. ALLEN GINSBERG (on left, with Timothy Leary, center, and Ralph Mezner) became the poet laureate of the Beat Generation, influencing many artists and entertainers.

On the advice of anarchist poet Kenneth Rexroth, Ginsberg moved to San Francisco and began experimenting with a technique similar to Jack Kerouac's spontaneous prose:

> I thought I wouldn't write a *poem* but just write what I wanted to without fear, let my imagination go, open secrecy, and scribble magic lines from my real mind—sum up my life—something I wouldn't be able to show anybody, write for my own soul's ear and a few other golden ears.[10]

Ginsberg's 1955–56 classic poem *Howl* used the "new vision" style he had developed. The poem noted that Ginsberg saw the best minds of his generation destroyed by "madmen," as they were "dragging themselves" down "negro streets" searching for an "angry fix...contemplating jazz ..." In this fourteen-page, one-sentence poem, he describes his generation as those who "howled on their knees" as they were taken away "waving genitals and manuscripts."

On October 13, 1955, Ginsberg gave his historic reading of the poem at the Gallery Six, a cooperative art gallery in San Francisco. Michael McClure, who also gave a reading, described the atmosphere the night of Ginsberg's recitation:

COLOR PLATE 1. Rembrandt van Rijn, *Adoration of the Shepherds* (Munich, Alte Pinakothek, Guraudon/Art Resource, NY). In a stable, surrounded by Mary, Joseph, and the adoring shepherds, the baby Jesus glows with a supernatural light, but he is depicted as an actual person who existed in real space-time history. Rembrandt and the society for which he painted made no distinction between the historical truth of Christ's life and the spiritual truth of his deity; the natural and the supernatural interact in a meaningful—and understandable—way.

COLOR PLATE 2. Morton Schamberg, *God* (c. 1917, Philadelphia Museum of Art). Merely a disconnected and impersonal "concept," Schamberg's god has no personal influence and imbues humankind with no intrinsic worth.

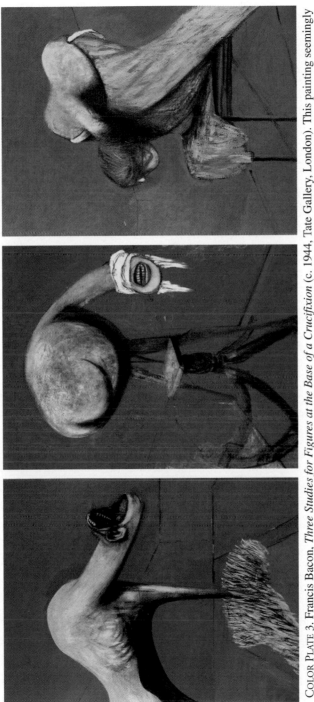

COLOR PLATE 3. Francis Bacon, *Three Studies for Figures at the Base of a Crucifixion* (c. 1944, Tate Gallery, London). This painting seemingly depicts the loss of all hope for a humanity grasping for some sort of meaning in a world where people appear destined merely to be carcasses. As biographer Andrew Sinclair described the triptych: "[The] figures in the three canvases were joined in the theme of the violence that men did to one another by the power of sex and hatred. The body on the right, lying head down, suggested an inverted crucifixion by Cimabue, which Bacon thought was like 'a worm crawling…just moving, undulating down the cross.'"

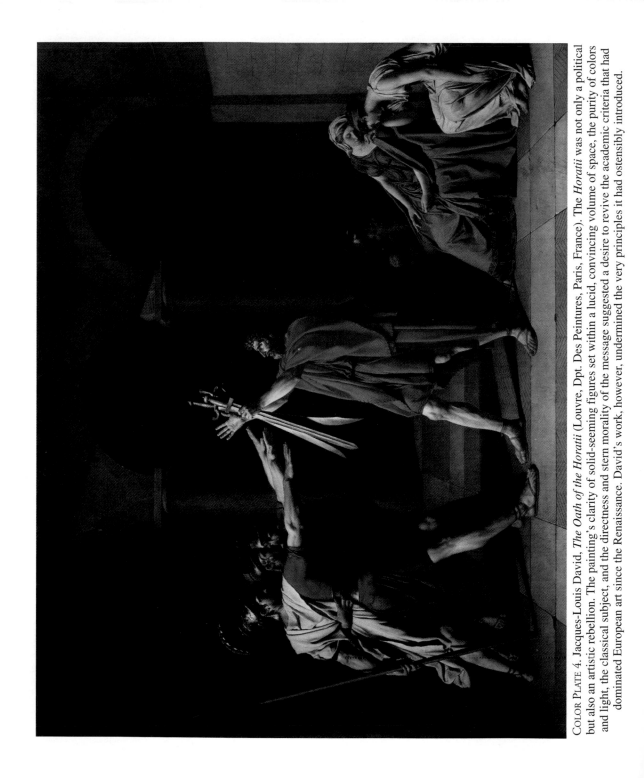

COLOR PLATE 4. Jacques-Louis David, *The Oath of the Horatii* (Louvre, Dpt. Des Peintures, Paris, France). The *Horatii* was not only a political but also an artistic rebellion. The painting's clarity of solid-seeming figures set within a lucid, convincing volume of space, the purity of colors and light, the classical subject, and the directness and stern morality of the message suggested a desire to revive the academic criteria that had dominated European art since the Renaissance. David's work, however, undermined the very principles it had ostensibly introduced.

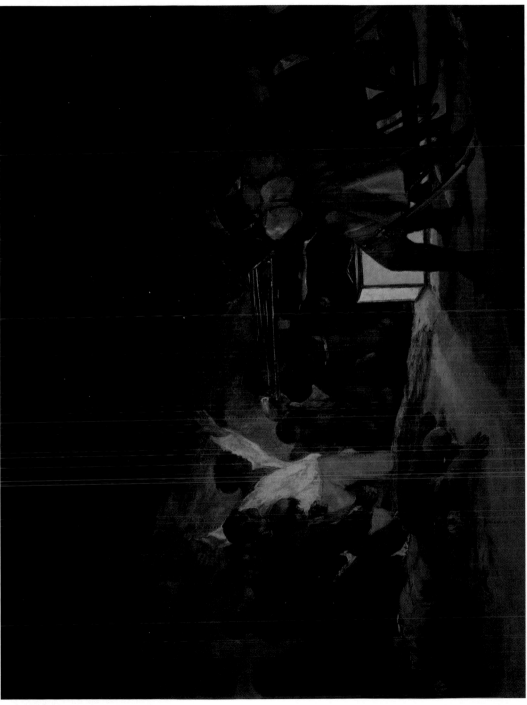

COLOR PLATE 5. Francisco de Goya y Lucientes. *The Third of May* (c. 1808, Academia, Madrid). Goya treats the French firing squad as a many-legged, faceless, dehumanizing monster raising bayoneted guns to groups of helpless victims. The first group has already been shattered by bullets and is streaming with blood. The next group is gesticulating wildly in the last seconds of life. The lantern lights the execution while a man, arms lifted in Christian symbolism, awaits crucifixion by gunfire. The third assemblage of victims are hiding the horror from their eyes with their hands, and in the dimness of evening, the nearest houses and a church tower of the city blend into the night sky.

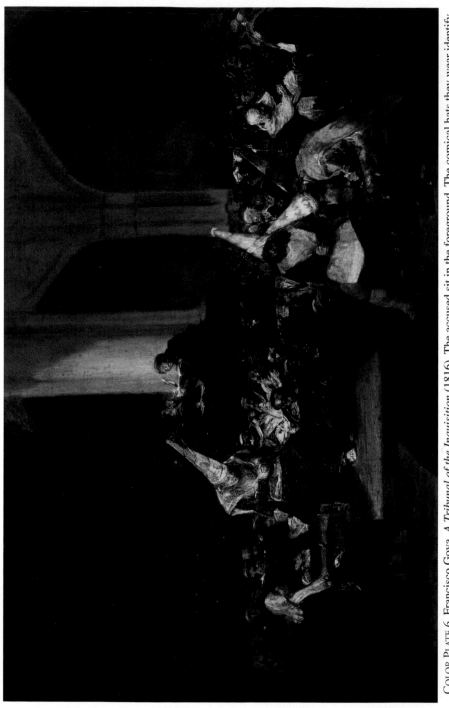

COLOR PLATE 6. Francisco Goya, *A Tribunal of the Inquisition* (1816). The accused sit in the foreground. The comical hats they wear identify and humiliate those accused by the Inquisition. A seemingly endless sea of monks of various orders epitomizes the ubiquitous and repressive power of the Church. Yet a torch illuminates the figure at the pulpit to show that he reads with eyes closed: his lines are memorized. The authority represented is literally blind.

COLOR PLATE 7. Gustave Courbet, *A Burial at Ornans* (c. 1849–50, Musée d'Orsay, France). The titles of Courbet's paintings became increasingly lengthy and descriptive in contrast with the rather minor incidents the paintings portrayed. The incident or event no longer pointed to a general theme and larger meaning but instead was itself the total focus of the work of art.

COLOR PLATE 8. Georges Seurat, *A Sunday Afternoon on the Island of La Grande Jatte* (c. 1884–1886, The Art Institute of Chicago). La Grande Jatte was a small grassy island in the Seine River where Parisians liked to picnic, fish, and take children on weekends. Seurat completed the painting two years after the work began, from some twenty drawings and two hundred art sketches, ranging from individual figures to whole compositions.

COLOR PLATE 9. Paul Gauguin, *Where Do We Come From? What Are We? Where Are We Going?* (c. 1897, Museum of Fine Arts, Boston, Tompkins Collection). The imagery suggests that life and the supernatural confront each other and merge imperceptibly in a primeval setting. The painting is both a cyclical allegory of life, from birth to death, and a philosophical meditation played out on a darkening stage.

Color Plate 10. Pablo Picasso, *Les Demoiselles d'Avignon* (c. 1907, © 2000 The Museum of Modern Art, New York). A friend of Picasso recorded his reactions upon viewing this large painting (almost eight feet by eight feet): "It contains… [five] huge female nudes: the drawing of them has a rugged accent. For the first time in Picasso's work, the expression of the faces is neither tragic nor passionate. They are masks almost entirely freed from humanity. Yet these people are not gods, nor are they Titans or heroes; not even allegorical or symbolical figures. They are naked problems, white numbers on the blackboard. Thus Picasso has laid down the principle of the picture-as-equation." Another of Picasso's friends spontaneously christened the new canvas "the philosophical brothel."

COLOR PLATE 11. Jacob Epstein, *Torso in Metal from "The Rock Drill"* (Tate Gallery, London). Epstein understood the implications of the development of Futurism and the glorification of the machine. In commenting on *The Rock Drill*, Epstein said: "This is the sinister armoured figure of today and tomorrow. Nothing human, only the terrible Frankenstein's monster into which we have transformed ourselves."

COLOR PLATE 12. Marcel Duchamp, *The Bride Stripped Bare by Her Bachelors, Even (The Large Glass)*
(c. 1915–23, Philadelphia Museum of Art). In one sense, *The Large Glass* is a glimpse into hell,
a peculiarly modern hell of repetition, frustration, nonfulfillment, and loneliness. *The Large Glass* is also
a tragic machine, a testament to indifference and defiance—the state of mind Duchamp suggested in his
"Readymades," sculptures that converted ordinary objects into art pieces and achieved memorable public
scandals in his day.

COLOR PLATE 13. Giorgio de Chirico, *The Nostalgia of the Infinite* (c. 1913–14, dated on painting 1911. © 2000 The Museum of Modern Art, New York). Many of the images in de Chirico's work are real and came from actual places, mostly Turin. Several of these appear in *The Nostalgia of the Infinite*. The tower in this painting, however, becomes a desolate and forlorn image; the townscape is emptied; human society has either ceased to exist or has been shrunken to tiny, faraway figures which cannot communicate with the human occupant of the townscape, who is de Chirico himself, the Onlooker, whose eye is the root of all perspectives. The tower, remote and inaccessible to the artist's diminutive and impotent, dehumanized human phantoms, also seems to carry, according to art historians Sam Hunter and John Jacobus, "Freudian overtones in its phallic power, although the associations seem almost innocent and naive by comparison with Dali's later self-conscious eroticism."

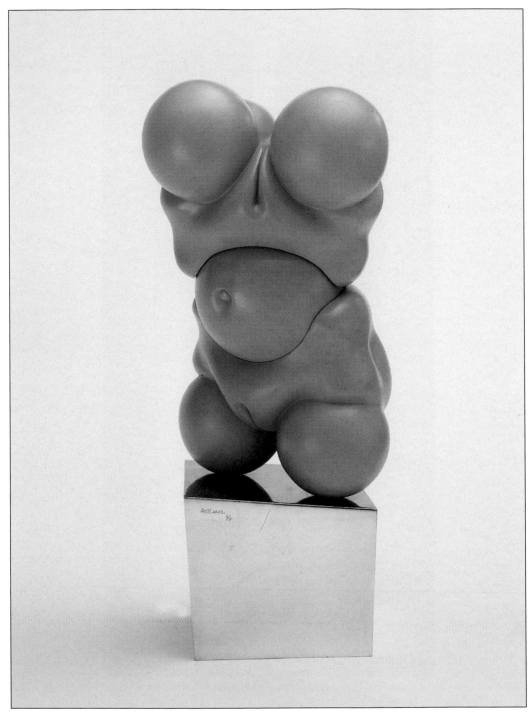

COLOR PLATE 14. Hans Bellmer, *The Doll* (c. 1936. Painted aluminum on bronze base. The Sidney and Harriet Janis Collection. © 2000 The Museum of Modern Art, New York). Bellmer's work represents the pathological side of the more usual Surrealist exaltation of romantic love. The mythology of sexual violence, most generally aimed at women, may be the result.

COLOR PLATE 15. Chuck Berry. Berry's guitar playing is based on country riffs, but also incorporates the sounds of '40s jazz stars. And as Katherine Charlton notes in *Rock Music Style: A History* (1990): "The greatest influences on his guitar style were T-Bone Walker and Muddy Waters (whom he met in Chicago in 1955), but his singing style clearly showed the influence of any of a number of white country-and-western singers. It was partly the fact that he derived his sound from both blues and country roots that made it neither of those, but instead their fusion, rock and roll."

COLOR PLATE 16. Edward Hopper, *Nighthawks* (c. 1924, The Art Institute of Chicago, Friends of American Art Collection). Hopper captured the alienation and loneliness of modern life. Nighthawks shows the shadowed, hollow eyes of a diner's customer (another man's back is turned and his face totally hidden) against the backdrop of a dark and haunted city, giving the impression that humanity could be swallowed up in the blankness of modernity.

COLOR PLATE 17. Mark Rothko, The Rothko Chapel North wall paintings (1966). Rothko explained his obsession with the qualities of light and its religious meaning: "I am not interested in relationships of color or form or anything else...I am interested only in expressing the basic human emotions—tragedy, ecstasy, doom, and so on—and the fact that lots of people break down and cry when confronted with my pictures shows that I communicate with those basic human emotions. The people who weep before my pictures are having the same religious experience I had when I painted them. And if you, as you say, are moved only by their color relationships, then you miss the point!"

COLOR PLATE 18. Actor James Dean. James Dean did not originate the pose of the doomed misfit. His reputation as insolent angel was built on an image that was already a teen paradigm by the early 1950s. However, Dean epitomized the image as a timeless icon.

COLOR PLATE 19. Willem de Kooning, *Woman and Bicycle*, c. 1952–53. (Collection of Whitney Museum of American Art, New York, photograph by Steven Sloman © 1984, New York.) "I look at them now," de Kooning remarked of paintings like *Woman and Bicycle*, "and they seem vociferous and ferocious. I think it had to do with the idea of the idol, the oracle, above all the hilariousness of it." The *Women* series comments on the indigestible vulgarity of dehumanized American mass images. The women are sex bombs without beauty or femininity, utterly horrifying demolitions of the woman's image.

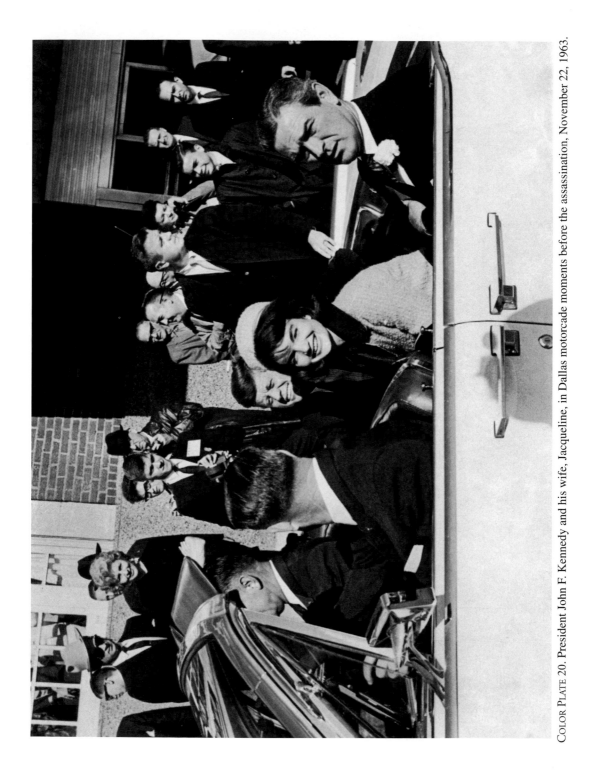

COLOR PLATE 20. President John F. Kennedy and his wife, Jacqueline, in Dallas motorcade moments before the assassination, November 22, 1963.

COLOR PLATE 21. Seminal folk rocker Bob Dylan is joined by Bruce Springsteen, right, during Dylan's set for the Rock and Roll Hall of Fame benefit concert, September 2, 1995, in Cleveland (AP photo/Tony Dejak). In his youth, Dylan was brilliant, expressing ideas and stories of the moment with exceptional strength. Pete Seeger, Joan Baez, and folk singer Phil Ochs witnessed Dylan instantly write topical songs that mixed the power and poetry of the best of Woody Guthrie, Hank Williams, Jimmie Rodgers, and a host of blues artists. Dylan's songs have endured for the quality of their writing; while they incorporated real events, they surpass a journalistic function and attain the level of art.

COLOR PLATE 22. A scene from the film *Apocalypse Now*. Willard (actor Martin Sheen) is a burnt-out government hit man with six kills to his credit whose mission is to terminate Colonel Kurtz (actor Marlon Brando), a rogue Green Beret colonel and self-proclaimed tribal god who has committed atrocities and engaged in a private war against the North Vietnamese and Viet Cong in the Cambodian jungle. Using Willard's pilgrimage as a framework, director Francis Ford Coppola constructs a hallucinatory, surreal Vietnam.

COLOR PLATE 23. Robert Rauschenberg, *Bed*, c. 1955. (The Museum of Modern Art, New York. Gift of Leo Castelli in honor of Alfren H. Barr Jr. © 2000, the Museum of Modern Art, New York.) Lacking sufficient canvas for *Bed*, Rauschenberg simply substituted the pillow, sheet, and patchwork quilt from his own cot. He stabbed and dripped various colors of paint from the top of the pillow down on the quilt. He then hung the work vertically to contradict the bedding's original function.

COLOR PLATE 24. Andy Warhol, *Two Hundred Campbell's Soup Cans*, c. 1962. (© 2000 The Andy Warhol Foundation for the Visual Arts, The Andy Warhol Foundation, Inc. Art Resource, New York.) Celebrity, Warhol understood, is just another form of advertising. Warhol believed advertising flattered the consumer, encouraging the consumer to view himself/herself as a discriminating connoisseur of sensation and taste. Thus, Warhol's early '60s work, such as *Two Hundred Campbell's Soup Cans*, balefully mimicked advertising while illustrating his view of culture's gluttony.

COLOR PLATE 25. Edward Kienholz, *The Future as an Afterthought* (1962). (Sammlung Reinhard Onnasch, Berlin.) The baby's head at the base appears sticky, as though in melt-down mode. Kienholz reinforces the notion that children are our future. But his warning is that science and technology may be out of control and, thus, endanger posterity.

COLOR PLATE 26. The Beatles, whose history mirrors not only the culture of their time but also impacts the present. From the early Hamburg-Liverpool days as punks in the Cavern to the lovable mop tops to the drug-inspired music to the brief fascination with Eastern religion to the individualized style of each Beatle, the composite of music history in terms of style seems to be repeating itself in the music and youth culture of the present.

COLOR PLATE 27. The original Woodstock Festival. August 15–17, 1969. The 400,000 young people who converged on the Yasgur farm created the second largest city in New York. As Abbie Hoffman was fond of pointing out, Woodstock had a crime rate much lower than the average city. Woodstock casualties included one accidental death and one death from a heart attack. Medical teams organized by Abbie Hoffman and Wavy Gravy of the Hog Farm commune were kept busy with drug overdoses and bad LSD trips. But, since there were few fights and no riots, the weekend was declared a triumph for peace.

COLOR PLATE 28. Jeff Koons, *Saint John the Baptist* (1988). (© Jeff Koons.) Koons here satirizes religion as he depicts John the Baptist with a cross at his back (symbolizing Christianity), holding a pig (capitalism), and pointing to heaven (the almighty dollar).

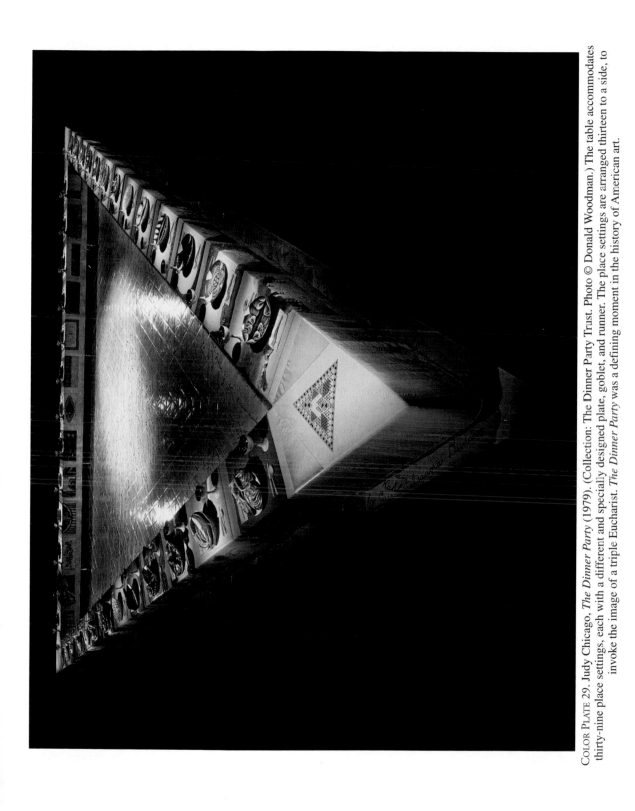

COLOR PLATE 29. Judy Chicago, *The Dinner Party* (1979). (Collection: The Dinner Party Trust. Photo © Donald Woodman.) The table accommodates thirty-nine place settings, each with a different and specially designed plate, goblet, and runner. The place settings are arranged thirteen to a side, to invoke the image of a triple Eucharist. *The Dinner Party* was a defining moment in the history of American art.

COLOR PLATE 30. Philip Guston, *The Street* (1977). (The Metropolitan Museum of Art. Photo © 1984 The Metropolitan Museum of Art.) Guston's depiction of what resembles a war between city gangs or bums is at once a parody and a stark warning. Here he combines in *The Street* an ethical statement while portraying an apocalyptic vision.

COLOR PLATE 31. A bloodied Tyler Durden (actor Brad Pitt) in a scene from *The Fight Club*. Through the mutual pummeling of one another, the men of Fight Club reach a new level of self-discovery. Fight Club gradually expands to men from all walks of life who convene in a basement to beat up on each other with bare knuckles, all in the name of brotherhood. Eventually, however, Tyler Durden turns the horrifying purity of Fight Club into something worse—a nationwide army of slave-like terrorists fighting class wars against corporate America.

COLOR PLATE 32. Actor Willem Dafoe in a scene from Martin Scorsese's *The Last Temptation of Christ*. The controversy engulfing this film, which was heavily protested and widely banned, tended to direct attention away from what is an exceptional statement of religious and artistic vision. An honest, thought-provoking exploration of God should be preferred to seemingly innocent depictions like actor George Burns' Yahweh in *Oh God* (1977), a film which exploits religion by emptying it of any substance except for a vague notion of divine nicety.

We were locked in the Cold War and the first Asian debacle—the Korean War. . . . We hated the war and the inhumanity of the coldness. The country had the feeling of martial law. An undeclared military state had leapt out of Daddy Warbucks' tanks and sprawled over the landscape. As artists we were oppressed. . . . We knew we were poets and we had to speak out as poets. We saw that the art of poetry was essentially dead—killed by war, by academies, by neglect, by lack of love, and by disinterest. We knew we could bring it back to life. We could see what Pound had done—and Whitman, and Artaud, and D. H. Lawrence in his monumental poetry and prose. . . . We wanted to make it new and we wanted to invent it and the process of it as we went into it. We wanted voice and we wanted vision.[11]

Howl delivered the necessary voice and vision for the emerging Beat movement. Everyone knew that a barrier had been broken, that a voice had been hurled against what many perceived to be the harsh wall of America, and against its network of supporting armies, navies, academies, institutions, ownership systems, and power-support bases.

The "old order" eventually tried to strike back. In May 1957, two San Francisco policemen bought a copy of *Howl* in a bookstore in an attempt to have the book declared obscene. They then obtained a warrant for the arrest of Lawrence Ferlinghetti (b. 1920), who was both the poem's publisher and the store's manager. In a landmark decision in October 1957, a California court ruled that the poem was not obscene, saying:

The first part of "Howl" presents a picture of a nightmare world; the second part is an indictment of those elements of modern society destructive of the best qualities of human nature; such elements are predominantly identified as materialism, conformity, and the mechanization leading to war. . . . It ends with a plea for holy living.[12]

Seventeen years after the *Howl* trial, Ginsberg received the National Book Award for poetry in 1974 for *The Fall of America*. In his acceptance speech, he lamented:

There is no longer any hope for the Salvation of America proclaimed by Jack Kerouac and others of the Beat Generation, aware and howling, weeping and singing Kaddish for the nation decades ago, "rejected yet confessing out the soul." All we have to work from now is the vast empty quiet space of our own Consciousness.

The Beats' popularity reflected a changing world order. Ginsberg himself influenced college students and rock musicians, including Bob Dylan, the Beatles, and the Rolling Stones. While a young student at Liverpool Art College, John Lennon produced a magazine called the *Daily Howl.* Lennon claimed that he had never read or understood the poem until hearing *Howl* one night on the radio. At that moment, Lennon said he then understood how much Ginsberg had influenced Dylan. Lennon's classic song "I Am the Walrus" (1967) seems to reflect the cadence and delivery of Beat poetry such as *Howl.*

By the 1990s, Ginsberg was a national icon. In 1994, Stanford University paid nearly $1 million for a collection of his papers and memorabilia. These included Ginsberg's old tennis shoes, snippets of his beard from various trimmings, thousands of old utility bills, paper napkins, old concert tickets, and anything else the poet had chosen to save. Some questioned the price Stanford paid for these items, given Ginsberg's longtime support of the North American Man/Boy Love Association (a pedophile group that advocates sex between adult males and young boys). In response, Ginsberg wrote: "I'm a member of NAMBLA because I love boys.... Everybody does who has a little humanity."[13]

KEROUAC AND ON THE ROAD

Ginsberg's success enabled other Beat writers to follow suit, most notably Jack Kerouac (1922–69). Kerouac's breakthrough work, the 1957 novel *On the Road,* offered a new vision of American life. As Bob Dylan would later proclaim: "I read *On the Road* in maybe 1959. It changed my life like it changed everyone else's."[14]

On the Road's hip opening sentences set the mood. Kerouac discusses meeting his sidekick Dean "after my wife and I split up." After getting over a serious illness of some kind that he doesn't bother to tell the reader about, the narrator goes on, "except that it had something to do with the miserably weary split-up and my feeling that everything was dead."[15] The book moves on from there to explore the theme of personal freedom and to challenge the promise of the "American Dream."

On the Road was fiction-as-nonfiction as Kerouac recounted real events from his life, focusing on one particular road trip with his friends. Initially, Kerouac changed nothing as he wrote the story, not even his friends' names (his publisher made him alter them because of legal concerns). One reason the sentences in *On the Road* are so long is the rush of sensation Kerouac derived from narcotics. Nevertheless, his ability to capture the moods and feelings of his characters surpassed that of traditional novelists.

The publication and huge success of *On the Road* in 1957 made the Beat writers a national phenomenon. Kerouac was dubbed the spokesman for the Beat Generation and was besieged with requests to explain it. In an article written for *Esquire* magazine in March 1958, Kerouac noted that although the small group that made up the Beat Generation had dispersed after the Korean War, in the early 1950s the

> postwar youth emerged cool and beat, had picked up the gestures and the style; soon it was everywhere, the new look...the bop visions became common property of the commercial, popular cultural world.... The ingestion of drugs became official (tranquilizers and the rest); and even the clothes style of the beat hipsters carried over to the new rock 'n' roll youth...and the Beat Generation, though dead, was resurrected and justified.[16]

36. CHALLENGING THE COMPLACENCY and prosperity of postwar America hadn't been Kerouac's intent when he wrote *On the Road*. However, he created a book that heralded a change of consciousness in the country.

Kerouac's autobiographical novel, *Vanity of Duluoz: An Adventurous Education, 1935–1946* (1960), later expressed reservations about his friends' wild behavior. He describes their association with criminals and drug dealers and his own Benzedrine and alcohol addiction. Kerouac, who clung to many of the beliefs of his Catholic upbringing, acknowledged that this "clique was the most evil and intelligent buncha [people] in America but had to admire in my admiring youth."[17]

Of all the Beat writers, Kerouac most effectively reached the popular mind. His characters, especially the ones evoking the real-life Neal Cassady, the high-adrenaline outlaw poet who became the hero of *On the Road,* continuously surface in contemporary pop culture. Actor Ethan Hawke's romantic lead character in the film *Reality Bites* (1994) invokes Kerouac's creations. The compressed mix of things sensual and philosophical in films such as Quentin Tarantino's *Pulp Fiction* (1994) and the hyperactive fusion of strange naïveté in director David Lynch's *Wild at Heart* (1990) also hint at Kerouac.

"I remember walking around in the eighth grade with a paperback copy of *On the Road* in my back pocket," says novelist and screenwriter Barry Gifford, who wrote *Wild at Heart.*[18] Gifford also coauthored a 1978 "oral biography" of Kerouac called *Jack's Book.* As one commentator notes: "Gifford came of age in the late '50s and early '60s. But the impact is intergenerational."

Kerouac died in 1969 at the age of forty-seven in St. Petersburg, Florida, after years of alcohol abuse. Although his estate was worthless at his death, it is now valued in the millions of dollars. This includes accruing royalties, personal effects, manuscripts, and other items related to Kerouac's work. An example of the value now placed on Kerouac occurred when Gen X-er movie star Johnny Depp (b. 1963) made a trip to Lowell, Massachusetts, Kerouac's birthplace, to reverently peruse Kerouac's artifacts and bought an old raincoat, once worn by Kerouac, for $15,000.

On the Road and other Beat works formed a cultural bridge to the 1960s. Kerouac's wild characters and gushing, all-embracing enthusiasm for ideas and action inspired artists from Bob Dylan to the rock group 10,000 Maniacs. In October of 1975, six years after Kerouac's death, Dylan and Ginsberg together traveled to Kerouac's grave in Lowell, Massachusetts, to pay homage to his influence—an influence that continues to gain momentum as the years go by. In 1990, for example, *Life* magazine named Kerouac one of the 100 most important Americans of the twentieth century.

Fred Fuchs, president of Zoetrope Studios, explained Kerouac's current popularity:

In an odd way, young people relate to this more than to the '60s. It's the restlessness, the introspectiveness. I think kids today have too much freedom in the world. So it's forcing them to look inward. That's why they're drawn to those '50s characters.[19]

Kerouac, however, was never able to convince his critics that the Beat Generation was basically a "religious" generation, as Steve Turner in his book on Kerouac, *Angelheaded Hipster* (1996), writes:

Ultimately, the reason for [Kerouac's] endurance is his work, which touches people with its honesty and compassion. He continues to inspire people to make art out of the substance of their daily lives, rather than to seek out "artistic" subjects. He continues to inspire ordinary people to break out of the narrow confinements of lives they have been handed down. He inspires the seekers, the peace-makers and the poor in spirit.[20]

THE CATCHER IN THE RYE

J. D. Salinger (b. 1919) wrote outside the Beat movement, but he too entered the popular mainstream with a message of alienation. Salinger depicted the goodness and innocence of childhood in his 1951 novel, *The Catcher in the Rye.* Holden Caulfield, the protagonist, is a teenager who finds the adult world ugly and depressing. He considers his younger sister, Phoebe, and dead younger brother, Allie, his only allies. Holden dreams of being the "catcher in the rye" who saves children from falling over "some crazy cliff." Wishing he could stick "certain things" in "one of those big glass cases and just leave them alone" so they would not change, Holden seeks escape from what he sees as a hopelessly phony adult world.[21] He's not a typical teenage rebel, however, because Holden feels sorry for his mother when he gets expelled from yet another school.

The book enjoyed instant critical success with positive comments in publications such as *Time* and *Newsweek,* though *The Christian Science Monitor* worried that it would open the way for more of the same, "as too easily happens when immorality and perversion are recounted by writers of talent whose work is countenanced in the name of art or good intention."[22]

By 1960, the book had been reprinted seventeen times and sold more than 1.5 million copies. As late as 1960, though, it was still being kept out of the reach of young people, in spite of the fact that *Newsweek* asserted that Salinger's name "probably bobs up oftener in current literary conversations than that of any other American writer—including Hemingway."[23] Despite attempts to censor it, sales tripled again by 1965, bringing the total copies sold to five million.

In an odd footnote to history, Mark David Chapman (b. 1955) apparently believed he could become Holden Caulfield by assassinating former Beatle John Lennon in December 1980, as Lennon entered his Dakota Apartment Building in New York City. Chapman first read the book when he was sixteen, Holden's age in the book. Like Holden, Chapman loved children and was a favorite counselor at a YMCA camp. Between spells of Christianity and Satanism, Chapman returned to the Caulfield character. While living in Hawaii, Chapman even requested a legal change of his name to Holden Caulfield.

Chapman reportedly believed Caulfield would have killed Lennon, believing him to be a phony. Leaving his wife in Hawaii, he traveled to New York to find Lennon. After murdering him, Chapman planned to hold up a copy of *Catcher* and shout, "I am Holden Caulfield, the catcher in the rye of the present generation."[24] Surprised that he did not turn into Caulfield after shooting Lennon, Chapman decided the purpose of killing Lennon was to draw attention to the book, as he compared himself to the likes of Moses and Jesus Christ. Chapman read the "catcher in the rye" passage aloud in the courtroom just before his sentencing.

After *Catcher*'s publication, Salinger became interested in Eastern mysticism—which was later confirmed by his daughter, Margaret A. Salinger, in her autobiography *Dream Catcher* (2000). His first story written under the influence of Zen, the 1953 "Teddy," presents a ten-year-old boy genius who explains higher truths to the narrator by referencing the biblical story of Adam and the apple in the Garden of Eden. The boy notes that the apple was made of logic and intellectual musings. "That was all that was in it. So—this is my point—what you have to do is vomit it up if you want to see things as they really are."[25]

THE ACTOR'S STUDIO

To "see things as they really are," three alumni from Harold Clurman's modernistic Group Theater founded the Actor's Studio in 1947 to be a workshop for professional actors. The workshop offered an advanced class with Robert Lewis and a beginner class with Elia Kazan, who became a renowned film director. In 1949, Kazan invited Lee Strasberg (1901–82) to the Actor's Studio. Kazan made him artistic director in 1952, and Strasberg went on to mold some of the greatest actors in history.

Strasberg helped the members see themselves as serious creative artists. He encouraged them to develop their subconscious and discover the reality of their dramatic situations. Strasberg demonstrated his own interpretations of Stanislavski's method of realism and permitted the actors to critique the various stage exercises. The studio created a collective in which directors, actors, and playwrights developed a vocabulary of their own, a distinctive language style and mentality foreign to outsiders. Method actors, often the antithesis of conventional actors such as John Wayne (1907–79), tended to be private, moody, intuitive, and deeply sexual. They interpreted scripts liberally and specialized in movies and plays of multidimensional, "real" characters.

The Actor's Studio became influential. For example, between 1947 and 1976, 112 Actor's Studio members received Academy Award nominations. Thirty won the coveted award, twenty-eight won Emmys, and twenty-six won Tonys. The members of the Studio read like a virtual who's who of Hollywood, including John Garfield, Montgomery Clift, Marlon Brando, James Dean, Paul Newman, Steve McQueen, Dustin Hoffman, Al Pacino, Robert DeNiro, Robert Duvall, Jack Nicholson, Julie Harris, Geraldine Page, Shelley Winters, Anne Bancroft, Lee Grant, Kim Stanley, Ellen Burstyn, Estelle Parsons, Sandy Dennis, and Shirley Knight. Two of the most famous Studio members skipped out on most of the sessions: James Dean and Marlon Brando (b. 1924) intuitively mastered the method, unlike many of the others.

ROCK 'N' ROLL COMES OF AGE

The Beats, Salinger, and a new form of music—rock 'n' roll—reflected a 1950s society in ferment and the emergence of a distinctive youth culture.

In August of 1954, Simon and Schuster published Evan Hunter's *The Blackboard Jungle,* a novel that painted a grim picture of troubled students at a fictional New York high school. Director Richard Brooks produced a film version and used a contemporary rock song he heard his daughter play—"Rock Around the Clock" by Bill Haley and the Comets—for the film's theme. Released on March 19, 1955, *Blackboard Jungle* became a must-see film for teenagers. Haley performed "Rock Around the Clock" on the *Ed Sullivan Show* on August 7, 1955.

Rock shocked many older Americans because it was loud and overtly sexual. But Chuck Berry, Buddy Holly, and Elvis Presley offered young people an energy, freedom, and earthiness that encouraged a new lifestyle and rebelled against the complacency and conformity of the 1950s.

The lifeless idols of their parents were replaced with James Dean, Presley, and others who became the communal images around which teenagers could define and defend themselves. They codified the uniform of youth that permeates adolescent culture even today. The wardrobe of Dean in particular expressed an attitude toward society. No tie, an unbuttoned shirt, blue jeans, and deliberate sloppiness all came to symbolize a rebellion against the social conventions of the adult world.

In the new rock 'n' roll subculture, the important authority figures were not statesmen or parents but disc jockeys. These radio sycophants confirmed the right to youthful independence and guided teenagers to their new rock heroes.

"BEFORE ELVIS, THERE WAS NOTHING"

Elvis Presley (1935–77) became the new teen idol, following Dean's example. Presley was a talented young man who arrived at the right place at the right time—and with virtually no political interests. Sam Phillips (b. 1923), a Memphis recording man and African-American music enthusiast, had been looking for someone like Presley—"a white boy who could sing like a black boy and catch the beat of black music."[27] He immediately liked Presley's early "greaser" style and recorded him on his now legendary Sun label.

Presley's 1954–55 soundtracks for Sun Records were some of his best recordings. These included "It's All Right, Mama" by black bluesman Arthur Crudup and "Blue Moon of Kentucky" by bluegrass singer Bill Monroe. Presley's music symbolized a reconciliation of the white and black cultures. Presley also had a general gospel flavor to his music, reflecting his early singing in church.

After Presley conquered the South with regional appearances, he perfected his act. For example, he added body gyrations similar to the movements of gospel singers. The first time Presley gyrated onstage, "he had been driven by pure instinct and the crowd began to shout."[28] From then on, it became part of his act.

Ministers publicly attacked Presley and threatened to lead a crusade to have him arrested if he set foot in their communities. His performances were often described as "demon rock as jungle music" in local newspapers.[29] But religious and parental disapproval only increased his popularity. After Presley performed his first national hit, "Heartbreak Hotel," on the *Milton Berle Show* on April 3, 1956, the song became number one in *Billboard* for eight weeks starting April 21, 1956. This appearance was followed by the *Steve Allen Show* in July 1956. Allen persuaded Presley to wear a tuxedo and limit his movements, and then he only shot Presley above the waist. For the first time, Steve Allen beat the legendary Ed Sullivan in the ratings.

Ed Sullivan's (1902–74) variety show mesmerized America. Sullivan disliked rockers, however, and said he wanted nothing to do with Presley, believing Presley's act in particular was too sexually suggestive. But after Steve Allen's success, Sullivan signed Presley for three shows for the unprecedented sum of $50,000. On the first Sullivan show, the producers, like those of Steve Allen's show, intentionally shot Presley only from the waist up. Sullivan told the audience after the third show that Presley was a "real decent, fine boy."[30]

Sullivan's statement resembled the generous speech of a man receiving a surrender. In reality, however, Sullivan himself had surrendered to market economics, and his decision to sign Presley augured a profound change in American taste. In the past, a white elite had appreciated black jazz, but the reaction to Presley was different. It was a visceral, democratic response by the masses and a critical moment for American society. The old order had been challenged and had not held. New forces were at work, driven primarily by technology. The young did not have to listen to their parents anymore.

Leonard Bernstein (1918–90), the distinguished American composer and conductor, called Presley "the greatest cultural force in the twentieth century." He continued: "He introduced the beat to everything—music, language, clothes, it's a whole new social revolution—the Sixties comes from it. Because of him a man like me barely knows his musical grammar anymore."[31] Or as John Lennon once said, "Before Elvis, there was nothing."[32]

By the late 1960s, however, most observers considered Elvis outdated. The British rock invasion, led by the Beatles, had dated the music and stance of the '50s rockers like Elvis. But the classic 1968 *Singer Television Special* for NBC proved that Presley could still perform. In the mid-1970s, with a couple of new hits, Presley made an impressive comeback.

After his 1972 divorce brought on violent mood swings, however, Elvis began to eat voraciously, sometimes consuming a dozen cheeseburgers and a pound of bacon at a time. Literally ballooning to about 250 pounds, Elvis was forced to cancel all-important Las Vegas and Lake Tahoe shows. After hints of drug dependence circulated, he secluded himself in Graceland or his Palm Springs home. And finally, in August of 1977 he died—an event that shocked and saddened his fans worldwide.

Like his idol, James Dean, Elvis's image after his death became larger than his own existence. The Elvis cult that began shortly after his death has now become, in essence, a religion. In fact, thousands of people still believe Presley is alive.

In Presley's life, we see an allegory of the entire American experience during the 1950s, 1960s, and beyond. A youthful and dynamic beginning ends in premature old age and a bloated, overweight body. Presley, thus, became a parody of himself and of modern, materialistic America.

DE KOONING AND THE SEX SYMBOL

Adolescents of the 1950s and 1960s tried to escape the dehumanization of their culture through rock 'n' roll and idols such as James Dean and Elvis Presley. Intuitively, many of the young were beginning to see the hypocrisy of the Fat Dream. During the early 1950s, various visual artists were coming to a similar conclusion. Willem de Kooning (1904–97), for one, believed a work of art was an act rather than a configuration, a by-product of some existential face-off between Will and Fate. De Kooning, who was born in Rotterdam, approached sexuality and women with a ferocity few artists had shown, with the exception of Picasso.

From 1950 to 1953, de Kooning's *Women* series became his greatest work. (See color plate 19 for his *Woman and Bicycle*, 1952–53.) The paintings comment on the indigestible vulgarity of American mass images. The women are sex bombs without beauty or femininity, utterly horrifying demolitions of the female image. They are emblems of otherness and domination. In the distorted vigor of their surface, the brush drags the forms of breast, grin, buttocks, and belly like a thick disturbed membrane.

The series seems to have drawn on other paintings of women such as Edvard Munch's (1863–1944) 1893 *Vampire*. Munch's fear, even hatred, of women was overt in much of his work. The series also recalls Picasso's series of paintings about women, including his 1932 *Girl Before a Mirror*.

De Kooning's repeated use of glamorous women as subjects for his paintings reflects the persistence of the female sex symbol in American society—from Mae West to Marilyn Monroe to Madonna and Sharon Stone. In fact, de Kooning titled his painting of a slightly dizzy, peach-skinned blonde after Monroe.

His painting *Monroe* dates from 1954—one of Marilyn Monroe's biggest years, during which she married and divorced Joe DiMaggio, entertained troops in Korea, finished the now-classic film *The Seven Year Itch* (1955), and appeared in five *Life* magazine picture spreads. De Kooning had seen Marilyn Monroe (1926–62) in the 1953 movie, *Gentlemen Prefer Blondes*. He kept her calendar in his studio, and when asked why he painted her, he replied it was "subconscious." He added, "I like beautiful women. In the flesh; even the models in magazines."[33] De Kooning's *Monroe,* however, is not a real woman but an object, a mannequin, closer to a puppet than a living being.

De Kooning struggled with the image of women. For example, in *Woman III* (1951–52), stab-like wounds above the subject's breasts appear to be displaced stigmata from a contemporary crucifixion. This is a theme de Kooning used in his drawings in the 1950s and '60s. Some of de Kooning's later paintings of women, such as *Woman, Sag Harbor* (1964) and *Woman on a Sign* (1967), are voyeuristic, if not pornographic. He caught on canvas cultural changes in the area of sexuality not yet obvious to the casual observer.

As a foreigner, de Kooning was intrigued by the imagery of *Life* magazine and the Times Square billboards of New York City, while the more theological Abstract Expressionists, like Mark Rothko, scorned them. According to art historian Robert Hughes, de Kooning's toothy Women were a "version of the girl in the old Camel cigarette ads being kind to her T-Zone. In creating this Doris Day with shark teeth, an amphibian living between the atavistic and the trivial, de Kooning had come up with one of the most memorable images of sexual insecurity in American culture."[34]

HEFNER AND THE PLAYBOY REVOLUTION

Hugh Hefner (b. 1929) launched an empire on the theme of sexual insecurity. An admirer of Alfred Kinsey, Hefner believed Americans were hypocritical about sex. He despised the strict Calvinism that had made his parents cold and undemonstrative. Hefner envisioned a men's magazine that would print "high-class" pictures of nude women next to good writing. In other words, he wanted to create "respectable" pornography. His initiative and timing guaranteed *Playboy* magazine's success.

Before the first issue's publication, Marilyn Monroe leaked to the press that she had once posed nude for a calendar and that Hefner had bought the rights for $500. He printed 70,000 copies of the first issue, hoping it would sell at least 30,000 at 50 cents an issue. Bolstered by the Monroe image, it sold 53,000 copies. By December of the following year, the magazine's circulation had reached 175,000 copies. By 1955, Hefner was offered $1 million to sell the magazine. He refused. By the end of 1956, still operating with a skeleton staff, *Playboy* was a phenomenon with a circulation of 600,000.

Hefner's greatest strength may have been his lack of sophistication. *Playboy* was born in the Midwest, not New York. Hefner understood the squareness of his readers because it was his own squareness. Hefner's magazine answered the right questions because they were his questions. Hefner was not a complicated thinker. According to one of the *Playboy* editors of the early days: "When [Hefner] buys a pipe, he buys two dozen of the same pipe. He likes his mashed potatoes to have a dimple of gravy on them. He is mid-America personified. The Marquis de Sade would have told him to wait in a corner, though he is, in a healthy way, sex possessed."

Hefner and his magazine introduced American men to a new American dream—an idealized lifestyle made up of the right clothes, the right women, and the right "adult" toys. Hefner believed he was filling a publishing need only

> slightly less important than the one just taken care of by the Kinsey Report...
> *Playboy* will emphasize entertainment. Affairs of state will be out of our province.
> We don't expect to solve any world problems or prove any great moral truths. If we
> are able to give the American male a few extra laughs and a little diversion from the
> anxieties of the Atomic Age, we'll feel we've justified our existence.[35]

The readership was described as sharp-minded business executives, workers in the arts, university professors. In the first issue of *Playboy,* Hefner wrote: "We like our apartment. We enjoy mixing up cocktails and an hors d'oeuvre or two, putting a little mood music on the phonograph, and inviting in a female for a quiet discussion on Picasso, Nietzsche, jazz, sex."[36] Whatever his profession, however, the reader was expected to see life not as a vale of tears but as a happy time, to find joy in one's work but not view it as everything. The reader was expected to be an "alert man, an aware man, a man of taste, a man sensitive to pleasure, a man who...can live life to the hilt."[37] Despite its common-man pretensions, however, the magazine reached a mostly middle-class audience.

Playboy's success reflected changing attitudes in America about sex and sexuality. The *Playboy* philosophy advocated sex outside the bonds of marriage, rejecting traditional religious codes and the Victorian ethic. The magazine shepherded a generation of young men to the "good life." For men who had not gone to college, the magazine provided an early, elementary tutorial on the new American lifestyle. The magazine celebrated indulgence and frivolity, with the central message being, "Celebrate your life. Free it up. Your sexuality can be as good as anybody else's if you take the inhibitions out, if you don't destroy yourself internally."[38]

Hefner realized that the pictures alone could easily sell the magazine, but only good prose could make it respectable. He hired August Comte Spectorsky, author of the best-selling novel *The Exurbanites* (1955), to improve the writing. Hefner also began offering a $1,000 award for fiction in 1957 and another for non-fiction in 1958. *Playboy* printed a short story by Jack Kerouac after *On the Road*'s success in the late 1950s, and a month later, the magazine's feature story addressed the "Beat Mystique," even though Hefner did not approve:

> The sandaled, dirty feet, unwashed aspects of the beats ran against the grain of the well-groomed, button-down, Aqua-Velva look our reader wanted. The anti-establishment attitude, lack of material ambition, or desire to get ahead, which typified the beats, was not what *Playboy* was all about. We were telling people how to make out, not just with girls, but in business and in their jobs.[39]

In his introduction to *Playboy*'s first political article, a 1959 piece protesting the advanced age of America's most influential politicians, Hefner wrote: "The knitted brow is not a common sight around *Playboy*. While not insensitive to the world's woes, we usually worry about them after office hours."[40] But in October 1959, the magazine printed one of the first anti-pollution articles published by a major periodical.

By the early '60s, Playboy printed some of the best literary criticism written in America by writers such as Norman Mailer and Henry Miller. It even published artwork by Picasso and a serialized novel by the renowned author John Steinbeck (1902–68). *Playboy* eventually became popular on college campuses. Students sporting bunny logo cuff links and a bunny carved of ice appeared at Dartmouth's winter carnival (and in newspapers across the country, thanks to an AP wire photo). Thus by the '60s, the *Playboy* philosophy had captured a generation of young male readers.

Reverend Harvey Cox lectured on the MIT campus about the proliferation of *Playboy* and later presented his findings in a May 1961 issue of *Christianity and Crisis*. He said the magazine appealed to the "male identity crisis" by "reducing the terrible proportions of sexuality, its power and its passion, to a packageable consumption item." Cox's attack on *Playboy* elevated the magazine to a serious cultural force and invited clerics nationwide to criticize its impact. Even major magazines discussed the phenomenon.

Delighted with the notoriety, Hefner published the first of twenty-five installments entitled "Playboy Philosophy" in the December 1962 issue. He wrote about individual freedom and the detrimental effects of organized religion but focused mostly on freedom for the pursuit of pleasure. While his "philosophy" hardly seemed controversial, the column established Hefner's magazine as a cultural think-tank. He soon added a religion section in 1963 and sent his religion editor, Anson Mount, to study for a summer at Episcopal Theological Seminary in Sewanee, Tennessee.

Hefner's influence cast an even wider net when, for example, Martin Luther King, Jr. visited the Playboy mansion. And in 1965, King granted an interview to *Playboy* just after collecting his Nobel Peace Prize. Eventually, Reverend Harvey Cox became a regular contributor. *National Review* compared his conversion to that of Saul of Tarsus.

By the mid-'60s, *Playboy* regularly ran articles on political and social issues, and in 1965, Hefner established the Playboy Foundation to provide financial support for causes espoused by the magazine. The Foundation's earliest recipients included lobbyists for legalized abortion and sex education. In 1970, the Foundation contributed $5,000 to help start the National Organization for the Reform of Marijuana Laws (NORML). In 1971, Hefner allotted an additional $100,000 to save NORML from financial ruin—he had recently discovered that marijuana enhanced his sex life.

Hefner's involvement with NORML, among other things, prompted the government to investigate him for narcotics. They arrested Hefner's personal secretary, hoping she would incriminate him, though she confessed only to her own cocaine use and later committed suicide while awaiting conviction. Hefner attacked the investigation as a witch hunt against him as a critic "of all forms of authoritarian repression in our society."[41]

In 1989, Hefner married that year's Playmate of the Year, with whom he now has two sons, although the couple later divorced. "Wouldn't it be unique," Hefner said at the time of his wedding, "if my life became a symbol of the conservative decade ahead, just as it was a symbol of the swinging '60s and '70s."[42]

A 1994 *MacLean's* article described the influence of Hugh Hefner on this century: "From the puritan Fifties to the Uptight Eighties, Hefner was an icon of libertinism, legitimizing the sexual revolution—for men at least—with an ideology of personal and economic freedom."[43]

INTO THE SIXTIES: BETTY FRIEDAN AND THE TRIUMPH OF FEMINISM

As the postwar era redefined sexuality, the role of women also changed. Traditionally, American women did not work outside the home for it was widely believed that women who competed against men became hard and aggressive and were doomed to loneliness. Real women reared their children, supported their husbands, kept their houses spotless and efficient, prepared dinner on time, and remained attractive and optimistic. This image was reinforced to the American public through television programs of the '50s such as *Leave It To Beaver* and *Father Knows Best.* Women's magazines such as *Ladies Home Journal, Redbook,* and *McCall's* also exerted much influence on women and reinforced these notions of traditional femininity. Women who felt unhappy or unfulfilled with this life were encouraged to believe they were an exception to normality.

One of the first women to challenge the prevailing notions of femininity was Betty Friedan (b. 1921). After graduating from Smith College in 1939, Friedan pursued her activist instincts in the political and social life of Greenwich Village, including Marxist discussion groups. After World War II, she married Carl Friedan, a war veteran and summer-stock theater manager. But unlike most wives of the '50s, Friedan took only brief leaves from work to give birth to her two sons and a daughter. The Federated Press, for whom she worked, fired her after she became pregnant for the second time. This enlightened her to the unequal treatment women received in the workplace.

Friedan's articles during the early years of her marriage extol the virtues of family life. While researching her college graduating class for their fifteenth reunion, however, she was surprised to find that most of her classmates were disillusioned housewives. After several magazines rejected her article about housewives with unfulfilled goals, she presented her idea to an editor at W. W. Norton and was offered a $1,000 advance on the project. After five years of writing and research, Friedan produced *The Feminine Mystique* (1963), in which she presented statistics to prove that women had actually lost social status during the '50s. Female college attendance had dropped, fewer women worked outside the home, and they worked at less prestigious occupations. Friedan blamed women's magazines and advertising, in part, for glamorizing the role of housewife to the exclusion of other female roles. The book received mixed reviews, but most recognized its publication as a landmark event in the women's movement. *The Detroit News* called Friedan's book "the Uncle Tom's Cabin of the women's liberation movement."[44]

Friedan next founded the National Organization for Women at an Equal Employment Opportunity Commission conference in 1966. She stated the organization's purpose: "To take the actions needed to bring women into the mainstream of

American society, now, full equality for women, in fully equal partnership with men."[45] During its first year, NOW concentrated on labor issues. At the 1967 NOW convention, however, Friedan introduced two new battlegrounds. First, she demanded "the long overdue amendment to the Constitution to provide that 'Equality of rights under the law shall not be denied by the United States or any state on account of sex.'" Thereafter, the push for the Equal Rights Amendment (ERA) became a NOW mainstay. Second, the "right of women to full sexual equality with men and to the dignity and privacy of their own person must be secured by federal statute recognizing the right of every woman to control her own reproductive life, and…removing contraceptive information and abortion from the penal code."

By 1973, NOW had won major victories in both the ERA and abortion. Congress ratified the ERA in 1972, but the amendment did not receive approval from the required 38 states before its June 30, 1982 deadline. The abortion fight was won with the 1973 *Roe v. Wade* Supreme Court decision that guaranteed women the right to an abortion.

In the early '70s, Friedan's split with feminist Gloria Steinem (b. 1935) revealed a conflict in the women's movement. According to Friedan, Steinem and her *Ms.* magazine exhibited female chauvinism and refused to acknowledge that a woman might happily choose homemaking and childrearing. Friedan spent the '70s and '80s attempting to reclaim women's issues from lesbian and militant feminist groups. In 1981, she published *The Second Stage,* which criticized the feminist movement for ignoring the important roles of the woman as wife and mother.

Friedan addressed problems of inequality again in *The Fountain of Age* (1993), but this time in relation to age. She argued that advertisers generally target younger audiences and often portray the elderly as burdens to society rather than contributors.

Like Sanger and Mead, Friedan has become an American icon. Her abortion advocacy has continuing ramifications, and her understanding of the issues of her time has kept her visible for more than sixty years.

KING AND RACIAL EQUALITY

In another key fight for equal rights, the Supreme Court joined the African-American struggle for equality with its 1954 *Brown v. Board of Education* decision against segregation in America's public schools. The landmark case began in five racially segregated schools, including one in Farmville, Virginia, where, in 1951, sixteen-year-old Barbara Johns led a student strike. The students and their parents only wanted facilities equal to those of white students. The NAACP lawyers, however, convinced them to sue for full integration with white schools. Although the decision was of critical importance, the ruling applied only to schools. Other public facilities and services could still be segregated lawfully. Mass transit, for instance, was increasingly the scene of public humiliation.

Mrs. Rosa Parks, a black woman in Montgomery, Alabama, had not planned to be arrested when she boarded a bus on December 1, 1955 and sat in a seat normally

37. AT HIS 1963 "I HAVE A DREAM" speech at the Lincoln Memorial in Washington, D.C., King proclaimed: "I have a dream that one day this nation will rise up and live out the true meaning of its creed: 'We hold these truths to be self-evident: that all men are created equal.' I have a dream that one day on the red hills of Georgia the sons of former slaves and the sons of former slaveowners will be able to sit down together at a table of brotherhood. I have a dream that one day even the state of Mississippi, a desert state, sweltering with the heat of injustice and oppression, will be transformed into an oasis of freedom and justice. I have a dream that my four children will one day live in a nation where they will not be judged by the color of their skin but by the content of their character. I have a dream today!"[46]

occupied by black passengers. Since Montgomery did not clearly separate the seats reserved for whites from those allowed for blacks, bus drivers reserved the power to force black passengers to give up their seats for whites. J. F. Blake exercised this power and commanded Mrs. Parks and three other black passengers to yield their row to a white man. Exhausted from her day's work as a seamstress and determined not to be mistreated, Mrs. Parks refused to get up. The driver demanded her arrest.

In response, black leaders led the Montgomery black community to litigate, boycott the bus system, and protest. As president of the Montgomery Improvement Association, the Reverend Martin Luther King Jr. (1929–68) called for action, tempered with love and respect for one's fellow man. Since blacks made up the majority of bus riders, the boycott of the bus system posed a significant economic threat.

Some whites in Montgomery responded by using obscure ordinances to detain car pool drivers such as King, who was arrested for exceeding the speed limit by five miles per hour. But the provocations extended to violence as well when African-American churches and homes, including King's, were bombed. These arrests and bombings brought the national media to Montgomery, and this exposure strengthened the movement. The entire nation witnessed the grand jury's indictment of eighty-nine of the bus-boycott leaders in February 1956 and saw the cheering crowds who accompanied the offenders as they were released on bail.

While the Montgomery boycotters had originally demanded only courtesy from bus drivers and a definite line of segregation, on November 13, 1956, the Supreme Court ruled that segregation of any kind on buses was unconstitutional. The Supreme Court decision brought renewed violence to Montgomery's black community. Snipers fired on integrated buses, and bombs destroyed more homes and churches. Within two years, King became a national hero, with a 1957 *Time* cover story focusing on his use of Ghandian, nonviolent tactics.

Despite the television and press coverage, the American public did not fully comprehend the racial conflicts until September 1957, when Arkansas Governor Orval Faubus defied the Supreme Court by sending the National Guard to prevent nine black students from attending classes at an all-white public high school in Little Rock. After meeting with President Eisenhower and receiving a contempt citation from a federal court, Faubus agreed to use the Arkansas National Guard to protect the black students from the white mob. On the appointed day, however, the National Guard failed to appear, and a white mob drove the black students away. In response, President Eisenhower sent armored vehicles and 1,000 riot-trained soldiers to Little Rock. Under guard, the nine black students entered the school without incident.

In June 1958, two years after the Montgomery bus boycott, Eisenhower invited King and three other black leaders to the White House, where they unsuccessfully attempted to convince the President to take a more active role in promoting black civil rights.

Still, King's fame did not protect him. Three months after speaking with the President in the White House, he was arrested for "loitering" outside a Montgomery courtroom where his friend Reverend Ralph Abernathy was testifying. After being brutalized by the police, King was convicted and sentenced to pay a $14 fine or spend fourteen days in jail. King shocked Montgomery authorities by choosing the jail sentence. When he arrived to serve his sentence, King was advised that his fine had been paid. Montgomery Police Commissioner Clyde Sellers later admitted paying the fine to prevent King's "publicity stunt."

King also supported the Freedom Riders, a group of blacks who rode buses across the country to test desegregation laws. He was jailed again after joining black citizens in Albany, Georgia, who were protesting the arrest of a group of Freedom Riders.

King was arrested other times, and these arrests had important ramifications for national politics. For example, after participating in a sit-in by students in Atlanta, King was sentenced to four months of hard labor for a former charge of driving without a license. Senator John F. Kennedy, in the heat of his presidential race, called King's wife, Coretta, to offer his sympathy. Robert Kennedy as well called the judge to suggest that his ruling may have been unjust. The judge relented and released King after eight days in jail.

The 1960 presidential election results revealed that a 30 percent shift from Republican to Democrat in the African-American vote had decided the election in favor of Kennedy over Richard Nixon. President Eisenhower blamed his protegé's defeat on the King case.

King's 1963 Birmingham youth marches evoked the most national sympathy the Civil Rights Movement had yet received. The national press published pictures of protesters. Some as young as six years were pictured being arrested, attacked by police dogs, and knocked off their feet with pressurized fire hoses. The Birmingham protests helped to energize the movement and brought white supporters of the Civil Rights Movement into the open. Later that same year, the August march on Washington, D.C. drew nearly 250,000 people, a third of whom were white. Folk singers Joan Baez, Bob Dylan, and Peter, Paul and Mary participated, as well as actors James Garner and Marlon Brando, among others. On that day, King gave his famous and inspirational "I Have a Dream" speech.

The high hopes of the D.C. march were dashed two weeks later when a bomb killed four young girls at the Sixteenth Street Baptist Church in Birmingham. Urging his followers to resist a violent counterattack, King earned *Time* magazine's "Man of the Year" award and the 1963 Nobel Peace Prize for his nonviolent example.

African-Americans had by now discovered a new form of protest: the sit-in. Neatly dressed black college students entered segregated lunch counters and politely asked for service. Although they were ridiculed, doused with drinks, and arrested, their protests remained strictly nonviolent.

Opponents of the Civil Rights Movement labeled it "Communist" since the Communist Party had been sympathetic to blacks as early as 1932 by sponsoring an African-American candidate for vice president of the United States. Although King's only contact with communism was his friendship with Communist Stanley Levison, the label was an attempt to redefine the Civil Rights Movement and its goals.

By the mid-'60s, King focused his efforts on lobbying for black voting rights. Although a constitutional amendment guaranteed black suffrage, local ordinances and practices often prevented blacks from voting. King led a march from Selma to Montgomery, Alabama, where he delivered a speech with the inspirational power second only to the "I Have a Dream" speech.

King saw the Watts riots of 1965 as a terrible blow to the cause of nonviolence. Investigating the causes, he realized that African-Americans were economically, as well as politically, oppressed. "The slum is little more than a domestic colony which leaves its inhabitants dominated politically, exploited economically, segregated and humiliated at every turn." But since issues of economic oppression are less clear-cut than those of civil rights, King began to lose white support for his work with unions.

When King was assassinated on April 4, 1968, in Memphis, Tennessee, while leading a sanitation workers' strike and planning a "Poor People's Campaign," the violent reaction in American black ghettos was one more indication of the schism within the African-American community on the proper response to oppression.

THE KENNEDY ASSASSINATION

With the Vietnam war, civil rights protests, bombings, and riots, the 1960s transformed American life. The tragedy and shock of the '60s was crystallized with the assassination of President John F. Kennedy on November 22, 1963. (See color plate 20.)

Kennedy was the most powerful man in the world at the time, and the world honored and mourned him at his death. Domestically, Kennedy commanded respect even from those who disagreed with him. The young president and his sophisticated wife were American pop idols, admired and imitated by millions of young people.

When Kennedy was shot, Americans felt personal outrage and sorrow. From Kennedy's conflict with Cuba to alleged assassin Lee Harvey Oswald's time in the Soviet Union, everything, some said, pointed to the Communists as the cause of Kennedy's death. Cold War hostility increased, and President Lyndon Johnson used it to justify escalating America's involvement in Vietnam, even while wild theories proliferated that the Central Intelligence Agency (CIA) or the Mafia had killed Kennedy.

Director Oliver Stone's controversial examination of the assassination in his 1991 film *JFK* continued to feed on conspiracy theories even in our recent history. The film sparked new calls to open the sealed government records from the 1977 House Select Committee on Assassinations investigation. While some call *JFK* a cinematic masterpiece, others criticize it as revisionist propaganda.

The Kennedy assassination temporarily suspended racial conflicts in many parts of the country. President Johnson urged the passage of Kennedy's Civil Rights Bill as the best possible tribute to the dead president. The death of the man who challenged, "Ask not what your country can do for you, but what you can do for your country," ushered in an age of suspicion. Kennedy's death was the first and most damaging of a series of events that killed American idealism. Following his assassination, one social upheaval led to another, and pessimism about the American way of life increased.

The literary and musical figures of the 1950s and '60s transformed an American society based on conservative, middle-class values to one at war with its own traditions. The '60s generation took two hundred years of ideas to the streets—radical ideas that were once mere speculation in the classroom became front-page news.

As traumatic as Kennedy's assassination was, America's problems were far more serious than the killing of a president. America appeared to be fragmenting. Two hundred years of assault on tradition had finally borne its fruit. In America of the 1960s, the ideas of the Romantic and Enlightenment movements had finally come to fruition. Soon their children would become members of the establishment itself.

CHAPTER 6
The Winds of Revolution

You gotta remember, establishment, it's just a name for—evil. The monster doesn't care whether it kills all the students or whether there's a revolution. It's not thinking logically, it's out of control, it's suffering from, it's a careless killer and it doesn't care whether the students all get killed or black power—it'll enjoy that.

JOHN LENNON[1]

W

"We are people of this generation, bred in at least modest comfort, housed now in universities looking uncomfortably to the world we inherit."[2] So began *The Port Huron Statement,* a manifesto proclaimed by fifty-nine people, including student activist Tom Hayden (b. 1939). *The Port Huron Statement* grew out of a meeting of the Students for a Democratic Society (SDS) in 1961 at a camp in Port Huron, Michigan, some forty miles north of Detroit.

Thus began the decade of the 1960s. Although pessimism would soon overtake it, the decade began with a sense of promise and the possibility for political change. During the '60s, the Socialists and Communists of the 1930s emerged on American university campuses as the "New Left." New Left ideology condemned the Cold War, issued a call to replace the arms race with a disarmament race, and criticized the permanent war economy and the burgeoning of the military-industrial establishment. It also called for corporations to be made responsible to the public and for democratically constructed foreign policy to guide private American foreign investment.

The Port Huron Statement radically rejected the '50s mentality and chronicled racial bigotry, the growing national affluence in contrast to worldwide poverty, the nuclear threat, and government hypocrisy regarding defense. It criticized anti-Communist "paranoia" and resistance to change and advocated a new system to

186 replace the "remote control economy." It criticized universities' reactions to modern issues and characterized them as bastions of "cumbersome academic bureaucracy" that employed "social and physical scientists" who worked "for the corporate economy" and "accelerate[d] the arms race." Finally, it broke away from the "old left." It disregarded traditional Communist ideals and addressed civil rights and personal liberties instead.

It was the first commentary from a new generation of white students. By expressing their utopian vision, they inspired an entire generation. As one SDS member declared about the *Statement*'s author: "Tom Hayden changed America.... He was the father to the largest mass protests in American history."[3] Little more than two years later, a much larger audience would see what the SDS member had predicted. In August 1963, nearly 250,000 people participated in the march on Washington, D.C., and watched Martin Luther King, Jr. deliver his stirring "I Have A Dream" speech. Demand for change had spread.

38. TOM HAYDEN in *The Port Huron Statement* proposed a new ideology for the 1960s: the New Left. In condemning the continuation of the Cold War, calling for an end to the arms race, and urging students to resist what he saw as the American Materialistic Machine, Hayden was the father to the largest mass protests in American history.

THE YOUNGSTERS BEGIN TO LEAD

Although the violent ghetto riots that engulfed many major cities in the '60s challenged white support for civil rights, nearly a third of the people who marched on Washington were white. White support of the black Civil Rights Movement remained strong, especially with the press coverage of violence in the South. But white resistance in the South and the hesitancy of the Democratic Party and labor unions to address racial issues resulted in black leaders being pressured to control blacks—especially students. During the first year of the sit-ins, for example, black college presidents expelled more than 140 students and dismissed almost 60 faculty members.

When attempts at suppression failed, opponents of civil rights turned to violence. Thousands of peaceful African-American students were arrested for "inciting a riot," and in many cities, white thugs were allowed to attack them while the authorities looked the other way. As a consequence, angry black leaders such as Malcolm X and Stokely Carmichael repudiated racial integration and advocated black nationalism and separatism.

Black students as well became increasingly restless. They began to believe they could effectively challenge the system, especially with the help of the national exposure they received every evening on television. During the next few years, the network evening news shows expanded from fifteen minutes to half an hour. Now, virtually every citizen could witness the day's events. What Americans saw on these programs inspired both southern and northern blacks to join the movement. The powerful images affected them. "They were kids my own age and I knew this had something to do with my life," said one African-American student.[4]

Both black and white young activists in the early '60s shared idealistic dreams and dismissed significant obstacles. As a professor wrote in the early '60s: "For the first time in our history, a major social movement, shaking the nation to its bones, is being led by youngsters."[5]

GROWING UP ABSURD

The civil rights struggle attracted and unified the student activists. They discovered they had many common experiences: liberal university or college educations, middle-class upbringing, and secure and egalitarian home environments in which they were reared to be democratic and questioning. They were more widely read than the average young adult, sometimes reading unorthodox journals such as *Dissent, Partisan Review, Liberation,* or the *Village Voice.* They also scorned most of the intellectuals of the '50s.

They found their heroes in campus radicals like the motorcycle-riding Columbia professor C. Wright Mills (1916–62). Mills combined the rebel lifestyle of James Dean and the moral passion of Albert Camus with the comprehensive portrayal of the American condition the students were seeking. Mills and others argued that the men who ruled America through money and influence did not represent the average American because their power did not derive from moral virtue. Mills hoped the "New Left" (a term he popularized) would be the new agent of historical change.

Herbert Marcuse (1898–1979) was probably the most respected thinker of the more extreme element of the student movement. Marcuse fled Nazi Germany after Hitler seized power, but he came to believe the United States was not much better than the Nazi regime. His antidote to the alienation of the machine age, as he argued in his books *Eros and Society* (1955) and *The One-Dimensional Man* (1964), was sexual freedom. Only if the human body was re-eroticized and the people were returned to the "polymorphous perversity" of children, he claimed, would they be "free."

Marcuse's emphasis on individual freedom fused the New Left with existentialism. The New Left opposed advanced technological societies regardless of their politics and believed that halting technological progress was the only way to regain the dignity of human life. As Marcuse wrote: "Freedom from the rule of merchandise over man is a precondition of freedom."[6] In turn, this caused students to identify with Third World freedom fighters such as Che Guevara (1928–67), and radical groups like the Weathermen eventually adopted Third World terrorist tactics.

STUDENTS IN REVOLT

In addition to fighting for black civil rights, the students also began to oppose the nuclear arms race. During the spring of 1960, a thousand Harvard students held a protest march for nuclear disarmament. Shortly thereafter, hundreds of students and more than 15,000 citizens held a Madison Square Garden rally in New York City. The protesters' aim was to end the nuclear arms race and create a test ban treaty. Peacemakers attributed the strong turnout to the students' awareness of the Civil Rights Movement and the atmosphere of action resulting from the southern sit-ins.

After the 1960 spring semester of activism, the House Un-American Activities Committee held hearings in California to investigate possible "Communist" activities. One thousand Berkeley students protested the investigations at City Hall in San Francisco. On the second day of the rally, police appeared with billy clubs and fire hoses, drenching the protesters. Students labeled the affair "Black Friday."

Many students of the '60s were inspired by the idealism of John F. Kennedy. Philosopher Frithjof Benjamin recalled the high expectations centered around Kennedy: "Kennedy created a climate of high idealism—it was evangelical. It was marvelous that we would make a beautiful world, a more compassionate world."[7]

This climate of high idealism was nowhere more evident than at the University of California at Berkeley. The University's attempts to suppress anti-discrimination and anti-segregation demonstrations in the fall of 1964 spawned a campus-wide rebellion and gave birth to the Free Speech Movement. The leaders of campus protests had learned at least one important lesson: by calling attention to the larger moral dimensions of a local issue, using the direct action techniques of the Civil Rights Movement, and enlisting the support of sympathetic liberal faculty members, a relatively small group of hardcore activists could pose a significant challenge to the administration of a university.

The Berkeley students staged sit-ins, invaded administration buildings, were arrested, held strikes, sang folk songs, and created slogans identifying the target of their protest. It was the dehumanizing aspect of modern society: "My Mind Is Not the Property of the University of California," "I Am A UC Student: Do Not Bend, Fold, Spindle or Mutilate," and "Don't Trust Anyone Over Thirty."

By February 15, 1965, however, the Berkeley student newspaper announced that the Free Speech Movement had, for all practical purposes, dissolved, though the *Daily Californian* also reported: "The campus and the entire nation has recently been immersed in conversation about the confusing situation in North and South Vietnam."[8] Vietnam now became the white student movement's cause.

LYNDON JOHNSON AND THE ESCALATION OF THE VIETNAM WAR

President Lyndon Johnson's (1908–73) February 1965 decision to launch reprisal bombing raids against Vietnam outraged students and marked a dramatic escalation in student opposition to this as yet undeclared war in Southeast Asia. Student protest was now gripped with urgency. For example, the Vietnam Day Committee was formed at Berkeley, and on May 21, 1965, 15,000 students attended a rally to protest the war, at which one of the most famous slogans of the '60s first appeared: "Make Love, Not War."

The Vietnam War dominated political debate and policymaking during the second half of the '60s. Instead of containing the Soviet-controlled Communist movement's expansion into South Vietnam, the United States found itself embroiled in a local civil war. Nonetheless, America's leaders chose to use the war as a way to extend America's "peace" to Asia and to test new military tactics in the post–World War II era through so-called "wars of national liberation." The government's political, military, and media activities were carefully calculated to achieve these goals.

Television networks initially supported the war and strengthened public backing of the Johnson Administration, but the coverage slowly began to expose some of the government's blatant manipulations. The televised "victories," which often clearly showed the tragedy and injustice of the war, shocked America, though television itself also manipulated the war to achieve the best television effects. Carefully selected footage portrayed "typical" events of the war, but it was soon discovered that some war correspondents had allegedly bribed participants to choreograph battle scenes. As a result, the press and television coverage of the war eventually destroyed Johnson's presidency. The differences between what Johnson knew to be true and the stories he saw on television paralyzed his ability to lead, and Johnson allowed the media and antiwar critics to get the best of him.

Perhaps more importantly, television coverage affected public insight and reflection on the war. One Vietnam veteran filmmaker said:

> If you really think about the war in Vietnam, there were about five still images that eventually persuaded everybody that what we were doing was wrong. The monk burning himself in Saigon. The police chief in Saigon shooting the Viet Cong suspect. The children running down a dirt road having been napalmed and their clothes burned off, and the little girl up front yelling in pain. Her mouth was like a black hole. The photograph of a protest at the Pentagon of a lovely little flower child putting a flower in the muzzle of a soldier's gun. And, of course, the photograph of the student at Kent State, lying dead on the ground, and the girl with her arms up in anguish over the body, crying out.[9]

THE WAR OF CHAOS

The public eventually learned that the Vietnam War was like no other war the United States had fought. There were no clearly defined fronts with trained male soldiers. There were no rules, norms, or mercy. Cruelty and torture by the Viet Cong (VC) and North Vietnamese Army (NVA) were widespread. Also, American captives and wounded were forced to endure psychological and physical torture. The torture spread to South Vietnamese villagers and American sympathizers. One soldier recalls a village boy whose skin had been peeled away from his chest in long, slender strips while his father was forced to watch. The father's head was then cut off in front of his wife, who was forced to hold the bloody, decapitated skull.

American soldiers reacted to such atrocities with deeds that were sometimes more severe and grotesque than those of their so-called "savage" enemy. Americans tortured VC captives, killed the enemy rather than move them to POW camps, and, frustrated because they could not differentiate between friend and enemy, tortured and tormented Vietnamese villagers. In response to the enemy's tactics, American soldiers desecrated dead bodies in the fury of revenge. They even killed one another. "Fragging"— using grenades to kill one's own unpopular officers—became all too common.

The nature of combat in Vietnam fed brutality. Frustration was caused by the torturous climate and the enormous obstacle that was "the bush." A war wallowing in strange guerilla tactics, invisible enemies, and unforeseen primitive weaponry naturally led to fatigue, loss of character, and violence. In addition, tiny autonomous platoons, led by young noncommissioned officers, often faced unimaginable strain and impossible tasks.

The March 1968 slaughter of 347 noncombatants in the small village of My Lai proved to be a key event in the war. Although twelve officers and enlisted men were charged with murder or assault with intent to commit murder for their horrific deeds, only Lt. William L. Calley (b. 1943) was found guilty and sentenced to life imprisonment in March 1971. In response to the public outcry to Calley's sentence, President Richard Nixon reduced Calley's life sentence to twenty years. Three years later, the sentence was reduced to ten years. In August 1974, Calley was released from prison on parole.

Apparently, most Americans at the time believed Calley was either innocent or his actions justified—or he was simply the fall guy for the high-ranking officers who permitted the massacre. War protesters used the event to justify their opposition. On either side, the My Lai incident profoundly influenced American attitudes of disillusionment and confusion toward the war. America had lost its innocence: "Used to thinking of their country as America the Good," writes author Marilyn Young, "Americans were shocked to see the streets filled with angry young people who insisted it was America the Bad. The massacre of My Lai, they accused, was neither impossible nor aberrational."[10]

The American public was not the only group that lost its innocence. Prolonged exposure to the horrific violence significantly affected the hearts and minds of American soldiers in Vietnam. Having witnessed the senseless violence, American soldiers who survived would bring their shock and disillusionment home with them. Various studies have shown that high levels of violent crimes were committed by returning servicemen, often against their own friends and family members. Many of these crimes resulted from flashbacks and could be directly attributed to the violence the soldiers had experienced in Vietnam. Director Michael Cimino's 1978 film, *The Deer Hunter,* depicts the grisly torture of American soldiers in Vietnam and shows the war's lasting impact on American culture.

THE ANTIWAR PROTESTS BACK HOME

The antiwar movement descended directly from the Berkeley Free Speech Movement and *The Port Huron Statement*. At SDS's first major antiwar demonstration, 20,000 protesters gathered in Washington, D.C., on April 17, 1965 to protest the introduction of American combat troops in Vietnam. SDS President Paul Potter asked during the rally:

> What kind of system is it that disenfranchises people in the South, leaves millions of people throughout the country impoverished and excluded from the mainstream and promise of American society...and still persists in calling itself free and finding itself fit to police the world?[11]

The military draft, which was the most visible and disruptive domestic policy during those years, became the lightning rod for mass demonstrations. There were draft card burnings, sit-ins, picketings at local draft boards, and so-called "teach-ins," which were campus meetings to discuss Vietnam. Congress toughened the legal penalties for acts of draft resistance, and the United States Justice Department investigated the anti-draft movement for Communist influence.

Means of evading and resisting the draft became more sophisticated as the war continued and as antiwar sentiment became more widespread. For example, in 1965 the Supreme Court expanded the definition of "conscientious objection" in response to a flood of lawsuits filed by people who opposed the war on moral grounds. Neither membership in an established church nor belief in God were requirements for conscientious objector status. A third of the potential draftees were deferred or exempted every year, with more than a quarter disqualified from military service. Five percent of the potential draftees served on the home front in the reserves and National Guard.

Another moral objection to the war was the fact that the people who actually fought the war, unlike those who were protesting it at home, were not well-educated, affluent, suburban-bred, post-war "baby boomers." The typical draftee came from a working-class family, lived in a city or small town, and had no education beyond high school. Factory neighborhoods, slums, and black ghettos were targets of the draft boards, according to one study done at the time.

RUBIN, HOFFMAN, AND THE YIPPIES

By early 1966, television was publicly broadcasting the congressional hearings on Vietnam, presented by Senator William Fulbright. Before they were over, most Americans had a strong opinion about the war, either for or against.

In the spring of 1967, the Mobilization Committee (MOBE) staged the largest antiwar protest to date: nonviolent protesters followed Rev. Martin Luther King Jr. and Dr. Benjamin Spock from New York's Central Park to the UN Headquarters. In October 1967, race riots broke out in Detroit and Newark, and bloody attacks on students in Madison, Wisconsin, and Oakland, California, occurred.

Then, Jerry Rubin (1938–94) and Abbie Hoffman (1936–89), as well as Allen Ginsberg and others, led a crowd in Washington, D.C., in an attempt to "levitate" the Pentagon—Hoffman had suggested levitation as a way of exorcising the Pentagon's evil demons. He offered to compromise and only raise the building ten feet in the air instead of the originally intended three hundred; that is, if the military would grant a

39. CHICAGO STREET FIGHTING during the 1968 Democratic Convention. There were four days and nights of ferocious police violence by the Chicago police, broadcast live to thirty million watching Americans by cameramen who had to wear gas masks in order to avoid breathing in the chemical fog and who themselves had to duck and run to escape from the indiscriminate clubbings and beatings of Mayor Daley's men. Michigan Avenue became a war zone, where photographers and reporters were just as likely to be clubbed senseless as demonstrators or innocent passers-by.

permit for the demonstration. Although the building did not budge, the demonstration was an all-night stand-off between protesters and United States marshals on the Pentagon steps. Norman Mailer, who also participated and was among the 683 people arrested, recorded his experiences in his 1968 Pulitzer Prize–winning book, *Armies of the Night.*

On New Year's Day 1968, Rubin and others came up with the idea for the Youth International Party, or "Yippies." They would continue to fight by "hurl[ing] themselves across the canvas of society like streaks of spattered paint."[12] The Yippies' first big event was at the Chicago Democratic Convention of 1968 where they nominated a pig—"Pigasus"—for president. They also threatened to put LSD in Chicago's water supply. The authorities in Chicago were not amused, and many of the convention demonstrators were beaten and many more arrested. Ironically, the trial of the "Chicago Eight" (the name given to the organizers of the demonstrations, including Hoffman and Rubin), on charges of conspiracy and crossing state lines with the intent to incite riots, ended up attracting more than the chaos they were accused of causing at the convention.

STUDENT REVOLTS IN WESTERN EUROPE

While American students had been caught up in the protest movement, European students were also demonstrating. In the tradition of Dada and Surrealism, French and German students sought to "achieve a radical rupture in the patterns of everyday life" as they protested the Vietnam War and other causes closer to home. British students protested Rhodesian white racist regimes as well as American involvement in Vietnam. Italian students demanded wider courses of study and a more democratic university system. And in Northern Ireland, students were inspired by Martin Luther King's "I Have A Dream" speech to liken their struggle for religious freedom to the black Civil Rights Movement. The turning point in European student revolts came in 1968. "The near revolution that occurred in Paris and the rest of France during May 1968," writes author Jon Savage, "had an immediate, galvanizing impact on youth throughout the world: partly because it marked a generation claiming its political rights."[13]

FINAL SPLINTERING

The student freedom movement, however, was not always internally consistent. Women participated in the discussions of freedom and equality, but their male fellow idealists often used and discarded them like chattel. And although lesbians found a place within the women's movement, gays eventually had to create their own activist group.

In 1969, police raided the Stonewall Inn, a gay bar in New York's Greenwich Village. The patrons and gays and lesbians from the surrounding community threw objects at police as they tried to take people into custody. The conflict escalated into a riot, which resulted in thirteen arrests, and the riots continued the next night when homosexuals chanted and advertised their new slogan—"Gay Power." The riots led directly to the formation of the Gay Liberation Front, and the homosexual community had its own militant radical movement.

On May 17, 1968, *Life* magazine appeared with a cover story on "The Generation Gap." Americans quickly seized on the notion as an explanation for the student insurrections around the world. One observer wrote:

> People who have been born in a nuclear world, in a computer world, are people with a different mental appetite. . . .It is a question of being open to a very complicated new world and to the complex questions of this world which demand new answers. Old answers are not accepted or acceptable.[14]

There were two ways to look for new answers. One was to drop out of society and smoke dope like the "hippies" or "flower children" did. The other was to confront the system, as the New Left did.

The assassinations of Martin Luther King Jr. in April of 1968 and Robert Kennedy (1925–68) two months later disillusioned some, while militarizing others into more radical tactics. The student movements began to dissolve over internal politics and disagreements about violence and militancy, especially as the government used increasing violence against them. In November 1969, police in Washington, D.C., used tear gas against a crowd of 300,000 at the largest antiwar demonstration to date. On May 4, 1970, at Kent State University in Ohio, National Guardsmen fired on a crowd of students, killing four. A similar event at Jackson State resulted in the deaths of two black students. Student strikes shut down almost nine hundred campuses. Other groups became militant as well—and the police responded in kind. Indeed, police killed a total of forty-four Black Panthers during the years 1970–75.

Finally, in January 1973, United States troops withdrew from Vietnam. As a result, the student protest movement lost its primary focus, though it left behind some powerful special-interest factions—the women's movement, Native American activists, environmentalist activists, and the Gay Liberation Front.

Another legacy of the student protest movement was a backlash of support for conservative politics. Richard Nixon's (1913–94) 1968 presidential campaign, for example, played on the fear that many Americans felt toward radicals and asked for the votes of conservatives—the "forgotten Americans" who were not "haters." Ironically, Nixon resurrected another basic fear that Americans had—fear of the federal government. After the illegal activities surrounding the Watergate break-in and its cover-up came to light, America faced a grave constitutional crisis that resulted in the resignation of its president in disgrace. Thereafter, many in the general public became as cynical and suspicious of the government as the student activists had been.

A CHORUS PROTEST

Music played a key role in both the black Civil Rights Movement and the antiwar protests of the '60s and early '70s. It came to symbolize an era. According to African-American singer Bernice Johnson Reagon (b. 1942),

> You couldn't call black people together in any committed way without a ritual that involved an enormous amount of singing. The singing was used to create the climate, to get people ready to address the issues. So any statement from lawyers, as a testimony from someone who'd been arrested, was always presented on a bed of song. And the song-leaders were absolutely essential.[15]

In 1962, the Freedom Singers, joined by Bernice Johnson and headed by Cordell Reagon (whom Johnson later married), publicized the racial problems in the South and raised money for the civil rights campaign. The music emerged from the southern communities with their powerful tradition of gospel singing.

On November 11, 1962, Pete Seeger gave a concert in Atlanta for the SNCC (Student Nonviolent Coordinating Committee), with which the Freedom Singers were aligned. In early 1963, the group conducted one of the most successful political campaigns ever launched by a pop band. The Freedom Singers often opened their concerts with "We Shall Not Be Moved." The group would then progress to new versions of songs that had been sung for over a hundred years and rhythm and blues songs from the jails and street corners.

The Singers toured the country, raising money, organizing local support committees, attracting publicity for the ongoing voter registration work, and telling audiences about racial segregation and discrimination in the South, participating, like so many others, in the historic March on Washington in August 1963. Perhaps most importantly, they introduced many listeners to the powerful sound of black gospel.

But the fit between ideals and style was not always complete. Pete Seeger, for example, who had first sung for Martin Luther King in the mid-'50s, found that traditional favorites like "If I Had a Hammer" did not move black audiences.

Bob Dylan (b. 1941) also experienced an inability to reach black audiences at various civil rights rallies, including the March on Washington. His masterpiece "Only A Pawn in the Game" (1963), for instance, sympathized with "poor white" racists whom Dylan saw as being exploited by the truly racist and evil politicians. The song recalled the death of Medgar Evers, who was shot and killed by the Ku Klux Klan in Mississippi. Dylan immortalized Evers, but while many young blacks liked his lyrics, they did not have much affinity with his singing. Dylan, however, gave the Civil Rights Movement one of its chief anthems, "Blowin' in the Wind" (1962), which the folk group Peter, Paul and Mary took to the top of the music charts in 1963.

Dylan consciously followed in the footsteps of his idol, Woody Guthrie, who had sung of the working man in the '30s and Pete Seeger, one of the first "flower children." In the early '60s, many of the Greenwich Village coffee house artists such as Dylan, Joan Baez, and Peter, Paul and Mary sang songs of peace and social justice. In 1966, the Byrds, a folk-rock quintet heavily influenced by Dylan, sang an Old Testament passage from Ecclesiastes put to music by Pete Seeger. The song "Turn, Turn, Turn" became a hit and showed that, with a rock beat, folk music could reach a much wider audience.

Peter, Paul and Mary also focused on politics and social activism, although their music imitated the new pop music style. Albert Grossman, who assembled and managed the group, intended them to be Kingston Trio-like, with a "sexy girl singer." Peter, Paul and Mary earned their initial success in 1962 with Pete Seeger's song "If I Had a Hammer." And in 1963, their top ten hits included two Dylan songs, "Blowin' in the Wind" and "Don't Think Twice, It's Alright."

DYLAN

Bob Dylan expressed ideas and stories of the moment with exceptional strength and brilliance. His prescience captivated his early audiences, and in the eyes of many, Dylan's song "The Times They Are A-Changin'" solidified his role as a prophet. (See color plate 21.) Much of Dylan's impetus through his poetry and music came from his Jewish heritage. He grew up in Hibbing, Minnesota, where many devout Jews lived. At his bar mitzvah in 1954, he read from the *haftorah* (a selection of readings from the Jewish prophets) in Hebrew and talked on the moral duty of the Jew.

From the beginning, Dylan's songs taught that there is an incestuous relationship between authoritarianism, social evils, militarism, and materialism and that the solutions to corruption are spiritual. Dylan proclaimed the existence of a personal God who brings judgment, a "hard rain" as one of his songs puts it, on people who perpetrate evil. Dylan's topical songs mixed the power of Beat poetry with the folk style of Guthrie and Seeger—all with prophetic overtones. Although his songs often incorporated real events, they went beyond mere journalism.

The "establishment," however, was slow to understand Dylan's attraction. In May 1963, *Time* magazine described him as "faintly ridiculous" because of his idiosyncrasies and a voice that sounded "as if it were drifting over the walls of a tuberculosis sanitarium." The magazine ridiculed Dylan's fans, saying they had "an unhappy tendency to drop their g's when praisin' him—but only because they cannot resist imitatin' him."[16] Dylan responded with the song "The Times They Are A-Changin'," which not only addressed the magazine's mockery but outlined the growing rift between Dylan's audience and the cultural elite. The battle lines of the '60s had been drawn.

In 1963, Dylan was catapulted to fame with his album *The Freewheelin' Bob Dylan,* which contained some of his most enduring work: "Blowin' in the Wind," "A Hard Rain's A-Gonna Fall," and "Don't Think Twice, It's All Right." About that time, he began a lifelong friendship with Beat poet Allen Ginsberg. More than ten years later, he expressed his respect for Ginsberg: "You're the king, you're the king, but you haven't found your kingdom. But you've always been the king. . . . People get off on your energy."[17] Two years later, the first song on Dylan's 1965 album *Bringing It All Back Home,* "Subterranean Homesick Blues," contained the unmistakable rhythmic cadence of Beat poetry put to music.

Dylan also admired the work of Jack Kerouac. One of the most poignant scenes in *Renaldo and Clara,* Dylan's documentary film of his Rolling Thunder Revue tour (1975–76), was his visit to Kerouac's grave in Lowell, Massachusetts. Ginsberg and Dylan approached the grave to read the inscription on a small marble plaque set in the earth. Ginsberg then quoted one of Kerouac's favorite lines from Shakespeare. They sat cross-legged on the grass before the plaque, as Dylan tuned his guitar and Ginsberg quoted a few lines from Kerouac's book *Mexico City Blues* (1959). Then, trading verses back and forth, they improvised a slow blues song for Kerouac.

Another influence on Dylan was the poetry of nineteenth century French symbolist poet Arthur Rimbaud. The similarity between the two artists, though a century apart, was first suggested by Ginsberg. Dylan was no doubt flattered by the comparison, for he even compares himself to the French poet in his song "You're Gonna Make Me Lonesome When You Go" (1974).

The Beatles also influenced Dylan. Dylan remembered driving across the country in 1964 listening to the Beatles: "Their chords were outrageous, just outrageous, and their harmonies made it all valid. You could only do that with other musicians. . . . I knew they were pointing the direction where music had to go."[18]

Even though Dylan always maintained a strong commitment to civil rights, he became deeply disillusioned with the petty squabbling and elitism of the New Left. But the alienation worked in both directions. In late 1963, soon after the assassination of John F. Kennedy, Dylan was invited to accept the Thomas Paine Award of the Emergency Civil Liberties Committee for his work in the Civil Rights Movement. Feeling the effects of alcohol and more than a little alienated from his audience, which included many wealthy and aging left-wing activists from the '30s, Dylan insulted them, confusedly saying, "It's not an old people's world."[19] He baffled them with a speech about race, class, and the establishment and attacked liberals, patriots, and the "Negroes" who had participated in the March on Washington. Dylan even drew parallels between himself and Lee Harvey Oswald, expressing his view that all people are victims of the men who control the system. Amidst an uproar, he left to a chorus of boos, as well as applause.

Not insignificantly, Dylan was absent from the final and grandest civil rights event at which black and white protesters and musicians came together—the march from Selma to Montgomery, Alabama in March of 1965, where more than 5,000 people sang Dylan's song, "The Times They Are A-Changin'."

Instead, Dylan's record company was releasing his first partially "electrified" album, *Bringing It All Back Home* (1965), which seemed to be about his bitterness that the times were not changing as he had expected them to. One song from that album, "It's Alright, Ma (I'm Only Bleeding)," revealed a deep cynicism, lambasting modern materialism's denigration of what was once venerated. Mentioning "flesh-colored Christs that glow in the dark," Dylan concluded that very little is held sacred anymore. His work from this point on began to concentrate on the message that dehumanizing forces treat modern people as mere business investments.

Dylan, the prophet, condemned what he saw: "All along the way," writes Dylan biographer Robert Shelton, we encounter Dylan's condemnation of the modern assembly line: mad human robots out of Chaplin's *Modern Times....* Then, almost as an aside, Dylan makes a shambles of simpleminded political commitment. What difference which side you're on if you're sailing on the *Titanic?* Irony and sarcasm are street lamps along "Desolation Row," keeping away total, despairing darkness. Gallows humor for a mass hanging.[20]

By 1965, Dylan had abandoned the civil rights campaigns and was moving away from the folk scene into rock. He was preparing to show his new, electric, non-folksy and non-protest style at the Newport Folk Festival, which would cause a scene and reduce Pete Seeger to tears. Dylan's breakthrough album, *Highway 61 Revisited* (1965), and his next, *Blonde on Blonde* (1966), revealed the many different influences on his life and crystallized his new plugged-in sound.

For the most part, Dylan turned his back on protest and politics. Like many pioneering mid-'60s thinkers, he explored subjects of personal radicalization such as consciousness, values, and freedom rather than public issues. "I don't want to write *for* people anymore. You know—be a spokesman," Dylan told Nat Hentoff in a 1964 *New Yorker* profile. "From now on I want to write from inside me."[21]

Dylan released the single "Like a Rolling Stone" in the summer of 1965 (off the *Highway 61 Revisited* album). Riding the organ effect of Al Kooper and a throbbing bass guitar, Dylan spits out a cryptic diatribe saturated with vengefulness toward some unnamed woman who once believed herself safe from life's existential horrors. The six-minute song (cut into two parts to fit the then three-minute format allowed by Top 40 radio stations) defined a new kind of music known as "folk rock." With this, Dylan abandoned traditional folksinging and created a new idiom—and a new pop culture. "Like a Rolling Stone" and subsequent songs introduced lyrics with substance to pop music. Previously, most serious-minded people considered pop songs meaningless and moronic.

The *Highway 61 Revisited* album introduced numerous biblical overtones. The title song suggested that humanity's slightest mistake could bring destruction. Another song, "Desolation Row," cries for people to renounce materialism. Robert Shelton asserts that it belongs beside Eliot's *The Waste Land* and Ginsberg's *Howl* as one of the strongest twentieth century expressions of apocalypse. Thousands would later imitate Dylan's counterculture style, including the punk rockers of the 1970s and many of those who followed in the last years of the century. By 1966, Dylan, although only twenty-five years old, was a major poet whose works were later studied at the university level. And in 1970, Princeton University awarded him an honorary doctorate.

After what was reported as a motorcycle accident in 1966, Dylan withdrew. He did not tour again for eight years, although he continued to write and record. By 1967, Dylan had produced what some called the first "biblical rock album," *John Wesley Harding*. This album, which had its roots in country music, also stood in stark contrast to the electronic and "psychedelic" sounds of the Beatles' *Sgt. Pepper's Lonely Hearts Club Band* that had recently preceded it. Dylan's well-known song from *Harding*, "All Along the Watchtower," begins with a conversation between two men within a walled city: the "joker" and the "thief." The joker warns the thief that the world is coming to an end, as "the hour is getting late." Their exchange resembles the conversation recorded in the Bible between the two men crucified with Christ.

Although Dylan had not been touring, his appeal remained. When it was announced that he and the Band (the name of his back-up group at the time) would do a concert tour in the U.S. in early 1974, five million fans turned in ticket applications. For the first time in years, Dylan sang his old songs but with new, often startling arrangements. The tour's album was released in 1975, with the apocalyptic title *Before the Flood*.

Dylan gave what now seem to be indications of his coming Christian conversion on his next album, *Blood on the Tracks* (1975), probably his most popular album among fans. In "Idiot Wind" he sings of a "lone soldier on the cross" who finally wins out in the end. And in "Shelter from the Storm" God is arguably referred to in the feminine gender. She takes Dylan's "crown of thorns" while promising to give him shelter from an impending tumult.

By mid-November of 1978, Dylan was in a poor state of mind and at a low point in his career. Although *Blood on the Tracks* had been critically acclaimed, the songs and albums to follow did not match it. His four-hour film *Renaldo and Clara* (1978) was highly criticized, and Dylan faced personal and marital problems—his wife was finally divorcing him.

At a concert in San Diego on November 17, someone threw a silver cross on the stage. Dylan picked it up and put the cross in his pocket. He took it to the next stop in Arizona and, in a Tucson motel room, had an intense religious experience. As Dylan said in 1980:

> There was a presence in the room that couldn't have been anybody but Jesus. . . . I truly had a born-again experience, if you want to call it that. . . . Jesus put his hand on me. It was a physical thing. I felt it. I felt it all over me. I felt my whole body tremble. The glory of the Lord knocked me down and picked me up.[22]

Dylan's conversion was evident on his next album, *Slow Train Coming* (1979). On the first track, he maintains that whether it's "the devil" or "the Lord," everyone must serve a spiritual entity. And on the reverent and worshipful "When He Returns," Dylan portrays an omnipotent God who knows and sees all. But the apocalyptic tone remained, as in the album's title track "Slow Train," which seems to represent the cumulative judgment of God.

In his 1981 *Shot of Love,* Dylan continued his warning in "Trouble," where he sings of persecution and "governments out of control," as if it were some portent of troubled times to come. He wove a similar tone into a number of albums that followed, including *Infidels* (1983), on which biblical references are present on "Man of Peace," where Satan comes as a deceiver of humankind.

Since his 1978 conversion, Dylan has returned to some of his Jewish roots but, apparently, with a mixture of Christianity. Whatever his beliefs, his prophetic calling and spiritual development seem to have continued. In a 1991 interview in Budapest, Dylan said he regularly reads the Bible: "I believe everything the Bible says." When asked about the Apocalypse, Dylan replied: "It will not be by water, but by fire the next time. It's what is written."[23]

Dylan's staying power has been remarkable. He was included in *Life* magazine's 1990 list of the twentieth century's one hundred most influential Americans. And in 1998, he made *Time* magazine's list of one hundred most influential entertainers of the century.

Dylan's tribute concert at Madison Square Garden in 1994 brought out the best of the young and old music worlds in celebration of him and his music. And his 1997 album, *Time Out of Mind,* won three Grammy Awards, including album of the year, and reestablished Dylan as a leading cultural voice.

It has been Dylan's success as a teacher of ethics that sets him apart. For a generation failed by traditional religion and in need of a moral compass, Dylan has been one of their greatest voices.

THE NEW WAVE

The 1960s also saw a new spirit in filmmaking and brought an end to the studio system in Hollywood. By the end of the decade, studios were responsible only for marketing and financial support. Court rulings and relaxed social standards erased former sexual taboos, and soft-core pornography quickly took advantage of the new freedom.

Alfred Hitchcock's (1899–1980) 1960 classic film *Psycho,* which is erotic, violent, and macabre, reflected the change in Hollywood's code of acceptability. Using the iconography of the horror film, Hitchcock aroused feelings of terror with a chilling musical score. *Psycho,* which featured a psychotic transvestite, redefined the limits of sex and violence in films.

In another important development known as the French "New Wave," directors Jean-Luc Godard (b. 1930) and François Truffaut (1932–84) created the notion of film "authorship." They claimed directors Hitchcock and Howard Hawks, among others, as their inspiration. The director was now considered to be as fully artistic as any of the great novelists, painters, and poets. As "auteur," the director was the ultimate authority and sole arbiter of a film's meaning, to the extent that a director's personality dominated the film's style and story line. As a result, critics began to view any given film in the context of the full body of that particular director's work.

40. WARREN BEATTY AND FAYE DUNAWAY in *Bonnie and Clyde.*

Aesthetically pleasing performances were not a goal of New Wave directors. Audiences often could no longer identify with "good" or "bad" characters. Viewers as such were forced to witness complex interactions between characters who were both good and bad. The New Wave resulted in innovative films coming from almost every country. On the negative side, however, some filmmakers and critics began to excuse technical sloppiness as reflecting deep feeling and criticized technical polish as the sign of a commercial sell-out.

The New Wave influence can be seen in many American films but perhaps nowhere more than in the 1967 classic, *Bonnie and Clyde,* directed by Arthur Penn (b. 1922). With this picture, the American film industry finally took notice of the youth movement engulfing the world. Bonnie and Clyde stand as symbols for the rebellious and high-spirited youth of the 1960s, while the banks, police, and authorities represent the callous, rigid, and hypocritical adult world. The film fed many young people's contempt for the adult world. It also gave symbolic sanction to certain nihilistic values within the counterculture and the New Left and set new standards for violence in film.

The film, however, also spoke to other overriding concerns of the '60s. For example, film historians Leonard Quart and Albert Auster assert: "There are suggestions in the exaggerated, murderous use of police firepower (for example, the bloody shoot-out where the police use an armored car), of the American military's penchant for overkill in Vietnam."[24] Other films by Arthur Penn, such as *The Left-Handed Gun* (1962), *The Chase* (1967), and *Little Big Man* (1973), commented on the conflict between law and violence in America. They addressed the public's disillusionment with corrupt government, racial discord, and the military machine.

Mike Nichols' (b. 1931) *The Graduate* (1967) was commercially and critically successful in portraying the crumbling of traditional values. The movie's most compelling moment—the abduction of young Elaine Robinson from a church in the middle of her wedding ceremony—was a shrewd attack on the sanctity of the marriage vow and on the values of affluent, upper-middle-class Americans. The movie created a world of honest young people surrounded by stereotyped adults who were either predators or fools. But the couple's blank, ambiguous stares as they leave the wedding in the back of a bus cause one to wonder if they will live happily ever after.

Other films addressed the war and political events more directly, as in John Wayne's 1968 movie, *The Green Berets.* Sam Peckinpah's (1925–84) 1969 classic

Western masterpiece, *The Wild Bunch,* undermined Wayne's hawkish values and covertly evoked a Vietnam War that had horror rather than honor as its dominant motif. *The Wild Bunch*'s good guys are barely distinguishable from its bad guys. Unfortunately, the women in the film are all whores, sluts, betrayers, or madonnas, all of whom either frustrate the male world or serve as its pleasure objects. The graphic, sensational violence raised serious questions about the blend of moralism and nihilism.

Dennis Hopper's (b. 1936) 1969 *Easy Rider* (which foreshadowed the independent film movement of the latter twentieth century) depicted an "us" versus "them" theme and struck a powerful emotional chord. Jack Nicholson (b. 1937), playing an articulate, witty, alcoholic lawyer, sets the despairing tone of the film when he says: "This used to be a helluva country."

Released the same year, the film *Medium Cool,* directed by Haskell Wexler (b. 1922), portrays an apolitical television cameraman who discovers that merely pointing the camera is a political gesture. The title of the film is derived from Marshall McLuhan's description of television as the "cool" medium, as opposed to "hot" media such as movies and radio. *Medium Cool,* in retrospect, was an illustration of how television itself became the subtext of film and an alternative to movies.

APOCALYPSE NOW

A number of films attempted to put the Vietnam struggle in perspective, including Oliver Stone's (b. 1946) *Platoon* (1986), Stanley Kubrick's *Full Metal Jacket* (1987), and John Irvin's *Hamburger Hill* (1987). Stone's powerful *Born on the Fourth of July* (1989) examines the real-life experiences of Ron Kovic, a Marine who was paralyzed during the war.

Perhaps the most haunting and lasting Vietnam-era film is Francis Ford Coppola's (b. 1939) 1979 *Apocalypse Now.* (See color plate 22). Coppola based his film on Joseph Conrad's (1857–1924) classic novella, *Heart of Darkness* (1902), which Orson Welles had planned to make into a film in the '30s but never succeeded.

Marlow, the central character in Conrad's book, is commissioned to travel to Africa to join a cargo boat. He grows disgusted by the greed of the ivory traders and their brutal exploitation of the natives. At a company station, Marlow hears of the remarkable Mr. Kurtz, who is stationed in the very heart of the ivory country. Although he is the company's most successful agent, the mysterious Kurtz has grown seriously ill.

Marlow sets off on a two-month journey to find Kurtz. Nearing Kurtz's outpost, Marlow learns that Kurtz exercises semi-divine powers over the local people. In fact, a row of severed heads on stakes around a hut reveals the barbaric rites by which Kurtz has achieved his ascendancy. Kurtz, an educated, civilized man, has used his knowledge and his gun to reign over this dark kingdom.

While Marlow attempts to get the ill Kurtz back down the river, Kurtz tries to justify his actions and motives. Kurtz has seen into the very heart of things, and his dying words are: "The horror! The horror!"

Coppola sets *Apocalypse Now* in Vietnam. Changing the setting from a British colonial ivory trading operation in the African Congo to Vietnam is less a stretch than might be expected, for in both stories the location is largely symbolic. Marlow (Conrad's protagonist) and Willard (Coppola's protagonist, played by Martin Sheen) journey into a world where society's moral standards do not apply. And at the heart of that world each finds Kurtz, the essence of unrestrained human egotism. "Charging a man with murder in this place was like handing out speeding tickets at the Indy 500," says Willard in *Apocalypse Now.* Willard recognizes that the Army officials who want him to kill renegade Colonel Kurtz are trying to impose morality in a place where all laws have already been broken.

The amorality of the men who were running the war and those fighting the war is obvious during Willard's journey toward Cambodia. He joins a helicopter attack led by Colonel Kilgore (actor Robert Duvall), to whom napalm is the perfume of victory ("I love the smell of napalm in the morning"). Kilgore is passionate about surfing and is willing to kill or risk lives in his quest for a good wave. Willard also witnesses a frenzied crowd of sex-starved soldiers rushing the stage after a USO bump and grind show of undulating Playboy bunnies. And at the last American outpost on the border between Vietnam and Cambodia, anxious African-American soldiers shoot at an unseen enemy to the accompaniment of atonal music, with disembodied voices on the film's soundtrack and flares lighting up the sky.

These apocalyptic scenes allow Willard to identify with Kurtz, who writes to his son: "I am beyond their timid, lying morality, and so I am beyond caring." In Conrad's *Heart of Darkness,* Marlow witnesses the atrocities the ivory traders commit. He too looks forward to meeting Kurtz, the man whose methods these exploiters of the jungle condemn as "unsound." Conrad's strength was being able to show that society operates on an arbitrary set of rules and judgments, a house of cards built over an abyss. Kurtz has the courage to plunge voluntarily into the abyss of horror, madness, and power. Conrad believed that the darkness that consumed Kurtz was in the heart of every man. He wrote to his socialist friend H. G. Wells: "The difference between us, Wells, is fundamental. You don't care for humanity but think they are to be improved. I love humanity but know they are not."[25]

Marlow and Willard both see their own potential to become Kurtz. In fact, Coppola originally wanted to leave *Apocalypse Now* open-ended, allowing the viewer to assume that Willard takes Kurtz's place after killing him. Marlon Brando (who played Kurtz) and others disliked the idea. Coppola himself identified with Kurtz as he was making the film. His wife Eleanor recorded in her journal: "Now he is struggling with the themes of Willard's journey into self and Kurtz's truths that are in a way themes he has not resolved within himself." While shooting *Apocalypse Now* in the Philippines, Coppola had an affair and considered ending his marriage. He also set up such an extravagant mini-civilization for the cast and crew that his wife warned him he was "turning into Kurtz—going too far."

The filming temporarily inflated the economy of the town of Pagsanjan, north of Manila, where the crew stayed. The high school principal toured the bars every night, urging the workers to save their money rather than throw it away on women and alcohol. "Our people have lost their sense of values," he said. "Everything I've taught them they've forgotten." After the crew and its money left, the community supported its new standard of living through a male child prostitution ring. According to Estanfania Aldaba-Lim, a former minister of social welfare in the Philippines, "Some gays with the crew fell in love with young macho boatmen, and then it went to much younger boys, down to nine, ten, eleven years old, and the whole town got into it." By 1989, a flourishing trade in boy prostitution had become a way of life. Tacitly supported by the community, boy prostitution had "brought economic advantages to the children and their families."[26]

THE CULTURE OF CONGESTION

The winds of revolution also blew over the world of visual art during the 1960s. Unlike previous generations, the post–World War II generation lived in a world of its own making. Up until the mid-twentieth century, natural images had been at the center of emotion in art. Nature's cycles of growth and decay, the wind, weather, light, and the infinite complexity of form and behavior from the molecule to the galaxy provided the metaphors for almost every relationship of men and women to their surroundings and the Deity.

Rembrandt's 1638 *Landscape With an Obelisk* exemplified the relationship between the artist and nature. The sense of a natural order corrected the onlooker's pretensions of ego and the self. This sense has now dimmed, partly because "Nature," for most people, has been replaced by a culture of congestion: of cities and the mass media. The post-'50s art world struggled to survive in this rapidly changing world.

In a medieval monastic community, random noise did not pollute the listener's ear. The silence of nature swallowed up the random noises of society and dominated medieval life. Against the quiet that enveloped the ear, any designed structure of sound seemed rare and unique. Because nothing could be retrieved or reproduced, the pre-technological ear listened to one thing at a time. As art historian Robert Hughes notes in *The Shock of the New* (1993), in a world not yet inundated with images and designed objects, the beauty of a medieval choir's voices resonating in a Gothic cathedral might well have exceeded any modern cultural experience. Today, we see the same cathedral through a vast filter that includes our eclectic knowledge of all other cathedrals and all other styles of building, the secular essence of our culture and even the memory of so-called medieval sideshows at modern-day theme parks such as Disney World. In our present day, however, a choir competes in our unconscious with jackhammers, car brakes, and passing 747s, not merely with the rattle of a cart or the lowing of cattle. The chant is no longer unique. One can go home and listen to something very similar on the stereo.

CAGE AND CHANCE

Musician John Cage (1912–92) greatly helped to smash the concept of uniqueness and majesty, not just in music but in art in general. A dedicated student of Marcel Duchamp and Zen Buddhism, Cage objected to the limitations of traditional music and grieved that "if a sound is unfortunate enough not to have a letter…it is tossed out of the system on the grounds: it's a noise or unmusical."[27] Calling traditionally composed music a product of the composer's vanity, he claimed: "By flipping coins to determine facets of my music, I chain my ego so that it cannot possibly affect it."

Cage's use of nontraditional sounds can be heard in his *Third Construction* (1940), which used rattles, tin cans, a lion's roar, and conch shells. Another composition recorded seven percussionists playing on bowls, pots, tin sheets, gongs, and metal bars. In the mid-'40s, Cage developed the "prepared piano." "Preparation" meant placing bolts, nuts, strips of rubber, and other foreign objects across and among the piano strings. Washers would clatter when certain keys were pressed. If a pencil was wedged between adjacent strings, a bell-like chord could be produced by striking only one note on the keyboard.

In the early '50s, Cage turned to "accidental" or "aleatory" composition. Influenced heavily by Zen Buddhism and the ancient Tibetan book *I Ching,* Cage "discovered that tosses of a coin could be translated into abstract patterns."[28] He composed the classic aleatory work *Imaginary Landscape No. 4* for "twelve portable radios and twenty-four players." A turn of the knob produced the next unpredictable sound, and in a defined time span any sound could appear.

Cage's music reached its apex in 1953 with his revolutionary work, *4'33".* "The pianist walked onto the stage and sat silently in front of the piano for the length of time indicated by the title," writes author Joan Peyser in *The New Music* (1970):

> Cage's "music" here is the collection of unintentional sounds that occur during this particular period. His point is that silence is never absolute, that even in a room designed to eliminate sound reverberation, one hears the sound of one's own body. Cage's piece is literally that, a "piece" taken from the sound continuum without beginning, middle, or end.[29]

Claiming that his favorite piece is "the one we hear when we are quiet," Cage argued that all sounds have value and that the traditional notion of a God-given frame of reference did not exist. Also, there was no natural synthesis with melody, harmony, or rhythm. He refuted the Abstract Expressionists' holy elitism. Instead, Cage made his art an integral part of everyday life, like Marcel Duchamp's *Readymades.* He insisted that it was the everyday physical environment that fueled art, not the so-called "creative process." Like

41. IN THE LATE FORTIES as a young composer, John Cage attended Daisetz Teitaro Suzuki's lectures on Zen Buddhism. Cage had previously read about Zen, and he studied eagerly under the famous Zen theorist.

Duchamp, Cage believed that art's purpose was to blur the distinction between art and life. He thought that the all-powerful element of chance required the artist to avoid the rational creation of patterns, hierarchies, and points of climax in favor of repetition and a kind of "all-over relatedness." Ultimately, Cage's philosophy helped to provide the basis for Pop Art, Minimal Art, Happenings, and Performance and Conceptual Art.

POP ART

Pop Art first appeared in Great Britain in the 1950s, a decade before attaining a distinctive artistic style or method. The Institute of Contemporary Art in London encouraged Pop Art discussions and exhibitions. By the winter of 1954–55, the word *pop* was popular in England, where young '50s artists did not share the American artists' pessimism for mass culture. They believed that the landscape of commercial America—that vast sea of neon signs and commercial messages that flourished on the far shore of the Atlantic—was deeply intriguing.

In 1956, a London exhibit called "This Is Tomorrow" showed a series of contemporary environments developed from photographs of architecture and imagery from ads. Richard Hamilton's (b. 1922) *Just What Is It That Makes Today's Homes So Different, So Appealing?* (1956) was exhibited there and gave the word *pop*—emblazoned on the hilarious phallic sucker a muscle-man is holding—its first physical appearance in art. The collage presented pictures of a tape recorder, a canned ham, a television, a comic book cover, a Ford advertisement, a vacuum cleaner, a motel bed, and a physically ideal couple displaying their bodies, especially their pectoral muscles and breasts, as "products"—giving a view through a window onto a movie marquee touting Al Jolson in *The Jazz Singer.*

The profound changes Pop Art brought became clear. This is mirrored in a statement of Hamilton's in which he irreverently listed its qualities as "popularity, transience, expendability, wit, sexiness, gimmickry, and glamour."[30]

In the early 1960s, English Pop artists such as David Hockney (b. 1937), Allen Jones (b. 1937), and Peter Blake (b. 1932) created an original style. The all-time most popular media figures, the Beatles, provided ideal subject matter. Blake designed the album cover for *Sgt. Pepper's Lonely Hearts Club Band* (1967), which became the most recognized pop-rock cover in history.

Pop Art achieved success in the '60s by mastering the cult of replication. Stripping humanity of its need for memory, the mass media created instant history by contracting time and space into a blurry, continuous present. This suggested that even the recent past was as remote as ancient archaeology. Mass production robbed images of their singularity. Resembling signs, modern images presented complete messages at one time. Art, on the other hand, portrayed more complicated messages of relationships, hints, uncertainties, and contradictions. While a sign dictated meaning, a work of art provided a process to discover it. Paintings educated but signs disciplined, always speaking in the imperative voice. Pop Art proliferated by emulating advertising and the media. It cast itself as a detached, amused, and lenient spectator in the vast theater of twentieth century mass media illusion.

RAUSCHENBERG, JOHNS, AND WARHOL

The Pop Art of Robert Rauschenberg, Jasper Johns, Andy Warhol, and others reflected John Cage's influence. Their work was accessible to kindred spirits, but not to the masses. That was to come later.

Robert Rauschenberg (b. 1925), who studied at the influential Black Mountain College, is one of the most wildly unpredictable artists in American history. His 1955 *Bed* was a composite of his own pillow, sheet, and patchwork quilt, stabbed and dripped with various colors of paint from the top of the pillow down onto the quilt. (See color plate 23.) He hung the work vertically to contradict the bedding's original function. The art was shocking because it challenged a consumerist society that valued gleaming, ersatz newness. By forcing the viewer to confront outcast and despicable fragments of objects, Rauschenberg and the other artists countered a culture maniacally geared for new and soon-to-be-obsolete products.

Rauschenberg further developed the alliance between the image world of popular culture and the articles of daily life. For example, he incorporated Coke bottles, stuffed animals, rubber tires, and other debris into his work, seeking to preserve the identity of the objects without distortion. Like Duchamp before him, Rauschenberg sometimes embedded an ironic lechery in his images. The 1955–59 *Monogram* shows a stuffed angora goat in a tire, inviting a provocative sexual reading. Robert Hughes described this work as one of the "few great icons of male homosexual love in modern culture: the Satyr in the Sphincter, the counterpart to Meret Oppenheim's fur cup and spoon."[31]

Rauschenberg also used silkscreened photo-journalism imagery. He was perhaps the first artist to test these new technical and aesthetic frontiers. Art historian Robert Rosenblum asserts: "Every artist after 1960 who challenged the restrictions of painting and sculpture and believed that all of life was open to art is indebted to Rauschenberg."[32]

Although his art is often compared to Rauschenberg's, Jasper Johns (b. 1930) was unlike him in temperament or style. Between 1955 and 1961, Johns developed principal motifs, as in his well-known paintings of flags and targets. These, along with maps and rule-and-circle devices, created new forms of representation from commonplace imagery.

Target with Plaster Casts (1955) exemplifies Johns' distinction between signs and art. A target is the simplest of signs, and its sole purpose is receptivity. To reflect the impersonality and dehumanization of modern society, Johns set plaster casts of bits of the human body in boxes above the painting. The body bits are twice removed from life—first cast, then fossilized in monochrome paint. The apparent body pieces defy labels. They are only signs. Human emotion is suspended between waxworks and a dehumanized geometry, the body's cage and a mental prison.

Three Flags (1958) appears to faithfully depict the American flag, but Johns insisted they were not flags. In the fashion of René Magritte—whose painting of a pipe carried the inscription "This is not a pipe"—Johns' flags were not flags, but paintings of flags. Johns' work influenced American art in the '60s because it defended painting in the face of a mass-culture environment. That defense was becoming more difficult than ever before.

Andy Warhol (1930–87) also attempted to deal with his pre-packaged, ready-made, repetitive culture: "I want to be a machine," he proclaimed, "to print, to repeat, repetitiously to bring forth novelties."[33] His 1962 *Two Hundred Campbell's Soup Cans* illustrated the culture's gluttony and mimicked advertising, which he believed flattered consumers. Warhol's point was to encourage consumers to view themselves as discriminating connoisseurs of sensation and taste. (See color plate 24.)

Warhol understood the modern exaltation of celebrity. In contrast, the true heroism of the Renaissance had been based on ability or accomplishment. The celebrity, whose notoriety is often short-lived, is famous only for his fame. Warhol contributed to the sociology of art, rather than art itself. By turning himself into a pure product, Warhol dissolved the traditional ambitions and pretensions of the avant-garde and helped turn the art world into a business.

Others emerged to carry Pop Art experimentation further. For example, Roy Lichtenstein (b. 1923) incorporated the print media into his art. He exaggerated the relationship between dots and contour, as had Georges Seurat in the late nineteenth century. His obsession with dots recalled the microscopic dots of a television image's mosaic. His *Drowning Girl* (1963), for example, is a conglomeration of dots arranged in a recognizable image. Lichtenstein was primarily concerned with art and style. His later paintings represent an effort to reconcile comic strip conventions with such twentieth century masterpieces as Matisse's. This is reflected in his *The Artist's Studio: The Dance* (1974).

James Rosenquist (b. 1933) painted billboards for a living before becoming an artist. The giant images he was accustomed to dealing with surfaced in his art as a montage of huge, bland fragments. He claimed that the inspiration for his most ambitious painting, *The F–111* (1965), arose from the jokes of workmen in Times Square, where he was painting signboards. *The F–111* was named after an American fighter bomber being used in Vietnam. The workmen said that the center of the Soviets' rocket target was around Canal Street and Broadway. Rosenquist's work was a recreation of the Beat writers' fear of the bomb being immediately dropped on humanity.

Claes Oldenburg (b. 1929) was one of the most radical and inventive Pop artists of the '60s. Instead of imitating the slick, processed surface of popular culture, Oldenburg converted unlikely objects into metaphors of the body and self. "I am for an art that is political-erotical-mystical," he wrote in 1967, "that does something other than sit on its ass in a museum."[34] His recurring theme of food suggests the infantile, oral obsessions of many consumerized Americans. Oldenburg's *Two Cheeseburgers, with Everything (Dual Hamburgers)* (1962) memorializes the excruciating banality of American fast food. His mockery of desire invites sensual frustration by combining appetite and repulsion. Oldenburg said: "I try to make the art look like it is part of the world around it. At the same time I take great pains to show that it doesn't *function* as part of the world around it."[35]

Later, Oldenburg designed imaginary urban monuments. These included a toilet ball-float for the polluted Thames, a teddy bear for Central Park, and a gargantuan Good Humor Bar for Manhattan's Park Avenue. A few of these have actually been built, such as the colossal *Clothespin* (1976) in Philadelphia. Oldenburg's visionary works graft childhood fantasies to a dehumanized, overcrowded civilization. They suggest that the problems of litter, traffic, congestion, crime, and air pollution resist rational solutions.

Edward Kienholz's (1927–94) remarkable work depicted the dehumanizing effects of modern culture. His *State Hospital* (1964–66) presented violation, loss, and entrapment imagery. And in his profound work, *The Future as an Afterthought* (1962), a bundle of baby doll heads, black, white, and brown, are shaped into the familiar mushroom cloud of the atomic bomb. (See color plate 25.) One head lies on the base of the piece; it is sticky, as though in melt-down mode. Kienholz reinforces the notion that children are our future. His warning seems to be that science and technology can get out of control and, thus, endanger posterity.

THE HAPPENINGS

By the early '60s, painting was no longer the primary form of artistic expression. It had lost the competition with mass media because painting could not be as vivid, far-reaching, or powerfully iconic as television or print. Modern people would believe what was seen in a photograph or on television, but few would conduct their lives on the basis of a work of art. Once art gave up its claim to seriousness, its essential role as an arena for free thought and unregenerate feeling was lost. The Pop artists further reduced painting's ability to reach the mass modern audience with true intellectual stimulation. This confirmed media analyst Marshall McLuhan's (1911–81) thesis that "the medium is the message."

"Happenings," a forerunner to Performance Art, attempted to create relevant art. They were animated collages of events involving people and materials in a theatrical setting, requiring no specific participation or response on anyone's part. Their purpose, however, was to alter the consciousness of audience and performers alike.

Allen Kaprow (b. 1927) invented the Happenings to bring visual artists into more fertile interaction with the world, arguing that art must not be separate from life. He said:

> Objects of every sort are materials for the new art: paint, chairs, food, electric and neon lights, smoke, water, old socks, a dog, movies, a thousand other things which will be discovered.... These bold creators...will disclose entirely unheard-of happenings and events, found in garbage cans, police files, hotel lobbies, seen in store windows and on the streets, and sensed in dreams and horrible accidents.[36]

His 1965 *Calling* reduced people to props. Three people wrapped in sheets lay silent and motionless against an information booth in New York's Grand Central Station amidst commuters.

Soon Kaprow's ideas made their way to Europe and found an outlet in the experimental, even political, art of Yves Klein (1928–62) and Joseph Beuys (1921–86). Kaprow's notions survive today in Performance Art and in a new generation of environmental works.

Europe's "new realism" movement paralleled the American Happenings. Frenchman Yves Klein directed a troupe of twenty musicians, who played his one-note *Monotone Symphony* (1960) while two naked women smeared in blue paint rolled over canvases on the floor. A sequence from this event was recorded for the 1963 film, *Mondo Cane*.

THE BEATLES: A DAY IN THE LIFE

A key event in pop music history took place in a New York hotel room during the Beatles' first tour of the United States in 1964: the Beatles and Bob Dylan met for the first time. The "Fab Four" had never smoked marijuana, and Dylan introduced it to them that night. Thereafter, the Beatles got high at virtually every opportunity, and drug references began to pop up in their songs. Paul McCartney (b. 1942) noted that marijuana triggered "the U-turn" in the Beatles' attitude toward life. After Dylan introduced them to marijuana, the Beatles dropped their heavy beer drinking "simple as that," said John Lennon (1940–80). Drugs would now be their main avenue to get high, including psychedelic drugs such as LSD.

The Beatles' mainstay in history would not be their drug use, however. It is the fact that the Beatles raised rock music to an art form. They influenced everything in the '60s from haircuts and fashion to the political and spiritual beliefs of a generation. This is true despite the fact that their career lasted only eight years, with a mere ten and a half hours of recorded music (twenty-two singles and fourteen albums). (See color plate 26.)

The Beatles have been routinely criticized for causing a widespread loosening of American moral codes, especially among the young. But by the time they landed in the United States, traditional moral codes were already disintegrating. As an Ohio State senior explained: "We've discarded the idea that the loss of virginity is related to degeneracy. Premarital sex doesn't mean the downfall of society, at least not the kind of society that we're going to build."[37]

The Beatles did not just come to America in 1964; they invaded it. In February, the group was met at Kennedy International Airport by three thousand screaming fans, mostly teenage girls. They required the help of two hundred policemen to get through the crowds. "Beatlemania" gripped America for a month as the Beatles performed before shrieking, squealing audiences. When they made their American television debut on the *Ed Sullivan Show* on February 9, the program received the highest ratings in history, attracting 72 percent of the New York audience. Soon, many of the '60s generation abandoned crew cuts for long bangs and black boots.

When the Beatles released the single "I Want to Hold Your Hand" on December 26, 1963, the number-one hit on the pop chart was "Dominique" by Sister Sourire, the Singing Nun. Many who first heard the wisecracking Beatles with their mushroom haircuts and matching slim-cut lapel-less jackets assumed they were just another musical novelty. By April 1964, however, the Beatles held the top five spots on the Hot 100 Billboard Chart ("Can't Buy Me Love," "Twist and Shout," "She Loves You," "I Want to Hold Your Hand," and "Please Please Me"). No other artist has since achieved such a feat.

The sounds and lyrics of the Beatles were similar to American popular music of the '60s. American groups such as Jan and Dean, the Beach Boys, the Temptations, and others sang about teen love won and lost. But the Beatles looked and acted differently. For many young Americans, the Beatles and other British groups symbolized a rejection of 1950s morality and a revolt against parental authority. "My mother hates them, my father hates them, my teacher hates them," said a young fan. "Can you think of three better reasons why I love them?"

The Beatles' first film, *A Hard Day's Night* (1965), irreverently mocked middle-class materialism and authority. This surrealist film, now considered a classic, was one of the earliest rock videos and appealed especially to youth: "[The film was] almost all joy," a student critic wrote, because "all the dreary old adults are mocked and brushed aside."[38] The film also was an inspiration to many aspiring young artists who imitated the Beatles and started rock bands.

Songs off the *Rubber Soul* album, released on December 3, 1965, such as George Harrison's (b. 1943) "Think For Yourself," exhibited a biting cynicism, particularly toward women. As Mark Hertsgaard in his book on the Beatles writes: "With the exception of the empty sweetness of 'Michelle' and forgettable formulaics of 'Wait,' the emotions directed toward women in the 'love' songs of *Rubber Soul* are angry, cutting, and occasionally violent."[39] For example, "Norwegian Wood" tells the story of a male antagonist who burns down a woman's house.

Although by 1966 public demand for the Beatles seemed insatiable, a furor arose over Lennon's now-famous statement that

> Christianity will go. It will vanish and shrink. I needn't argue about that. I'm right, and I will be proved right. We're more popular than Jesus Christ right now. I don't know which will go first, rock 'n' roll or Christianity. Jesus was alright, but his disciples were thick and ordinary. It's them twisting it that ruins it for me.[40]

Some defended Lennon, including a Wisconsin minister who said that anyone outraged by the remark should "take a look at their own values and standards. There is much validity in what Lennon said. To many people, the golf course is also more popular than Jesus Christ."[41]

Others used the statement to attack the Beatles as evil. In South Carolina, the Ku Klux Klan put a Beatles record on a wooden cross and set it on fire. The Birmingham, Alabama radio station WAQY broadcast announcements every hour urging listeners to turn in their Beatles records and souvenirs for a great community bonfire. The Grand Wizard of the Ku Klux Klan exhorted: "Get out there, you teenagers, and cut off your Beatle-style long hair. Join those at the bonfires and throw your locks into the fire! Burn, burn, burn everything that is Beatle!"

Lennon soon publicly retracted his statement, and the *Chicago Daily News* proclaimed him forgiven. But the "Christianity statement" brought death threats, and the Beatles realized that their fame was not only distracting but dangerous. The San Francisco Candlestick Park concert in August 1966 proved to be their last.

Thereafter, the Beatles retreated to the studio and produced more introspective songs, such as the technologically innovative "Rain" single in 1966, which presented the first stirrings of pop psychedelia. The song's phrases "I can show you" and "Can you hear me?" indicated that Lennon had begun to take his role as spokesman for his generation seriously.

Revolver, the first album of the Beatles' "psychedelic" period, clearly qualified as art, containing sounds no one else had produced. The pervasive mood was that something was dramatically wrong with the traditional culture. "Eleanor Rigby," a combination of rock and classical forms, proclaims that Eleanor Rigby lives in a surreal dreamworld where she wears a false face she stores in a jar. Traditional religion, the Beatles seem to say in the song, has little to offer modern society. As Paul McCartney sings, "no one was saved."

Largely drug-inspired, the *Revolver* album, released in August 1966, was possibly the Beatles' best collected work. It made Beatlemania irrelevant because there was no longer any need for touring to keep the idea of the Beatles alive. *Revolver* was clearly the work of recording artists. Thus, it seemed ridiculous to the Beatles to compromise the creative progress they had made in the studio by embarking on another tour.

WHEN THE WORLD STOPPED TO LISTEN

Sgt. Pepper's Lonely Hearts Club Band (released in June of 1967) is the Beatles' most notorious record. It embraced a psychedelic vision and was their most audacious and inspired leap into the avant-garde: their self-presentation as fictional characters.[42] The

Beatles' concept was to produce an album that was a show and then send themselves on tour as a record. They hoped the album's concept would be a way around the problem of their not touring anymore.

The album cover by Peter Blake was the first fusion of Pop Art and pop music and is now one of the best-known Pop Art works. Inverting fantasy and reality, Blake places the Beatles among notable figures and artists the Beatles themselves had chosen. These include, among a few dozen others, George Bernard Shaw, Edgar Allen Poe, Aldous Huxley, Lenny Bruce, Mae West, and Bob Dylan. The cover is also a funeral pose, where art romanticizes celebrity. The Beatles are wearing Victorian band uniforms, and the graveside memorial they are attending is for their former image. They are paying respect to their own late live career.

The album ends with a reprise of the title track that fades into the climactic classic "A Day in the Life." The British Broadcasting Company banned this song, along with "Lucy in the Sky with Diamonds," because of what the BBC believed were drug references. As a postlude, "A Day in the Life" sets the other songs on the album and the Beatles' career in perspective. A collection of vignettes that are somewhat tragic, the song is punctuated with the phrase "I'd love to turn you on"—either a reference to drugs or the need to tune in to the Beatles' message. No doubt drugs were an intended reference in "A Day in the Life." As Hertsgaard writes, "Indeed, John and at least one other Beatle were tripping—or flying, as John put it—during the photo session for the *Sgt. Pepper* album cover."[43]

The Beatles underscored the verses of that final song with a dark, tumultuous orchestra crescendo. McCartney had wanted to include an instrumental passage with the avant-garde feel of John Cage and others, a spiraling ascent of sound, beginning with all instruments, each climbing to the highest in their own time. Lennon wanted the song to end with "a sound like the end of the world"[44] so the Beatles simultaneously struck an E-major chord on three grand pianos, drawing out the sound as long as possible with electronic enhancement. The effect of the crashing E-major chord, followed by some fifty-three seconds of gradually dwindling reverberation, brings to mind nothing so much as the eerily spreading hush of the mushroom cloud—visions of nuclear holocaust.

Neither Lennon nor McCartney could read or notate music. Therefore, George Martin had to explain their vision for "A Day in the Life" to the forty musicians summoned to Abbey Road Studios on the evening of February 10, 1967. Trained to play as a coherent unit, the orchestra was disconcerted when told by McCartney, under the influence of John Cage's music, that the essential thing was not to play like the musician next to them. According to Martin, they laughed and "all looked at me as though I was mad."[45] The recording session was festive. Martin and the orchestra had been requested to wear full evening dress with silly party disguises. The leader of the violins, for example, wore a gorilla's paw on his bow hand.

The evening was recorded for a music video, which shows the Beatles and company in the semi-darkness of the studio chatting, drinking, and playing to the camera before the session. A dove flies back and forth across a darkened sky, as strangely marked faces zoom in and out of the picture. Martin conducts the orchestra wearing a Pinocchio nose. The film, in exquisite synchronization with the sound track, gradually builds to a fantastic climax. It cuts faster and faster from image to tripping image as the orchestra madly charges up the hill to the end of the song—a "riveting visual experience," as Hertsgaard put it.

The album took the world by storm. As one observer recounts:

> The closest Western Civilization has come to unity since the Congress of Vienna in 1815 was the week the *Sgt. Pepper* album was released.... For a brief while the irreparable fragmented consciousness of the West was unified, at least in the minds of the young.[46]

THE SUMMER OF LOVE

The hippies inherited the Beat counterculture and gravitated to the Beat mecca, San Francisco. There they improved on the Beat formula with stronger drugs and drug-inspired music. Rent was inexpensive and business space readily available in the Haight-Ashbury district. The gay community tested the area in 1964 and found it tolerant of gay bars, although the neighborhood drove out a gay movie theater. Haight-Ashbury as well tolerated the hippie invasion in 1965–66.

Some of the key Beat figures easily evolved into hippies. Allen Ginsberg presided over many hippie (and yippie) Happenings. And Neal Cassady (1926–68), Kerouac's inspiration for *On the Road*, drove Kenneth Kesey's (b. 1935) drugged-out Merry Pranksters across the country in a Day-Glo bus.

The San Francisco hippie culture gathered in January 1967 for a "Human Be-In" at Golden Gate Park. The program included Ginsberg, political activist Jerry Rubin, drug guru Timothy Leary (1920–96), and the Grateful Dead. The Diggers, an anarchist group based in the Haight, provided free food, and August Owsley Stanley III, the Bay Area's drug czar, supplied free LSD. News of the party spread nationally and inspired a popular song about going to San Francisco and wearing flowers in your hair. When school ended the following spring, more than 75,000 young people took the song's advice. It was called the "Summer of Love," and its music was *Sgt. Pepper's*.

Unfortunately, "free love" excused the victimization of hippie women and spread a variety of sexually-transmitted diseases. Overpopulation, counterfeit drugs, and poor sanitation made the Haight-Ashbury district one of the earliest casualties of the hippie movement. The Diggers closed down their free food program, and hippie capitalists exploited starving drug addicts. The scene attracted people such as the eventual mass murderer, Charles Manson (b. 1934). By 1968, the neighborhood was too dangerous to house college students.

The wider psychedelic revolution dwarfed Haight's decline. Mainstream America neutralized the hippie rebellion with commercialism, and by the late '60s, virtually everyone wore paisley prints, bell-bottomed pants, and long hair. Consumer America had stolen the hippie identity.

HELTER SKELTER

On June 25, 1967, the Beatles represented the BBC in the first world television satellite link-up, with a potential audience of 400 million viewers. They sang Lennon's "All You Need Is Love," the perfect encapsulation and embodiment of the summer of 1967. But the August 1967 death of Beatles manager Brian Epstein (1934–67) upset the group's internal dynamics. Partly from necessity, McCartney asserted greater leadership and forever altered the group's cohesiveness.

Their next project, the 1967 *Magical Mystery Tour* film and album, reflected the change. The tour was

42. JERRY GARCIA (left) of the legendary rock band the Grateful Dead and Phil Lesh at Haight-Ashbury in San Francisco in the late 1960s. In the Haight-Ashbury district of San Francisco, rent was inexpensive and business space readily available. The gay community tested the area in 1964 and found it tolerant of homosexual bars, although the neighborhood drove out a gay movie theater. Haight-Ashbury apathetically tolerated the hippie invasion in 1965 and 1966.

badly organized, but songs such as Lennon's "I Am the Walrus," with its childlike aspects that affirmed human unity, partially redeemed the production. The opening mantra of the song came to Lennon during an LSD drug trip. "I Am the Walrus" inspired later artists such as the Electric Light Orchestra, which was formed, the group said, to continue where "I Am the Walrus" left off.

The 1968 double single, "Hey Jude" and "Revolution," is considered one of the best single releases by Lennon and McCartney. "Revolution" was released during the same week that police clubbed protesters outside the Chicago Democratic Convention. "Revolution" urged change but not destruction—or else, as Lennon sings, "you can count me out." The underground Left saw this phrase as a compromise of radicalism and criticized Lennon for it.

"Revolution" advocated trust in people, however, not systems. Lennon knew that any form of government is as frail as the people who construct it. Therefore, he stressed individuals and causes more than radical ideologies.

An unnamed album, dubbed *The White Album,* reflected the influence of Indian guru Maharishi Mahesh Yogi (whom the Beatles would later denounce as dubious, at best). Its songs are simple, straightforward, and apparently the opposite of *Sgt. Pepper.* Yet *The White Album*'s "Helter Skelter," a John Cage-like cacophony of sound named after a spiral fairground slide in London, was to inspire mass murderer Charles Manson. When Manson heard the album in December 1968, he thought the Beatles were warning America of a racial conflict through the lyrics, "I'm coming down fast but don't let me break you." A frustrated musician himself, the criminally psychotic Manson believed the album had been written for him and his followers. They smeared key lyrics in blood at the scene of murders committed at his behest.

FLUXUS AND THE ONO FACTOR

Rock, which was a derivative of jazz, blues, rhythm and blues, classical, and Far Eastern music, also borrowed heavily from art movements such as Fluxus. Fluxus began in the 1950s and flourished in America in the 1960s. Influenced by the 1920s Dadaism that concentrated on Performance Art, Fluxus performances explored the absurd.

The audience might build and watch a fire or feed a piano, as in the *Piano Piece for David Tudor #1* by La Monte Young in October 1960. A bale of hay and a bucket of water were brought on stage for the piano to eat and drink. The performer could either feed the piano or leave it to eat by itself. The piece concludes after the piano finishes eating.

222

When rocker Jimi Hendrix (1942–70) set his guitar on fire at the Monterey Pop Festival, he was merely performing a variation of an earlier Fluxus performance in which a violin was set on fire. The mega-rock group the Who and the later grunge group Nirvana similarly destroyed their instruments on stage.

Fluxus performance altered the treatment of the audience. Patrons were doused with water, pelted with pennies, choked with sneezing powder, singed with acetylene torches, ordered to walk the plank, locked in cattle cars, and otherwise treated as impersonally as possible. Various musicians, including the Rolling Stones, have also

43. THE ROLLING STONES, whose real genius lay in their cult-rated contempt for their audience. Instead of grinning at the camera, they scowled. Instead of signing autographs, they spat. Instead of ending their televised performance at the London Palladium with the show business ritual of going out on the revolving stage to greet the fans, they turned their backs and stalked off.

been inspired by these tactics to exhibit arrogant rudeness toward their audience as part of their performance.

John Lennon and Yoko Ono (b. 1933), one of the most visible couples in the world in the early '70s, encouraged the combination of Fluxus art and music. They planted two acorns for peace in pots at a sculpture exhibit at Coventry Cathedral. One faced East and the other West, to symbolize that East and West had met through them. In early 1967, Lennon sponsored an Ono exhibition at London's Lisson Gallery. This included her "Half-Wind" project displaying a furnished room with each piece of furniture cut exactly in half.

Ono first encountered the Fluxus group while living in New York's avant-garde community. She gained the group's respect by lending her loft apartment for Happenings and by performing antics such as "Cut Piece" (circa 1964), in which the audience was invited to cut away her clothing a little at a time.

In 1964, Ono published a book of Fluxus instructions—projects such as: "Decide not to use one particular syllable for the rest of your life. Record things that happened to you as a result of that."[47]

In May 1968, with Lennon's wife, Cynthia, out of town, Ono and Lennon met at his country house and recorded the avant-garde and rather disconnected assortment of sounds known as *Two Virgins.* Thus began a relationship that changed their lives and music history. They had moved in together by June, and Lennon's first wife divorced him by August.

Their arrest later that year for drug possession was eclipsed when the *Two Virgins* album appeared on the market with a

44. John Lennon and Yoko Ono. The union of John Lennon and Yoko Ono, who in the early '70s were one of the most visible couples in the world, further encouraged the combinatinon of Fluxus art and music. Ono had been greatly impacted by the work of musician John Cage.

cover displaying Lennon and Ono completely nude. The nude photo was one of their first joint shock projects.

Yoko Ono was the first Beatle wife to influence their music and is often credited with contributing to the break-up of the Beatles. Ono followed John Cage's noise-is-music ideal. She acknowledged Alban Berg's (1885–1935) opera and traditional Japanese, Indian, and Tibetan singing as her most important influences. Ono experimented with original and nontraditional sounds in voice and instrument. This often resulted in her banshee-like screaming, which anticipated punk music and its later derivatives.

WOODSTOCK NATION

The Woodstock Rock Festival bridged the '60s to the '70s. The Festival was originally scheduled to take place in Woodstock, New York, a hip artists' community. Woodstock Ventures, however, cut a deal instead with Max Yasgur for the use of his dairy farm in Bethel. Abbie Hoffman blackmailed the event's organizers for $10,000; in return, he worked with them instead of disrupting the Festival. The organizers conceded because they understood that the Festival would "have to be nonpolitical to be political."[48] Hoffman generally limited his activities to organizing medical and food services for concert-goers.

The 400,000 young people who converged on the Yasgur farm on August 15–17, 1969, created the second largest city in New York, but with a crime rate much lower than the average city. (See color plate 27.) Despite drug overdoses and bad LSD trips, there were few fights, no riots, one accidental death, and one death from a heart attack. Woodstock was about peace, sex, and drugs—not necessarily in that order. Aware that they were making history, the Woodstock partners arranged for press coverage and negotiated a deal for a film. They even filmed the Festival preparations.

Less than six months after Woodstock, the Festival's name was synonymous with an entire generation. At his Chicago Eight trial, Abbie Hoffman claimed to reside in "Woodstock Nation." The Woodstock agenda had prevailed: the Dionysiac triad of sex, drugs, and rock 'n' roll now dominated private life and popular culture.

HIPPIES TO YUPPIES

Most people realize that an impossible-to-repeat national climate created Woodstock. America has now had peace so long that the culture counterbalances it with media violence. Free sex and cheap drugs are nothing to celebrate, since they can easily be obtained anywhere. With Bill Clinton's presidency, the Woodstock Nation became the Establishment.

Woodstock's commercial undertones foreshadowed the reality that the hippies of the 1960s would soon become the yuppie entrepreneurs of the materialistic 1970s and '80s. The counterculture's rebellious ideals eventually became just another facet of American consumerism.

The student and New Left rebels became the backbone of the so-called tenured Left, the establishment professors who came to control the universities in the '80s. Unfortunately, the political correctness movement of the '90s that yet permeates many university campuses imitates many things the New Left once opposed. Political correctness is an ironic twist to a movement that espoused free speech.

In spite of the hippies' and New Left's return to conventional life and American-style consumerism, the '60s generation unleashed a spirit of moral anarchy and political chaos that has shaped Western society ever since. The rebellious mood of the old counterculture now manifests itself in such areas as the white supremacy movement, the black separatist movement, and their many extremist offshoots. America has become tribalized in the process, a nation of competing interest groups.

Terrorism, such as the bombing of the Federal Building in Oklahoma City in April 1995 or the senseless shooting of students in April 1999 at Columbine High School in Littleton, Colorado, may be the face of the new revolution. These events may signify the final sequel to the social fragmentation of the 1960s. Today there is little talk of peace and love. Many of today's revolutionaries speak only of paranoia, power, and violence. Idealism seems to have given way to raw competition for the ability to control others.

Still from the video series *Grasping for the Wind*. John Whitehead discusses some of the pivotal figures that influenced modern thought. Included here are Hitler, Wagner, Nietzsche, and a scene from *Blade Runner*.

CHAPTER 7
The Narcissistic Culture

We now live in an age in which science is a court from which there is no appeal. And the issue this time around, at the end of the twentieth century, is not the evolution of the species... but the nature of our own precious inner selves.

TOM WOLFE[1]

For the Woodstock Generation, even public movements and events reflected the personal. This group imagined a world of several billion people defined and governed by their individual, subjective desires, the restraints of the past having been abolished in favor of unrestrained freedom to "do your own thing." But in the long run, that generation was not able to offer a social structure to replace the old one it wanted to destroy. Some disillusionment set in. And the most obvious way to shatter the bonds of the state and the power of parents, laws, and convention was a movement inward with sex and drugs. Thus, the '60s reaped a culture of narcissism that would extend through the '70s, '80s, '90s, and into the Third Millennium.

THE BIG CHILL

Director Lawrence Kasdan's 1983 film *The Big Chill* portrays the Woodstock Generation as it moved into adulthood. The film is about a reunion of '60s friends following the suicide of their comrade and guru, Alex, the only single member of the group who had kept the '60s faith. Harold, their generous weekend host, owns a chain of shoe stores and is the only one who is happily married. He is at home in the '80s—an investor, money-maker, and an integral part of his small town's community.

Nick is the antithesis of Harold. He is a bitter insomniac, graduate school dropout, and, for good measure, a Vietnam veteran who was wounded and became

228

impotent as a result. Nick sells drugs from his run-down sports car, feels totally adrift, and hates life. He inherits the deceased Alex's cabin and girl. There is nothing in Nick's fragmented life, however, that offers an alternative vision to Harold's complacent well-being.

Most of the characters have achieved some upper-middle-class, albeit superficial success—pop journalist, store owner, real estate lawyer, and television actor. None of them, though, works in social activist professions. Although they express some regret about betraying their '60s ideals, there is little sign that these characters—except for the dead Alex and the burned-out Nick—ever had any real politics to betray, except smoking dope, wearing their hair long, and attending the odd anti-war rally. The malaise most of them feel has more to do with their own psychic make-up than with conflicting values and ideals.

The film seems to affirm materialistic, middle-class yuppie values and to reject adherence to the ideals of the past. In other words, it represents the sell-out of the '60s counterculture as life faded into the yuppie-ism of the '70s and beyond. It is a perfect

45. SCENE FROM *THE BIG CHILL*. This well-crafted film affirms materialistic, middle-class yuppie values and rejects the notion of clinging to the ideals of the past.

expression of the temporary truce between bourgeois and bohemian individualism, as they joined together in a celebration of private life during the '80s and early '90s. This truce may have reached its symbolic climax when Bob Dylan performed at Bill Clinton's inaugural celebration.

Former yippie Jerry Rubin was a real-life manifestation of the truce. Best-selling books gave him new fame and earned him a lot of what he had once burned outside the New York Stock Exchange—money. "Money in my pockets mellowed out my radicalism," he said.[2] His creation, Network Party Inc., which staged a weekly party for young professionals at New York's Palladium, required a cover charge and business card for admittance. In his new life as a Wall Street market analyst and marketer for a health drink, Rubin explained without apology that he "change[d] lives every ten years."[3] Rubin died in 1994 at the age of fifty-six after he was hit by a car while jaywalking—his final small act of nonconformity.

Jimmy Carter's failed presidency of the late '70s marked the death of the mores of the '60s and introduced Ronald Reagan's culture of materialism. Indeed, the tone for the decade was set by Reagan's first inaugural. The event cost $8 million and opened with an $800,000 fireworks display at the Lincoln Memorial, followed by two nights of show business performances and topped off by nine inaugural balls serving 14,400 bottles of champagne. The inaugural exemplified both Reagan's aesthetic and moral perspective (anchored primarily in a '50s frame of reference), which was based on the notion that the beautiful was the expensive, the good was the costly. Thus, the '80s emphasis on financial success, consumption, and self-development defined the decade and set the tone for the '90s.

JOSEPH BEUYS: ARTIST AS SHAMAN

The art and music of the '80s attempted to deal with the culture of materialism. After 1970, painting became an increasingly specialized, academic activity, and computer games and the Internet were more interesting than paint dabs. Painting as a form of public discourse was dying.

Painters such as Frank Stella (b. 1936), however, with his three-dimensional or painted sculptures, and Keith Haring (1958–90), who died at thirty-two from AIDS but left the profound 1989 graffiti art painting *Silence-Death* (1989), sought to find a niche in public dialogue.

Artist Joseph Beuys (1921–86) dreamed that society could be transformed through art. A German sculptor-activist-teacher-guru, Beuys may be the most influential

230

post-modern artist. During World War II, Beuys had been shot down while on a mission over the blizzard-swept Crimea. He was rescued by nomadic Tartars who cared for him in their warm, felt-insulated tents. Afterward, Beuys viewed the human experience and organic life mystically. The courage and spiritual power he saw in the Tartars and the metaphoric meaning he found in the wild fauna they hunted and mythologized—especially the swan, stag, and hare—permeated his work.

Beuys eventually sought to rehumanize art and politics by creating untraditional works such as "Thinking Forms" and "Spoken Forms." He particularly worked at creating "Social Sculpture," which reflected how people mold the world they live in. For example, hoping to heal a country wounded by the Vietnam War, as the Tartars had healed him, Beuys came to New York in 1974 to perform his memorable and photogenic Performance Art piece, *Coyote: I Like America and America Likes Me.* This was a five-day "dialogue" with a live coyote from the American wild. Both "actors" were housed in a gallery and surrounded by folded sheets of felt, a bed of hay, and fifty copies daily of the latest *Wall Street Journal.* As the coyote slept on the felt, fouled on, or ate the *Wall Street Journal,* peered out the window in wonder at Manhattan's stone wilderness, or glowered at the gaggle of staring spectators, Beuys silently followed and mimicked, secure inside a felt tent that he held aloft like a tall sculpture. Beuys carried a kind of shepherd's-crook walking stick, before concluding with a smoke while he relaxed on the hay next to his now-companionable protagonist. Gradually, a flashlight shining from the pile of felt dimmed as its battery ran down, a poignant symbol of the human condition.

In the Native American's veneration of the coyote and the white man's persecution of the animal, Beuys saw a ruinous polarity of instinct and intellect that cried out for resolution. Beuys believed that everyone is an artist, and

46. JOSEPH BEUYS, *Coyote: I Like America and America Likes Me.* As the coyote slept on the felt, fouled on or ate the *Wall Street Journal,* peered out the window in wonder at Manhattan's stone "wilderness," or glowered at the gaggle of staring spectators, Beuys silently followed and mimicked, secure inside a felt tent that he held aloft, like a tall sculpture, with a kind of shepherd's-crook walking stick, before concluding with a smoke while he relaxed on the hay next to his now-companionable protagonist.

everything is in a stage of change. He allowed chemical reactions, fermentations, color alterations and decay to complete his art. This belief eventually introduced a political dimension to his work, for he transformed political agitation into a form of artistic activity, designating it Social Sculpture. In 1971, he founded the Organization for Direct Democracy through Referendum (People's Free Initiative) to challenge the existing political structure and party system: "Minorities [or top officials]...dominate unhindered the millions who make up the productive majority of the people. We call that a democracy. We consider it to be party dictatorship, pure and simple."[4] A wide range of museums and galleries hosted Beuys' political and social discourse. Some, such as the Museum of Modern Art, even preserved and displayed the blackboards upon which he had drawn diagrams to illustrate his points.

SULAMITH

Many artists imitated Beuys' new approach, although some of his followers, such as German Anselm Kiefer, reverted to more conventional means of artistic expression. The fatal collision of German and Jewish history fascinated Kiefer. For example, Romanian poet Paul Celan's famous poem "Death Fugue," written in a German concentration camp, inspired his 1983 painting, *Sulamith.* The poem states that "death is a master from Germany, your golden hair Margarete, your ashen hair Shulamith."[5]

Kiefer presents the blonde Margarete (the personification of Aryan womanhood) and the cremated Jewess, Shulamith (who is also the archetypal Beloved of the Song of Solomon) hauntingly and obliquely. Neither is portrayed as a figure. Margarete's presence is signaled by long wisps of golden straw, while Shulamith's emblem is a charred substance and black shadow.

THE FALL OF THE AVANT-GARDE

Beuys' work contrasted sharply with the mainstream absorption of avant-garde art. Like the Romantics of the early nineteenth century, the Modernists had defined themselves negatively. They opposed the bourgeoisie and regarded rejection and the ability to shock as a necessary condition for genius. While the first Modernists were alienated from the contemporary museum culture, by the mid-1960s they enjoyed strong support. Modernism became the official culture of America and Europe in the 1970s. Supported by tax breaks, enshrined in museums, scrutinized by a growing number of academics and students, underwritten by corporations and government agencies, and collected with ever-increasing interest, Modernist art enjoyed the strongest support that living art has ever known from its own society.

A vivid symbol of accessible modernism is the East Wing of the National Gallery in Washington, D.C. It was built in the late 1970s at a cost of more than $100 million—only a third the price of a nuclear submarine, to put it one way, but more than twice the gross national product of some African states, to put it another. All of this destroyed the "outsider" status of what used to be the vanguard. American museums, in particular, made rebel art fashionable. The official nature of the museum setting, however, inevitably compromised the avant-garde message. For example, Carl Andre's 1978 *Equivalent VIII* achieved status as art simply through its placement in a museum. While a Rodin sculpture in a parking lot would no doubt be a misplaced Rodin, *Equivalent VIII* in the same lot is simply a heap of bricks.

The 1929 founding of the Museum of Modern Art (MOMA) in New York City united the previously incompatible worlds of the museum and modern art. MOMA treated modern art as "historical" and thus resolved the tension that existed within the movement. By the '70s, modernism would look accessible, not problematic. Moreover, the historical study of modern art had expanded to the point where students were searching for unexploited thesis subjects. According to art historian Robert Hughes, "By the mid-eighties, twenty-one-year-old art-history majors would be writing papers on twenty-six-year-old graffists. The modernist ethos was no longer a side issue in art history; it had become an industry."[6]

Art's aesthetic value does not traditionally arise from its ability to shock or predict the future. Instead, it comes from deep within the work—its vitality, its intrinsic qualities, and its effect on the senses, intellect, and imagination. It is also important how a particular work uses the concrete body of tradition. In modernism, however, one usually finds only paradoxes. All that remain are the various reworkings of tradition in their outermost shell. Art, as such, is virtually incapable of speaking in utopian terms anymore.

The question is no longer how to make art, but whether it should be made at all—at least in the form familiar to us since the emergence of modernism. The age-old question "Why bother with art?" is no longer rhetorical. Instead, the veil is being lifted from its radical implications as a question of fundamental principle. Thus, contemporary artists continually search for new points of reference—politics and communication, eroticism and the human body, reality and the media, *ad infinitum.*

NEW IMAGES

The financial euphoria of the Reagan era boosted the art market and created an unprecedented link between art and commerce. Philip Guston (1913–80), Jean-Michel Basquiat (1960–88), Keith Haring, and Jeff Koons (b. 1955) all built on the work of Andy Warhol and created the American School of New Image. It promoted itself with industrial marketing strategies and used public relations techniques to present artists as stars and celebrities.

Object art replaced painting as the dominant medium in the late '80s and early '90s, highlighting art's manufactured quality and its proximity to the world of commodities. Art introspectively reflected its relationship with tradition and consumer capitalism. Thus, Koons' 1988 *Saint John the Baptist* (See color plate 28) depicts John the Baptist with a cross at his back (symbolizing Christianity) holding a pig (to symbolize capitalism) and pointing to heaven (the "almighty dollar"). The obvious import of Koons' work here is to satirize the often materialistic gloss of modern religion.

This introspection, combined with a new frankness concerning sexuality, inaugurated a distinctly erotic and openly gay art. Director Neil Jordan's 1992 film *The Crying Game* showed that these themes could be accessible to the general public. With the popularity of films such as *In and Out* (1997), *Boys Don't Cry* (1999), and others, homosexuality has moved closer to being an acceptable theme in popular culture.

Robert Mapplethorpe's (1946–89) rise as one of America's leading photographic artists underscored the growing gay art culture. Mapplethorpe's graphic photographs stunned audiences and were the subject of Congressional hearings on public art funding. His works include photographs of a man urinating into another man's mouth (1977), the fist of one male inserted in the anus of another (1978), and Mapplethorpe himself with a bullwhip inserted in his anus in mock simulation of Satan (1978).

Cindy Sherman (b. 1954), another pre-eminent photographer, also gained attention for her unusual works. Beginning with self-portraits that moved from the stereotypical to the bizarre, Sherman then photographed masks, false breasts and bellies, and bits of mannequins arranged as contorted allegorical figures of sexual horror. Her 1992 *Untitled (No. 264—Woman with Mask)* combines assembled body parts to criticize male attitudes toward female sexuality. *Untitled* shows a woman leering at the viewer as she gives birth to a grotesque, unidentifiable object.

Judy Chicago (b. 1939) introduced the most spectacular wave of feminist art with her massive environment-cum-installation *The Dinner Party* (1974–79) in homage to thirty-nine women she classified as major figures in Western history. (See color plate 29.) A triangular table accommodates thirty-nine place settings, each with a specially designed plate, goblet, and runner. The place settings are arranged thirteen to a side to invoke the image of a triple Eucharist. *The Dinner Party* includes an illuminated manuscript of a revised version of the biblical account of Genesis: a goddess replaces the traditional male God as the supreme creatrix, and feminist healing replaces Christ's second coming. The plates at Chicago's *Dinner Party* were inspired by the form of the female vulva and sought to celebrate women's achievements, long hidden in history. The work made the point of using skills that have been thought of as specifically female, such as stitchery and china painting, as an integral part of the presentation. *The Dinner Party* is now recognized as both a key event in the history of the women's movement and also a defining moment in the history of American art. As such, it signaled a return to content, long in abeyance since the Minimal Art movement of the late '60s.

Much feminist art depends heavily on transcendentalism and Christian theology and often depicts female deities. For example, Edwina Sandys' 1975 bronze *Christa* transforms the traditional male crucifix into a nude female figure.

It was obvious by the early '70s that women were producing some of their best new art. They had, so to speak, assumed the mantle of creativity previously reserved for male artists.

Male artists, however, also addressed subject matter by contravening traditional religious themes. For example, photographer Andre Serrano's 1987 *Piss Christ* showed a crucifix submerged in bright yellow urine. AIDS victim David Wojnarowicz's 1979 *Untitled* depicted Christ with a heroin needle in his arm and fueled opposition to federal funding for art.

Eventually, however, the viewing public became somewhat anesthetized by the striking images. By the 1990s, art shows such as "True Phallacy: The Myth of Male Power" could not garner much controversy. As one art critic noted: "Works of art of these sorts—that refer to pain and porn and other zones of the forbidden—today are rather chic."[7]

DEHUMANIZATION IN ART

Art such as Polish artist Magdalena Abakanowicz's *Backs* (1976–80) expresses more introspectively the tragic depths of the universal human condition. Made from coarse brown burlap, *Backs* shows a huddled mass of hunched-over half-figures, downtrodden, headless, limbless, and sexless. Abakanowicz suggests that modern regimentation and repression reduces people to pathetic victims.

Dehumanization also gives way to prophecies of a cracked-up culture in Philip Guston's (1913–80) 1977 painting *The Street*, which resembles a war between city gangs or bums. (See color plate 30.) A cluster of knobby legs in boots opposes a phalanx of arms with trash-can lids as shields. In American painting of the '70s, Guston stands out above all others in terms of his intensity. His leap back into figure painting from abstract work, such as *Painting* (1954), to classic works such as *Painting, Smoking, Eating* (1973) or *Pit* (1976), influenced an entire new generation of painters.

Because of the bankruptcy of innovation, many artists in the '80s attempted to delve into feeling, even at the risk of appearing "conservative." This was expressed in painting, almost unnoticed at first, by artists in England. For example, Great Britain produced some of the best figurative artists in the world, including Francis Bacon, David Hockney, R. B. Kitaj, Frank Auerbach, and Lucian Freud (b. 1922).

Lucian Freud was a master of detachment, and his 1980 *Naked Portrait with Reflection* details every vein, inch of sagging flesh, and tuft of body hair. He left the face until last, wanting the "expression to be in the body. The head must be just another limb."[8]

Realist painting also re-emerged in America, as in Philip Pearlstein's (b. 1924) 1977–78 *Female Nude on a Platform Rocker*, which analytically dehumanizes its subject. Eric Fischl's (b. 1951) paintings portray the crisis of American identity, the failure of the American dream. His 1981 *Bad Boy*, with a young man peering at a naked prostitute whose legs are spread on a bed, is an adult-hating sour farce packed with erotic misery.

POSTMODERNISM

By the 1980s, postmodernism arose as a reaction against modernist art. The movement denied all previous arts criteria. For example, the rise of Pop Art obliterated architectural hegemony, as architects like Philip Johnson adorned skyscrapers with Chippendale pediments. Johnson, the co-inventor of the term "international style," also designed the AT&T Building (1978–83) in New York City, giving the Manhattan skyline an unstructured horizon.

Postmodernism eventually spread outside the arts. By the 1990s, there were postmodern artists, philosophers, social scientists, anthropologists, and historians. Literary criticism enthusiastically adopted postmodernism. Just as the Romantics had retreated from the structured world of Swift, Pope, and Samuel Johnson, the postmodernists departed from T. S. Eliot and James Joyce. They turned to barbarian and titillating popular literature instead.

While modernist writers had attempted to restructure a society plagued by war, loss of religious faith, and general chaos, postmodernists produced blatantly self-centered works and abandoned the goal of improvement. Henry Miller, for example, an early trendsetter, wrote almost exclusively about himself. Postmodernism, by contrast, reduced literature to the level of the common man, closing the gap between entertainment and serious art. Like Pop Art, literary postmodernism imitated whatever sold to the general public and posed a fundamental skepticism about the existence of an objective reality. The essence of postmodernism was to search for ways to express what could not possibly be expressed in terms of the past—the reality of the twentieth century.

CULTURE OF NARCISSISM

In July 1979, President Jimmy Carter, a self-professed "born again" Christian, gave a speech ostensibly on energy policy. The speech, however, actually addressed the ills of self-indulgence: "The erosion of our confidence in the future is threatening to destroy the social and political fabric of America...we have learned that piling up material goods cannot fill the emptiness of lives which have no confidence or purpose."[9]

The collapse of the New Left and the '60s counterculture contributed to a collective narcissism. Western culture now craved intimacy but refused sacrifice; demanded material plenty but rejected productivity; sought success but denied accomplishment. Hedonistic consumerism and self-preservation were celebrated. This was sometimes reflected in an obsessive interest in the body through exercise and natural diets and in personal identity and authenticity issues. Activists simply replaced political action with personal therapy and sought peace and fulfillment in the self.

Traditional religions like Judaism and Christianity seemed outdated and irrelevant, even to many who continued to believe. For example, Erhard Seminars Training, or EST—$300 two-weekend conferences at luxury hotels—was supposedly one way to reach higher levels of consciousness. Strict rules about food and bathroom breaks, revelations of personal pain to the group, and the leader's consistent response of "So what?" allegedly convinced participants that adversity was simply a matter of perspective that could be overcome. Predicated on the destruction of the ego, EST promised that "until you know that who you are is empty and meaningless, you don't know anything." Once the trainee discovered the empty "space" of his being, he was supposedly prepared to transform his life and create his own reality.

Popular literature also reflected a narcissistic preoccupation, as evidenced by self-actualization guru Dr. Wayne W. Dyer, whose well-known books *Your Erroneous Zones* (1976), *Pulling Your Own Strings* (1978), and *The Sky's the Limit* (1980) provided a self-test for determining whether the reader was a "victim" or "non-victim."

While Dyer advised Americans on how to reorder all areas of their lives, other best-selling authors concentrated on business. Robert J. Ringer's *Winning Through Intimidation* encouraged the average businessman to trample competition, client, and co-worker alike, in the name of profit. Ringer's 1977 *Looking Out for Number One* and his 1979 *Restoring the American Dream* both made the best-seller lists. Thomas Peters' and Robert Waterman's 1982 *In Search of Excellence* and biographies of financial wizards Donald Trump and former Chrysler CEO Lee Iacocca celebrated business success stories.

Nostalgia, however, tinged the unprecedented material wealth of the '70s and '80s. Historical fiction like Peter Jenkins' 1979 memoir *Walk Across America* and Garrison Keillor's humorous *Lake Wobegon Days* (1985) recaptured the charm of small-town America. At the same time, horror writers such as Stephen King (b. 1947), who is believed to be the best-selling author of all time, appealed to modern insecurities that infested even the rural countryside. "We make up horrors," wrote King in *Danse Macabre* (1981), "to help us cope with the real ones."[10]

One of the most popular books of the 1970s was about a seagull who perfected his flying by propelling himself to higher levels of being. Richard Bach's 1970 *Jonathan Livingston Seagull,* the top-selling fiction book in 1972 and 1973, mixes Eastern mysticism and European psychology with the consciousness movement. After conquering time and space by climbing to new levels of consciousness, Jonathan returns to his flock as messiah-rejected and earns the title "Son of the Great Gull." Bach suggested that the messiahs of the world religions simply achieved a higher consciousness that every person could reach. As if in response, Kenneth Taylor's *The Living Bible* hit the top of the nonfiction best-seller list for 1972. It maintained that position in 1973 with its readable modern prose paraphrases of the Bible.

Before the Beatles popularized Transcendental Meditation, the majority of religious Americans were either Jewish or Christian. But in the 1970s, the young Aquarians of the '60s heralded a new age of consciousness, as epitomized by two 1972 best-sellers: Ruth Montgomery's *A World Beyond* and Carlos Castaneda's *Journey to Ixtlan*. By 1975, Transcendental Meditation's instruction manual, *TM: Discovering Energy and Overcoming Stress*, also made the best-seller list.

Thomas Harris' 1969 *I'm O.K., You're O.K.* made the best-seller list for three years beginning in 1971, encouraging readers to see themselves as three separate people: the selfish, irrational Child, the tyrannical Parent, and the rational Adult. It became the premiere self-help book of the '70s. Other best-sellers reflected the sexual and mystical preoccupations of the '70s, including David Reuben's *Everything You Always Wanted to Know About Sex but Were Afraid to Ask* (1969), "J's" *The Sensuous Woman* (1969) and *The Sensuous Man* (1971), Alex Comfort's *The Joy of Sex* (1974), Shere Hite's *The Hite Report* (1976), Irene Kassorla's *Nice Girls Do* (1980), and Gay Talese's *Thy Neighbor's Wife* (1980).

Alex Haley's (1921–92) *Roots* told the major nonwhite success story of the '70s. It was made into a phenomenally successful television mini-series, with Nielsen ratings reporting more than 40 percent of television households. Female African-American authors such as Toni Morrison (b. 1931) and Alice Walker (*The Color Purple,* 1982) depicted black women's struggle for identity and produced some of the most important literature of the '70s and '80s.

THE ERA AND THE RISE OF THE NEW RIGHT

Many women returned to the battle for political power in the '70s. After the women's movement had secured the right to vote in 1920, many of the activists simply returned to their homes. The ones who remained active in the women's movement were divided in their goals. On the one hand, the League of Women Voters, formerly the National American Woman Suffrage Association, dedicated itself to lobbying for better working conditions for women and children. On the other, activists such as Alice Paul (1885–1977) advocated more militancy. Paul proposed the first Equal Rights Amendment in 1923, which simply said: "Men and women shall have equal rights throughout the United States and every place subject to its jurisdiction."

Attempts to pass an ERA consistently failed. During the late '70s, Phyllis Schlafly (b. 1924) led one of the first New Right pressure groups to oppose the last ERA proposed. By uniting her Catholic faith with politics, Schlafly turned the debate into a moral battle. Religious conservatives might have ignored her campaign had it not been for the other great issue of the early '70s—abortion. The 1973 *Roe v. Wade* Supreme Court decision jolted religious conservatives from their confidence that the ERA would be defeated. Schlafly's New Right used the government's legalization of abortion to condemn the feminists. Her organization virtually singlehandedly defeated the ratification of the ERA in 1982. It fell three states short of the thirty-eight needed for ratification.

American feminists, however, have succeeded in achieving many of the goals of the ERA through court decisions and laws benefiting women and banning discrimination. Legalized abortion, for instance, was a major feminist victory, even though opposition to it provided both the impetus and the ideological basis for the Christian Right, as the movement came to be known. By the late '70s, the Christian Right had emerged full-force by influencing Republican Party politics and helping to usher Ronald Reagan into the White House.

But by the late '80s, the Christian Right's influence seemed to wane. The first sign that it was diminishing came with the dismantling of the Moral Majority in 1989. And with Bill Clinton's ascendancy to the presidency and his survival of the impeachment process, the Christian Right was all but finished. The splintering of the Christian Coalition in 1999 may be evidence that in the Third Millennium the Christian Right may have little, if any, influence. George W. Bush's ascendancy to the White House in the 2000 election, however, with his outspokenness about his "born again" experience and his opposition to abortion, can be seen as a survival, of sorts, of the Christian Right's yet lingering political potency.

Although abortion continues to be one of America's social concerns, feminist and abortion issues are even more critical in other countries. For example, in China, a society historically more patriarchal than Western culture, the Communist revolution supposedly afforded women equal rights before the women had even sought them. The Great Leap Forward of the late 1950s established communal child care, laundry, sewing, and food services in cities and villages throughout China. But traditional family and social structures were dismantled.

Leaders who hoped to increase production by mobilizing the largely untapped female labor force encouraged women to "liberate" themselves by proving their productive and commercial equality. It was ultimately a governmental economic ploy. The Chinese state quickly asserted its "right" to control every aspect of the family, including the "right" to end a woman's pregnancy through forced abortion and sterilization. Today, aborted fetuses are a lucrative commodity in China, with some reports claiming that aborted fetuses have been sold to be eaten as a health remedy. The Chinese government exercises the same inhumane economic expediency through executing its

240

prisoners and selling their organs. Yet one Chinese official, defending his country's human rights violations, has asserted that China surpasses the United States in sexual equality.

A CLOCKWORK ORANGE

In addition to the feminists, the splintered Western culture of the 1970s included marginal punk groups that celebrated chaos and anarchy. The now classic film *A Clockwork Orange* anticipated this intense youth movement. Anthony Burgess's original 1968 book and Stanley Kubrick's 1971 film version of it portray an anarchistic and nihilistic future in which people are all potential destroyers and lovers of violence.

47. Scene from *A Clockwork Orange* with Alex (actor Malcolm McDowell). Concerning his film, director Stanley Kubrick remarked: "We have a highly complex civilization which requires an equally complex social structure and political authority... yet against that the goal should be to destroy all authority, so man in his natural goodness may emerge...this Utopian view is a dangerous fallacy...[All such efforts] eventually fall into the hands of thugs.... The weaknesses [don't stem] from an improperly structured society.... The fault is in the very imperfect nature of man himself."[11]

A gang of youth punks called "droogs" conduct orgies of destruction. The police must themselves resort to periodic violence and technological manipulation in order to keep the peace.

Alex, the head tough, brilliantly played by actor Malcolm McDowell, is particularly sadistic. In one scene, the gang members enter the home of a writer. Wearing a grotesque phallic face mask, Alex throws books and a typewriter to the floor. Casually singing "Singin' in the Rain," he does a violent soft-shoe to the writer's stomach and face, leaving him writhing on the floor. After mocking the man, he viciously rapes his wife, while another gang member restricts her.

Several more acts of sexual violence and brutality result in Alex's imprisonment, during which he agrees to undergo a special experimental treatment. The electrodes and pain of the treatment have their intended effect: Alex is so afraid of physical pain that he is no longer violent.

The prison chaplain, however, objects to the obviously dehumanizing process, voicing his concern that Alex's fear has deprived him of the ability to make choices on a moral basis. A state official responds: "Padre, these are subtleties. We're concerned with cutting down crime." The official is applauded and puts his arm around a now shy Alex. "He will be your true Christian, ready to be crucified rather than crucify! Reclamation! The point is that it works!" At the end of the film, the operation is reversed, however, and Alex reverts to his previous violence.

Kubrick believed the film's most powerful meaning was its "psychological myth":

> Alex represents natural man in the state in which he is born: unlimited, unrepressed. When Alex is given the Ludovico Treatment, you can say that this symbolizes the neurosis created by the conflict between the structures imposed by our society, and our primal natures. This is why we feel exhilarated when Alex is "cured" in the final scene.[12]

Some critics viewed the film as criminally irresponsible and stupidly naive. They feared that Alex would become a folk hero for a generation raised on the adventures of Bonnie and Clyde. Most critics, however, missed the fundamental concept of the novel and the film, which was the basic paradox of free will—the importance of a human being's power to choose, even if it is only violence and destruction.

Kubrick suggests the traditional religious concept of original sin (that people are innately bad), but without invoking any kind of redemption. Thus, Kubrick presents a problem without a solution. Later films such as Abel Ferrara's insightful *Bad*

Lieutenant and Quentin Tarantino's violent *Reservoir Dogs,* both released in 1992, as well as Oliver Stone's *U Turn* (1997), David Fincher's *Fight Club* (1999), Mary Harron's disturbing *American Psycho* (2000), and Darren Aronofsky's *Requiem for a Dream* (2000), equally disconcerting, also present a chaotic world with doomed, unredeemable characters.

SETTING THE STAGE FOR PUNK

As some critics anticipated, many members of the rising youth subculture identified with *A Clockwork Orange* and its character Alex. This was true especially in Great Britain, where the punk movement extended the impact of the film. Zandra Rhodes, a punk fashion designer, noted: "Punk was an antidesign movement. Isn't the movement from punk just an extension of the *Clockwork Orange* film by Stanley Kubrick that came around a bit before that period?"[13] The film combined with other cultural events to establish the punk style.

Punk initially gleaned its impetus from the New York punk scene of the late '60s. Singer/songwriter Lou Reed (b. 1944) emerged as a leader in what would eventually become punk. Reed, for instance, named his band the Velvet Underground after a pornographic book. The group produced a sound, notes author Martha Bayles, with "dark, devastating glamour that absolutely reflects a time and place—New York City in the mid to late '60s—that are gone forever."[14] In his songs, Reed recounted, in a dry, dispassionate voice, details of his mundane life, which just happened to be full of drag queens, pimps, and hypodermic needles. His songs represented the complete rejection of the spiritual high ground that the 1960s counterculture had staked out, however ineptly.

Andy Warhol engineered much of what the New York scene became and helped set the tone for the punks. Oliver Stone caught the essence of Warholian thinking in a scene from his 1991 film, *The Doors,* in which Warhol hands a toy phone to Jim Morrison at a party, saying "I can talk to God on this phone, but I don't have anything to say."

Iggy Pop and Richard Hell proved that the avant-garde New York scene wanted Performance Art and eventually "noise rock," not rock music. Iggy Pop assembled the Stooges, a band of non-musicians, to explore primitivism and create chaos. Their "concerts" were, for all practical purposes, one big noise that throbbed and filled the room. The music-noise provided a context for Iggy, who engaged in random acts on stage such as rubbing his chest with a drumstick until he started to bleed or inflicting a gash on his head.

Richard Hell, the vocalist for the semi-punk, art-rock group Television, added a new element that would become a staple of the British punk movement: ripped clothing. The point of these performances was to shock. In the words of shock-rock performer Alice Cooper: "We were upper middle class suburban brats that had anything we wanted. We never had a blues. The whole end is that we are what we are now—a living social criticism."[15]

Frank Zappa's (1940–93) work would also exude an influence on the punk movement. In Los Angeles in 1966, Zappa released *Freak Out!*, one of the first rock double albums. The record included sentimental pop, social protest, and audience provocation ("You're Probably Wondering Why I'm Here"). Between tracks, Zappa and producer Tom Wilson inserted dialogue and sound effects. Zappa was a multi-talented and innovative musician whose career yielded patches of brilliance. His musical taste was ever in thrall to his compulsive need to satirize virtually everything. His album, *We're Only In It For The Money* (1967), satirized two sacred cows of his day: the hippies and the Beatles' *Sgt. Pepper.*

During the mid-'60s, Zappa's group, the Mothers of Invention, deliberately aggravated audiences with their bizarre onstage antics. Zappa reflected the Performance Art of the early Dadaists and the musical ideology of John Cage. He also popularized the use of obscene lyrics. Zappa sang "Why Does It Hurt When I Pee" and "Shove It Right In," while the Beatles sang "All You Need Is Love." Zappa helped to further "shock rock" by signing such acts as Alice Cooper to his record label. In turn, John Lydon (aka Johnny Rotten) of the Sex Pistols cited Cooper for helping to inspire his punk music and lifestyle.

48. FRANK ZAPPA (left) and the Mothers of Invention. On stage there is the possibility that anything can happen. Dolls are mutilated. A gas mask is displayed. A bag of vegetables is unpacked and examined. There are spaced intervals of "honks" and suddenly the Mothers perform "Dead Air." They stop, sit down, and ignore the audience. Zappa might get a shoeshine from Motorhead, the percussionist. They keep this going for as long as it takes for the audience to become unsettled, uncomfortable, and angry. Then Zappa calmly approaches the mike and says: "It brings out the hostilities in you, doesn't it?"

244 American punk, however, not only introduced a new sound but also a new racism. At clubs such as New York's CBGB, performers wore swastikas and other Nazi regalia like that sported by Iggy Pop and the New York Dolls. Nico, the female singer for the Velvet Underground, told a reporter in 1979 that she thought of blacks as "a whole different race.... I don't like the features. They're so much like animals...it's cannibals, no?"[16] The Ramones (named after an early pseudonym of Beatle Paul McCartney) also popularized racism and abuse with songs such as "Beat the Brat," "Gimme Shock Treatment," and "Now I Wanna Sniff Some Glue."

THE SEX PISTOLS

The emerging British punk movement found its first home in the "Sex" clothing and apparel shop run by art fashion designer Malcolm McLaren (b. 1946). McLaren had visited New York and was inspired by what he saw and heard there. According to Johnny Rotten (b. 1956), the Sex Pistols' lead singer, "Sex" sold "rubber wear and bondage gear which, of course, was highly appealing to any teenager who wanted to be decadent." "Sex" stocked pornographic T-shirts, whips, and vises. Its walls were festooned with hardcore pornography. The gear, however, was not supposed to stimulate in the sexual sense; it was more of a statement. As rocker Chrissie Hynde recognized: "[It was] two fingers up at the Establishment."[17] Thus, with all its rips and safety pins, punk was a creative movement that began largely in the streets. Young people were expressing themselves with something within their price range.

Although their recording career lasted less than three years, the Sex Pistols, some rock historians believe, had a greater impact

49. THE SEX PISTOLS. The Pistols stood for no rules and a negativity toward the establishment. Although anarchy was their stance, the Pistols, contrary to what some have written, claimed they were not nihilists. They wanted something other than the total destruction of all of society's institutions. As Johnny Rotten writes: "What we wanted as a band was not mass acceptance, but understanding."[18]

on British rock than anyone since the Beatles. Morever, the Pistols' 1978 American tour, although a financial disaster for the group, burst the seams of American culture and opened the door for punk, grunge, and all that was to follow in the music world. The Pistols expressed an intense negativity toward the Establishment. But not intending to be nihilists, they wanted something other than the total destruction of all social institutions. According to Johnny Rotten: "We weren't there to destroy their way of life or anything like that. Quite the opposite. We sought to bring a little freshness into their boring, daily routines."[19]

Hoping to challenge the established order, the group sang songs like "God Save the Queen." The British political hierarchy was understandably concerned when the lyrics called the Queen a fascist and indicated that she was "not a human being." The song, however, was more than a broadside against the Queen. The lyrics argued that the system had made people "morons." Thus, there is "no future," as Rotten would opine. Not surprisingly, "God Save the Queen" was banned on British radio stations.

The Sex Pistols projected anger and rock-bottom working-class hate. As black rappers and hip-hop singers would do years later, the Pistols seethed with frustration for class injustice and at the hypocrisy they saw in the "rock star" status of the music establishment. The Pistols defied students, addressing instead teenagers and the working class. Rotten notes: "Our worst enemies were university students and the general public."[20] The Sex Pistols were the Theatre of Rage, and Johnny Rotten directed his anger at the church and traditional religion as well: "The smell of church used to annoy me.... Church was a place where women wore hideous hats.... That's my view of religion. I've never had any godlike epiphanies or thought that God had anything to do with this dismal occurrence called life."[21]

Eventually, punk's obscenity and sadomasochistic violence overshadowed its philosophical aspects. McLaren's partner, Vivienne Westwood, said: "If there is one thing that frightens the Establishment, it's sex. Religion you can knock, but sex gives them horrors."[22] Denying the emotional, psychological, spiritual, and even physical intimacy of sex, Rotten defined sex as merely two and a half minutes of squeaky noises—thus dehumanizing something once thought to be sacred and truly human. Sid Vicious (1955–79), the Sex Pistols' bass guitarist, became the prototype self-destructive individualist, dying of a heroin overdose after being charged with fatally stabbing Nancy Spungen, his live-in lover, a prostitute who had hooked him on heroin.

FROM PUNK TO GRUNGE TO BECK

The Sex Pistols, however, earned respect from key members of the older avant-garde. The legendary Pete Townshend of the Who told Sex Pistol John Lydon that he was "his hero." Former Beatle Paul McCartney, according to Lydon, was also entranced by him.

British and American post-punk or "new wave" groups such as Blondie, the Talking Heads, and Elvis Costello quickly mainstreamed punk. The Clash and the Police experimented with African-American music and Jamaican reggae under the guise of punk style. Music television and music videos further popularized the punk mode.

50. NIRVANA. Bandleader Kurt Cobain's suicide cut short the group's phenomenal rise.

Post-'70s avant-garde rock, such as "noise," "thrash," and "hardcore," is a direct offshoot of punk. Hardcore and heavy metal eventually fused into "thrash metal," which is heavy metal played at 78 rpm with sweltering sheets of electronic noise. Although their concerts often erupt into mayhem, thrash groups such as Anthrax, Motorhead, and Pantera claim their music addresses important cultural issues.

Alternative rock gave way to grunge, which emerged full-force in 1991 with the mega-group Nirvana. By that time, it seemed the music was no longer the point. Instead, it was noise compounded with violent and often obscene lyrics. Nirvana's first album, *Nevermind,* was expected to sell 200,000 copies but actually sold over 10 million, knocking Michael Jackson off the top of the album chart. After *Nevermind's* fame, however, Nirvana crossed the forbidden line from punk into "pop" by writing melodic and harmonic songs. They retained their morbid themes, however, singing about rape, violence, and suicide.

The 1994 suicide of Nirvana's talented leader, Kurt Cobain (1967–94), at age twenty-seven stalled the group's roller coaster ride. Cobain in part inspired the nihilism and pessimism of the groups to follow, including Pearl Jam, Hole, and Stone Temple Pilots, along with Nirvana replicas Bush and Silverchair. Pearl Jam continued the grunge tradition. Lead singer Eddie Vedder has a strong, expressive voice reminiscent of Jim Morrison. Pearl Jam's music and noise, however, sometimes suffocate Vedder's often startling and depressing lyrics. In the same way that Bob Dylan once protested war and racism, Nirvana publicly backed homosexuality. And Pearl Jam, like the group U2, took strong stands on social issues such as abortion, even distributing condoms at its concerts.

U2, one of the most influential bands of the '80s and quite possibly the '90s, was a direct offshoot of punk. By the '90s, however, U2 had departed from punk's original "do it yourself" ethic by using high-tech devices and mimicking the Pop Art of the '60s. In 1997, for example, U2's Popmart Tour featured a twelve-foot-wide internally-lit, stuffed olive on a 100-foot-tall toothpick and a 35-foot-high lemon-shaped mirror ball that rolled into the crowd. The mirror ball opened to reveal U2, who strolled down a staircase singing "discothèque," the opening song off their Pop album. The concert-goer found U2 had gone more than full circle, incorporating the '70s music and scene that punk had rebelled against.

Despite the new styles of rock music, the audience seems to respond primarily to the message, not the medium. The obscure genre of "industrial rock" has recently flourished because of its lyrical content. Industrial rockers rarely mention the nihilist origin of their music because, as Martha Bayles notes, "they don't want to be associated with fascism or (worse) optimism."[23] The rockers frequently cite Dada, however. Their music's pure noise and the grotesque, surreal character of videos by groups such as Nine Inch Nails and Marilyn Manson clearly reflect Dadaism.

"Techno" or "electronica" stresses the medium over the message. Proffered by groups such as the Chemical Brothers, the Underworld, and Prodigy and borrowed by U2, techno songs often have no words at all and rely instead on electronic repetition and the oldest of musical forms, the beat.

Beck Hansen (b. 1970) has emerged as a transitional figure, a bridge. Although often linked with Nirvana's Kurt Cobain—primarily for his 1993 song "Loser" with its self-deprecating refrain "I'm a loser baby, so why don't you kill me?"—Beck actually shares little with Nirvana's former frontman. Where Cobain's lyrics and tone are consistently straightforward and pessimistic, Beck's (while sometimes dark) border on the undecipherable and are suffused with humor. Musically, the differences continue. While Nirvana played primarily guitar-driven rock 'n' roll, Beck displays a multi-dimensionality. His 1996 album *Odelay* managed to combine nearly every type of music imaginable—folk, blues, jazz, rock, rap, R&B, lounge, etc.—so that each song is a mishmash of musical styles. Producing music in the electronic, techno age, Beck, therefore, is heavily influenced by the past. Also of note is Beck's connection to Fluxus and Andy Warhol. His grandfather, Al Hansen, was a celebrated artist and member of an experimental Fluxus performance group.

Beck, who won two Grammys in 1997, has stated his affinity for older forms of music. He supposedly wanted his album *Odelay* to "be the kind of album they made in the '60s, when people experimented with whatever they felt like—folk, country, chamber music, Eastern sounds."[24] Beck is also important for his link between white and black music, which he has continued to demonstrate in grand fashion on two further albums, the folk-drenched *Mutations* (1998) and the rhythm and blues–flavored *Midnite Vultures* (1999). This was something the Beatles, Rolling Stones, and Bob Dylan were so adept at providing.

One of the more important musical developments in the latter half of the twentieth century was the emergence of rap, or hip-hop. Originating in the late '70s and early '80s, rap experienced its most creative time in the mid- to late '80s when a number of groups advanced musically. Run-DMC and the Beastie Boys both reached incredible commercial and critical success by fusing rap with rock.

Led by groups like Public Enemy and NWA, rap also became a primary vehicle of black social commentary, whether embracing Nation of Islam's Louis Farrakhan (Public Enemy's "Bring the Noise") or criticizing police brutality (NWA's "F—Tha Police"). By the early '90s, former NWA member Dr. Dre had emerged as one of the leading producers in music. Along with rappers Ice Cube (also of NWA) and Ice-T, Dr. Dre—on his own projects and with Snoop Doggy Dogg—established "gangsta rap" as a popular musical form, known as much for its offensive lyrics as for its musical sophistication. Despite the objections of political pundits (for songs like Ice-T's "Body Count," which advocated the genocide of police), by the end of the decade, hip-hop was the highest selling form of music in the world. As the blues music of the '30s and '40s led to the advent of rock 'n' roll, rap and hip-hop spawned a group of white-led rap-rock groups such as Limp Bizkit, Korn, and Kid Rock (who dubbed the music "Hick Hop"). Produced by Dr. Dre, white rapper Eminem has emerged in the Third Millenium as both a critical and commercial success. But like his precursors, he faces severe criticism for what is deemed offensive content. His reference to gays as "faggots" and demeaning women as "sluts" to be abused and killed on his album *The Marshall Mathers LP* (2000) has generated a storm of protest from gay rights and feminist groups.

The punk freshness of groups like Nirvana and Pearl Jam, the electronic sound of Beck, and even the brashness of some of the hip-hop artists present viable alternatives to the bland, commercially motivated, videogenic generation of singers such as Prince, Madonna, Mariah Carey, and the Spice Girls. Punk's initial popularity and lasting impact, however, seem to prove a new maxim: the underground music of one generation is the pop music of the next.

MTV: SURREALISM AND THE MASSES

The music of everything from punk to the Spice Girls, Britney Spears, 'N Sync, Christina Aguilera, the Backstreet Boys, and others has been magnified by music television. The progenitor of the medium, MTV, introduced surrealism to the masses. Its advertising announcement in *Billboard* magazine promised advertisers a very desirable demographic group: "The best of both worlds—the 'low taste' audience selectivity of radio and magazines, and the broader reach of television."[25]

The MTV audience has faithfully consumed not only the recordings of Nirvana, Marilyn Manson, Nine Inch Nails, Pearl Jam, Madonna, and others but also athletic shoes, hair mousse, breath freshener, jeans, and all the must-have items for a street-smart lifestyle. MTV style—with its quick cuts, extravagant imagery, and aggressive music beats—has saturated television and is now used to sell not only pop recordings and lifestyle paraphernalia but also cake mix, dog food, automobiles, and deodorant. MTV even has its own line of memorabilia.

MTV was already the hot venue for pop music when Michael Jackson's (b. 1958) *Thriller* album sold an unmatched 40 million copies in 1983. After *Thriller*'s seven top-ten singles and accompanying videos, music required successful videos in order to compete. Image had overpowered music.

Madonna (b. 1958) has released more videos on MTV than any other artist. She extended the punk legacy of exhibitionism to the extreme through her videos and interviews. As one commentator noted: "Madonna is impressive.... The black-leather bimbo cracks her whip, and the media lion jumps through her hoop."[26] Madonna has also become one of the most potent mythmakers in pop history. Besides constantly remodeling herself, she changed how people think—especially about sexuality and sexual stereotypes. Her 1992 book *Sex* provoked readers to reexamine their definitions of what is permissible, of what is and is not "pornographic," "erotic," and, in an era of sexual risk, "responsible." As the Third Millennium dawned, Madonna adopted the image of "motherhood"; however, without relinquishing her former image.

Though MTV may not go as far as artists such as Madonna would like, it sanctions exhibitionism in a theater of the surreal. French surrealists of the 1930s incorporated sound technology into films to create bizarre juxtapositions and activate the subconscious. This same concept permeates MTV videos and art rock films. A classic example is Pink Floyd's film *The Wall* (1982), a surreal, impressionistic tour de force about a British boy who grows up to become a Nazi-like rock star.

As a result of promoting exhibitionism and surrealism, MTV, as authors Jane and Michael Stern

51. MADONNA ON MTV. The most successful woman in the history of popular music, Madonna was able to reach a level of wide popularity while exploring all sorts of explosive subjects, including sex, family, female identity, and Catholicism.

note, has earned a reputation for promoting "occult and degenerate perverts whose leering, sweat-drenched, snake-kissing, tongue-wagging, microphone-stand-humping performances encourage viewers to think evil thoughts and presumably to become immoral people."[27] The National Coalition on Television Violence found that 40 percent of the videos they studied contained acts of aggression, and 39 percent of the aggressive acts were sexual.

THE MANUFACTURED REALITY OF TELEVISION

The claims that were once made for television—its educational, cultural, and informative values—have virtually all proven false. The entertainment component of the equation has so thoroughly dominated every aspect of television, and the mass media generally, that literally everything has become reduced to slick and powerful images. The medium has indeed become the message. The simple lesson is that no technology, however beneficial, comes without serious consequences.

TV has thoroughly permeated Western culture through the general and widespread adoption of its general format and look by such newspapers as *USA Today* and magazines like *Business Week.* It is now virtually impossible to distinguish where television leaves off and general culture begins. As such, television not only generally informs Western culture, it creates its own reality.

Although some television content makes positive contributions, its detrimental effects may be more dominant. Television blurs the boundaries between fact and fiction. For example, a 1989 *Times-Mirror* poll revealed that 50 percent of those who watched so-called "reality" or crime re-creation television shows such as *Rescue 911* believed they were watching the actual event, despite a televised disclaimer. This deliberate creation of unreality is one of the most pivotal social forces shaping our times.

Shows that are infused with sensationalism such as *Cops, Caught On Tape, Most Amazing Videos, Confessions,* and others shamelessly violate people's privacy in order to amuse audiences and appeal to the basest in human nature. And with shows such as *Survivor* and *Big Brother,* viewers became voyeurs as they invaded the most intimate and private areas of human behavior.

Unfortunately in the West, television has, in part, caused what seems to be a virtually psychopathic fascination with violence and fantasy. As a consequence, our inability to face problems directly, honestly, and intelligently raises the possibility that manufactured, sensationalist reality is psychologically crippling us.

COMIC BOOKS

Television, movies, video games, and the popular media intersect in an interesting and often overlooked place: the unreality of comic books. During the 1950s, comics were regulated by the federal "Comics Code," which banned sex, violence, and anti-establishment propaganda from the comics market. In the 1960s, however, comic books dealing with drugs, sex, and the psychedelic counterculture—called "comix"—appeared underground from the pens of pioneers such as Robert Crumb (b. 1943), who mixed misogyny and sometimes pornography in his groundbreaking work.

The mainstreaming of the '60s counterculture during the '70s relaxed censorship codes and brought most of the underground above ground. The French magazine *Metal Hurlant* signaled a new age for comic books in 1975, with occult and hippie stories that were soon copied in the United States. The new comics merged violence, spiritualism, science fiction, and sex in attractive artistic formats and created America's own massive comic book subculture.

Comic books have served as a main catalyst for science fiction's transition to popular culture. While science fiction and fantasy genres traditionally claimed a limited audience, they now attract diverse television, movie, video game, and popular culture audiences—as with television shows such as *The X-Files* and its numerous imitators.

The range of what comic books can now do is greater than ever before. Art Spiegelman (b. 1948) won a Pulitzer Prize for his graphic novel *Maus,* an animated version of his father's Holocaust experiences. And Robert Crumb now creates comic adaptations of classics such as Kafka's *Metamorphosis.* Certainly one of the most controversial comic titles is Garth Ennis' *The Preacher.* While comics have historically dealt with religious issues, *The Preacher* confronts religion, specifically Catholicism, from a nontraditional view. Set in the Western genre, the story begins where God has left heaven to roam the earth in disguise. God did not tell anyone where he was going, however, and the earth is thrown into chaos. The comic's hero, Jesse Custer, a priest, vows to find God and make him confess and explain why he left. The book has been attacked as blasphemous, and Ennis himself conceded that it might be "anti-religious."

The mix of comedy and violence of the 1994 film *Pulp Fiction* has been a longstanding comic book staple. And films like *Batman* (1989), *The Crow* (1993), *The Mask* (1994), *Spawn* (1997), and *X-Men* (2000) bring comic book characters to life on the large screen. The sophistication of computer imaging further facilitates comic book characters coming to life in film in both animated and live-action formats in such hits as *Spawn* and *Blade* (1998). The funneling of such talent as former Marvel comics writers Larry and Andy Wachowski, who directed the innovative *Bound* (1996) and *The Matrix* (1999), further fuels the comic book conversion to film. The comics industry has become a multimillion-dollar business, producing such magnates as Todd MacFarlane, who directed the film version of *Spawn* and produced a best-selling soundtrack CD, line of toys, and Grammy-nominated music video for Pearl Jam.

Curiously, some directors have moved the other direction—from film to writing comics. This can be seen in the work of Kevin Smith, writer-director of the critically acclaimed *Clerks* (1994) and *Chasing Amy* (1997), and J. Michael Stracynski, creator

52. ROBERT CRUMB. The troubling aspect of Robert Crumb's work is that it is savagely misogynistic and pornographically explicit. In *Crumb* (1995), director Terry Zwigoff's documentary on the artist, Crumb admits his hostility toward women and the fact that he is sometimes sexually stimulated by his own erotic and pornographic cartoon images of women. The film, thus, is telling as it offers an astonishingly unguarded portrait of Crumb and his seriously dysfunctional family. It succeeds in showing us how one man's psychic wounds contributed to an art that transmits personal pain into garish visual satire.

and producer of the television series *Babylon 5*. Both have written best-selling comic books such as *Daredevil* and *Rising Stars,* which Stracynski also created. The cycle will undoubtedly continue.

TELEVISION AND FILM

Perhaps because television appeared to be cutting into their profits, the filmmakers of the early '50s movies seemed to enjoy satirizing television's blatant commercialism. *Callaway Went Thataway* (1951), *It's Always Fair Weather* (1955), Elia Kazan's classic *A Face in the Crowd* (1957), and *Will Success Spoil Rock Hunter?* (1957) all generally portrayed television as the merchant of false consciousness and television producers and celebrities as the greedy slaves of advertisers.

In the late '60s, Haskell Wexler's (b. 1925) film *Medium Cool* went so far as to deal with the conflict between the camera and the very subjects it tackled—generation wars, class wars, race wars, the Vietnam War, and the war between corporations and independents. Mixing documentary footage with rehearsed scenes played by natural-looking actors, *Medium Cool* presented an impersonal television-camera reading of the world, simultaneously imitating and criticizing television. For example, actor Robert Forster, the protagonist in the film, remarks that "the typewriter doesn't really care what's being typed on it," in reference to the role of a cameraman in his shooting of footage.

Still, ultimately unable to conquer television, cinema eventually joined it. Studios sold the rights of hundreds of recently made movies to television and thereby saved themselves, as often as not, from bankruptcy. The major studios even began making thirty- and sixty-minute weekly shows for television and producing commercials. By 1956, movies and television coexisted peacefully. In fact, television production occupied 75 percent of the film footage shot in Hollywood. FOX, Warner Bros., and other film studios are now major players in their own right, owning their individual networks. This blending, coupled with new technologies such as computer digitization and sophisticated animation, opened even greater possibilities for the distortion of reality.

Films, however, continued to satirize television. Director Sidney Lumet's (b. 1924) 1976 *Network,* for instance, made it clear that television was turning humanity into morons and humanoids and accused television of confusing news and show business. Screenwriter Paddy Chayefsky's (1923–81) message was that since television's advent, people have forgotten how to connect emotionally as human beings. And by the '80s, the formation of reality had shifted to the computer screen. Now what is real and true or what may be "true lies" is in the hands of whoever has the right keyboard—and it may be Generation X.

GENERATION X

While they have been called the "MTV Generation," "Generation X," "Slackers," "13ers," "Twentysomethings," and "Baby-busters," their image is one of Doc Marten's boots, flannel shirts, and ripped jeans. They are a large group of young people born between the early 1960s and 1980 or so and characterized, according to some, by short attention spans shaped by television and little desire for conventional occupations— the most misrepresented, over-hyped generation in American history. The unofficial guide to understanding these young adults is a 1991 book by Douglas Coupland (b. 1961), who has been called the Jack Kerouac of his generation. In *Generation X: Tales of an Accelerated Culture,* Coupland tells the story of three corporate drop-outs in their twenties who move to Palm Springs to find themselves.

Corporations invited Coupland to lecture, pleading with him to explain how to deal with and market to the problem X generation. John Fraser, a friend of Coupland's and a writer for the magazine *Saturday Night,* describes Coupland's overnight success:

> Doug has been a major literary and sociological event, especially in North America. In the States, he's cruising around in guru stratosphere: the Jack Kerouac of his generation (the post boomer generation of disaffected techno punks who don't know the words to either "God Save the Queen" or "O Canada"), a new-minted McLuhan, Homer to the micro serfs.[28]

The Xers are the most racially diverse American generation, and they generally come from the worst home lives. Forty percent are children of divorce, and even more were latchkey kids. They grew up immersed in a culture shifting from G to R to NC-17 film ratings, amid new public health dangers and the nightmare of self-absorbed parents. Fifty-eight percent of all unmarried singles between the ages of twenty and twenty-four still live with their parents, and many have turned to "McJobs," low-paying positions such as cashier, janitor, or waiter, which give them more time for recreational activities.

The possible salvation of the Xers, however, may ultimately be their technological ability. They are leading the growth of the Internet, and their fluency with computers has even created a new traditional publishing renaissance, with small presses that have become successful publishers of experimental, youth-oriented fiction.

FIGHT CLUB AND THE SEARCH FOR MEANING

Timothy McVeigh was twenty-seven years old when he vented his rage against society by massacring one hundred sixty-eight people in the Oklahoma City bombing in April 1995. In April 1999, a mere four years later, eighteen-year-old Eric Harris and seventeen-year-old Dylan Klebold walked into a Colorado high school and vented their rage by murdering thirteen people. These two tragic instances illustrate the longing, almost desperation that mars the psyche of Generation X, a desperation portrayed in the remarkable film *Fight Club*.

The story begins with Generation Xer Jack, a miserable, white-collar lackey for an auto manufacturer. Jack, worn out from his job and unable to sleep, is a slave to his crass consumer lifestyle. Soon, however, Jack's life is radically altered when he gains a new friend, the virile Tyler Durden, another Xer. Tyler is the type of person who at first glance seems a rare breed: he complains about the way we're all lapdogs to corporate culture in the endless working-spending cycle of consumerism. "You have a class of young men and women, and they want to give their lives to something," Tyler proclaims. "Advertising has these people chasing cars and clothes they don't need. Generations have been working in jobs they hate, just so they can buy what they don't really need." Tyler, however, has found a way out of this materialistic cycle. (See color plate 31).

Jack and Tyler begin Fight Club, inspired by Tyler's commitment to near-death experiences as a source of heightened consciousness. Through the mutual pummeling of one another, Jack and Tyler reach a new level of self-discovery. Soon, the club expands to men from all walks of life who convene in a basement to beat up on each other with bare knuckles, all in the name of brotherhood. Gradually, however, Tyler turns the horrifying purity of Fight Club into something worse—a nationwide army of slave-like terrorists fighting class wars against corporate America.

Director David Fincher's film exposes a raw nerve about the fear that many of today's males have about their manhood becoming increasingly irrelevant in the face of feminism and political correctness. It also explores the pervasiveness of exploitive forces in our corporate economy. But this despairing film is about something much deeper that is set forth with clarity in the novel by Chuck Palahniuk, from which the film was adapted. "I'm breaking my attachment to physical power and possession," Tyler announces, "because only through destroying myself can I discover the greater power of my spirit."

Then Tyler addresses the real problem: "We don't have a great war in our generation, or a great depression, but we do, we have a great war of the spirit. We have a great revolution against the culture. The great depression in our lives. We have a spiritual depression."

The Xers are victims of a philosophical shift in Western culture from traditional religion's concept of absolute truth to modern philosophy's reliance on human reason and postmodernism's claim of unattainable truth. Thus, we are faced with a rootless generation seeking desperately for something to believe in. And, having grown up in the midst of headlines about fallen televangelists and crooked politicians, the Xers' trust in authority figures is low. Therefore, cynicism about anything organized, such as church and political power, is high.

"What you have to consider," Tyler says to Jack, "is the possibility that God doesn't like you. Could be, God hates us. This is not the worst thing that can happen." Thus, getting God's attention for being bad is better than not getting God's attention at all. "We are God's middle children, according to Tyler Durden," Jack says, "with no special place in history and no special attention. Unless we get God's attention, we have no hope of damnation or redemption. Which is worse, hell or nothing?"

The Xers are a generation in search of something, and they don't want to be taken lightly. "It's not enough to be numbered with the grains of sand on the beach and the stars in the sky," Jack notes. This search has led many to communities of submission where the person is relieved of the burdens of individuality and freedom. This is a substitute for a new form of bondage where an exclusive ideology injects meaning into an otherwise empty existence. As expressed in various religious cults and certain extremist strains of militia organizations, violence is often the result. In fact, the new revolutionaries against culture, like those in *Fight Club,* often validate their existence with violent acts. Accordingly, the generation leading us into the Third Millennium is finding, as Milton writes in *Paradise Lost,* that "Long is the way and hard that out of hell leads up to light."

In the end, however, easy definitions fail to capture the complexity of human beings. Gallup surveys show that 48 percent of those between eighteen and twenty-four do volunteer work—the largest percentage of Americans in history, while 60 percent of college freshmen provide some kind of community service for their entire four years. Perhaps more than any other generation, the Xers have developed a talent for getting the most out of a bad hand.

THE MILLENNIALS

Even while Generation X stereotypes are crumbling, the media has created a label for the next generation—the Millennials. Born after 1982, this generation will come of age after the year 2000. Supposedly, they are "cute," "cheerful," and "scout like," and their parents dress them in military uniforms and educate them to be children of "civic virtue." The 1989 film *Parenthood* marks the contrast between cynical teenage Xers and Millennial "Babies on Board." While the Millennials were in their infancy, "kids-as-devil" films, such as 1984's *Children of the Corn* and *Firestarter,* were rapidly being replaced by "cuddly-baby" movies—*Raising Arizona* (1987), *Three Men and a Baby* (1987), *Baby Boom* (1987), *For Keeps* (1988), and *She's Having a Baby* (1988). This trend continued with *Baby Geniuses* (1999).

Xers' parents took them to R-rated movies, while Millennials' parents take them to G-rated movies. Fortysomething Baby-boomer parents protect their children from the same drugs they introduced in the '60s and '70s. Xer and young Baby-boom fathers now demand "daddy-track" work schedules to spend time at home with their children. New laws make parents civilly or criminally liable for their children's misbehavior. Kindergartens are more academic; elementary schools stress good works, along with academic performance; teachers' paychecks are growing; and PTAs are thriving.

Millennials, in contrast to Xers, however, seem to be assertive, independent, sure of themselves, and capable of making decisions of their own at an early age. As a result, areas such as film and television concentrated on the teen culture at the end of the '90s. Unlike previous eras, though, teens are presented with subjects traditionally reserved for adults such as birth control, teen pregnancy, homosexuality, and other topics once thought too cumbersome for young minds. Television is a primary purveyor of the heavier material. Shows like 1994's *My So-Called Life* is an early example. But programs like *Dawson's Creek, Buffy the Vampire Slayer,* and reruns of *Beverly Hills 90210, Party of Five,* and *Felicity* confront the teenage mind with discussions and topics on a daily basis that many adults do not even consider on a regular basis.

A number of school shootings—students killing other students—in the late '90s raised serious questions about the stability of the Millennial Generation, however. The senseless violence of the 1999 Colorado shootings may indeed point to a reconsideration of what the young view as entertainment and how parents and teachers disseminate knowledge. To understand youth today, one must realize that, unlike prior generations, these young people are like fish swimming in a bowl. Although previous generations lived in the present, they had the past and its undergirding values to give meaning and structure to their existence. But today's youth have little historical or cultural memory. They live only in the present and often in the context of the thirty-minute "sit-com" they have just finished watching. Thus, often only the present gives them meaning. Unfortunately, the present seems to be either a joke or a dead end for many young people.

Moreover, in the overstimulated Western culture, every materialistic and variant idea is in some way or other presented to the young. Caught in their fish-bowl world of the present, they have little defense. And because the traditional family structure is greatly weakened and the schools no longer teach moral values consistently, children have little guidance. As a result, contemporary youth have virtually no idea of where they came from, who they are, or where they are going. And with little parental leadership and failing political leaders, young people have almost no moral bank account from which to withdraw when necessary.

CONFUSED SEXUALITY

Although AIDS and the family-values rhetoric of the Reagan Administration seemed to have quelled the sexual revolution of the '60s and '70s, America of the 1990s showed a surprising surge in sexual openness and a catastrophic confusion regarding sex and gender roles.

Gays have forged the most visible paths through and beyond the abstinence that AIDS at first induced. Overtly gay sexual expression—which first flourished after the Stonewall Inn riot on Christopher Street in New York in 1969—is now an established way of life. Indeed, since the '70s, when they first became wildly popular, public meeting spots for possible sex—bathhouses, movie theaters, bookstores, and sex clubs—have never really gone away. Gay characters now populate television, movies, and the news. Information proliferates about the gay rights movement and gay surrogate parenting and adoption. Prominent figures who are homosexual, from local AIDS volunteers to Congressmen, provide role models for gay youth. AIDS has made many Americans recognize that a gay subculture exists and is becoming mainstream. The current sexual openness has not greatly increased the number of gays, however. Apparently only between 1 and 6 percent of women are lesbians, and a mere 3 to 10 percent of men are gay. But gays have made a great impact in the entertainment industry, and the number of gay sympathizers has grown. Alternative sexual expression has increased as well.

Society now generally defines "sex" as the factual chromosomal and anatomical make-up of a person and "gender" as a mental and social construct. Thus, transsexuals define themselves as "gender gifted," "gender creative," and "whole gendered." In the '90s, American culture celebrated transsexuals much as ancient cultures did, with a bevy of movies exploring the theme: *The Crying Game* (1992), *Orlando* (1992), *House of Angels* (1992), *The Ballad of Little Jo* (1993), *M. Butterfly* (1993), *Farewell My Concubine* (1993), and the top box office hits *Mrs. Doubtfire* (1993), *In and Out* (1997), and *Boys Don't Cry* (1999). A theme similar to *Mrs. Doubtfire* was played out successfully by Dustin Hoffman in 1982's *Tootsie* and has carried over into the Third Millennium.

"Gender tourism," or exploring one's sexual identity through such things as cross-dressing, has been used by many rock musicians, among them Little Richard, David Bowie, Mick Jagger, Lou Reed, Elton John, Madonna, Boy George, Michael Jackson, Annie Lennox, Kurt Cobain, and Marilyn Manson. Of anyone, David Bowie employed this concept to its extreme with his alter ego Ziggy Stardust in the early 1970s. His songs also spoke of gay themes; for example, "Rebel Rebel": "You got your mother in a whirl because she's not sure whether you're a boy or a girl." All this was while being married to wife, Angie, and with a newborn son, Zowie. Even though it was often unclear what level of Ziggy/Bowie was camp or part of his act, the effect was profound. As Mark Paytress recounts in *The Rise and Fall of Ziggy Stardust and The Spiders From Mars* (1998), in the 1980s, Boy George recalled Bowie's importance for him coming to terms with the nature of his sexuality in the '70s. For many, Bowie made homosexuality attractive.

A more recent example of gender tourism is Courtney Love (b. 1965) of the rock band Hole. Love, who was the wife of the late Kurt Cobain of the group Nirvana, claims she was raised "gender free," with her mother forbidding her to wear dresses. As an adult, she has become somewhat of a contradiction. Though a woman, she possesses many of the traits of a male rock star. At her shows, Love often assaults the crowd with insults and obscenities. This is usually followed by a stage dive into the crowd, where she is groped and pulled at until her clothes are torn off.

Love seems a radical feminist at times but a "traditional" woman at others. She claims to be a lesbian, but then denies it. Love presents herself as a strong, aggressive woman but then appears as a little girl. "A sort of rag doll stitched together from past and present notions of womanhood," writer Nicole Arthur notes, "Love mirrors the paradox of contemporary feminism. Old models of femininity have outlived their usefulness, but nothing satisfactory has arisen to take their place. Love is a near-perfect transitional figure."[29]

Some see gender blurring as a result of a global paradigm shift of both the body and the body politic—a strain of the emerging global-village philosophy. As part of an independent Great Chain of Being, many believe that we are all one, all male and female. Even religious denominations are reinterpreting the Bible to include a growing variety of sexual perspectives, while others claim there is no biblical sex ethic at all. Instead, there is only a "love ethic," which should be changed to fit the sexual mores of whichever cultural period people find themselves in.

Yet every year in the United States, five thousand young people between the ages of fifteen and twenty-four kill themselves, and 30 percent of these cases are related to confusion about sexual orientation. Sexual confusion causes higher dropout rates, higher levels of drug and alcohol abuse, parental rejection, hopelessness, and prostitution. Open sexuality and competing messages of proper sexual fulfillment seem to have traumatized thousands of children. A number of contemporary singers/entertainers increase the confusion by blurring the differences between public and private, gay and straight, and "kinky" and normal.

TECHNOLOGY AND THE POST-HUMAN

Like new sexual messages, America's new technologies are also changing how we see the world. The adage "to a man with a hammer, everything looks like a nail" is now more appropriately "to a man with a computer, everything looks like data." The twentieth century has been distinguished by transforming technologies: the automobile, airplane, atomic bomb, television, and finally—and perhaps most profoundly—the computer. Advances such as artificial intelligence, mechanical implants, biotechnology, voice-activated programming, virtual reality, robotics, and computer graphics blur the distinction between human and machine. The films *Robocop* (1987), *Johnny Mnemonic* (1995), *Virtuosity* (1995), and *ExistenZ* (1999) depict a kind of historical reality/cyborg future, the fusion of humans and machines. "At the same time that the cyborg represents a triumph of the intellect," Claudia Springer argues in her book *Electronic Eros,* "it also signifies obsolescence for human beings and the dawn of a post-human, post-Enlightenment age."[30] And with the emergence of virtual reality, the door is more open than ever to the possible synthesis of human beings and computer technology.

The computer is billed as the first thinking machine, and yet, the difference between humans and machines is that the mind thinks with ideas, not information. Those master ideas—the religious and philosophical teachings at the center of our culture and consciousness—are not based on information but are produced by that marvel of intuition and epiphany, the human mind. Moreover, the so-called computer revolution may drive culture further inward. The technology resistance movement argues that we are joining virtual communities while our real cities crumble, at least partly because our sense of common purpose has frayed.

The information industry, unlike past inventions, has created a new, nearly exclusive dependence on the products of our own ingenuity. We have moved into a "techno sphere." In his book *In the Absence of the Sacred* (1991), Jerry Mander states:

> Technologies have organized themselves in relation to other technologies to create an interactive web, of which we're only one part. We feel it, and we serve it, and we interact with it, and we co-evolve with it, and we slowly become it. We're practicing a form of intra-species suicide.[31]

A MATTER OF DEATH AND LIFE

While small businesses and factory jobs disappear and inner cities decay, the participants in the computer revolution create virtual communities. As a result, we seem to be losing the traditional meaning of life. Our public moral discourse has become a cacophony, rather than a symphony. Courts, legislatures, and universities argue about the definition of a person and the worthiness of life, and many contort moral theories to fit preferred behavioral outcomes.

Dr. Jack Kevorkian (b. 1928), for one, continues to pursue his euthanasia goals with the same zeal that Margaret Sanger fought for birth control. In light of what Kevorkian describes as life's mission, questions of who should decide when life is no longer worth living are being raised with more and more urgency. This continues, despite Kevorkian being found guilty of second-degree murder in March of 1999 for an "assisted suicide."

In countries like the Netherlands, euthanasia is now considered a part of the "living" process. It has even entered Dutch popular culture. For example, the popular television series *A Matter of Life and Death,* co-sponsored by the Dutch Ministry of Health, asked the studio audience to vote on which of two patients should receive life-saving treatment. The patients pleading for their lives were not actors but real people.

In one broadcast, both patients were female and both wanted to be treated with an expensive new drug, which could possibly prolong their lives. Violet Falkenburg, the host, dutifully told the audience that doctors would actually make the decision about the women's futures. "However," notes American columnist Nat Hentoff, "the enthusiasm of the viewing audience for having, even vicariously, the power to end one life and save another, was not diminished. The results of the studio audience's vote were shown to the country on a flashing electronic scoreboard."[32] A spokesman for the Dutch Ministry of Health was honest in stating why the government was co-sponsoring the show: "Our goal was to make people think about health care costs, how important they are, and where choices must be made."[33]

Insidiously, it seems that human life is being redefined in economic terms. Ending an unwanted life may soon become much easier. As Hentoff recognizes, Americans may one day have a "duty" to die when they grow old or get sick.

MANIPULATION OF LIFE

Despite the warning signs, the United States government relaxed its standards on DNA research in 1994 to allow scientists conducting human gene therapy experiments to bypass the previously required review before the Recombinant DNA Advisory Committee. The Committee is also investigating whether to allow genetic altering of human fetuses, an area of research banned since the 1970s. August 2000 guidelines to allow federal funding of human embryo cell research by the United States government will, according to many, lead a revolution in science. The guidelines allow federal funding for research with stem cells that have been removed from human embryos. The rules forbid research on the embryo itself. The effect, some believe, will be that privately-funded researchers will remove stem cells from embryos—which has been done at several universities—and that these stem cells could then be used in federally-funded studies.

Much of the push for this type of research came from those who see such work as helping those with certain ailments, such as Parkinson's Disease. The longstanding political discussion over the moral status of embryos, however, will continue. Recent experiments on sheep and mice have proven that a gene altered in a fetus may be passed on to the next generation. Although the process could possibly cure inherited diseases, on the reverse side it could severely contaminate the gene pool.

The concept of cloning burst upon the world with Dolly, the cloned sheep. From there, other animals have been cloned. Moral concerns have been raised in regard to cloning, however. "To produce replica animals on demand would be to go against something basic and God-given about the nature of life," notes Donald Bruce, chairman of the Church of Scotland committee that examines ethical crises raised by advances in science and technology. Moreover, "history suggests we could never rest assured that no human being would dream of exploiting genetics or embryology to evil ends."[34]

Still, a British government commission of experts called for a lifting of the ban on human cloning in the summer of 2000. The commission urged that scientists be allowed to create cloned embryos to study the manufacture of cells and tissues for transplant. The key benefit of cloning for transplants, scientists argue, comes from stem cells. An embryo is essentially a ball of stem cells that becomes a fetus when the stem cells start specializing to create a nervous system, spine, and other features. Scientists hope that by extracting the stem cells from the embryo before they start to specialize, their growth can be directed in a lab to become any desired cell or tissue type.

Some realized early on that if mammals, especially monkeys, which are thought to be closest to humans biologically, can be cloned, what will stop the next inevitable step—human clones? The January 2001 announcement of a genetically-altered rhesus monkey by a group of American scientists marked the first time anyone had so altered a primate—a grouping that also includes humans. Thus, the situation that Aldous Huxley (1894–1963) described in his landmark novel *Brave New World* (1932), which many believed was far off in the future, now seems extremely imminent. Within the next few years, there could possibly be human clones. Some have posited that such clones would be "soul-less" and could be treated as sub-humans, to be used as servants, warriors, entertainment devices, or organ storage places ready to be utilized when a "real" human needs a new liver or pancreas.

Gene manipulation raises many ethical questions as well. If, as the United States Supreme Court has decided, the pre-born have no rights, their genes may be altered. But if genetically-altered fetuses are eventually born, they will have been genetically changed without their consent. Although current research concentrates on curing inherited diseases, the research may also enable scientists to change basic human characteristics—such as a baby's sex.

In June 2000, Celera Genomics completed the first assembly of the human genome—the company had determined the correct alphabetical order of the 3.1 billion letters of the human genetic code. The human genome is the biological map of

3.1 billion pairs of chemical "letters" (G, C, T, and A) that make up the DNA in each human cell. These chemicals are arranged in specific ways to create the 80,000 to 100,000 genes that carry the instructions for human life. This is known as genetic mapping, and most have no idea what this means in scientific terms. Yet ethical questions were raised immediately. The most important question of all: Who should own this information?

A few years ago, the United States Patent Office decided to allow sequenced segments of DNA to be patented. DNA sequences can be used as testing devices for the purpose of, for example, developing new medical cures or obtaining genetic information for use by the government or employers or genetic counselors. This information could replace the hit or miss of today's diagnostic medicine with preventative medicine. The owner of patents on DNA sequences may prevent competitors from using their sequences to make further developments or force the payment of royalties in order to market medical or other products that incorporate their segments. Worse, they could prohibit their use entirely. The Human Genome Organization (HUGO) has squarely opposed such patents.

HUGO is not alone. James Watson, perhaps the grandfather of human genome discoveries and the Nobel prizewinning co-discoverer of the DNA structure in 1953, worked from the start to ensure that no single nation or private group could control the human genome and that the information—perhaps the most important scientific breakthrough of all time—would be available without cost to all the people of the world.

Medical transplant advances have redefined sudden death into an opportunity for improved health—or even life for others. Andrew Kimbrell's 1993 book *The Human Body Shop* cites an incident where a young man's body parts were distributed among fifty-two people. While demonstrating the possibilities for organ transplants, this story also warns of the dangers. The young man was HIV-positive, and at least four of the people who received his body parts contracted AIDS.

In developing countries, poor people are finding that their kidneys are their most valuable possession. Involuntary participation in transplants, however, is a real danger. For example, staff members of a state-run mental hospital in Argentina killed patients (possibly more than a thousand) in order to sell their organs. One of the recovered bodies, which had both eyes missing, belonged to a sixteen-year-old boy.

The demand for organs has pushed doctors to redefine death itself. In America, for instance, a person is declared dead when his or her brain ceases to function, even if machines still allow that person to breathe and maintain a heartbeat. The definition now, however, is being pushed to include patients in permanent comas with self-maintaining body functions.

FEAR AND THE EXTREMIST SWING

The collapse of Marxism created an ideological vacuum for the twentieth century. The easiest replacement may be a worldview that soothes the pain of modern complexity. Unfortunately, many seek an ideology to solve their fears, and people often hate what they fear. For some, fear itself has become the answer—fear of the government. The heavily-armed militia groups that have sprung up in rural America and the rise of white supremacy groups reflect the need of a public outlet for government opposition. Director Tony Kaye's film *American History X* (1998) is a character study of white supremacists and their destructive tendencies.

Several weeks after the April 1995 bombing of the Federal Building in Oklahoma City, Gallup pollsters asked 1,008 Americans: "Do you think the federal government has become so large and powerful that it poses an immediate threat to the rights and freedoms of ordinary citizens?" Thirty-nine percent of the conservatives answering said "yes," and 42 percent of the liberals polled perceived that their government was "out to get them."[35]

The media coverage of the Oklahoma tragedy introduced many people to the military nature of America's federal agents. As polls show, Americans are increasingly fearful of their government, especially branches like the FBI and the Bureau of Alcohol, Tobacco, and Firearms (ATF). For example, an April 1995 *Time* magazine photograph showed five FBI agents in training to provide security at a World Cup soccer game. The image was menacing, the kind of picture one associates with Special Forces, commando units, or the guards outside foreign government buildings.

According to costume experts, popular culture plays a crucial role, though often an unconscious one, in uniform design. Margaret Vining, a specialist in the military collection at the National Museum of American History, says the trend in military uniforms has been away from spit-and-polish formality and toward camouflage and other casual dress—the SWAT-team dress adopted by the federal agencies. "They leave the impression of a stealth Darth Vader look-alike," she says. "I wonder if they were influenced by current entertainment."[36]

Paranoia, in turn, increases with the way that government agencies mishandle certain situations. For example, in April 1994, ninety-two men, women, and children were burned alive in the federal government's siege of a religious commune headed by David Koresh in Waco, Texas. This was the result of what many now consider a government "mistake."

Paranoia seems to be gripping Western societies. This in part explains the popularity of television programs such as *The X-Files* (and those like it), a decidedly paranoid program about the government's involvement in people's daily lives. Not only fear of the government but also the fear of viruses, AIDS, and antibiotic-resistant strains of tuberculosis is added to the matrix of cultural suspicion. The troubled American psyche is captured in the 1993 film *Falling Down*, where Michael Douglas stars as a defense worker, a normally law-abiding, white-collar citizen who violently snaps with pent-up frustration and rage. At the end of the film, he asks incredulously, "Am I the bad guy?"

The disordering of society is not an exclusively American problem. The collapse of communism raised dreams of freedom and economic stability that too often matured into the ethnic cleansing and genocide that occurred in Bosnia and Belgrade and the massacre of idealistic, unarmed students in China. Germany continues to struggle with right-wing extremism and xenophobia.

While there appears to be no equivalent to Third Reich Germany on the horizon, the scenario today for Eastern Europe is no less perilous. Some believe that the same dynamic is at work that led the post–World War I successor states down the road of extreme nationalism and war. When extreme nationalists take the logic of the ethnic nation to its radical conclusion, as in former Yugoslavia, an all-inclusive, homogeneous ethnic nation-state emerges. The price is war, complete with forcible mass expulsions, concentration camps, and genocide.

Therefore, a diverse spectrum of extremist forces is surfacing in every country, including the United States, each brandishing nationalist ideologies with authoritarian and racial underpinnings. A newly charged discourse of ancestry and tradition, of suffering and fate, of lost territories and thwarted ambitions, seems to be replacing the rhetoric of Marxism-hedonism.

GOD AND FILM

In this chaotic age, people are increasingly seeking something outside themselves to give order and meaning to their lives. While painting once tackled these questions, modern film now addresses this search, which inevitably includes the subject of God. Of all the artistic forms throughout the ages, film may be the most suitable forum for the discussion of religion and God.

Traditionally, film has focused on Christ and Christ figures. Some more recent films, however, have pushed the dialogue toward Eastern mysticism and religion—which can be seen in Bernardo Bertolucci's (b. 1940) trilogy in search of the Other: *The Last Emperor* (1987), *The Sheltering Sky* (1990), and *Little Buddha* (1993). Martin Scorsese's (b. 1942) classic *Kundun* (1997) is a spiritual journey that focuses on the life of the Dalai Lama. A visually exhilarating film, *Kundun* details the perseverance of the spirit in the material world.

Hollywood's earliest forays into religion were D. W. Griffith's 1916 *Intolerance* and Cecil B. DeMille's 1923 *The King of Kings*. These were the original biblical film epics. Both presented visual representations of Christ as pious, sugary, soft, and surrounded by an artificially colored aura. Later films, such as the 1959 version of *Ben-Hur* and 1961's *King of Kings*, were more realistic but devoid of religion. Pier Paolo Pasolini's 1964 film *The Gospel According to St. Matthew* presented Christ as an authentic human being, while retaining the holiness and divinity that previous movies provided. But its lack of commercial success (and the box office failure of other films like it) proved that religious motifs do not succeed unless they are sugarcoated.

Still, "Christ figures" and Christian mysticism appeared in a number of popular films through the decades: *The Day the Earth Stood Still* (1951), *Shane* (1953), *Cool Hand Luke* (1967), *Taxi Driver* (1976), *E. T.* (1982), *Amadeus* (1984), *U Turn* (1997), *The Matrix* (1999), and *The Cell* (2000), as well as independent films such as *Jesus' Son* (2000).

William Friedkin's (b. 1939) *The Exorcist* (1973) thrust the debate about the existence of God and Satan into mainstream conversation and also seemed to signal the end of the death-of-God movement that had emerged in the '60s. Movies like Scorsese's 1988 *The Last Temptation of Christ*, however, may be the culmination of all the cinematic genres. It combines symbolism and realistic accounts of historical events in an effort to understand the core of the religious beliefs of one particular director. (See color plate 32.) The images of Peter eating the Last Supper with blood dripping from his mouth, Christ's sacred heart, Christ's guardian angel who is really Satan, and the crucifixion hallucination may be the very things to stir the minds of twentieth century searchers.

TRANSCENDENCE

Ultimately, it seems that people are generally hungry for transcendence. Many want to know God or a God-force. Seeking spirituality, they investigate the occult, astrology charts, angels, UFOs, and extraterrestrial beings. This sometimes leads to tragedy, as in the March 1997 mass suicide of thirty-nine Heaven's Gate cult members who sought union with extraterrestrials supposedly following the Hale-Bopp Comet.

Some people have sought a form of transcendence in the modern horror film. Many believe this began in 1969 with the low-budget shocker *Night of the Living Dead,* which presented an apocalyptic vision of a worldwide plague of flesh-eating zombies. The startling spectacle of mindless cause-and-effect swallowing up everything provided an utterly amoral basis for this classic's horror.

Many similar horror films have exploited people's fears of the modern scientific world, which often seems to run through mechanics—with its apparently meaningless cause and effect. There is no meaning whatsoever to the horror—just terror for terror's sake. In this sense, the modern horror film perhaps has helped people unlearn metaphysical terror by showing them the horrific implications of the "God is dead" philosophy.

Horror film directors now appear to be moving away from this mold, though, perhaps because they have realized its inherent limitations. The influential television series *The X-Files* proved intoxicating because it posits a universe in which truth is objective and human choices have meaning. After all, what is more entertaining—a universe where life and death are absurd or a universe where life is sacred and some things are worse than death?

FORREST GUMP

Those attracted to conservative values also seek a framework of meaning and purpose. Phenomena like the massive male-bonding groups, such as Promise Keepers rallies and Million Man Marches, have attempted to provide validation in a confusing world. Such "communities of meaning" have great drawing power because they provide validation to people for who they are—not for what they have accomplished. Groups like the Christian Coalition make people feel good about themselves without having to do anything—except maybe vote for the "right" candidate.

This helps explain the success of director Roger Zemeckis's 1994 film, *Forrest Gump,* which offered a new redemptive vision of American history and a reconstructed image of the American people. Gump, through dogged adherence to his mother's principles, becomes rich, gets the girl, and raises a wonderful child. Everyone he touches is eventually transformed. In Gump's world, since everything is an act of God, no one has to do anything to achieve salvation.

Gump underlines the civil religion that has served as a pseudo-spiritual backdrop for much of twentieth-century America. Like Gump, many Americans have gone through the century without comprehending how deeply their good fortune depended upon the oppression of others.

Gump highlights the search for value that so many pursue. If the only way most people can feel validated is to be part of a xenophobic, nationalist, or extremist group, they will most likely embrace those avenues. Ultra-conservative talk show hosts successfully mobilize against gays, feminists, and liberals by exploiting listeners' frustration and allowing them to externalize their rage at some evil "Other."

CULTURELESS CULTURE

Violence, crime, and general disorder almost invariably strike foreign visitors as the most salient features of American life. Foreigners also discover a universal concern with self—"self-fulfillment" and, more recently, "self-esteem" slogans of a society incapable of generating a sense of civic obligation. Americans' disinclination to subordinate self-interest to greater concerns captures Americanism as we move into the Third Millennium.

Those in the West, in general, have failed to mature, looking for external reasons for their internal faults. The "Whiney Nineties" lumped personal problems with major political and social problems. Dissatisfied and distracted, today's Westerners are easy prey for movements that provide "direction."

Democratic society may be unable to flourish, or even survive, in the absence of the internal constraints once provided by traditional religion that formerly supported the work ethic and discouraged self-indulgence. Modernism's attempts to erase the past have robbed humanity of all guiding forces, except personal whim and authoritarian power. And although Western civilization has achieved a level of unparalleled complexity, it also yearns nostalgically for a bygone simplicity, which, for all practical purposes, is an illusion.

As historian Christopher Lasch suggests,

An exhaustive investigation would uncover a great number of influences [that have produced the modern state], but the gradual decay of religion would stand somewhere near the head of the list. . . . Public life is thoroughly secularized. The separation of church and state, nowadays interpreted as prohibiting any public recognition of religion at all, is more deeply entrenched in America than anywhere else. Religion has been relegated to the sidelines of public debate.[37]

The religious attitude of "the elites," which comprise governmental agencies, the media, the arts, and leaders of the major institutions of society, Lasch notes, "ranges from indifference to active hostility. It rests on a caricature of religious fundamentalism as a reactionary movement bent on reversing all the progressive measures achieved"[38] over the years.

Traditional religion has subsided in a permissive culture that replaces the concept of sin with the concept of sickness. The therapeutic Freudian worldview replaced religion with psychoanalysis. Sickness and health have replaced guilt, sin, and atonement as the dominant concerns guiding those who care for the soul and the mind. Psychiatric practice currently requires a suspension of moral judgment. "A 'nonjudgmental' habit of mind," writes Lasch, "easily confused with the liberal virtue of tolerance, came to be regarded as the *sine qua non* of sociability."[39]

Therapy infiltrated social and political arenas as well, creating a therapeutic state where blame shifts from the individual to society. Intellectual circles discuss the "society as patient."

If culture is a set of moral demands—deeply graven interdicts, etched in superior and trustworthy characters—then the United States today is a "cultureless society." American society claims that nothing is sacred and nothing is forbidden, except that which falls outside the bounds of what is considered politically correct.

Culture, by its very definition, is a life backed up by the will to ostracize those who defy its mores. As Lasch writes, "A 'way of life' is not enough. A people's way of life has to be embedded in 'sacred order'—that is, in a conception of the universe, ultimately a religious conception, that tells us 'what is not to be done.'"[40]

Without limitations, virtues, or morals, a society cannot protect itself or its institutions. Professor Gertrude Himmelfarb's *The Re-Moralization of Society* (1995) calls for a return to the older values, even if for merely pragmatic reasons. Religion, however, cannot be expected to provide a comprehensive, definitive code of conduct that settles every dispute and resolves every doubt. Religious faith issues from the heart and cannot be summoned up on demand. It is, thus, primarily individual. But when faith is allowed free and open expression—as reflected in the life and work of the likes of the Reverend Martin Luther King Jr.—it can influence thought and conduct on a societal level by encouraging moral inquiry.

At the same time, true religion is ultimately forgiving of human weakness and folly, but not because it ignores them or attributes them exclusively to unbelievers. As Lasch recognizes,

For those who take religion seriously, belief is a burden, not a self-righteous claim to some privileged moral status. Self-righteousness, indeed, may well be more prevalent among skeptics than among believers. The spiritual discipline against self-righteousness is the very essence of religion.[41]

Obviously, all cultures must narrow the range of choices available to citizens. A society, for example, that would not forbid murder or theft would fall into utter chaos. But such a narrowing of choices cannot be effectively imposed from the top-down by government agencies or coercive, authoritarian structures. As with religious faith, it should be a restraint on certain actions, acted upon voluntarily by the individual citizen. Moreover, while a culture's controls should not dehumanize its people, it cannot allow every impulse a public expression. The revolutionary slogan of 1968—"it is forbidden to forbid"—not only invites anarchy but also abolishes truth. When every expression is equally permissible, nothing is true.

Some of today's societal elitists are rediscovering the principle of limitation. Many recognize that modernism has run its course. Unfortunately, both the modern rightist and leftist movements generally replace the much-needed principle of limitation with repression, oppression, and dehumanization. Some groups even evoke such a change in the name of religion, as we saw with some of the "communities of meaning."

Religion itself is not culture. The best interpreters of Christianity, as historical analyst Philip Rieff has noted, have always distinguished "between faith and the institutions and attitudes by which it is transmitted at any given time."[42] Culture may depend on religion, but religion has no meaning if it is seen merely as a prop of culture. Unless it rests on a disinterested love of being, religious faith only clothes human purposes with spurious sanctity. Once "religion" establishes itself in a movement, such as a strident religious right or leftist movement, it can lead to repressive tactics. "This is why," Lasch states, "an honest atheist is always to be preferred to a culture Christian."[43]

AFTERWORD
Into the New Millennium

Now what is history? It is the centuries of systematic explorations of the riddle of death, with a view to overcoming death. That's why people discover mathematical infinity and electromagnetic waves; that's why they write symphonies. Now, you can't advance in this direction without a certain faith. You can't make such discoveries without spiritual equipment. And the basic elements of this equipment are in the Gospels. What are they? To begin with, love of one's neighbor, which is the supreme form of vital energy. Once it fills the heart of humanity it has to overflow and spend itself. And then the two basic ideals of modern man—without them human beings are unthinkable—the idea of free personality and the idea of life as sacrifice.

BORIS PASTERNAK, *Dr. Zhivago*[1]

The future, of course, is an illusion. Nothing has happened there yet. There does not yet exist. But hopefully, by studying the past, we can get a glimpse of what may be. Otherwise, there is no way to navigate a course and attain a sense of maturity. As the Roman philosopher Cicero recognized: "To know nothing of what happened before you were born is to remain ever a child."

There is no doubt that those of us caught in the clutches of modernity have been reeling from a spiritual crisis that does not seem to be lessening. As such, there has been no lack of commentary on our modern spiritual plight, which assumes, curiously enough, that doubt, moral relativism, and disillusionment are the price of progress. Many recognize that postmodernism, by its very definition, cannot produce a viable society. Postmodernism is defined by disillusionment with grand historical theories, including Marxism, and by personal freedom through an aesthetic revolt against middle-class culture. The postmodern sensibility simultaneously rejects modernism while standing on the modernist ideal of individuality as emancipation from convention.

Many troubled and disillusioned people seek to emulate a historical era when life was simple and religious values reigned supreme. We must be careful of simplistic assumptions, however. Indeed, such golden eras never existed. Americans in particular must realize that the tides of change have so altered society that a return to the political, social, and moral climate of 1776 is impossible, if not dangerous. Some see an inevitable decline in Western culture, while others predict the coming of a major crisis, as cultural analysts William Strauss and Neil Howe do in *The Fourth Turning* (1997).

It is clear that the older cultural and moral bulwarks of modern societies have disintegrated. As this continues to happen, Western society will need something beyond so-called "Republican" values to sustain any semblance of order, form, and freedom. Serious believers, agnostics, and atheists, in the words of author Michael Harrington, an avowed atheist himself, must consider that they "now have the same enemy: the humdrum nihilism of everyday life in much of Western society."[2]

Modernism's legacy, however, has not been altogether destructive. There are many positive elements in modernist movements. For example, the rise of the women's and Civil Rights movements, freedom in the arts, and the questioning of illegitimate authority have improved the human condition. Still, it is clear that our sense of community and shared values is disintegrating, and our moral accountability has been lost. This was epitomized in the legal and political troubles that plagued the presidency of William Jefferson Clinton (b. 1946).

Clinton, who was accused of lying to a federal grand jury and lying under oath in his deposition in the Paula Jones case, was subsequently impeached in 1999 by the United States House of Representatives. Although Clinton survived the final challenge in the Senate, he was later held in contempt of court and fined by a federal judge for lying under oath in the Jones case. The result of Clinton's troubles and other scandals in government is that, as we enter the new millennium, confidence and trust in elected leaders is at an all-time low.

We seem to be at the end of a long experiment, which began in the eighteenth century with such Enlightenment philosophers as Voltaire and the Romantic movement that followed. The experiment has altered the traditional concepts of religion, art, music, and life itself. People now appear to be mere parts in the so-called machinery of life, and science threatens to tinker with and possibly rearrange the concept of what it means to be human. Modern technologies, however, have failed to create new answers to our search for meaning.

If there is to be a restoration of hope and beauty, it must begin with the recovery of an appreciation for the uniqueness of each human being. Until then, behind the opaque cloud of our ignorance and uncertainty, the historical forces that shaped the twentieth century will continue to operate. One thing is certain: we have reached a heightened state of historical crisis, wherein the techno-scientific community's forces are now great enough to destroy all the material foundations of life. In the end, therefore, only the spiritual will remain.

Thus, the questions confronting us as we begin the Third Millennium are these:

Can we regain a spiritual hope comparable to the one that enlightened Western culture for so many centuries?

Can we rediscover religious or moral certainties of the magnitude that inspired artists such as Rembrandt to paint magnificent works like *Adoration of the Shepherds*?

Can we retain our dignity, worth, and uniqueness as human beings?

Only time will tell.

BIBLIOGRAPHY

Aberback, Alan David. *The Ideas of Richard Wagner*. Lanham, New York and London: University Press of America, 1984.

Abernathy, Ralph David. *And The Walls Came Tumbling Down*. New York: Harper & Row, 1989.

Abraham, Gerald. *A Hundred Years of Music*. London: Duckworth, 1974.

Abrams, M. H., et al., eds. *The Norton Anthology of English Literature*, 3d ed. New York: Norton, 1975.

Adler, Jerry. "Sex in the Snoring '90s," *Newsweek*, 16 April 1993.

Agar, Herbert. *The Price of Union*. Boston: Houghton Mifflin, 1950.

Aiken, Stephen. *Joseph Beuys' Coyote: An American Action*, vol. 10, Provincetown Arts, 1994.

Albini, Steve. *Beavis and Butthead Experience*. David Geffen, 1993.

Aldridge, Alan, ed. *The Beatles Illustrated Lyrics*. Boston: Houghton Mifflin, 1969.

Allen, Frederich Lewis. *Only Yesterday: An Informal History of the Nineteen Twenties*. New York: Harper & Row, 1931.

Anderson, Terry H. *The Movement and the Sixties*. New York: Oxford University Press, 1995.

Anderson, Christopher. *Hollywood: The Studio System in the Fifties*. Austin: University of Texas Press, 1994.

Anderson, Jon Lee. *Che: A Revolutionary Life*. New York: Grove, 1997.

Anderson, Terry H. *The Movement and the Sixties*. New York: Oxford University Press, 1995.

Aranda, Francisco. *Luis Buñuel: A Critical Biography*. London: Seeker & Warburg, 1975.

Armour, Robert A. *Fritz Lang*. Boston: Twayne, 1977.

Arnason, H. H. and Marla F. Prather. *History of Modern Art*, 4th ed. New York: Abrams, 1998.

Arthur, Nicole. "The Hole Truth: What Courtney Love Is and What She Isn't," *The Washington Post,* 21 May 1995.

Ascheim, Steven E. *The Nietzsche Legacy in Germany 1890–1990.* Berkeley: University of California Press, 1992.

Auiler, Dan. *Vertigo: The Making of a Hitchcock Classic.* New York: St. Martin's Press, 1998.

Ayer, A. J. *Philosophy in the Twentieth Century.* New York: Vintage, 1984.

Bach, Richard. *Jonathan Livingston Seagull.* New York: Macmillan, 1970.

Bakan, David. *Sigmund Freud and the Jewish Mystical Tradition.* Princeton, N.J.: Van Nostrand, 1958.

Baker, Carlos. *Ernest Hemingway: A Life Story.* New York: Macmillan, 1969.

———. *Hemingway: The Writer as Artist.* Princeton, N.J.: Princeton University Press, 1980.

Baker, James N. "Coming Out Now," *Newsweek,* Summer/Fall, 1990.

Ball, Hugo. "Gadji Beri Bimba," in *The Dada Market: An Anthology of Poetry,* trans. Willard Bohn. Carbondale, Ill.: Southern Illinois University Press, 1993.

Barnaby, Karin and D'Acierno, Pellegrino, eds. "Popular Culture Symposium," in *C. G. Jung and the Humanities.* Princeton, N.J.: Princeton University Press, 1990.

Barnouw, Erik. *Tube of Plenty.* New York: Oxford University Press, 1975.

Barzun, Jacques. *Classic, Romantic, and Modern.* Chicago: University of Chicago Press, 1961.

Baty, S. Paige. *American Monroe: The Making of a Body Politic.* Berkeley: University of California Press, 1995.

Bauche, Freddy. *The Cinema of Luis Buñuel.* London: Tanting, 1973.

Baxter, John. *Fellini.* New York: St. Martin's Press, 1993.

Bayles, Martha. *Hole in Our Soul: The Loss of Beauty and Meaning in American Popular Music.* New York: Macmillan, 1994.

Bayley, Edwin R. *Joe McCarthy and the Press.* Madison, Wis.: University of Wisconsin Press, 1981.

Bazin, Andre. *Orson Welles: A Critical View.* Los Angeles: Acrobat, 1991.

Beatles, The. *The Beatles Anthology.* New York: Chronicle Books, 2000.

Beck. *Mellow Gold.* David Geffen, 1994.

Becker, Ernest. *Escape From Evil.* New York: Free Press, 1975.

Becker, Raymond de. *De Tom Mix a James Dean.* Paris: Librarie Antheme Fayard, 1959.

Berendt, Joachim. *The Jazz Book.* Westport, Conn.: Laurence Hill, 1975.

Berger, Kathleen Stassen, with Ross A. Thompson. *The Developing Person Through the Life Span,* 3d ed. New York: Worth, 1994.

Bernard, Oliver, ed. *Rimbaud: Collected Poems.* Middlesex, England: Penguin, 1986.

Bernstein, Amy. "Where Have You Gone, Jughead?" *U.S. News & World Report,* 15 August 1994.

Berry, Jason, Jonathan Foose, and Tad Jones. *Up from the Cradle of Jazz.* Athens: University of Georgia Press, 1986.

Bianculli, David. *Teleliteracy: Taking Television Seriously.* New York: Continuum, 1992.

Biskind, Peter. *Easy Riders, Raging Bulls*. New York: Simon & Schuster, 1998.

Bjork, Daniel W. *B. F. Skinner: A Life*. New York: Basic Books, 1993.

Blackwell, Mark. *Raygun*, April 1997.

Blake, William. *The Complete Poetry and Prose of William Blake*, ed. David V. Erdman. Berkeley: University of California Press, 1981.

————. *The Marriage of Heaven and Hell*. Coral Gables, Fl.: University of Miami Press, 1963.

Blau, Justine. *Betty Friedan*. New York: Chelsea House, 1990.

Blaug, Mark. *John Maynard Keynes: Life, Ideas, Legacy*. London: Macmillan, 1990.

Bloom, Amy. "The Body Lies," *The New Yorker*, 18 July 1994.

Blum, John Morton. *Years of Discord: American Politics and Society, 1961–1974*. New York: Norton, 1991.

Bohn, Willard. *Apollinaire and the Faceless Man*. Cranberry, N.J.: Associated University Presses, 1991.

Bolton, Richard and Robert, eds. *Culture Wars: Documents from the Recent Controversies in the Arts*. New York: New Press, 1992.

Booth, Stanley. *The True Adventures of the Rolling Stones*. New York: Vintage, 1985.

Bouzereau, Laurent. *Ultraviolent Movies: From Sam Peckinpah to Quentin Tarantino*. Toronto: Citadel, 1996.

Bowman, John S. *The World Almanac of the Vietnam War*. New York: Pharos, 1985.

Boyer, Jay. *Sidney Lumet*. New York: Twayne, 1993.

Boyer, Paul. *By the Bomb's Early Light: American Thought and Culture at the Dawn of the Atomic Age*. New York: Pantheon Books, 1985.

Braestrup, Peter. *Big Story*. California: Presidio, 1994.

Branch, Taylor. *Parting the Waters: America in the King Years, 1954–63*. New York: Simon & Schuster, 1988.

Brandy, Leo. *Focus On the Piano Player*. New Jersey: Prentice-Hall, 1972.

Brantlinger, Patrick. *Bread & Circuses: Theories of Mass Culture as Social Decay*. Ithaca: Cornell University Press, 1983.

Brendan, Piers. *The Dark Valley: A Panorama of the 1930s*. New York: Knopf, 2000.

Breskin, David. "Bono: The Rolling Stone Interview," *Rolling Stone*, 8 October 1987.

Breslin, James E. B. *Mark Rothko: A Biography*. Chicago: University of Chicago Press, 1993.

Breton, André. *Manifestoes of Surrealism*, trans. Richard Seaver and Helen R. Lane. Ann Arbor: University of Michigan Press, 1969.

————. *What is Surrealism?*, ed. Franklin Rosemont. New York: Pathfinder, 1978.

Brill, A. A., trans. *The Basic Writings of Sigmund Freud*. New York: Modern Library, 1938.

Brockett, Oscar G. and Robert R. Findlay. *Century of Innovation: A History of European and American Theatre and Drama Since 1870*. Englewood Cliffs, N.J.: Prentice-Hall, 1973.

Brooks, Cleanth. *Modern Poetry and the Tradition*. Chapel Hill: University of North Carolina Press, 1939.

Brooks, Van Wyck. *On Literature Today*. New York: E. P. Dutton, 1941.

————. *An Autobiography*. New York: E. P. Dutton, 1965.

Brosnan, John. *Future Tense: The Cinema of Science Fiction*. New York: St. Martin's Press, 1978.

Brown, J. D. "Henry Miller" in *Dictionary of Literary Biography*, vol. 4, ed. Karen Lane Rood. Detroit: Gale Research, 1980.

Brown, Michael E., et al. *New Studies in the Politics and Culture of U.S. Communism*. New York: Monthly Review Press, 1993.

Brown, Peter and Steven Gaines. *The Love You Make: An Insider's Story of The Beatles*. New York: McGraw-Hill, 1983.

Brown, Royal S. *Focus On Godard*. Englewood Cliffs, N.J.: Prentice-Hall, 1972.

Broyard, Anatole. *Kafka Was the Rage: A Greenwich Village Memoir*. New York: Vintage, 1997.

Bruccoli, Matthew J. and Jackson R. Bryer, eds. "Self-Interview: An Interview with F. Scott Fitzgerald," in *F. Scott Fitzgerald in His Own Time: A Miscellany*. Kent, Ohio: Kent State University Press, 1971.

Bruun, Geoffrey. *Revolution and Reaction: 1848–1852, A Mid-Century Watershed*. Princeton, N.J.: D. Van Nostrand, 1958.

Byrds, The. "Turn! Turn! Turn!" *20 Essential Tracks From the Boxed Set: 1965–1990*. New York: Sony Music Entertainment, 1992.

Byron, Lord George Gordon. "Cain," in *The Poetical Works of Byron,* Cambridge ed. Boston: Houghton Mifflin, 1975.

Calinescu, Matei. *Five Faces of Modernity*. Durham, N.C.: Duke University Press, 1987.

Callow, Simon. *Orson Welles: The Road to Xanadu*. New York: Viking, 1995.

Camus, Albert. *The Myth of Sisyphus and Other Essays* [1942], trans. Justin O' Brien. New York: Knopf, 1955.

Canby, Vincent. "*A Clockwork Orange* Dazzles the Sense and the Mind," *The New York Times*, 20 December 1971.

———. "*Orange*—Disorienting But Human Comedy. . . ," *The Sunday New York Times*, 9 January 1972.

Capon, Paul, trans., *Surrealism*. Yves Duplessis. New York: Walker, 1962.

Carlin, Richard. *Rock and Roll: 1955–1970*. New York and Oxford, England: Facts on File Publications, 1988.

Carter, John F. Jr. "'These Wild Young People' by One of Them," *Atlantic Monthly*, September 1920.

Cassidy, Robert. *Margaret Mead: A Voice for the Century*. New York: Universe Books, 1982.

Cavan, Sherri. *Hippies of the Haight*. St. Louis, Mo.: New Critics Press, 1972.

Cawelti, John G. *Focus on Bonnie and Clyde*. Englewood Cliffs, N.J.: Prentice-Hall, 1973.

Chang, Iris. *The Rape of Nanking: The Forgotten Holocaust of World War II*. New York: Penguin, 1997.

Chao, Jennifer. "Dutch see crippled man die by injection in first televised mercy killing," *The Washington Times*, 22 October 1994.

Charlton, Katherine. *Rock Music Styles: A History*. Dubuque, Ia.: William C. Brown, 1990.

Charters, Ann, ed. Introduction: "Variations on a Generation," *The Portable Beat Reader*. New York: Penguin, 1992.

Chicago, Judy and Edward Lucie-Smith. *Women Art: Contested Territory*. London: Weidenfeld & Nicolson, 1999.

Chidley, Joe. "Hef at Home," *MacLean's,* 15 August 1994.

Chilvers, Ian, Harold Osborne, and Dennis Farr, eds. *The Oxford Dictionary of Art*. Oxford: Oxford University Press, 1988.

Chion, Mischel. *David Lynch*. London: British Film Institute, 1995.

Chipp, Herschel Browning, ed. *Theories of Modern Art: A Source Book by Artists and Critics*. Berkeley: University of California Press, 1968.

Christenson, Cornelia V. *Kinsey: A Biography*. Bloomington, Ind.: Indiana University Press, 1971.

Christy, Jim. *The Long Slow Death of Jack Kerouac*. Toronto: ECW, 1998.

Ciment, Michael. *Kazan on Kazan*. New York: Viking, 1973.

Clark, Kenneth. *The Romantic Rebellion: Romantic Versus Classic Art*. London: Omega, 1973.

Clarke, Donald. *The Rise and Fall of Popular Music*. New York: St. Martin's Press, 1975.

Clausen, Christopher. "Welcome to Postculturalism," *The Key Reporter,* Autumn 1996.

Clover, Carol J. *Men, Women and Chainsaws*. Princeton, N.J.: Princeton University Press, 1992.

Collier, James Lincoln. *Jazz: the American Theme Song*. New York: Oxford University Press, 1993.

———. *The Rise of Selfishness in America*. New York: Oxford University Press, 1991.

Cone, James J. *Martin & Malcolm & America: a dream or a nightmare*. Maryknoll, N.Y.: Orbis, 1991.

Conrad, Joseph. *Heart of Darkness*, Norton Critical Edition, ed. Robert Kimbrough. New York: Norton, 1988.

———. *The Collected Letters of Joseph Conrad*, vol. 2, eds. Frederick R. Karl and Laurence Davies. London: Cambridge University Press, 1986.

Conrad, Peter. "The Devil's Disciple: The art and artifice of Robert Mapplethorpe," *The New Yorker*, 5 June 1995.

Corrigan, Robert, ed. *Masterpieces of the Modern German Theatre*. New York: Collier, 1967.

Costello, John. *Virtue Under Fire: How World War II Changed Our Social and Sexual Attitudes*. Boston: Little, Brown, 1985.

Coupland, Douglas. *Generation X: Tales For An Accelerated Culture*. New York: St. Martin's Press, 1991.

Courthion, Pierre. *Manet*. New York: Abrams, 1984.

Crichton, Michael. *Jurassic Park*. New York: Ballantine, 1993.

Crick, Bernard. *George Orwell: A Life*. Boston: Little, Brown, 1980.

Crisafulli, Chuck. *The Doors: When the Music's Over*. New York: Thunder's Mouth, 2000.

Cronin, Anthony. *Samuel Beckett: The Last Modernist*. New York: HarperCollins, 1996.

Crow, Thomas. *The Rise of the Sixties*. New York: Abrams, 1996.

Crunden, Robert M. *Body and Soul: The Making of American Modernism*. New York: Basic Books, 2000.

Crystal, David, ed. *The Barnes & Noble Encyclopedia*. New York: Barnes & Noble, 1993.

Cunard, Nancy, ed. *Negro: An Anthology*, ed. and abr. New York: Frederick Ungar, 1970.

Cunningham, Frank R. *Sidney Lumet: Film and Literary Vision*. Lexington: University Press of Kentucky, 1991.

Dachy, Marc. *The Dada Movement, 1915–1923*. New York: Rizzoli International, 1990.

Dali, Salvador. *Diary of a Genius* [1964]. London: Creation, 1998.

Dalton, David. *El Sid: Saint Vicious*. New York: St. Martin's Press, 1997.

———. *James Dean: The Mutant King*. New York: St. Martin's Press, 1974.

Darnton, Nina. "The End of Innocence Special Edition: How Kids Grow: Health, Psychology and Values," *Newsweek*, Summer 1991.

Darwin, Charles. *The Autobiography of Charles Darwin, 1809–1882*, ed. Nora Barlow. New York: Norton, 1958.

———. *The Life and Letters of Charles Darwin*, ed. Francis Darwin. New York: D. Appleton, 1904.

———. *Descent of Man*. London: John Murray, 1871.

Davenport-Hines, Richard. *Gothic: Four Hundred Years of Excess, Horror, Evil and Ruin*. New York: North Point, 1999.

Davidson, Phillip B. *Vietnam at War: The History 1946–1975*. New York: Oxford University Press, 1991.

Dawson, Christopher. *Religion and the Rise of Western Culture*. New York: Doubleday, 1957.

Dawson, N. P. "Enjoying Poor Literature" in *Critical Essays on T. S. Eliot's The Waste Land*, eds. Lois A. Cuddy and David H. Hirsch. Boston: G. K. Hall, 1991.

Delbanco, Andrew. *The Death of Satan: How Americans Have Lost the Sense of Evil*. New York: Farrar, Straus & Giroux, 1995.

Dempsey, David. "Review of *The Naked and the Dead*." *New York Times Book Review*. 9 May 1948.

Denisoff, R. Serge. *Great Day Coming*. Urbana, Ill.: University of Illinois Press, 1971.

Denselow, Robin. *When The Music's Over: The Story of Political Pop*. London: Faber & Faber, 1989.

Denton, Jeremiah A. Jr. *When Hell Was In Session*. New York: Reader's Digest Press, 1976.

Descartes, Rene. "Discourse on Method," in *Discourse on Method and the Meditations*, trans. F. E. Sutcliffe. New York: Penguin, 1968.

Dewar, Douglas and H. S. Shelton. *Is Evolution Proved?* London: Hollis & Carter, 1947.

Dewey, John. *The Quest for Certainty*. New York: Minton, Balch, 1929.

Dougan, Clark and Samuel Lipsman. *A Nation Divided*. Boston: Boston Publishing, 1984.

Dowlding, William J. *Beatlesongs*. New York: Simon & Schuster, 1989.

Downs, Phillip G. *Classical Music: the Era of Haydn, Mozart, and Beethoven*. New York: Norton, 1992.

Drabble, Margaret, ed. *The Oxford Companion to English Literature*. London: Oxford University Press, 1985.

Duddy, Marianne. "Different From Norm, We Reflect a God Who Delights in Surprises," *National Catholic Reporter*, 2 September 1994.

Durant, Will. *The Story of Philosophy: The Lives and Opinions of the Great Philosophers of the Western World*. New York: Simon & Schuster, 1961.

Durant, Will, ed. *The Works of Schopenhauer*. New York: Simon & Schuster, 1928.

Durant, Will and Ariel. *The Age of Napoleon*. New York: Simon & Schuster, 1975.

———. *The Age of Voltaire*. New York: Simon & Schuster, 1965.

———. *The Age of Reason Begins*. New York: Simon & Schuster, 1961.

Dylan, Bob. *Lyrics, 1962–1985*. New York: Knopf, 1985.

Ebert, James R. *A Life In a Year: The American Infantryman in Vietnam, 1965–1972*. Novato, Calif.: Presidio, 1993.

Edwards, Paul, ed. *The Encyclopedia of Philosophy*, vols. 5 and 6. New York: Macmillan, 1967.

Ehrenreich, Barbara and John. *Long March, Short Spring*. New York: Monthly Review Press, 1969.

Einstein, Albert. *Out of My Later Years*. London: Thames & Hudson, 1950.

Eisner, Lotte H. *Fritz Lang*. New York: Oxford University Press, 1977.

Elegant, Robert. "How to Lose a War: Reflections of a Foreign Correspondent" in *The American Experience in Vietnam* by Grace Sevy. Norman, Okla.: University of Oklahoma Press, 1989.

Eliot, T. S. *The Complete Poems and Plays, 1909–1950*. New York: Harcourt, 1980.

———. *The Letters of T. S. Eliot*, vol. I. New York: Harcourt, 1988.

———. *The Waste Land*. London: Faber & Faber, 1971.

———. "Thoughts after Lambeth," in *Selected Essays 1917–1932*. New York: Harcourt, 1932.

———. "Ulysses, Order, and Myth," *The Dial*. November 1923.

Eliot, Valerie, editorial notes in T. S. Eliot, *The Waste Land*. London: Faber & Faber, 1971.

Elliott, Anthony. *The Mourning of John Lennon*. Berkeley: University of California Press, 1999.

Engel, Joel. *Rod Serling: The Dreams and Nightmares of Life in The Twilight Zone*. Chicago: Contemporary Books, 1989.

Epstein, Jacob. *Let There Be Sculpture: An Autobiography*. London: Michael Joseph, 1940.

Erhard, Werner. *Current Biography Yearbook 1977*, ed. Charles Moritz. New York: Thomas W. Wilson, 1978.

Etherington-Smith, Meredith. *The Persistence of Memory: A Biography of Dali*. New York: Random House, 1992.

Farson, Daniel. *The Gilded Gutter Life of Francis Bacon*. New York: Pantheon, 1993.

Fast, Julian. *The Beatles: The Real Story*. New York: Berkeley Medallion Books, 1968.

Faunce, Sarah. *Gustave Courbet*. New York: Abrams, 1993.

Faust, Wolfgang Max. "Shattered Orthodoxy: The Energy of Transformation," *American Art in the 20th Century: Painting and Sculpture, 1913–1993*. Berlin: Zeitgeist-Gesellschaft, 1993.

Fejto, Francois. "Conclusion," in *The Opening of an Era 1848: An Historical Symposium*, ed. Francois Fejto. New York: Howard Fertig, 1966.

Fell, John L. *Film: An Introduction*. New York: Praeger, 1975.

Ferris, Paul. *Dr. Frued: A Life*. Washington, D.C.: Counterpoint, 1997.

———. *Dylan Thomas: The Biography* [1977]. Washington, D.C.: Counterpoint, 2000.

Finkle, David. "High Performance," *Village Voice*, 5 January 1993.

Fitzgerald, F. Scott. "Echoes of the Jazz Age," in *The Fitzgerald Reader*, ed. Arthur Mizner. New York: Charles Scribner's Sons, 1963.

Fong-Torres, Ben. "A Chronology," in *The Ballad of John and Yoko*, eds. Jonathan Cott and Christine Doudna. New York: Doubleday, 1982.

Foster, John Burt Jr. *Heirs to Dionysus*. Princeton, N.J.: Princeton University Press, 1981.

Foster, William Z. *History of the Communist Party of the United States*. New York: International Publishers, 1952.

Fowlie, Wallace. *Rimbaud and Jim Morrison: The Rebel as Poet*. Durham: Duke University Press, 1993.

Fraser, John. "The Dalai Lama of Generation X," *Saturday Night*, March 1994.

Fraser, Ronald, et al. *1968: A Student Generation in Revolt*. London: Chatto & Windus, 1988.

Freud, Ernst L., ed. *Letters of Sigmund Freud*, trans., Tevin and James Stern. New York: Basic Books, 1960.

Freud, Sigmund. *Civilization and its Discontents*, trans., James Strachey. New York: Norton, 1961.

———. *A General Introduction to Psychoanalysis*. New York: Garden City, 1938.

———. "From the History of an Infantile Neurosis," *Collected Papers*, vol. III, trans. Joan Riviere. New York: Basic Books, 1959.

———. *Moses and Monotheism*, trans., Katherine Jones. New York: Vintage, 1955.

———. *New Introductory Lectures on Psycho-Analysis.* New York: Norton, 1933.

Frey-Rohr, Liliane. *From Freud to Jung: A Comparative Study of the Psychology of the Unconscious*. Boston: Shambhala, 1990.

Fricke, David. "Life After Death: Courtney Love," *Rolling Stone*, 15 December 1994.

Fried, Michael. *Courbet's Realism*. Chicago: University of Chicago Press, 1990.

Fried, Richard M. *Nightmare in Red: The McCarthy Era in Perspective*. New York: Oxford University Press, 1990.

Friedan, Betty. *It Changed My Life: Writings on the Women's Movement*. New York: Random House, 1976.

Friedlander, Henry. *The Origins of Nazi Genocide: From Euthanasia to the Final Solution*. Chapel Hill: University of North Carolina Press, 1995.

Friedrich, Thomas. *Berlin: Between the Wars*. New York: Vendome Press, 1991.

Fry, E. F. *Cubism*. London: Thames & Hudson, 1966.

Fulton, Robert and Greg Owen. "Death and Society in Twentieth Century America," *Omega Journal of Death and Dying*, vol. 18, no. 4. 1987–1988.

Furness, R. S. *Expressionism*. London: Methuen, 1973.

Gabler, Neal. *An Empire of Their Own: How the Jews Invented Hollywood*. New York: Doubleday, 1988.

———. *Life The Movie: How Entertainment Conquered Reality*. New York: Knopf, 1998.

Gaines, James R. "The Man Who Shot John Lennon," *People Weekly*, 23 February 1987.

———. "In the Shadows a Killer Waited," *People Weekly*, 2 March 1987.

————. "The Killer Takes His Fall," *People Weekly*, 9 March 1987.

Garfield, David. *A Player's Place*. New York: Macmillan, 1980.

Garrow, David J. *Martin Luther King, Jr., and the Southern Christian Leadership Conference*. New York: Quill, 1986.

Gasset, José Ortega y. *The Dehumanization of Art* [1925]. Garden City, N.Y.: Doubleday, 1956.

Gates, David. "Twenty-Five Years Later, We're Still Living in Woodstock Nation," *Newsweek*, 8 August 1994.

Gibson, Ian. *The Shameful Life of Salvador Dali*. New York: Norton, 1998.

Giles, Jeff. "Generalizations X," *Newsweek*, 6 June 1994.

Gleick, Elizabeth. "The Maker We've Been Waiting For," *Time*, 7 April 1997.

Glennor, Lorraine, ed. *Our Times: An Illustrated History of the 20th Century*. Atlanta: Turner, 1995.

Gold, Jonathan. "Trent Reznor of Nine Inch Nails Preaches the Dark Gospel of Sex, Pain and Rock & Roll: Love It to Death," *Rolling Stone*, 8 September 1994.

Goldberg, Rose Lee. *Performance Art: From Futurism to the Present*. New York: Abrams, 1988.

Goodman, Paul. *Growing Up Absurd: Problems of Youth in the Organized Society*. New York: Random House, 1960.

Goodwin, Richard N. *Remembering America: A Voice from the Sixties*. Boston: Little, Brown, 1988.

Gordinier, Jeff. "On A Ka-Ching! & A Prayer: In the Wake of 'Gump' the Entertainment Industry Gets Spiritual and the Profits are Heaven-Sent," *Entertainment Weekly*, 7 October 1994.

Gorney, Cynthia. "A Sex-Changing Odyssey," *Harper's Bazaar*, September 1994.

Gottesman, Ronald. *Focus on Orson Welles*. Englewood Cliffs, N.J.: Prentice-Hall, 1976.

Gould, Michael. *Surrealism and the Cinema*. South Brunswick and New York: A. S. Barnes; London: Tantivy, 1976.

Gould, Stephen Jay. *The Mismeasure of Man* [1981]. New York: Norton, 1996.

Gowing, Laurence and Sam Hunter. *Francis Bacon*. London: Thames & Hudson, 1990.

Grant, Zalin. *Survivors: Vietnam P.O.W.'s Tell Their Stories*. New York: Da Capo, 1994.

Grauerholz, James and Ira Silverberg, eds. *World Virus: The William Burroughs Reader*. New York: Grove, 1998.

Gray, Paul. "The Assault on Freud," *Time*, 29 November 1993.

Grebanier, Bernard D., et al., eds. *English Literature and Its Backgrounds*, vol. 2. New York: Dryden, 1949.

Green, Martin. *New York 1913: The Armory Show and the Patterson Strike Pageant*. New York: Charles Scribner's Sons, 1988.

Greenberg, Martin. *The Terror of Art: Kafka and Modern Literature*. London: Lowe & Brydone, 1968.

Greer, Germaine. *The Female Eunuch*. New York: McGraw-Hill, 1970.

Gregor-Dellin, Martin. *Richard Wagner: His Life, His Work, His Century*, trans. J. Maxwell Brown John. San Diego and New York: Harcourt, 1980.

Gregory, Dick. *Nigger*. New York: Washington Square Press, 1964.

Grenier, Richard. *Capturing the Culture: Film, Art and Politics*. Washington, D.C.: Ethics and Public Policy Center, 1991.

Grenville, J. A. S. *A History of the World in the Twentieth Century*. Cambridge, Mass.: Belknap Press of Harvard University, 1994.

Gross, David M. and Sophronia Scott. "Proceeding With Caution: The Twentysomething Generation is Balking at Work, Marriage, and Babyboomer Values, " *Time,* 16 July 1990.

Guerin, Wilfred L., et al., eds. *A Handbook of Critical Approaches to Literature*, 3d ed. New York: Oxford University Press, 1992.

Guralnick, Peter. *Last Train to Memphis: The Rise of Elvis Presley*. Boston: Little, Brown, 1994.

Guthrie, Woody. *Dust Bowl Ballads*, sound recording. New York: Folkways Records, 1964.

————. *Pastures of Plenty: A Self-Portrait*, eds. Dave Marsh and Harold Leventhal. New York: HarperCollins, 1990.

Haertel, Joe. "Rock's 'Clock' Turns Forty: On a Spring Day in 1955, 'Blackboard Jungle' Changed the Times," *The Washington Post*, 19 March 1955.

Halberstam, David. *The Best and the Brightest*. New York: Fawcett, 1973.

————. *The Fifties*. New York: Villard, 1993.

Hamilton, George Heard. *19th and 20th Century Art*. New York: Abrams, 1970.

————. *Painting and Sculpture in Europe: 1880–1940*, 6th ed. New Haven: Yale University Press, 1993.

Hamilton, Ian. *In Search of J. D. Salinger*. New York: Random House, 1988.

Hammond, Paul. *Constellations of Miró, Breton*. San Francisco: City Lights, 2000.

————, ed. and trans. *The Shadow and Its Shadow: Surrealist Writings on the Cinema* [1978]. San Francisco: City Lights, 2000.

Hampton, Wayne. *Guerilla Minstrels*. Knoxville: University of Tennessee Press, 1986.

Hamsher, Jane. *Killer Instinct*. New York: Broadway Books, 1997.

Hanke, Ken. *Tim Burton: An Unauthorized Biography of the Filmmaker*. Los Angeles: Renaissance, 1999.

Hardy, Phil and Dave Laing, eds. *The Faber Companion to 20th-Century Music*. London: Faber & Faber, 1990.

Harrington, Michael. *The Politics at God's Funeral: The Spiritual Crisis of Western Civilization*. New York: Holt, Rinehart & Winston, 1983.

Harrington, Richard. "The Core of Rotten: 15 Years of Silence, John Lydon Talks About His Career as a Sex Pistol," *The Washington Post*, 10 July 1994.

Harris, Daniel. *The Rise and Fall of Gay Culture*. New York: Hyperion, 1997.

Harrison, Lawrence E. and Samuel P. Huntington. *Culture Matters: How Values Shape Human Progress*. New York: Basic Books, 2000.

Hartt, Frederick. *Art: A History of Painting, Sculpture, Architecture*, 4th ed. New York: Abrams, 1993.

Hawkins, Joan. *Cutting Edge: Art-Horror and the Horrific*. Minneapolis: University of Minnesota Press, 2000.

Hayden, Tom. *Port Huron Statement*. New York: Students for a Democratic Society, 1964.

Hayman, Ronald. *Nietzsche: A Critical Life*. New York: Oxford University Press, 1980.

Headington, Christopher. *The Bodley Head History of Western Music*. London: Bodley Head, 1974.

Hegel, Georg Wilhelm Friedrich. *Philosophy of Right*, trans. T. M. Knox. London: Oxford Press, 1967.

———. *The Philosophy of History*, rev. ed., trans. J. Sibree. New York: Colonial Press, 1900.

Helprin, Mark. "Modernism and Fascism: Sleeping With the Enemy," *The Washington Post*, 29 May 1994.

Hemingway, Ernest. *A Farewell to Arms* [1929]. New York: Macmillan, 1957.

———. *The Sun Also Rises*. New York: Macmillan, 1954.

Henderson, George. *A Religious Foundation of Human Relations: Beyond Games*. Norman: University of Oklahoma Press, 1977.

Hendricks, Jon. *Fluxus Codex*. Detroit: Gilbert and Lila Silverman Fluxus Collection, 1988.

Henry, Tricia. *Break All Rules!: Punk Rock and the Making of a Style*. Ann Arbor: University of Michigan Press, 1989.

Hentoff, Nat. "Health Reform: You Bet Your Life," *The Washington Post*, 14 May 1994.

———. *Jazz Is*. New York: Limelight, 1983.

———. "Profiles," *New Yorker*, 24 October 1964.

Herman, Arthur. *The Idea of Decline in Western History*. New York: Free Press, 1997.

Herrera, Hayden. *Matisse: A Portrait*. New York: Harcourt, 1993.

Hertsgaard, Mark. *A Day In The Life: The Music and Artistry of the Beatles*. New York: Delacorte, 1995.

Hess, Thomas B. *Willem de Kooning: Drawings*. Greenwich: New York Graphic Society, 1972.

Hethmon, Robert H. *Strasberg at the Actors Studio*. New York: Viking, 1965.

Higgenbotham, Virginia. *Luis Buñuel*. Boston: Twayne, 1979.

Hill, Geoffrey. *Illuminating Shadows: The Mythic Power of Film*. Boston: Shambhala, 1992.

Hill, Lee. *Easy Rider*. London: British Film Institute, 1996.

Hiller, Jim. *Cahiers du Cinema: The 1950's: Neo-realism, Hollywood, New Wave*. Cambridge, Mass.: Harvard University Press, 1985.

Himmelfarb, Gertrude. *The Re-Moralization of Society: From Victorian Virtues to Modern Values*. New York: Knopf, 1995.

Hinson, Hal. "And The Winner Is. . .Us," *The Washington Post*, 1 November 1992.

Hirsch, Foster. *A Method to Their Madness*. New York: Norton, 1984.

———. *Detours and Lost Highways: A Map of Neo-Noir*. New York: Limelight Editions, 1999.

Hobbes, Thomas. *Leviathan*. New York: Dutton, 1931.

Hobsbawm, Eric. *The Age of Extremes: A History of the World, 1914–1991*. New York: Pantheon, 1994.

Hockemos, Paul. *Free to Hate: The Rise of the Right in Post-Communist Eastern Europe*. New York: Routledge, 1993.

Hodgson, Godfrey. *America in Our Time: From World War II to Nixon, What Happened and Why*. New York: Vintage, 1978.

Hoffman, Abbie. *Soon to be a Major Motion Picture*. New York: Putnam's, 1980.

Hofstadter, Richard. *Anti-Intellectualism in American Life*. New York: Vintage, 1963.

Holland, Vyvyan. *Oscar Wilde: A Pictorial Biography*. New York: Viking, 1960.

Homans, Peter. *Jung in Context*. Chicago: University of Chicago Press, 1979.

Horn, Miriam. "Goings-on Behind Bedroom Doors," *U.S. News and World Report*, 10 June 1991.

Hopkins, Jerry and Danny Sugerman. *No One Here Gets Out Alive*. New York: Warner Brothers, 1980.

Horowitz, Joseph. "Mozart as Midcult: Mass Snob Appeal," *Musical Quarterly*, Spring 1992.

Hoskyns, Barney. *Mojo*, March 1997.

Houghton, Walter E. and G. Robert Stange, eds. *Victorian Poetry and Poetics*. Boston: Houghton Mifflin, 1968.

Huelsenbeck, Richard. *Memoirs of a Dada Drummer*, ed. Hans J. Kleinschmidt, trans. Joachim Neugroschel. New York: Viking, 1974.

Huffington, Arianna Stassinopoulos. *Picasso: Creator and Destroyer*. New York: Simon & Schuster, 1988.

Hughes, Robert. *American Visions: The Epic History of Art in America*. New York: Knopf, 1997.

———. "Days of Antic Weirdness," *Time*, 27 January 1997.

———. *The Shock of the New: Art and the Century of Change*. London: Thames & Hudson, 1993.

Hull, S. Loraine. *Strasberg's Method as Taught by Lorrie Hull: A Practical Guide for Actors, Teachers and Directors*. Woodbridge, Conn.: Ox Bow, 1985.

Hunter, Sam and John Jacobus. *Modern Art,* 3d ed. New York: Abrams, 1992.

Hyams, Joe (with Jay Hyams). *James Dean: Little Boy Lost*. New York: Warner Books, 1992.

Hynes, Samuel, ed. *The Complete Short Fiction of Joseph Conrad*, vol. 2. Hopewell, N.J.: Ecco, 1992.

Iannone, Carol. "The Last Temptation Reconsidered," *First Things*, February 1996.

Insdorf, Annette. *François Truffaut*. Boston: Twayne, 1978.

Isaacs, Reginald. *Gropius: An Illustrated Biography of the Creator of the Bauhaus*. Boston: Little, Brown, 1991.

"Jack Kevorkian," *Current Biography,* September 1994.

James, William. "What Pragmatism Means," in *Essays in Pragmatism*, ed. Alburey Castell. New York: Hafner, 1951.

Janis, Harriet and Rudi Blesh. *De Kooning*. New York: Grove Press, 1960.

Janis, Pam. "Welcome to 'The Whiney Nineties,'" *USA Weekend*, 5–7 May 1995.

Janowitz, Hans. "Caligari—The Story of a Famous Story (Excerpts)," in *The Cabinet of Dr. Caligari: Texts, Contexts, Histories*. ed., Mike Budd. New Brunswick, N.J.: Rutgers University Press, 1990.

Jarry, Alfred. *The Supermale*. London: Jonathan Cape, 1968.

Jaspers, Karl. *The Future of Mankind*. Chicago: University of Chicago Press, 1958.

Jenkins, Janet, ed. *In the Spirit of Fluxus*. New York: Distributed Art Publishers, 1993.

Jezer, Marty. *Abbie Hoffman: American Rebel*. New Brunswick, N.J.: Rutgers University Press, 1992.

Joachimides, Christos M. and Norman Rosenthal, eds. *American Art in the 20th Century: Painting and Sculpture, 1913–1993*. Berlin: Zeitgeist-Gesellschaft, 1993.

Johnson, Brian D. "Body Doubles," *MacLean's*, 10 March 1997.

Johnson, Paul. *A History of Christianity*. New York: Atheneum, 1979.

———. *Intellectuals*. New York: Harper & Row, 1988.

———. *Modern Times: The World from the Twenties to the Eighties*. New York: Random House, 1983.

Jones, Amelia, ed. *Sexual Politics: Judy Chicago's Dinner Party in Feminist Art History*. Berkeley: University of California Press, 1996.

Jones, E. Michael. *Dionysos Rising: The Birth of Cultural Revolution Out of the Spirit of Music*. San Francisco: Ignatius, 1994.

Jones, Ernest. *The Life and Work of Sigmund Freud*, vol. II. New York: Basic Books, 1955.

Jones, Jack. *Let Me Take You Down: Inside the Mind of Mark David Chapman, The Man Who Killed John Lennon*. New York: Villard, 1992.

Jung, Carl G. *Four Archetypes,* trans., R. F. C. Hull. Princeton, N.J.: Princeton University Press, 1969.

———. *The Modern Man in Search of a Soul*. London: Routledge & Kegan Paul Ltd., 1933.

Jung, Carl G. and M. L. von Franz, eds. *Man and His Symbols*. Garden City, N.Y.: Doubleday, 1964.

Kael, Pauline. *For Keeps: Thirty Years at the Movies*. New York: Dutton, 1994.

Kafka, Franz. *I Am Memory Come Alive*, Nahum N. Glatzer, ed. New York: Schocken, 1974.

———. "The Judgment," in *The Penal Colony: Stories and Short Pieces*, trans. Willa and Edwin Muir. New York: Schocken Books, 1976.

Kagan, Norman. *The Cinema of Stanley Kubrick*, rev. ed. New York: Continuum, 1989.

Kaleta, Kenneth C. *David Lynch*. New York: Twayne, 1993.

Kant, Immanuel. *Gessamelte Schriften*, Prussian Academy ed. Berlin: George Reiner, 1911.

Karaim, Reed. "Technology and Its Discontents," *Civilization*, May/June, 1995.

Katsiaficas, George. *The Imagination of the New Left: A global analysis of 1968*. Boston: South End, 1987.

Kaufman, Walter, trans. and ed. *The Portable Nietzsche*. New York: Viking, 1968.

Kazan, Elia. *Elia Kazan: A Life*. New York: Knopf, 1988.

Kazantzakis, Nikos. *The Last Temptation of Christ*, trans. P. A. Bien, New York: Touchstone, 1960.

Kearns, Doris. *Lyndon B. Johnson and the American Dream*. New York: Signet, 1976.

Kelly, Mary Pat. *Martin Scorsese: A Journey*. New York: Thunder's Mouth, 1991.

Kennedy, David. *Birth Control in America: The Career of Margaret Sanger*. New Haven: Yale University Press, 1970.

Kennedy, David M. *Over Here: The First World War and American Society*. New York: Oxford University Press, 1980.

290

Kerouac, Jack. *On the Road*. New York: Viking, 1957.

———. "The Philosophy of the Beat Generation," *Esquire,* March 1958.

———. *Vanity of Duluoz*. New York: Coward-McCann, 1968.

Keynes, John Maynard. *The General Theory of Employment, Interest and Money*. New York: Harcourt, 1936.

Keyssar, Helene. *Robert Altman's America*. New York: Oxford University Press, 1991.

Kienholz, Edward and Nancy Reddin. *Keinholz: A Retrospective*. New York: Whitney Museum of Modern Art, 1996.

Kimbrell, Andrew. *The Human Body Shop*. New York: HarperCollins, 1993.

Klein, Joe. *Woody Guthrie: A Life*. New York: Knopf, 1980.

Klemperer, Victor. *I Will Bear Witness: A Diary of the Nazi Years, 1942-1945*. New York: Random House, 1999.

Knowlson, James. *The Life of Samuel Beckett*. New York: Touchstone, 1996.

Kolker, Robert. *A Cinema of Loneliness,* 3d ed. New York: Oxford University Press, 2000.

Kracauer, Siegfried. *From Caligari to Hitler*. Princeton, N.J.: Princeton University Press, 1947.

———. "The Making of Caligari," in *The Classic Cinema*, ed. Stanley J. Solomon. New York: Harcourt, 1973.

Kramer, Hilton. "Stuart Davis at the Met," *The New Criterion*, vol. 10, no. 5, January 1992.

LaCapra, Dominick. *A Preface to Sartre*. Ithaca, N.Y.: Cornell University Press, 1978.

Laing, Dave, Karl Dallas, Robin Denselow, and Robert Shelton. *The Electric Muse: The Story of Folk into Rock*. London: Eyre Metheun Ltd., 1975.

Lanning, Michael Lee. *Vietnam at the Movies*. New York: Fawcet-Columbine, 1994.

Larkin, Philip. *All What Jazz: A Record Diary 1961–1977*. New York: Faber & Faber, 1970.

Lasch, Christopher. *The Revolt of the Elites and the Betrayal of Democracy*. New York: Norton, 1995.

Lasky, Melvin J., ed. *The Hungarian Revolution*. New York: Frederick A. Praeger, 1957.

LaValley, Al, ed. *Invasion of the Body Snatchers*. New Brunswick, N.J.: Rutgers University Press, 1999.

Lawson, Don. *The United States in the Vietnam War*. New York: Thomas Y. Crowell, 1981.

Leaming, Barbara. *Marilyn Monroe*. New York: Crown, 1998.

Ledeen, Jenny. *Prophecy in the Christian Era*. St. Louis: Peaceberry of Webster Groves, 1995.

Leeming, David Adams. *Mythology: The Voyage of the Hero*. New York: HarperCollins, 1981.

Leish, Kenneth W. *Cinema*. New York: Newsweek Books, 1974.

Leland, John. "Bisexuality," *Newsweek*, 17 July 1995.

Lelby, Richard, "Paranoia," *The Washington Post*, 5 May 1995.

Lelby, Richard and Jim McGee. "Still Burning: Four Years After Waco, The Question Hasn't Been Extinguished," *The Washington Post*, 18 April 1997.

Lemârtre, Georges Édouard. *From Cubism to Surrealism in French Literature*. Cambridge, Mass.: Harvard University Press, 1941.

Leonard, Neil. *Jazz: Myth and Religion*. New York: Oxford University Press, 1987.

Lerner, Michael. "In 'Gump' We Trust," *The Washington Post*, 14 August 1994.

Lettis, Richard and William E. Morris, eds. *The Hungarian Revolt*. New York: Charles Scribner's Sons, 1961.

Levin, Gail. *Edward Hopper: An Intimate Biography*. Berkeley: University of California Press, 1995.

Levine, Richard M. "Crossing the Line," *Mother Jones*, May-June 1994.

Levy, Charles J. *Spoils of War*. Boston: Houghton Mifflin, 1974.

Lewis, David L. *King: A Biography*. Urbana: University of Chicago Press, 1978.

Lewisohn, Mark. *The Beatles: Recording Sessions*. New York: Harmony Books, 1988.

Lewy, Guenter. *The Cause that Failed: Communism in American Political Life*. New York: Oxford University Press, 1990.

Lipmann, Samuel. *Music After Modernism*. New York: Basic Books, 1979.

Lipsky, David and Alexander Abrams. "The Packaging (And Re-Packaging) of a Generation," *Harper's Magazine*, July 1994.

Littlewood, Thomas B. *The Politics of Population Control*. Notre Dame: University of Notre Dame Press, 1977.

Livingston, Paisley. *Ingmar Bergman and the Rituals of Art*. Ithaca, N.Y.: Cornell University Press, 1982.

Lobrutto, Vincent. *Stanley Kubrick: A Biography*. New York: Donald I. Fine Books, 1997.

Locke, John. *On The Reasonableness of Christianity* [1695]. Chicago: Henry Regnery, 1965.

Loshitsky, Yosefa. *The Radical Faces of Godard and Bertolucci*. Detroit: Wayne State University Press, 1995.

Lucie-Smith, Edward. *Race, Sex, and Gender In Contemporary Art*. New York: Abrams, 1994.

Lueken, Verena. *Cindy Sherman*. Rotterdam: Museum Boijmans Van Beuningen, 1997.

Luhan, Mabel Dodge. *Movers and Shakers* [1936]. Albuquerque: University of New Mexico Press, 1985.

Lydon, John. *Rotten: No Irish, No Blacks, No Dogs*. New York: St. Martin's Press, 1994.

Lydon, Michael. *Rock Folk*. New York: Dial Press, 1971.

MacBeath, Rod. "Looking Up Dylan's Sleeves," *The Telegraph*, Winter 1994.

Macdonald, Dwight. *On Movies*. New Jersey: Da Capo, 1969.

MacDonald, Ian. *Revolution in the Head: The Beatles' Records and the Sixties*. New York: Henry Holt, 1994.

MacDonald, J. Fred. *One Nation Under Television*. New York: Pantheon, 1990.

Mailer, Norman. *The Naked and the Dead*. New York: Henry Holt, 1976.

————. "Norman Mailer on Madonna: Like A Lady," *Esquire*, August 1994.

Maitre, Georges Le. *From Cubism to Surrealism in French Literature*. New York: Russell & Russell, 1941.

Makower, Joel. *Woodstock: The Oral History*. New York: Doubleday, 1989.

Mallove, Eugene T. "Einstein's Intoxication with the God of the Cosmos," *Washington Post*, 22 December 1985.

Malone, Bill C. *Country Music U.S.A.* Austin: University of Texas Press, 1985.

Malone, Peter. *Movie Christs and AntiChrists*. New York: Crossroad, 1990.

Mann, Thomas. *Doktor Faustus: Das Leban des dentscher Tonsetzers Adrian Leverkuhn orzahlt von einum Frende*, in *Gesammelte Werke*. Frankfut um Main: S. Fischer Verlag, 1980.

———. *Pro and Contra Wagner*, Allen Blunder, trans. Chicago: University of Chicago Press, 1985.

Manso, Peter. *Brando: The Biography*. New York: Hyperion, 1994.

Manson, Marilyn (with Neil Strauss). *The Long Hard Road Out of Hell*. New York: Regan Books/Harper Perennial, 1999.

Marcus, Greil. *Lipstick Traces: A Secret History of the Twentieth Century*. Cambridge, Mass.: Harvard University Press, 1989.

Marcuse, Herbert. *An Essay on Liberation*. Boston: Beacon, 1969.

Marinetti, Filippo Tommaso. *Selected Writings*, ed. R. W. Flint and trans. R. W. Flint and Arthur A. Coppotelli. New York: Farrar, Straus & Giroux, 1972.

Marquis, Alice G. *Hopes and Ashes: The Birth of Modern Times, 1929–1939*. New York: Macmillan, 1986.

Marshall, Eliot. "One Less Hoop for Gene Therapy," *Science*, 29 July 1994.

Marwick, Arthur. *The Sixties*. Oxford: Oxford University Press, 1998.

Marx, Karl and Friedrich Engels. *The Communist Manifesto*. New York: Monthly Review Press, 1964.

Mast, Gerald. *A Short History of the Movies*. New York: Macmillan, 1986.

Match, Richard. Review of *The Naked and the Dead*. *New York Herald Weekly Book Review*. 9 May 1948.

Mathews, Jay. "Morph for the Money: Hollywood and Computer Imagery Give Advertisers a Powerful New Tool," *The Washington Post*, 7 October 1994.

Mathieu, Bertrand. *Orpheus in Brooklyn: Orphism, Rimbaud and Henry Miller*. The Hague: Mouton, 1976.

Matthews, J. H. *Surrealism and Film*. Ann Arbor: University of Michigan Press, 1971.

Maughan, Shannon and Johnathon Bing, "Turning In To Twentysomething," *Publishers Weekly*, 29 August 1994.

May, Henry F. *The End of American Innocence: A Study of the First Years of Our Time, 1912-1917*. New York: Knopf, 1959.

McCabe, Bob. *The Exorcist: Out of the Shadows*. London: Omnibus Press, 1999.

McCarthy, Abigail. "Generations Aren't Scamless: Altruism Among the Twentysomethings," *Commonweal*, 3 June 1994.

McCarthy, Kevin, ed. *"They're Here. . .": Invasion of The Body Snatchers*. New York: Berkeley Boulevard Books, 1999.

McDonald, Marci. "From Yippies to Yuppies," *MacLean's*, 7 April 1986.

McGilligan, Patrick. *Robert Altman: Jumping Off the Cliff*. New York: St. Martin's Press, 1984.

McKay, Claude. "On Hemingway," in Linda W. Wagner, ed. *Ernest Hemingway: Six Decades of Criticism*. East Lansing, Mich.: Michigan State University Press, 1987.

McKenna, Kristine. "The Feminine Mistake: Being Picasso's Mistress Was Enough To Make

You Cry," *The Washington Post*, 27 February 1994.

McLuhan, Marshall. *Understanding Media: The Extensions of Man*. New York: McGraw-Hill, 1964.

Mead, Margaret. *Coming of Age in Samoa*. New York: Random House, 1953.

————. "From Popping the Question to Popping the Pill," *McCalls*, April 1976.

Megill, Donald D. and Richard S. Demory. *Introduction to Jazz History*. Englewood Cliffs, N.J.: Prentice-Hall, 1984.

Melles, Wilfred. *Twilight of the Gods: The Music of the Beatles*. New York: Viking, 1974.

Mello, Greg. "The Birth of a New Bomb: Shades of Dr. Strangelove! Will We Learn to Love the B61–11?" *The Washington Post*, 1 June 1997.

Miles, Barry. *Ginsberg: A Biography*. New York: Simon & Schuster, 1989.

————. *Paul McCartney: Many Years From Now*. New York: Henry Holt, 1997.

Miller, J. Hillis. *Poets of Reality*. Cambridge, Mass.: Harvard University Press, 1965.

Miller, Jim. "Bob Dylan," *Witness* (Summer/Fall 1988), reprinted in *The Dylan Companion: A Collection of Essential Writings About Bob Dylan*, eds. Elizabeth Thomson and David Gutman. New York: Dell, 1990.

Miller, Russell. *Bunny: The Real Story of Playboy*. New York: Holt, Rinehart & Winston, 1984.

Mills, C. Wright. "The New Left," in *Power, Politics and People: The Collected Essays of C. Wright Mills*, ed. Irving Louis Horowitz. New York: Oxford University Press, 1963.

————. *The Power Elite*. New York: Oxford Univeristy Press, 1956.

Mills, Kathryn. *C. Wright Mills: Letters and Autobiographical Writings*. Berkely: University of California Press, 2000.

Milne, Tom, ed. *Godard on Godard*. New York: Da Capo, 1972.

Mitroff, Ian I. and Warren Bennis. *The Unreality Industry: The Deliberate Manufacturing of Falsehood and What it is Doing to Our Lives*. New York: Oxford University Press, 1989.

Mizener, Arthur, ed. *The Fitzgerald Reader*. New York: Scribner's, 1963.

Monaco, James. *American Film Now: The People, the Power, the Money, the Movies*. New York: Oxford University Press, 1979.

Mordden, Ethan. *Medium Cool: The Movies of the 1960's*. New York: Knopf, 1990.

Moritz, Charles, ed. "Werner Erhard," *Current Biography Yearbook 1977*. New York: Thomas W. Wilson, 1978.

Morris-Keitel, Peter. "Karl Marx" in *Dictionary of Literary Biography*, vol. 129, eds. James Hardin and Siegfried Mews. Detroit: Gale Research, 1993.

Morrisoe, Patricia. *Mapplethorpe: A Biography*. New York: Random House, 1995.

Morrison, Joan and Robert K. *From Camelot to Kent State: The Sixties Experience in the Words of Those Who Lived It*. New York: Times Books, 1987.

Morrison, Wilbur H. *The Elephant and the Tiger: The Full Story of the Vietnam War*. New York: Hippocrene, 1990.

Mulvey, Laura. *Citizen Kane* [1992]. London: British Film Institute, 1994.

294

Murry, John Middleton. "Eliot and the 'Classical' Revival," in *T. S. Eliot: The Critical Heritage,* vol. 1, ed. Michael Grant. London: Routledge & Kegan Paul, 1982.

Mydans, Seth. "In Philippine Town, Child Prostitution, Despite Protests, Is a Way of Life," *New York Times*, 5 February 1989.

Naifeh, Steven and Gregory White Smith. *Jackson Pollock: An American Saga.* New York: Clarkson N. Potter, 1989.

Naremore, James. *More Than Night: Film Noir In Its Contexts.* Berkely: University of California Press, 2000.

Nasaw, David. *The Chief: The Life of William Randolph Hearst.* Boston: Houghton Mifflin, 2000.

Neely, Kim. "Where Angels Fear to Tread," *Rolling Stone*, 5 May 1994.

Neimark, Jill. "They've Got to Have It: The Twentysomethings Take Over," *Mademoiselle*, December 1990.

Nelson, James B. "Needed: A Continuing Sexual Revolution," *The Christian Century*, 1 June 1988.

Nicosia, Gerald. *Memory Babe: A Critical Biography of Jack Kerouac.* Berkeley: University of California Press, 1983.

Nietzsche, Friedrich. *Beyond Good and Evil*, trans. Helen Zimmern. Buffalo, N.Y.: Prometheus, 1989.

————. "The Birth of Tragedy from the Spirit of Music" in *The Birth of Tragedy and the Genealogy of Morals*. trans. Francis Golffing. New York: Doubleday, 1956.

————. *Thus Spake Zarathustra*, trans. Thomas Common, New York: Random House, 1982.

————. *Werke in Drei Banden*. Munich: Carl Hansler Verlag, 1954.

"NIH to Study 'Germ-line' Therapy," *Science*, 9 December 1994.

Nirvana, *In Utero*. David Geffen, 1993.

Norman, Philip. *Rave On: The Biography of Buddy Holly*. New York: Simon & Schuster, 1996.

————. *Shout! The Beatles in Their Generation*. New York: Warner Books, 1982.

O'Brien, Tom. *The Screening of America.* New York: Continuum, 1990.

O'Hanlon, Redmond. *Joseph Conrad and Charles Darwin.* Edinburgh: Salamander Press, 1984.

Okun, Milton, ed. *The Compleat Beatles*, vol. II. Toronto: Delilah/ATV/Bantam Books, 1981.

On the Harvesting of Organs from Executed Prisoners in the People's Republic of China: Hearings before the Senate Committee On Foreign Relations, 104th Cong., 1st Sess., testimony of Harry Wu, Executive Director, Laogai Research Foundation, 1995.

O'Neill, William L. *Coming Apart: An Informal History of America in the 1960s.* New York: Quadrangle, 1971.

Ono, Yoko. *Grapefruit.* New York: Simon & Schuster, 1970.

Orwell, George. *1984* [1949]. New York: Harcourt, 1977.

Orwell, Sonia and Ian Angus, eds. *The Collected Essay, Journalism and Letters of George Orwell*, vol. IV. London: Secker & Warburg, 1968.

Ostrander, Gilman. "The Revolution in Morals," in *Change in Continuity in Twentieth-*

Century America: The 1920's, eds. John Braeman, et al. Columbus, Ohio: Ohio State University Press, 1968.

Oumano, Ellen, ed. *Film Forum: Thiry-Five Top Filmmakers Discuss Their Craft*. New York: St. Martin's Press, 1985.

Pach, Chester J. Jr. "And That's the Way it Was: The Vietnam War on the Network Nightly News," in *The Sixties: From Memory to History by David Farber*. Chapel Hill: University of North Carolina Press, 1994.

Pawel, Ernst. *The Nightmare of Reason: A Life of Franz Kafka*. New York: Farrar, Straus & Giroux, 1984.

Paytress, Mark. *The Rise and Fall of Ziggy Stardust and the Spiders from Mars*. New York: Schirmer Books, 1998.

Peary, Danny. *Cult Movies*. New York: Delta Books, 1981.

Perloff, Marjorie. *The Futurist Moment*. Chicago: University of Chicago Press, 1986.

Perry, Bruce. *Malcolm: The Life of a Man Who Changed Black America*. Barrytown, N.Y.: Station Hill, 1991.

Petitfils, Pierre. *Rimbaud*. Charlottesville, Va.: University of Virginia Press, 1987.

Peyser, Joan. *The New Music: The Sense Behind the Sound*. New York: Delacorte Press, 1971.

Pickering, Stephen. *Bob Dylan Approximately*. New York: David McKay, 1975.

Pillai, A. Sebastian Dravyam. *Post-Modernism: An Intorduction to Postwar Literature in English*. Tiruchirapalli, India: Theresa, 1991.

Pioli, Richard J. *Stung by Salt and War*. New York: Peter Lang, 1987.

Plantinga, Leon. *Romantic Music: A History of Musical Style in Nineteenth Century Europe*. New York: Norton, 1984.

Plessix Gray, Francine du. *At Home With the Marquis de Sade*. New York: Simon & Schuster, 1998.

Poellner, Peter. *Nietzsche and Metaphysics*. Oxford: Oxford University Press, 1995.

Polizzotti, Mark. *Revolution of the Mind: The Life of André Breton*. New York: Farrar, Straus & Giroux, 1995.

Pollock, Jackson. "My Painting," *Possibilities*, vol. I. Winter 1947–48.

Postman, Neil. *Technopoly*. New York: Knopf, 1992.

———. *Building a Bridge to the Eighteenth Century*. New York: Knopf, 1999.

Pound, Ezra. "Letter to Felix Schelling, 8–9 July 1922," in *Selected Letters 1907–1941*, ed., D. D. Paige. New York: New Directions, 1971.

———. "Vortex," *Blast*, vol. I., 20 June 1914.

Powers, John. "The Death of the Actor," *The Washington Post*, 17 July 1994.

Powers, Richard Gid. "Introduction" in Jack Finney, *The Body Snatchers*. Boston: Gregg Press, 1976.

Powers, William F. "Dressed to Kill?" *The Washington Post*, 4 May 1995.

Presnell, Don and Marty McGee. *A Critical History of Television's The Twilight Zone, 1959–1964*. Jefferson, N.C.: McFarland, 1998.

Prince, Stephen. *Savage Cinema: Sam Peckinpah and the Rise of Ultraviolent Movies*. Austin: University of Texas Press, 1998.

"Pro-Pedophile Poet Paid $1 M By Stanford," *Campus Report,* November 1994.

Protopsaltis, E. G. "Byron's Love of Classical Greece and His Role in the Greek Revolution," in *Byron's Political and Cultural Influence in Nineteenth Century Europe*, ed. Paul Graham Trueblood. London: Macmillan, 1981.

Putnam, Robert D. *Bowling Alone: The Collapse and Revival of American Community.* New York: Simon & Schuster, 2000.

Quart, Leonard and Albert Auster. *American Film and Society Since 1945*, 2d ed. New York: Praeger, 1991.

Quinn, Jane Bryant. "The Luck of the Xers: Comeback Kids: Young People Will Earn More and Live Better Than They Think," *Newsweek*, 6 June 1994.

"Radical Evolutionary," *People Weekly*, 12 December 1994.

Rebello, Stephen. *Alfred Hitchcock and the Making of Psycho*. New York: St. Martin's Griffin, 1990.

Reid, Ogden R. "The Day-Care Veto: A Republican Congressman's Challenge to the President," *Redbook*, April 1972.

Reincourt, Amaury de. *The Coming Caesars*. New York: Coward-McCann, 1957.

Reisner, Robert George. *Bird: The Legend of Charlie Parker*. New York: Da Capo, 1987.

Report of the President's Research Committee on Social Trends, in *Recent Social Trends in the United States*. New York: McGraw-Hill, 1933.

Revill, David. *The Roaring Silence: John Cage: A Life*. New York: Arcade, 1992.

Reynolds, Simon and Joy Press. *The Sex Revolts: Gender, Rebellion and Rock 'n' Roll*. Cambridge, Mass.: Harvard University Press, 1995.

Rhodes, Richard. *Dark Sun: The Making of the Hydrogen Bomb*. New York: Simon & Schuster, 1995.

Richard, Paul. "Phallic Phrenzy," *The Washington Post*, 4 December 1993.

Ricketts, Mac Linscott. "Bob Dylan's Church: The Vineyard Christian Fellowship," *On the Tracks*, Fall 1994.

Rifkin, Jeremy. *Algeny*. New York: Viking, 1983.

Riley, Clayton. "...Or 'A Dangerous, Criminally Irresponsible Horrorshow'?" *The Sunday New York Times Drama Section*, 9 January 1972.

Riley, Tim. *Tell Me Why: A Beatless Commentary*. New York: Knopf, 1988.

Riordan, James. *Stone: The Controversies, Excesses, and Exploits of a Radical Filmmaker*. New York: Hyperion, 1995.

Riordan, James and Jerry Prochnicky. *Break on Through: The Life and Death of Jim Morrison*. New York: William Morrow, 1991.

Robb, Graham. *Rimbaud: A Biography.* New York: Norton, 2000.

Roberts, J. M. *History of the World*. New York: Oxford University Press, 1993.

Robinson, Paul. *The Modernization of Sex*. New York: Harper & Row, 1976.

Rodley, Chris. *Cronenberg On Cronenberg*. London: Faber & Faber, 1993.

Rodman, Seldon. *Conversations With Artists*. New York: Devin-Adair, 1957.

Rookmaaker, H. R. *Modern Art and the Death of Culture*. Downers Grove, Ill.: InterVarsity Press, 1970.

Rose, Barbara. *American Art Since 1900*. New York: Praeger, 1967.

Rosentheil, Thomas B. "Viewers Found to Confuse TV Entertainment With News," *Los Angeles Times*, 17 August 1989.

Rousseau, Jean-Jacques. "The Social Contract," in *The Social Contract and Discourses*, trans. G. D. H. Cole, New York: E. P. Dutton, 1950.

Rowland, Anna. *Bauhaus Source Book*. New York: Van Nostrand Reinhold, 1990.

Rubin, Jerry. *Growing (Up) at Thirty-Seven*. New York: M. Evans, 1976.

Runes, Dagobert D., ed. *Treasury of World Philosophy*. Patterson, N.J.: Littlefield, Adams, 1959.

Sabin, Richard. *Adult Comics: An Introduction*. New York: Routledge, 1993.

Salinger, J. D. *The Catcher in the Rye*. New York: Random House, 1951.

Salinger, Margaret A. *Dream Catcher: A Memoir*. New York: Washington Square Books, 2000.

Salisbury, Mark, ed. *Burton On Burton*. London: Faber & Faber, 1995.

Salzberg, Joel, ed. *Critical Essays on Salinger's The Catcher in the Rye*. Boston: G. K. Hall, 1990.

Sandbank, Shimon. *After Kafka*. Athens: University of Georgia Press, 1989.

Sander, Gordon F. *Serling: The Rise and Twilight of Television's Last Angry Man*. New York: Dutton, 1992.

Sandoz, Ellis. *Political Apocalypse: A Study of Dostoevsky's Grand Inquisitor,* 2d ed., rev. Wilmington, Del.: ISI Books, 2000.

Sanger, Margaret. *An Autobiography* [1938]. New York: Dover, 1971.

Saul, John Ralston. *Voltaire's Bastards: The Dictatorship of Reason in the West*. New York: Free Press, 1992.

Savage, Jon. *England's Dreaming: Anarchy, Sex Pistols, Punk Rock and Beyond*. New York: St. Martin's Press, 1992.

Scaduto, Anthony. *Bob Dylan*. New York: Grosset & Dunlap, 1971.

Schaeffner, Neil. *The Marquis de Sade: A Life*. New York: Knopf, 1999.

Schaffner, Nicholas. *The Beatles Forever*. Harrisburg, Penn.: Stackpole Books, 1977.

Schatz, Thomas. *The Genius of the System: Hollywood Filmmaking in the Studio Era*. New York: Pantheon, 1988.

Schelde, Per. *Adroids, Humanoids, and other Science Fiction Monsters*. New York: New York University Press, 1993.

Scheuer, Jeffrey. *The Sound Bite Society: Television and the American Mind*. New York: Four Walls Eight Windows, 1999.

Schindehette, Susan, Todd Gold, and Barbara Kleban Mills. "Hef Gains a Bride, Loses a Reputation," *People Weekly*, 17 July 1989.

Schmidt, Paul, trans. *Arthur Rimbaud: Complete Works*. New York: Harper & Row, 1976.

Schoemer, Karen. "Woodstock '94: Back to the Garden," *Newsweek*, 8 August 1994.

Schuller, Gunter. *Early Jazz: Its Roots and Musical Development.* New York: Oxford Univeristy Press, 1986.

Schumacher, Michael. *There But for Fortune: The Life of Phil Ochs.* New York: Hyperion, 1996.

Scott, Otto. *Robespierre: The Voice of Virtue.* New York: Mason & Lipscomb, 1974.

Selby, Spencer. *Dark City: The Film Noir.* Jefferson, N.C.: McFarlane, 1984.

Sessums, Kevin. "Love Child," *Vanity Fair*, June 1995.

Sexton, Jim. "No Rest for the Eerie," *USA Weekend*, 12–14 May 1995.

Shadwick, Keith. *The Illustrated Story of Jazz.* New York: Crescent Books, 1991.

Shapiro, Joseph P. "Just Fix It: The Twentysomething Rebels' Battle Plan is to Repair the Damage Their Elders Wrought and Chart a New Course," *U.S. News and World Report*, 22 February 1993.

Shapiro, Nat and Nat Hentoff. *Hear Me Talkin' to Ya.* New York: Dover, 1966.

Sharpe, Tony. *T. S. Eliot: A Literary Life.* London: Macmillan, 1991.

Sheed, Wilfred and Jacques Lowe. *The Kennedy Legacy.* New York: Penguin, 1988.

Shelton, Robert. *No Direction Home: The Life and Music of Bob Dylan.* New York: Ballantine, 1986.

Showalter, Elaine. *Sexual Anarchy: Gender and Culture at the Fin de Siecle.* London: Bloomsbury, 1991.

Siegel, Don. *A Siegel Film: An Autobiography.* London: Faber & Faber, 1993.

Siegel, Fred. "Blissed Out and Loving It," *Commonweal*, 9 February 1990.

Simpson, Louis. *Three on the Tower.* New York: William Morrow, 1975.

Sinclair, Andrew. *Francis Bacon: His Life and Violent Times.* London: Sinclair-Stevenson, 1993.

Singer, Peter. *Rethinking Life and Death: the Collapse of Our Traditional Ethics.* New York: St. Martin's Press, 1995.

Skal, David J. *The Monster Show: A Cultural History of Horror.* New York: Penguin Books, 1994.

Skinner, B. F. *About Behaviorism.* New York: Knopf, 1974.

———. *Beyond Freedom and Dignity.* New York: Knopf, 1971.

Sloan, Louise. "Do Ask, Do Tell: Lesbians Come Out at Work," *Glamour*, May 1994.

Slott, Dan, Mike Kazaleh, et al. *The Ren & Stimpy Show: I Scream Clones*, vol. 1, no. 12. November 1993.

Smith, Joe. *Off the Record: An Oral History of Popular Music.* New York: Warner, 1988.

Sobchack, Vivian. *Meta-Morphing: Visual Transformation and the Culture of Quick-change.* Minneapolis: University of Minnesota Press, 2000.

Solomon, Stanley J. *The Classic Cinema: Essays in Criticism.* New York: Harcourt, 1973.

———. *The Film Idea.* New York: Harcourt, 1972.

Sowell, Thomas. *Marxism: Philosophy and Economics.* New York: William Morrow, 1985.

Span, Paula. "The Man Who Cried Wolf," *The Washington Post*, 14 April 1997.

Sperber, A. M. and Eric Lax. *Bogart.* New York: William Morrow, 1997.

Spigel, Lynn and Michael Curtin, eds. *The Revolution Wasn't Televised: Sixties Television and Social Conflict*. New York: Routledge, 1997.

Spoto, Donald. *The Dark Side of Genius: The Life of Alfred Hitchcock*. Boston: Little, Brown, 1993.

———. *Rebel: The Life and Legend of James Dean*. New York: HarperCollins, 1996.

Springer, Claudia. *Electronic Eros: Bodies and Desire in the Postindustrial Age*. Austin: University of Texas Press, 1996.

Stackelhaus, Heimer. *Joseph Beuys*. New York: Abbeville, 1991.

Stambler, Irwin. *The Encyclopedia of Pop, Rock and Soul*, rev. ed. New York: St. Martin's Press, 1989.

Star, Alexander. "The Twentysomething Myth," *The New Republic*, 4 January 1994.

Starkie, Enid. *Arthur Rimbaud*. New York: New Directions, 1961.

Stella, Frank. "Painting Is Dead . . . ," *The Washington Post*, 21 November 1993.

Stepp, Laura Sessions. "Youth Say TV Shapes Values: Poll Shows Majority Want Moral Guidance on Issues," *The Washington Post*, 27 February 1995.

Stern, Jane and Michael. *Encyclopedia of Pop Culture*. New York: Harper Perennial, 1992.

Stokstad, Marilyn. *Art History*. New York: Abrams, 1995.

Stone, Oliver and Zachary Sklar. *JFK: The Book of the Film*. New York: Applause Books, 1992.

Storr, Anthony. *Music and the Mind*. New York: Ballantine, 1992.

Strachery, James, ed., *On the History of the Psychoanalytic Movement, Standard Edition of the Complete Psychological Works of Sigmund Freud*. London: The Hogarth Press and the Institute of Psychoanalysis, 1953–66.

Strauss, William and Neil Howe. *The Fourth Turning: An American Prophecy*. New York: Broadway Books, 1997.

———. *Generations: The History of America's Future 1584 to 2069*. New York: William Morrow, 1991.

Sugarman, Danny, ed. *The Doors: The Complete Lyrics*. New York: Delta, 1991.

Sullivan, Henry W. *The Beatles with Lacan: Rock & Roll as Requiem for the Modern Age*. New York: Peter Lang, 1995.

Sullivan, William J. "Peter Shaffer's *Amadeus*: The Making and Un-Making of the Fathers," *American Imago*, Spring 1988.

Sulpy, Doug and Ray Schweighardt. *Drugs, Divorce and a Slipping Image*. Princeton Junction, N.J.: The 910, 1994.

"Summer of Love: George Martin's New Book Gives An Account of the Making of the Sgt. Pepper Album," *Beatle Monthly*, November 1994.

Sweetman, David. *Paul Gauguin: A Life*. New York: Simon & Schuster, 1995.

Sylvester, David. *Francis Bacon: The Human Body*. Berkeley: University of California Press, 1995.

———. *Interviews with Francis Bacon*. London: Thames & Hudson, 1975.

"The Complexities of Tomorrow's Medicine," *Healthcare Forum*, September/October 1994.

The Illustrated History of Country Music. Garden City, N.Y.: Doubleday, 1979.

The Washington Post Magazine, 2 February 1997.

The World Almanac & Book of Facts 1978. New York: Newpaper Enterprise Association, 1977.

Taffel, Ron. "How to Protect Your Kids From Madonna," *McCalls*, January 1993.

Tapia, Andres. "Reaching the First Post-Christian Generation X," *Christianity Today*, 12 September 1994.

Taylor, Ella. *Prime Time Families: Television Culture in Postwar America.* Los Angeles: University of California Press 1989.

Taylor, John Russel. *Orson Welles: A Celebration.* Boston: Little, Brown, 1986.

Tebbel, John and Mary Ellen Zuckerman. *The Magazine in America, 1741–1990.* New York: Oxford University Press, 1991.

Thomas, Dana. "A Nude Wraps," *The Washington Post*, 28 June 1995.

Thompson, Hunter. *Fear and Loathing in Las Vegas.* New York: Vintage, 1971.

Thomson, David. *A Biographical Dictionary of Film*, 3d ed. New York: Knopf, 1994.

———. *Rosebud; The Story of Orson Welles.* New York: Knopf, 1996.

Tomkins, Calvin. *Duchamp.* New York: Henry Holt, 1996.

Tonetti, Claretta Micheletti. *Bernardo Bertolucci.* New York: Twayne, 1995.

Tosches, Nick. *Unsung Heroes of Rock 'n' Roll: The Birth of Rock in the Wild Years Before Elvis.* New York: Harmony Books, 1984, 1991.

Trescott, Jacqueline and Roxanne Roberts. "A Weekend All About R-E-S-P-E-C-T," *The Washington Post*, 5 December 1994.

Truffaut, Francois. *The Films In My Life.* New York: Da Capo, 1994.

Turner, Steve. *Angelheaded Hipster: A Life of Jack Kerouac.* New York: Viking, 1996.

———. *A Hard Day's Write: The Story Behind Every Beatle Song.* New York: Harper Perennial, 1994.

Twitchell, James B. *Lead Us Into Temptation: The Triumph of American Materialism.* New York: Columbia University Press, 1999.

Tzara, Tristan. *Seven Dada Manifestos and Lampisteries*, trans. Barbara Wright. London: John Calder, 1977.

Unger, Irwin and Debi. *Turning Point: 1968.* New York: Charles Scribner's Sons, 1988.

Vincent, Richard C., Dennis K. Davis, and Lily Ann Boruszkowski. "Sexism on MTV: The Portrayal of Women in Rock Videos," *Journalism Quarterly*, Winter 1987.

Vogel, Amos. *Film as a Subversive Art.* New York: Random House, 1974.

Volz, Pia Daniela. *Nietzsche in Labyrinth seiner Krankheit: Eine medizinischbiographische Untersuchuns.* Wurzburg: Konighausen und Neumann, 1990.

Wagner, Richard. *Prose Works*, William Ashton Ellis, trans., vol. 1, in *The Artwork of the Future.* New York: Bronde Brothers, 1966.

———. *Prose Works*, William Ashton Ellis, trans., vol. 2, in *Opera and Drama.* New York: Bronde Brothers, 1966.

———. *Tristan and Isolde*, English vocal score by Henry Grafton Chapman. New York: G. Schirmer, 1934.

Walker, Gregg B., David A. Bella, and Steven J. Sprecher, eds. *The Military-Industrial Complex*. New York: Peter Lang, 1992.

Wallace, Bruce. "The Dolly Debate," *MacLean's*, 10 March 1997.

Washington, James M., ed. *A Testament of Hope: The Essential Writings and Speeches of Martin Luther King, Jr.* San Francisco: HarperCollins, 1986.

Watkins, T. W. *The Great Depression: America in the 1930's*. New York: Little, Brown, 1993.

Watson, Ben. *Frank Zappa: The Negative Dialectics of Poodle Play*. New York: St. Martin's Press, 1993.

Watson, John B. *The Ways of Behaviorism*. New York: Harper & Brothers, 1928.

Waxman, Sharon. "The Dutch Way of Death," *The Washington Post*, 21 January 1995.

Wayne-Davies, Marion, ed. *The Bloomsbury Guide to English Literature*. New York: Prentice-Hall, 1990.

Weiss, Stephen. *A War Remebered: Voices from Vietnam*. Boston: Boston Publishing, 1986.

West, Geoffrey. *Charles Darwin; A Portrait*. New Haven, Conn.: Yale University Press, 1938.

Weyr, Thomas. *Reaching for Paradise: The Playboy Vision of America*. New York: Times Books, 1978.

Whitehead, John W. "Slaughterhouse Earth: The Crucifixion of Francis Bacon," *Gadfly*, March 1998.

———. "Who's Afraid of *The Exorcist?*" *Gadfly*, October 1998.

Whitford, Frank. *Bauhaus*. London: Thames & Hudson, 1984.

Wilde, Oscar. *The Works of Oscar Wilde*, G.F. Maine, ed. New York: E. P. Dutton, 1954.

Wilshire, Bruce. *Romanticism and Evolution*. New York: G. P. Putnam's Sons, 1968.

Wilson, A. N. *God's Funeral*. New York: Norton, 1999.

Wilson, Edmund. "The Poetry of Drouth," *The Dial*, December 1922.

Wilson, Sloan. *The Man in the Gray Flannel Suit*. New York: Simon & Schuster, 1955.

Wineapple, Brenda. *Sister Brother: Gertrude and Leo Stein*. New York: G. P. Putnam's Sons, 1996.

Wolfe, Donald H. *The Last Days of Marilyn Monroe*. New York: William Morrow, 1998.

Wolfe, Tom. *From Bauhaus to Our House*. New York: Farrar, Straus & Giroux, 1981.

———. "Sorry, But Your Soul Just Died," *Forbes ASAP*, 2 December 1996.

Woloch, Nancy. *Women and the American Experience*. New York: Knopf, 1984.

"Women's Liberation Revisited," *Time*, 20 March 1972.

Woodward, Kenneth L. "Roll Over John Calvin," *Newsweek*, 6 May 1991.

World Almanac. Manwah, N.J.: Funk & Wagnalls, 1995.

Wyatt, Charles R. *Paper Soldiers: The American Press and the Vietnam War*. New York: Norton, 1993.

Wyver, John. *The Moving Image: An International History of Film, Television and Video*. New York: Basil Blackwell, 1989.

302

Yard, Sally. "Francis Bacon," *Francis Bacon: A Retrospective*. New York: Abrams, 1999.

Young, Marilyn B. *The Vietnam Wars: 1945–1990*. New York: HarperCollins, 1991.

Yue, Meug, "Female Images and the National Myth," in *Gender Politics in Modern China*, ed. Tani E. Barlow. Durham: Duke University Press, 1993.

Yurchenco, Henrietta. *A Mighty Hard Road: The Woody Guthrie Story*. New York: McGraw-Hill, 1970.

Zahn, Gordon. "Abortion and the Corruption of the Mind," *New Perspectives on Human Abortion*. Frederick, Md.: University Publications of America, 1981.

Zicree, Marc Scott. *The Twilight Zone Companion*. New York: Bantam, 1982.

Zinn, Howard. *SNCC: The New Abolitionists*. Boston: Beacon, 1965.

NOTES

CHAPTER ONE: BREAKING WITH THE PAST

1. Oscar Wilde, *The Works of Oscar Wilde* (New York: Dutton, 1954), p. 931.

2. Otto Scott, *Robespierre: The Voice of Virtue* (New York: Mason & Lipscomb, 1974), p. 164.

3. Will and Ariel Durant, *The Age of Napoleon* (New York: Simon & Schuster, 1975), p. 579.

4. Gerald Abraham, *A Hundred Years of Music* (London: Duckworth, 1974), p. 26.

5. George Gordon, Lord Byron, "Cain" in *The Poetical Works of Byron* (Boston: Houghton Mifflin, 1975), p. 630.

6. Byron quoted in M. H. Abrams, et al., eds., *The Norton Anthology of English Literature*, 3d ed. (New York: Norton, 1975), p. 1603.

7. Oscar Wilde, op. cit., p. 19.

8. Ibid, p. 857.

9. Sarah Faunce, *Gustave Courbet* (New York: Abrams, 1993), p. 8.

10. As quoted in ibid., p. 17.

11. Sam Hunter and John Jacobus, *Modern Art: Painting, Sculpture, Architecture* (New York: Abrams, 1992), p. 18.

12. As quoted in Oliver Bernard, ed., *Rimbaud: Collected Poems* (Middlesex, England: Penguin, 1986), pp. 5–6 (emphasis in original).

13. As quoted in ibid., pp. 10–11 (emphasis in original).

14. Arthur Rimbaud, *Complete Works,* trans. Paul Schmidt (New York: Harper & Row, 1976), pp. 84–5.

15. As quoted in Yves Duplessis, *Surrealism,* trans. Paul Capon (New York: Walker, 1962), p. 10.

16. As quoted in Richard Harrington, "The Core of Rotten: Fifteen Years of Silence, John Lydon Talks about His Career as a Sex Pistol," *The Washington Post* (July 10, 1994), p. G1.

CHAPTER TWO: WHERE ARE WE GOING?

1. As quoted in Charles Binderman, "Charles Darwin" in *Dictionary of Literary Biography,* vol. 57 (Detroit: Cale Research, 1987), p. 63.

2. Charles Darwin, *Descent of Man* (London: John Murray, 1871), p. 9.

3. Douglas DeWar and H. S. Shelton, *Is Evolution Proved?* (London: Hollis & Carter, 1947), p. 4.

4. As quoted in Amaury de Reincourt, *The Coming Caesars* (New York: Coward-McCann, 1957), p. 179.

5. As quoted in Herbert Agar, *The Price of Union* (Boston: Houghton Mifflin, 1950), p. 522.

6. Geoffrey Bruun, *Revolution and Reaction: 1848–1852: A Mid-Century Watershed* (Princeton: Van Nostrand, 1958), p. 83.

7. Georg Wilhelm Friedrich Hegel, *The Philosoophy of History,* rev. ed., trans. J. Sibree (New York: Colonial, 1900), p. 39.

8. J. M. Roberts, *History of the World* (New York: Oxford Univ. Press, 1993), p. 637.

9. As quoted in Robert Hughes, *The Shock of the New: Art and the Century of Change* (London: Thames and Hudson, 1993), pp. 113-14.

10. As quoted in Sam Hunter and John Jacobus, *Modern Art: Painting, Sculpture, Architecture* (New York: Abrams, 1992), p. 20.

11. As quoted in Sam Hunter, *Modern French Painting, 1855–1956* (New York: Dell, 1956), p. 75.

12. As quoted in Hunter and Jacobus, op. cit., p. 28.

13. As quoted in Hughes, op. cit., p. 18.

14. Arthur Keith, *Evolution and Ethics* (New York: G. P. Putnam's Sons, 1949), p. 230.

15. Stephen Jay Gould, *The Mismeasure of Man* (New York: Norton, 1996), p. 416.

16. Charles Darwin, *The Descent of Man and Selection in Relation to Sex* (New York: D. Appleton, 1896), p. 564.

17. Michael Crichton, *Jurassic Park* (New York: Ballantine, 1993), p. x.

18. Arthur Schopenhauer, *The Works of Schopenhauer,* ed. Will Durant (New York: Simon & Schuster, 1928), p. 454.

19. As quoted in Richard Grenier, *Capturing the Culture: Film, Art and Politics* (Washington, D.C.: Ethics and Public Policy Center, 1991), p. 10.

20. As quoted in Emile Faguet, *On Reading Nietzsche* (New York: Moffat, Yard, 1918), p. 71.

21. As quoted in John Burt Foster, Jr., *Heirs to Dionysus* (Princeton, NJ: Princeton Univ. Press, 1981), p. 5.

22. James Riordan and Jerry Prochnicky, *Break On Through: The Life and Death of Jim Morrison* (New York: Morrow, 1991), p. 39.

23. Friedrich Nietzsche, *Beyond Good and Evil,* trans. Walter Kaufman (New York: Random House, 1966), p. 153.

24. Riordan and Prochnicky, op. cit., p. 301.

1. Robert Hughes, *The Shock of the New: Art and the Century of Change* (London: Thames & Hudson, 1993), p. 11.

2. Frederick Harrt, *Art: A History of Painting, Sculpture, Architecture,* 4th ed. (New York: Abrams, 1993), p. 962.

3. Hughes, op. cit., p. 24.

4. As quoted in Kristine McKenna, "The Feminine Mistake: Being Picasso's Mistress Was Enough to Make You Cry," *The Washington Post* (February 27, 1994), p. G6.

5. As quoted in Sam Hunter and John Jacobus, *Modern Art: Painting, Sculpture, Architecture* (New York: Abrams, 1992), p. 152.

6. As quoted in Hughes, op. cit., p. 44.

7. Ibid., p. 48.

8. As quoted in Hunter and Jacobus, op. cit., p. 250.

9. As quoted in Henry F. May, *The End of American Innocence: A Study of the First Years of Our Time, 1912–1917* (New York: Knopf, 1959), p. 245.

10. As quoted in Hunter and Jacobus, op. cit., pp. 250–51.

11. As quoted in Hughes, op. cit., p. 56.

12. Ibid., p. 58.

13. As quoted in J. M. Roberts, *History of the World* (New York: Oxford Univ. Press, 1993), p. 720.

14. David M. Kennedy, *Over Here: The First World War and American Society* (New York: Oxford Univ. Press, 1980), p. 57.

15. As quoted in Marc Dachy, *The Dada Movement, 1915–1923* (New York: Rizzoli International, 1990), p. 43.

16. As quoted in Rose Lee Goldberg, *Performance Art: From Futurism to the Present* (New York: Abrams, 1988), p. 26.

17. David Finkle, "High Performance," *Village Voice* (January 5, 1993), p. 54.

18. As quoted in Hughes, op. cit., p. 61.

19. As quoted in Dachy, op. cit., p. 176.

20. As quoted in Hughes, op. cit., p. 63.

21. As quoted in R. S. Furness, *Expressionism* (London: Methuen, 1973), p. 48.

22. As quoted in Hunter and Jacobus, op. cit., p. 121.

23. Ibid.

24. Ernest L. Freud, ed., *Letters of Sigmund Freud,* trans. Tevin and James Stern (New York: Basic Books, 1960), p. 307.

25. As quoted in Freddy Bauche, *The Cinema of Luis Buñuel* (London: Tanting, 1973), p. 9.

26. Edmund Wilson, "The Poetry of Drouth," *The Dial* (December 1922), p. 613.

27. T. S. Eliot, "Thoughts after Lambeth," *Selected Essays, 1917–1932* (New York: Harcourt Brace, 1932), p. 332

CHAPTER FOUR: THE LOST GENERATION

1. T. S. Eliot, *The Complete Poems and Plays, 1909–1950* (New York: Harcourt, Brace and World, 1971), p. 56.

2. John B. Watson, *The Ways of Behaviorism* (New York: Harper & Brothers, 1928), p. 20.

3. Albert Einstein, *Out of My Later Years* (London: Thames & Hudson, 1950), p. 41.

4. Mabel Dodge Luhan, *Movers and Shakers* (Albuquerque: University of New Mexico Press, 1985, orig. 1936), p. 69.

5. As quoted in David Halberstam, *The Fifties* (New York: Villard, 1993), p. 286.

6. As quoted in Thomas B. Littlewood, *Birth Control in America: The Career of Margaret Sanger* (New Haven: Yale University Press, 1970), p. 16.

7. Margaret Sanger, *An Autobiography* (New York: Dover, 1971, orig. 1938), p. 217.

8. As quoted in Halberstam, op. cit., pp. 605–6.

9. Margaret Mead, "From Popping the Question to Popping the Pill," *McCalls* (April 1976), p. 260.

10. As quoted in Nat Hentoff, *Jazz Is* (New York: Limelight, 1983), p. 68.

11. Ibid.

12. As quoted in Gary Giddens, *Satchmo* (New York: Doubleday, 1988), p. 33.

13. As quoted in Keith Shadwick, *The Illustrated Story of Jazz* (New York: Crescent Books, 1990), p. 110.

14. Patrick Carr, ed. *The Illustrated History of Country Music* (Garden City, NY: Doubleday, 1979), pp. 54–55.

15. F. Scott Fitzgerald, "Self-Interview: An Interview with F. Scott Fitzgerald," in *F. Scott Fitzgerald in His Own Time: A Miscellany,* eds. Matthew J. Bruccoli and Jackson R. Bryer (Kent, OH: Kent State Univ. Press, 1971), p. 162.

16. As quoted in F. Scott Fitzgerald, "Echoes of the Jazz Age, " in *The Fitzgerald Reader* (New York: Scribner's, 1963), pp. 327–28.

17. As quoted in Matthew J. Bruccoli, *Some Sort of Epic Grandeur* (New York: Harcourt Brace Jovanovich, 1981), p. 229.

18. John F. Carter, Jr., "'These Wild Young People' by One of Them," *Atlantic Monthly* (September 1920), p. 303.

19. Frank Whiteford, *Bauhaus* (London: Thames & Hudson, 1984), p. 196.

20. Ernest Hemingway, *A Farewell to Arms* (New York: Macmillan, 1957; orig. 1929), p. 327.

21. Eric J. Hobsbawm, *The Age of Extremes: A History of the World, 1914–1991* (New York: Vintage, 1996), p. 195.

22. John Russel Taylor, *Orson Welles: A Celebration* (Boston: Little, Brown, 1986), p. 56.

23. As quoted in Cornelia V. Christenson, *Kinsey: A Biography* (Bloomington, IN: Indiana Univ. Press, 1971), p. 280.

24. David Dempsey, review of *The Naked and the Dead,* in *New York Times Book Review* (May 9, 1948), p. 6.

25. Sloan Wilson, *The Man in the Gray Flannel Suit* (New York: Simon & Schuster, 1955), p. 109.

26. Robert Hughes, *The Shock of the New* (London: Thames & Hudson, 1993), p. 323.

27. As quoted in David Sylvester, *An Interview with Francis Bacon* (London: Thames & Hudson, 1995), p. 23.

28. As quoted in Andrew Sinclair, *Francis Bacon: His Life and Violent Times* (London: Sinclair-Stevenson, 1993), p. 101.

29. As quoted in Daniel Farson, *The Gilded Gutter Life of Francis Bacon* (New York: Pantheon, 1993), p. 276.

30. As quoted in ibid., p. 239.

31. As quoted in Sinclair, op. cit., p. 100.

CHAPTER FIVE: THE FAT DREAM

1. Jack Kerouac, *On the Road* (New York: Penguin, 1991, orig. 1957), p. 54.

2. As quoted in Dominick LaCapra, *A Preface to Sartre* (Ithaca, NY: Cornell Univ. Press, 1978), p. 97.

3. Albert Camus, *The Myth of Sisyphus and Other Essays,* trans. Justin O'Brien (New York: Knopf, 1955, orig. 1942), p. 6.

4. As quoted in Richard Lattis and William E. Morris, eds., *The Hungarian Revolt* (New York: Scribner's, 1961), p. 60.

5. Edwin R. Bayley, *Joe McCarthy and the Press* (Madison, WI: Univ. of Wisconsin Press, 1981), p. 193.

6. As quoted in Michel Ciment, *Kazan on Kazan* (New York: Viking, 1973), p. 110.

7. As quoted in John Brusnan, *Future Tense: The Cinema of Science Fiction* (New York: St. Martin's Press, 1978), p. 127.

8. As quoted in Erik Barnouw, *Tube of Plenty* (New York: Oxford Univ. Press, 1975), p. 180.

9. As quoted in J. Fred MacDonald, *One Nation Under Television* (New York: Pantheon, 1990), p. 75.

10. As quoted in Ann Charters, ed., *The Portable Beat Reader* (New York: Penguin, 1992), p. 61 (emphasis in original).

11. As quoted in ibid., p. xxvii.

12. As quoted in David Halberstam, *The Fifties* (New York: Villard, 1993), p. 307.

13. As quoted in "Pro-Pedophile Poet Paid $1 M by Stanford," *Campus Report* (November 1994), p. 1.

14. As quoted in Steve Turner, *Angelheaded Hipster: A Life of Jack Kerouac* (New York: Viking, 1996), p. viii.

15. Kerouac, op. cit., p. 9.

16. Jack Kerouac, "The Philosophy of the Beat Generation," *Esquire* (March 1958), pp. 24, 26.

17. Jack Kerouac, *Vanity of Duluoz: An Adventurous Education, 1935–1946* (New York: Coward-McCann, 1968, orig. 1960), p. 207.

18. As quoted in Ben Brown, "A Restless Generation Finds a Muse," *USA Today* (October 19, 1994), p. 2D.

19. Ibid.

20. Turner, op. cit., (New York: Viking, 1996), p. 213.

21. J. D. Salinger, *The Catcher in the Rye* (New York: Random House, 1951), pp. 225, 224.

22. As quoted in Joel Salzberg, *Critical Essays on Salinger's The Catcher in the Rye* (Boston: Hall, 1990), p. 31.

23. "The Mysterious J. D. Salinger," *Newsweek* (May 30, 1960), p. 92.

24. James R. Gaines, "The Man Who Shot John Lennon," *People* (February 23, 1987), p. 60.

25. Ian Hamilton, *In Search of J. D. Salinger* (New York: Random House, 1988), p. 131.

26. David Dalton, *James Dean: The Mutant King* (New York: St. Martin's, 1974), p. 340.

27. As quoted in Halberstam, op. cit., p. 457.

28. Ibid., p. 477.

29. Ibid., p. 473.

30. Ibid., p. 479.

31. Ibid., p. 257.

32. Ibid.

33. As quoted in Seldon Rodman, *Conversations with Artists* (New York: Devin-Adair, 1957), p. 102.

34. Robert Hughes, *The Shock of the New: Art and the Century of Change,* rev. ed. (London: Thames & Hudson, 1993), p. 296.

35. As quoted in Russell Miller, *Bunny: The Real Story of Playboy* (New York: Holt, Rinehart & Winston, 1984), p. 39.

36. As quoted in Halberstam, op. cit., p. 573.

37. As quoted in Thomas Weyr, *Reaching for Paradise: The Playboy Vision of America* (New York: Time Books, 1978), p. 37.

38. As quoted in Halberstam, op. cit., p. 576.

39. As quoted in Weyr, op. cit., p. 49.

40. As quoted in ibid., p. 51.

41. As quoted in Miller, op. cit., p. 230.

42. As quoted in Susan Schindehette, Todd Gold, and Barbara Kleban Mills, "Hef Gains a Bride, Loses a Reputation," *People Weekly* (July 17, 1989), p. 39.

43. Joe Chidley, "Hef at Home," *MacLean's* (August 15, 1994), p. 40.

44. As quoted in Justine Blau, *Betty Friedan* (New York: Chelsea House, 1990), p. 49.

45. As quoted in ibid., p. 55.

46. James Melvin Washington, ed., *A Testament of Hope: The Essential Writings and Speeches of Martin Luther King, Jr.* (New York: HarperSanFransisco, 1986), p. 219.

CHAPTER SIX: THE WINDS OF REVOLUTION

1. Miles, ed., *John Lennon: In His Own Words* (London: Omnibus Press, 1994), p. 79.

2. Tom Hayden, *Port Huron Statement* (New York: Students for a Democratic Society, 1964), p. 3.

3. As quoted in Terry H. Anderson, *The Movement and the Sixties* (New York: Oxford Univ. Press, 1995), p. 64.

4. As quoted in ibid., p. 49.

5. As quoted in Howard Zinn, *SNCC: The New Abolitionists* (Boston: Beacon, 1965), p. 1.

6. Herbert Marcuse, *An Essay on Liberation* (Boston: Beacon, 1969), p. 91.

7. As quoted in Anderson, op. cit., p. 59.

8. As quoted in Clark Dougan and Samuel Lipsman, *A Nation Divided* (Boston: Boston Publishing, 1984), p. 70.

9. As quoted in Joan Morrison and Robert K. Anderson, *From Camelot to Kent State: The Sixties Experience in the Words of Those who Lived It* (New York: Time Books, 1987), p. 97.

10. Marilyn B. Young, *The Vietnam Wars: 1945–1990* (New York: HarperCollins, 1991), p. 244.

11. As quoted in Dougan and Lipsman, op. cit., p. 72.

12. Abbie Hoffman, *Soon to be a Major Motion Picture* (New York: C. P. Putnam's Sons, 1980), p. 102.

13. Jon Savage, *England's Dreaming: Anarchy, Sex Pistols, Punk Rock, and Beyond* (New York: St. Martin's, 1992), p. 27.

14. "De Gaulle's Great Mal de Tete," interview with Jean-Jacques Servan-Schreiber, *Life* (May 31,1968), p. 27.

15. As quoted in Robin Denselow, *When the Music's Over: The Story of Political Pop* (London: Faber & Faber, 1989), p. 31.

16. "Folk Singers: Let Us Now Praise Little Men," *Time* (May 31, 1963), p. 40.

17. As quoted in Barry Miles, *Ginsberg: A Biography* (New York: Simon & Schuster, 1989), pp. 458–59.

18. As quoted in Donald Clarke, *The Rise and Fall of Popular Music* (New York: St. Martin's, 1975), p. 462.

19. As quoted in Robert Shelton, *No Direction Home: The Life and Music of Bob Dylan* (New York: Ballantine, 1986), pp. 222–24.

20. Ibid., p. 324.

21. Nat Hentoff, "Profiles," *New Yorker* (October 24, 1964), p. 65 (emphasis in original).

22. As quoted in Clinton Heylin, *Bob Dylan: Behind the Shades* (New York: Summit, 1991), p. 316.

23. As quoted in Mac Linscott Ricketts, "Bob Dylan's Church: The Vineyard Christian Fellowship," *On the Tracks* (Fall 1994), p. 44.

24. Leonard Quart and Albert Auster, *American Film and Society Since 1945,* rev. ed. (New York: Praeger, 1991), p. 89.

25. As quoted in Redmond O'Hanlon, *Joseph Conrad and Charles Darwin* (Edinburgh: Salamander Press, 1984), p. 17.

26. Seth Mydans, "In Philippine Town, Child Prostitution, Despite Protests, Is a Way of Life," *New York Times* (February 5, 1989), p. 3.

27. As quoted in David Revill, *The Roaring Silence: John Cage: A Life* (New York: Arcade, 1992), p. 110.

28. As quoted in Joan Peyser, *The New Music: The Sense Behind the Sound* (New York: Delacorte, 1970), p. 177.

29. Ibid., p. 178.

30. As quoted in Sam Hunter and John Jacobus, *Modern Art,* 3d ed. (New York: Abrams, 1992), p. 333.

31. Robert Hughes, *The Shock of the New: Art and the Century of Change,* rev. ed. (London: Thames & Hudson, 1993) p. 335.

32. As quoted in ibid., p. 334.

33. As quoted in ibid., p. 348.

34. As quoted in ibid., p. 356.

35. As quoted in ibid., p. 357 (emphasis in original).

36. As quoted in Hunter and Jacobus, op. cit., p. 313.

37. As quoted in Anderson, op. cit., p. 92.

38. As quoted in ibid., p. 93.

39. Mark Hertsgaard, *A Day in the Life: The Music and Artistry of the Beatles* (New York: Delacorte, 1995), p. 156.

40. As quoted in Julian Fast, *The Beatles: The Real Story* (New York: Berkeley Medallion, 1968), p. 163.

41. Ibid., p. 165.

42. Hertsgaard, op. cit., pp. 212–23.

43. Ibid., p. 196.

44. Ibid., p. 9.

45. Ibid, p. 8.

46. Tim Riley, *Tell Me Why: A Beatles Commentary* (New York: Knopf, 1988), p. 205.

47. Yoko Ono, *Grapefruit* (New York: Simon & Schuster, 1970). No pagination.

48. Joel Makower, *Woodstock: The Oral History* (New York: Doubleday, 1989), p. 27

Chapter Seven: The Narcissistic Culture

1. Tom Wolfe, "Sorry, But Your Soul Just Died," *Forbes ASAP* (December 2, 1996), p. 214.

2. As quoted in "Radical Revolutionary," *People Weekly* (December 12, 1994), p. 53.

3. As quoted in Marci McDonald, "From Yippies to Yuppies," *MacLean's* (April 7, 1986), p. 7d.

4. As quoted in Edward Lucie-Smith, *Race, Sex, and Gender in Contemporary Art* (New York: Abrams, 1994), p. 60.

5. As quoted in Robert Hughes, *The Shock of the New: Art and the Century of Change,* rev. ed. (London: Thames & Hudson, 1993), p. 407.

6. Ibid., p. 372.

7. Paul Richard, "Phallic Phrenzy," *The Washington Post* (December 4, 1993), p. F8.

8. As quoted in Hughes, op. cit., p. 417.

9. As quoted in Leonard Quart and Albert Auster, *American Film and Society Since 1945,* rev. ed. (New York: Praeger, 1991), p. 107.

10. Stephen King, *Danse Macabre* (New York: Everest House, 1981), p. 13.

11. As quoted in Norman Kagan, *The Cinema of Stanley Kubrick,* rev. ed. (New York: Continuum, 1989), p. 181.

12. As quoted in ibid., pp. 181–82.

13. As quoted in John Lydon, *Rotten: No Irish, No Blacks, No Dogs* (New York: St. Martin's, 1994), p. 75.

14. Martha Bayles, *A Hole in Our Soul: The Loss of Beauty and Meaning in American Popular Music* (New York: Free Press, 1994), p. 291.

15. As quoted in ibid., p. 297.

16. As quoted in ibid., p. 302.

17. As quoted in ibid., pp. 70–71.

18. Lydon, op. cit., p. 238.

19. Ibid., p. 239.

20. Ibid., p. 87.

21. Ibid., p. 19.

22. As quoted in Bayles, op. cit., p. 310.

23. Ibid., p. 337.

24. As quoted in Barney Hoskyns, *Mojo* (March 1997), p. 78.

25. As quoted in Jane and Michael Stern, *Encyclopedia of Pop Culture* (New York: Harper Perennial, 1992), p. 344.

26. As quoted in Bayles, op. cit., p. 334.

27. Stern, op. cit., p. 346.

28. John Fraser, "The Dalai Lama of Generation X," *Saturday Night* (March 1994), p. 9.

29. Nicole Arthur, "The Hole Truth: What Courtney Love Is and What She Isn't," *The Washington Post* (May 21, 1995), p. G7.

30. Claudia Springer, *Electronic Eros: Bodies and Desire in the Postindustrial Age* (Austin: Univ. of Texas Press, 1996), p. 19.

31. As quoted in Reed Karaim, "Technology and its Discontents," *Civilization* (May/June, 1994), p. 49.

32. Nat Hentoff, "Health Reform: You Bet Your Life," *The Washington Post* (May 14, 1994), p. A23.

33. As quoted in ibid.

34. As quoted in Brian D. Johnson, "Body Doubles," *MacLean's* (March 10, 1997), p. 57.

35. Richard Leiby, "Paranoia," *The Washington Post* (May 5, 1995), p. D1.

36. As quoted in William F. Powers, "Dressed to Kill?" *The Washington Post* (May 4, 1995), p. D8.

37. Christopher Lasch, *The Revolt of the Elites and the Betrayal of Democracy* (New York: Norton, 1995), p. 215.

38. Ibid.

39. Ibid., p. 222.

40. Ibid.

41. Ibid., p. 16.

42. As quoted in ibid., p. 227.

43. Ibid., p. 228.

AFTERWORD: INTO THE NEW MILLENNIUM

1. As quoted in Jon Krakauer, *Into the Wild* (New York: Doubleday, 1996), p. 187.

2. Michael Harrington, *The Politics at God's Funeral: The Spiritual Crisis of Western Civilization* (New York: Holt, Rinehart, Winston, 1983), p. 11.

INDEX

A

Abakanowicz, Magdalena, 234–235; *Backs*, 234–235
Abernathy, Ralph, 181
Absurdism, 150–151
Addams, Jane, 116
Aguilera, Christina, 249
Albee, Edward, 151; *Sandbox, The*, 151
Albers, Josef, 137
Aldaba-Lim, Estanfania, 207
Allen, Steve, 170–171
Allen, Woody, 140, 154; *Front, The*, 154; *Radio Days*, 140
Andre, Carl, 232; *Equivalent VIII*, 232
Antiwar movement, 191
Apollinaire, Guillaume, 74, 102
Armstrong, Louis, 123, 124–125; *Cornet Chop Suey*, 124; *Heebie Jeebies*, 124
Aronofsky, Darren, 109, 242; *Pi*, 109; *Requiem for a Dream*, 242
Arp, Jean, 90, 91; *Birds in an Aquarium*, 91
Auerbach, Frank, 235
Auster, Albert, 204
Autry, Gene, 128

B

Bach, Richard, 237; *Jonathan Livingston Seagull*, 237
Backstreet Boys, 249
Bacon, Francis, 16–17, 145–147, 235; *After Velasquez's Portrait of Pope Innocent X*, 146; *Painting*, 146–147; *Three Studies for Figures at the Base of a Crucifixion*, 16–17, 146
Baez, Joan, 134, 181, 197
Ball, Hugo, 88–89
Ball, Lucille, 158; *I Love Lucy*, 158
Bancroft, Anne, 167
Basquiat, Jean-Michel, 233
Baudelaire, Charles, 40, 55–56; *Flowers of Evil, The*, 55
Bauhaus style, 136–137

Bayles, Martha, 242, 247–248
Beach Boys, 216
Beat generation, 159–165
Beatles, the, 129, 161, 171, 199, 201, 210, 215–219, 220–221, 224; *All You Need Is Love*, 220; *Beatles for Sale*, 129; *Can't Buy Me Love*, 216; *Day in the Life, A*, 218; *Eleanor Rigby*, 217; *Hard Day's Night, A*, 216; *Helter Skelter*, 221; *Hey Jude*, 221; *I Am the Walrus*, 221; *I Want to Hold Your Hand*, 216–217; *Lucy in the Sky with Diamonds*, 218; *Magical Mystery Tour*, 220–221; *Norwegian Wood*, 216; *Please Please Me*, 216; *Rain*, 217; *Revolution*, 221; *Revolver*, 217; *Rubber Soul*, 216; *Sgt. Pepper's Lonely Hearts Club Band*, 201, 210, 217–219; *She Loves You*, 216; *Twist and Shout*, 216; *White Album, The*, 221
Beatty, Warren, 203–204; *Bonnie and Clyde*, 203–204
Bebop, 125–126
Bechet, Sidney, 124
Beckett, Samuel, 115; *Waiting for Godot*, 115
Beckmann, Max, 92; *Night*, 92
Beethoven, Luwig van, 25–26; *Ninth Symphony*, 26
Behaviorism, 116–117
Bellmer, Hans, 104; *Doll, The*, 104
Benjamin, Frithjof, 188
Berg, Alban, 224
Berle, Milton, 170
Bernstein, Leonard, 171
Berry, Chuck, 129, 167
Bertolucci, Bernardo, 268; *Last Emperor, The*, 268; *Little Buddha*, 268; *Sheltering Sky, The*, 268
Beuys, Joseph, 214, 229–231; *Coyote: I Like America and America Likes Me*, 230
Blake, J. F., 180
Blake, Peter, 210, 218; *Sgt. Pepper's Lonely Hearts Club Band*, 210, 218
Blake, William, 29–32, 67–68, 160; *All Religions Are One*, 29; *America*, 30; *Body of Abel Found by Adam and Eve, The*, 31; *Everlasting Gospel, The*, 31; *French Revolution,*

The, 30; *Jerusalem*, 30–31; *Marriage of Heaven and Hell, The*, 31–32; *Songs of Experience*, 29; *Songs of Innocence*, 29; *Visions of the Daughters of Albion*, 30

Blériot, Louis, 75

Boas, Franz, 121

Boccioni, Umberto, 81; *City Rises, The*, 81; *Unique Forms of Continuity in Space*, 81

Bowie, David, 260

Boy George, 260

Branagh, Kenneth, 34

Brando, Marlon, 167, 181; *On the Waterfront*, 155

Breton, André, 44, 101–102

Brooks, Richard, 167; *Blackboard Jungle*, 167

Brooks, Van Wyck, 111

Brown, Ford Madox, 50; *Work*, 50

Bruce, Donald, 264

Bruce, Lenny, 218

Brummel, Beau, 29

Buñuel, Luis, 105–107; *L'Age d'Or*, 105, 106–107; *Un Chien Andalou*, 105–106

Burgess, Anthony, 105, 239–240; *Clockwork Orange, A*, 105, 239–240

Burroughs, William, 45, 159; *Naked Lunch*, 45

Burstyn, Ellen, 167

Burton, Tim, 95–96; *Batman*, 95; *Batman Returns*, 95–96; *Ed Wood*, 95; *Edward Scissorhands*, 95

Bush, George W., 239

Byron, Lord George Gordon, 26–29, 34, 37; *Cain*, 28; *Don Juan*, 26; *Giaour*, 34; *Prisoner of Chillon, The*, 34

C

Cage, John, 137, 208–210, 218–219, 221, 224, 243; *4'33*, 209; *Imaginary Landscape No. 4*, 209; *Third Construction*, 208–210

Calas, Jean, 18

Calley, William L., 191

Capra, Frank, 95; *It's a Wonderful Life*, 95

Carey, Mariah, 249

Carlisle, Cliff, 128

Carmichael, Stokely, 187

Carnegie, Andrew, 49

Carter, Jimmy, 229, 236

Cassady, Neal, 219

Castaneda, Carlos, 238; *Journey to Ixtlan*, 238

Celan, Paul, 231; *Death Fugue*, 231

Cézanne, Paul, 53, 54–55; *Great Bathers, The*, 77; *Mont Ste-Victoire*, 55

Chambers, Whitaker, 154

Chapman, Mark David, 166

Chayefsky, Paddy, 254; *Network*, 254

Chicago, Judy, 233–234; *Dinner Party, The*, 233–234

Cimino, Michael, 191; *Deer Hunter, The*, 191

Clift, Montgomery, 167

Clinton, Bill, 140, 225, 229, 274

Clurman, Harold, 166

Cobain, Kurt, 246–248, 260

Cold war, the, 151–157, 183

Coleridge, Samuel Taylor, 37

Comfort, Alex, 238; *Joy of Sex, The*, 238

Comic books, 252–254

Communism, 50–53, 131–135, 155–157

Comstock, Anthony, 119

Conrad, Joseph, 205–207; *Heart of Darkness*, 205–207

Constructivism, 135

Cooper, Alice, 243

Coppola, Francis Ford, 69, 205–207; *Apocalypse Now*, 69, 205–207

Costello, Elvis, 246

Country music, 128–129

Coupland, Douglas, 255; *Generation X: Tales of an Accelerated Culture*, 255

Courbet, Gustave, 38–40; *Burial at Ornans, A*, 39–40; *Origin of the World, The*, 40, 78; *Sleepers, The*, 40

Cox, Bill, 128

Cox, Harvey, 175, 176

Crichton, Michael, 59; *Jurassic Park*, 59

Cronenberg, David, 45

Crudup, Arthur, 129, 170

Crumb, Robert, 252–253

Cubism, 76–77, 79–80, 125

D

Dadaism, 88–91, 93, 221, 248

Dalí, Salvador, 103; *Lugubrious Game*, 103; *Metamorphosis of Narcissus*, 103

Dalton, David, 169; *James Dean: The Mutant King*, 169

Darwin, Charles, 47–50, 58; *Descent of Man*, 48; *Journal of Researches*, 47–48; *Origin of Species, The*, 48, 52, 59

David, Jacques-Louis, 21–23, 39; *Death of Marat, The*, 22; *Oath of the Horatii*, 21–22, 39; *Oath of the Tennis Court, The*, 22

Davies, Idris, 135

Davis, Stuart, 125; *Hot Still-Scape for Six colors—7th Avenue Style*, 125

Day, Doris, 173

de Chirico, Giorgio, 102–103; *Nostalgia of the Infinite, The*, 102–103, 108

de Haan, Jacob Meyer, 57

de Kooning, Willem, 172–173; *Monroe*, 172–173; *Woman and Bicycle*, 172; *Woman III*, 173; *Woman on a Sign*, 173; *Woman, Sag Harbor*, 173; *Women*, 172

de Sade, Donatien Alphonse François, 103–105; *Juliette*, 104, 105; *Justine*, 104

314

Dean, James, 167, 168–170, 172; *East of Eden*, 168; *Giant*, 168; *Rebel Without a Cause*, 168–169

Delaunay, Robert, 75

DeMille, Cecil B., 107, 268; *King of Kings, The*, 268; *Ten Commandments, The*, 107

DeNiro, Robert, 34, 167

Dennis, Sandy, 167

Depp, Johnny, 164

Descartes, René, 17–18

Dewey, John, 116; *Quest for Certainty, The*, 116

Diabolism, 57

DiMaggio, Joe, 172

Disney, Walt, 107; *Pinocchio*, 107; *Snow White and the Seven Dwarfs*, 107

Dix, Otto, 93; *Cardplaying War-Cripples*, 93

Dodge, Mable, 84

Doors, the, 66–69

Dorsey, Tommy, 126

Dostoyevski, Fyodor, 92

Douglas, Michael, 267; *Falling Down*, 267

Dove, Arthur, 84

Duchamp, Marcel, 82–83, 208–210; *In Advance of the Broken Arm*, 83; *Bride Stripped Bare by Her Bachelors, Even (The Large Glass)*, 82–83; *Comb*, 83; *Fountain*, 83; *Given: 1. The Waterfall, 2. The Illuminating Gas*, 83; *Nude Descending a Staircase No. 2*, 82, 84; *Readymades*, 209

Dunaway, Faye, 203–204; *Bonnie and Clyde*, 203–204

Duvall, Robert, 167; *Apocalypse Now*, 206

Dyer, Wayne W., 237; *Pulling Your Own Strings*, 237; *Sky's the Limit, The*, 237; *Your Erroneous Zones*, 237

Dylan, Bob, 44, 68, 126, 134, 160, 161, 162, 164, 181, 197–202, 215, 218, 229; *All Along the Watchtower*, 201; *Blonde on Blonde*, 200; *Blood on the Tracks*, 201; *Blowing' in the Wind*, 197; *Bringing It All Back Home*, 198, 199; *Don't Think Twice, It's Alright*, 197, 198; *Before the Flood*, 201; *Freewheelin' Bob Dylan, The*, 198; *Hard Rain's A-Gonna Fall, A*, 198; *Highway 61 Revisited*, 200; *Idiot Wind*, 201; *Infidels*, 202; *It's Alright, Ma (I'm Only Bleeding)*, 199; *John Wesley Harding*, 201; *Like a Rolling Stone*, 200; *Man of Peace*, 202; *Pawn in the Game, A*, 197; *Renaldo and Clara*, 198, 201; *Shelter from the Storm*, 201; *Shot of Love*, 202; *Slow Train Coming*, 202; *Subterranean Homesick Blues*, 198; *Time Out of Mind*, 202; *Times They Are A-Changin', The*, 197–199; *Trouble*, 202; *When He Returns*, 202; *You're Gonna Make Me Lonesome When You Go*, 199

E

Eastwood, Clint: *Bird*, 126

Einstein, Albert, 76, 117–118

Eisenhower, Dwight, 180–181

Eliot, T. S., 109–112, 113, 200, 236; *Hollow Men, The*, 111; *Waste Land, The*, 109–110, 200

Ellington, Duke, 123, 124

Ellis, Havelock, 98

Eminem, 249; *Marshall Mathers LP, The*, 249

Engels, Friedrich, 52; *Communist Manifesto*, 52

Ennis, Garth, 252; *Preacher, The*, 252

Epstein, Brian, 220

Epstein, Jacob, 81–82; *Rock Drill, The*, 81–82

Evers, Medgar, 197

Evolutionism, 47–50, 58–59

Existentialism, 149–151

Expressionism, 91–99

F

Facism, 131–135, 138

Falkenburg, Violet, 263

Farrakhan, Louis, 249

Faubus, Orval, 180

Fauve movement, 75–76

Feminism, 176–178, 233–234, 238–240

Ferlinghetti, Lawrence, 161

Ferrara, Abel, 240–241; *Bad Lieutenant*, 240–241

Ferris, Paul, 100; *Dr. Freud*, 100

Fincher, David, 114, 241, 255–256; *Fight Club*, 114, 241, 255–256

Finney, Jack, 156, 157; *Invasion of the Body Snatchers*, 155–157

Fischl, Eric, 41, 235; *Bad Boy*, 41, 235

Fitzgerald, F. Scott, 129–130; *Tender Is the Night*, 130; *This Side of Paradise*, 129–130

Fluxus, 221–224, 248

Franco, Francisco, 133

Fraser, John, 255

Freud, Lucian, 41, 235; *Naked Portrait with Reflection*, 41, 235

Freud, Sigmund, 60, 75, 97–100, 113–114; *International Journal of Psycho-Analysis*, 97; *Interpretation of Dreams, The*, 103

Friedan, Betty, 177–178; *Feminine Mystique, The*, 177; *Fountain of Age, The*, 178; *Second Stage, The*, 178

Friedkin, William, 109, 268; *Exorcist, The*, 109, 268

Fuche, Klaus, 154

Fuchs, Fred, 164–165

Fulbright, William, 192

Fuller, R. Buckminster, 137

Futurism, 80–81, 85–86

G

Gallo, Vincent, 109; *Buffalo 66*, 109

Garcia, Jerry, 219–220

Garfield, John, 167

Garner, James, 181

Gauguin, Paul, 55, 56–58; *Be in Love and You Will Be Happy*, 57; *Nirvana*, 57; *Where Do We Come From? What Are We? Where Are We Going?*, 57–58, 76

Gifford, Barry, 164; *Jack's Book*, 164

Ginsberg, Allen, 31, 44, 126, 160–162, 164, 193, 198, 200, 219; *Fall of America, The*, 161; *Howl*, 160–161, 200

Gleason, Jackie, 158; *Honeymooners, The*, 158

Godard, Jean-Luc, 203

Goebbels, Joseph, 95

Goethe, John Wolfgang von, 29; *Faust*, 29

Goodman, Benny, 126

Gould, Stephen Jay, 59

Goya y Lucientes, Francisco, 35–36; *Adoration of the Name of God*, 36; *Los Caprichos*, 35–36; *Procession of Flagellants*, 36; *Third of May, 1808, at Madrid: The Shootings on Principe Pio Mountain, The*, 36; *Tribunal of the Inquisition, A*, 36

Graham, Billy, 143

Grant, Lee, 167

Grateful Dead, 219–220

Griffith, D. W., 268; *Intolerance*, 268

Gropius, Walter, 136–137

Grossman, Albert, 197

Grosz, George, 93; *Republican Automatons*, 93

Grunge, 247

Guevara, Che, 188

Guston, Philip, 233, 235; *Painting, Smoking, Eating*, 235; *Pit*, 235; *Street, The*, 235

Guthrie, Woody, 134, 197

H

Haley, Alex, 238; *Roots*, 238

Haley, Bill, 127–128, 167; *(We're Gonna) Rock Around the Clock*, 127, 167

Hamilton, Richard, 210; *Just What Is It That Makes Today's Homes So Different, So Appealing?*, 210

Hansen, Beck, 248; *Midnite Vultures*, 248; *Mutations*, 248; *Odelay*, 248

Happenings, 214–215

Haring, Keith, 229, 233; *Silence-Death*, 229

Harrington, Michael, 274

Harris, Eric, 255

Harris, Julie, 167

Harris, Thomas, 238; *I'm O.K., You're O.K.*, 238

Harrison, George, 216; *see also* Beatles, the; *American Psycho*, 242; *Think For Yourself*, 216

Harron, Mary, 151, 242; *American Psycho*, 151

Hausmann, Raoul, 93; *Spirit of Our Time, The*, 93

Hawke, Ethan, 164; *Reality Bites*, 164

Hawks, Howard, 203

Hayden, Tom, 185–186; *Port Huron Statement, The*, 185–186

Hearst, William Randolph, 141

Heartfield, John, 93; *Adolf Hitler as Superman*, 93

Hefner, Hugh, 41, 173–176; *Playboy*, 41, 173–176

Hegel, Georg Wilhelm Freidrich, 50–51

Hell, Richard, 242–243

Helms, Jesse, 89

Hemingway, Ernest, 79, 85, 130, 139–140; *Farewell to Arms, A*, 139–140

Hendrix, Jimi, 222

Hennings, Emmy, 88–89

Hentoff, Nat, 263

Hertsgaard, Mark, 216

Himmelfarb, Gertrude, 271; *Re-Moralization of Society, The*, 271

Hippies, 219–221

Hiss, Alger, 154

Hitchcock, Alfred, 95, 107–108, 203; *Birds, The*, 107, 108; *Psycho*, 108–109, 203; *Spellbound*, 107–108; *Vertigo*, 108

Hite, Shere, 238; *Hite Report, The*, 238

Hitler, Adolph, 58–59, 61, 100, 134, 137–138; *Mein Kampf*, 58, 61

Hobbes, Thomas, 17, 19

Hobsbawm, Eric, 140; *Age of Extremes, The*, 140

Hockney, David, 210, 235

Hoffman, Abbie, 193–194, 224

Hoffman, Dustin, 155, 260; *Graduate, The*, 155, 204; *Midnight Cowboy*, 155; *Tootsie*, 260

Holland, Vyvyan, 33

Holly, Buddy, 128, 129, 167

Holmes, John Clellon, 159; *Go*, 159

Hopper, Dennis, 205; *Easy Rider*, 205

Hopper, Edward, 144; *Nighthawks*, 144

Houseman, John, 141; *Macbeth*, 141

Howe, Neil, 274; *Fourth Turning, The*, 274

Huelsenbeck, Richard, 89

Hughes, Robert, 138, 173, 208, 211, 232; *Shock of the New, The*, 138, 208

Hugo, Victor, 43

Hume, David, 17

Huncke, Herbert, 159

Hunter, Evan, 167; *Blackboard Jungle*, 127, 167

Huston, John, 95

Huxley, Aldous, 67, 97, 218, 264; *Brave New World*, 264; *Doors of Perception, The*, 67–68

Hynde, Chrissy, 244

I

Iacocca, Lee, 237

Impressionism, 53–54

Irvin, John, 205; *Hamburger Hill*, 205

J

J, 238; *Sensuous Man, The*, 238; *Sensuous Woman, The*, 238
Jackson, Michael, 250, 260; *Thriller*, 250
Jagger, Mick, 260
James, Harry, 126
James, William, 116
Janowitz, Hans, 94; *Cabinet of Dr. Caligari, The*, 93–95
Jazz age, the, 122–125
Jenkins, Peter, 237; *Walk Across America*, 237
John, Elton, 260
Johns, Barbara, 178
Johns, Jasper, 212; *Target with Plaster Casts*, 212; *Three Flags*, 212
Johnson, Lyndon, 189–190
Johnson, Philip, 235
Johnson, Robert, 127
Jolson, Al, 210; *Jazz Singer, The*, 210
Jones, Allen, 78, 105, 210; *Table Sculpture*, 78, 105
Jones, David, 114; *Trial, The*, 114
Jones, Ernest, 97, 98
Jones, James, 144; *From Here to Eternity*, 144
Jordan, Louis, 127; *Is You Is or Is You Ain't My Baby*, 127
Jordan, Neil, 233; *Crying Game, The*, 233
Joyce, James, 88, 111
Jung, Carl, 100–101, 144

K

Kafka, Franz, 113–115, 252; *Dearest Father*, 113; *Face in the Crowd, A*, 254; *Judgement, The*, 113; *Metamorphosis, The*, 114, 252; *Trial, The*, 114
Kant, Immanuel, 24–25
Kaprow, Allen, 214; *Calling*, 214
Kasdan, Lawrence, 227; *Big Chill, The*, 227–229
Kassorla, Irene, 238; *Nice Girls Do*, 238
Kaye, Tony, 266; *American History X*, 266
Kazan, Elia, 155, 166, 254; *On the Waterfront*, 155
Keats, John, 37
Keillor, Garrison, 237; *Lake Wobegon Days*, 237
Kennedy, John F., 181, 182–183, 188, 199
Kennedy, Robert, 181, 195
Kerouac, Jack, 44, 126, 149, 159, 160, 162–165, 175, 198; *Mexico City Blues*, 198; *On the Road*, 162–164; *Vanity of Duluoz: An Adventurous Education 1935–1946*, 164
Kesey, Kenneth, 219
Kevorkian, Jack, 262
Keynes, John Maynard, 73, 85, 131
Kiefer, Anselm, 231; *Sulamith*, 231
Kienholz, Edward, 213–214; *Future as an Afterthought, The*, 213–214; *State Hospital*, 213
Kimbrell, Andrew, 265; *Human Body Shop, The*, 265
King, Martin Luther, Jr., 176, 179–182, 193, 195

King, Stephen, 34–35, 237; *Danse Macabre*, 237; *Dark Half, The*, 101
Kinsey, Alfred, 143; *Modernization of Sex, The*, 143; *Sexual Behavior in the Human Female*, 143; *Sexual Behavior in the Human Male*, 143
Kitaj, R. B., 235
Klebold, Dylan, 255
Klein, Yves, 214–215; *Monotone Symphony*, 214
Knight, Shirley, 167
Koklova, Olga, 78
Kondratieu, N. D., 131
Koons, Jeff, 233; *Saint John the Baptist*, 233
Kooper, Al, 200
Koresh, David, 267
Kovic, Ron, 205
Kubrick, Stanley, 105, 153–154, 205, 239–240; *Clockwork Orange, A*, 105, 239–240; *Dr. Strangelove*, 153–154; *Full Metal Jacket*, 205
Kuhn, Walter, 83–84

L

Lamarck, Jean, 98
Lang, Fritz, 95; *Fury*, 95; *M*, 95; *Metropolis*, 95
Lasch, Christopher, 270–272
Leary, Timothy, 160, 219
Lenin, Vladimir Ilich, 86, 88
Lennon, John, 161–162, 166, 171, 185, 215–219, 220–221, 223–224; *see also* Beatles, the; *Daily Howl*, 162; *Two Virgins*, 223–224
Lennox, Annie, 260
Levison, Stanley, 182
Lewis, Jerry Lee, 129
Lewis, Robert, 166
Lichtenstein, Roy, 212–213; *Artist's Studio: The Dance, The*, 213; *Drowning Girl*, 213
Little Richard, 260
Locke, John, 17
Louis XVI, King, 21
Love, Courtney, 260
Love, Daddy John, 128
Lucas, George, 60; *Phantom Menace, The*, 60; *Star Wars*, 60, 101
Luce, Claire Booth, 121
Lumet, Sidney, 254; *Network*, 254
Lydon, John, 44, 243, 246
Lyell, Charles, 47; Importance of Being Earnest, The, 47
Lynch, David, 109, 164; *Blue Velvet*, 109; *Elephant Man, The*, 109; *Eraserhead*, 109; *Lost Highway*, 109; *Twin Peaks*, 109; *Twin Peaks: Fire Walk with Me*, 109; *Wild at Heart*, 109, 164

M

Maar, Dora, 78
MacFarlane, Todd, 253; *Spawn*, 253
Madonna, 172, 249–250, 260; *Sex*, 250
Magritte, Rene, 104, 212; *Rape, The*, 104
Mailer, Norman, 143–144, 175, 194; *Armies of the Night*, 194; *Naked and the Dead, The*, 143–144
Malcolm X, 187
Mallarmé, Stéphane, 55; *Afternoon of a Faun, The*, 56
Malthus, Thomas, 48–49; *Essay on the Principle of Population as It Affects the Future Improvement of Society, An*, 48–49
Mander, Jerry, 262; *In the Absence of the Sacred*, 262
Manet, Edouard, 40, 115–116; *Luncheon on the Grass*, 40; *Olympia*, 115–116
Mann, Thomas, 65, 97; *Doktor Faustus*, 65
Manson, Charles, 220–221
Manson, Marilyn, 249, 260
Mapplethorpe, Robert, 78–79, 233; *1977 X Portfolio, Jim and Tom, Sausalito*, 89; *Black Males*, 78–79; *Man in Polyester Suit*, 78–79; *Perfect Moment, The*, 89; *Phillip Prideau*, 79
Marat, Jean-Paul, 22
Marc, Franz, 92; *Fate of Animals, The*, 92
Marcuse, Herbert, 187–188; *Eros and Society*, 188; *One-Dimensional Man, The*, 188
Marinetti, Filippo Tommaso, 80–81, 85
Martin, George, 218–219
Marx, Karl, 50–53, 74, 133; *Communist Manifesto*, 52; *Das Kapital*, 51, 52
Matisse, Henri, 75–76; *Green Stripe, The*, 76; *Jazz*, 125; *Joy of Life*, 76
Mayer, Carl, 94; *Cabinet of Dr. Caligari, The*, 93–95
McCarthy, Joseph R., 134, 154–157, 158
McCartney, Paul, 215–219, 220–221, 246; *see also* Beatles, the
McClure, Michael, 160–161
McCormick, Katharine Dexter, 121
McDowell, Malcolm, 239–240; *Clockwork Orange, A*, 239–240
McLaren, Malcolm, 244–245
McLuhan, Marshall, 205, 214
McVeigh, Timothy, 255
Mead, Margaret, 121–122, 143; *Coming of Age in Samoa*, 121
Mezner, Ralph, 160
Miller, Henry, 44–45, 175, 236; *Tropic of Cancer*, 44–45
Miller, Tim, 89; *My Queer Body*, 89
Mills, C. Wright, 187
Modernism, 137–139, 231–232
Moholy-Nagy, László, 137
Mola, Emilio, 133
Monet, Claude, 53; *Haystack at Sunset Near Giverny*, 53
Monroe, Bill, 129, 170
Monroe, Marilyn, 172–173; *Gentlemen Prefer Blondes*, 173; *Seven Year Itch, The*, 172
Montgomery, Ruth, 238; *World Beyond, A*, 238
Moreas, Jean, 55; *Symbolist Manifesto*, 55
Moreau, Gustave, 55; *Apparition, The*, 55
Morrison, Jim, 66–69, 242; *End, The*, 68–69
Morrison, Toni, 238
Motherwell, Robert, 137
Mount, Anson, 176
Munch, Edvard, 56, 172; *Scream, The*, 56, 92; *Vampire*, 172
Murnau, F. W., 96; *Nosferatu*, 96
Murrow, Edward R., 154–155, 158; *See it Now*, 154–155
Murry, John Middleton, 111
Mussolini, Benito, 58, 85, 138

N

'N Sync, 249
Nagy, Imre, 151–152
Napolean, 29
Narcissism, 236–238
New Wave, 203–205, 246–248
Newton, Isaac, 118
Nichols, Mike, 204; *Graduate, The*, 204
Nicholson, Jack, 167, 205; *Easy Rider*, 205
Nietzche, Friedrich, 47, 59–60, 61–69; *Beyond Good and Evil*, 66; *Birth of Tragedy*, 68; *Case of Wagner, The*, 63; *Geneaology of Morals, The*, 66; *Thus Spake Zarathustra*, 63–64
Nightmare on Elm Street, A, 109
Nijinsky, Vaslav, 80
Nirvana, 246–248, 249, 260; *Nevermind*, 246–247
Nixon, Richard, 181, 191, 196
Novak, Kim, 108

O

Ochs, Phil, 134
O'Keefe, Georgia, 84
Oldenburg, Claes, 213; *Clothespin*, 213; *Two Cheeseburgers, with Everything (Dual Hamburgers)*, 213
Ono, Yoko, 223–224; *Cut Piece*, 223; *Half-Wind*, 223; *Two Virgins*, 223–224
Ortega y Gasset, José, 131; *Dehumanization of Art*, 131; *Revolt of the Masses, The*, 131
Orwell, George, 152; *Animal Farm*, 152; *Nineteen Eighty-Four*, 152
Oswald, Lee Harvey, 183, 199

P

Page, Geraldine, 167
Palahniuk, Chuck: *Fight Club*, 114, 241, 255–256
Parker, Charlie "Bird", 126
Parks, Rosa, 179–180

Parsons, Estelle, 167
Pasolini, Pier Paolo, 268; *Gospel According to St. Matthew, The*, 268
Patton, Charlie, 127
Paul, Alice, 238
Paxton, Tom, 134
Paytress, Mark, 260; *Rise and Fall of Ziggy Stardust and the Spiders From Mars, The*, 260
Pearl Jam, 248–249
Pearlstein, Philip, 41, 235; *Female Nude on a Platform Rocker*, 41, 235
Peckinpah, Sam, 204–205; *Wild Bunch, The*, 205
Penn, Arthur, 204; *Bonnie and Clyde*, 204; *Chase, The*, 204; *Left-Handed Gun, The*, 204; *Little Big Man*, 204
Peret, Benjamin, 102
Perkins, Carl, 129
Peters, Thomas, 237; *In Search of Excellence*, 237
Peyser, Joan, 209; *New Music, The*, 209
Phillips, Sam, 170
Picabia, Francis, 82; *La Fille Nee Sans Mere*, 82
Picasso, Pablo, 41, 76–79, 132–133, 172, 175; *Girl Before a Mirror*, 172; *Glass of Absinthe*, 79; *Guernica*, 132–133; *Head of a Woman*, 78, 79; *Head on a Red Background*, 78; *Kiss, The*, 78; *Les Demoiselles d'Avignon*, 41, 77–78; *Peeing Woman, The*, 78; *Seated Bather*, 78; *Weeping Woman, The*, 78
Pincus, Gregory Goodwin, 121
Pink Floyd, 250; *Wall, The*, 250
Poe, Edgar Allen, 218
Pollack, Jackson, 144–145; *Autumn Rhythm*, 144; *Blue Poles*, 145
Pommer, Eric, 94; *Cabinet of Dr. Caligari, The*, 93–95
Pop Art, 210–214
Pop, Iggy, 242, 244
Postmodernism, 235–236
Potter, Paul, 192
Pramatism, 116–117
Presley, Elvis, 126, 128, 129, 167, 169–172; *Heartbreak Hotel*, 170; *It's All Right, Mama*, 170
Prince, 249
Prisoner, The, 103
Punk, 242–245

Q

Quart, Leonard, 204

R

Racism, 59
Rap, 248–249
Rauschenberg, Robert, 137, 211–212; *Bed*, 211; *Monogram*, 211
Ray, Man, 104; *Monument to D.A.F. de Sade*, 104

Reagan, Ronald, 229, 239
Reagon, Bernice Johnson, 196
Reagon, Cordell, 196
Realism, 38–41
Redford, Robert, 159; *Quiz Show*, 159
Reed, Lou, 242, 260
Relativism, 117–118
Rembrandt: *see* van Rijn, Rembrandt
Renoir, Auguste, 53; *Le Moulin de la Galette*, 53
Reuben, David, 238; *Everything You Always Wanted to Know About Sex but Were Afraid to Ask*, 238
Rexroth, Kenneth, 160
Rhythm and Blues, 126–127
Rieff, Philip, 272
Rimbaud, Arthur, 42–44, 160, 198–199; *Drunks*, 42; *Savior Bumped Upon His Heavy Butt, The*, 42; *Season in Hell, A*, 43
Ringer, Robert J., 237; *Looking Out for Number One*, 237; *Restoring the American Dream*, 237; *Winning Through Intimidation*, 237
Robespierre, François-Maximilien-Joseph de, 23
Rock music, 127–128, 167
Rockefeller, J. D., 49
Rodes, Zandra, 242
Rodgers, Jimmie, 128–129
Rolling Stones, the, 161, 222–223
Romanticism, 24–38, 111
Roosevelt, Franklin D., 133, 139, 140
Roosevelt, Teddy, 84
Rosemblum, Robert, 211–212
Rosenquist, James, 213; *F–111, The*, 213
Rothko, Mark, 144, 145; *Centre Triptych*, 145; *Ochre and Red on Red*, 145
Rotten, Johnny, 44, 244–245
Rousseau, Jean-Jacques, 17, 19–21
Rubin, Jerry, 193–194, 219, 229
Russell, Bertrand, 29; *History of Western Philosophy*, 29

S

Salinger, J. D., 165–166; *Catcher in the Rye, The*, 165–166
Salinger, Margaret A., 166; *Dream Catcher*, 166
Sandy, Edwina, 234; *Christa*, 234
Sanger, Margaret, 118–121, 143
Sartre, Jean-Paul, 115, 150; *Myth of Sisyphus, The*, 150; *Nausea*, 115, 150
Savage, Jon, 194
Schamberg, Morton, 16; *God*, 16
Schiller, Johann, 26
Schlafly, Phyllis, 238–239
Schneck, Max, 96
Schopenhauer, Arthur, 59–61
Schwitters, Kurt, 90–91; *Cathedral of Erotic Misery*, 90–91

Scorsese, Martin, 268; *Kundun*, 268; *Last Temptation of Christ, The*, 268

Scott, Ridley, 35, 70–71; *Alien*, 35, 70; *Blade Runner*, 70–71; *Gladiator*, 70

Seeger, Pete, 134–135, 196–197

Seligmann, Kurt, 104; *Ultra-Furniture*, 104

Sellers, Peter, 153

Serling, Rod, 158–159; *Twilight Zone, The*, 103, 158–159

Serrano, Andre: *Piss Christ*, 234

Seurat, Georges, 54, 212; *Bathers*, 54; *Sunday Afternoon on the Island of La Grande Jatte, A*, 54

Severini, Gino, 85; *Armored Train*, 85

Sex Pistols, the, 44

Shaw, George Bernard, 49, 218

Sheen, Martin, 206; *Apocalypse Now*, 206

Shelley, Mary Wollstonecraft, 34; *Frankenstein, or the Modern Prometheus*, 34, 81

Shelley, Percy Bysshe, 28, 37

Shelton, Robert, 199–200

Sherman, Cindy, 105, 233; *Untitled (No. 264-Woman with Mask)*, 105, 233

Siegel, Don, 156–157

Sinatra, Frank, 126

Skinner, B. F., 117

Slee, J. Noah, 120

Smith, Kevin, 253; *Chasing Amy*, 253; *Clerks*, 253

Smith, Patti, 44

Snow, Hank, 128

Socialism, 50–53, 131 135

Sourire, Sister, 216

Southey, Robert, 37

Spears, Britney, 249

Spectorsky, August Comte, 175; *Exurbanites, The*, 175

Speer, Albert, 137–138

Spencer, Herbert, 47

Spice Girls, 249

Spiegelman, Art, 252; *Maus*, 252

Spielberg, Steven, 59; *Jurassic Park*, 59

Spock, Benjamin, 193

Springer, Claudia, 261; *Electronic Eros*, 261

Sprinkle, Annie, 89; *Post-Porn Modernist*, 89

Spungen, Nancy, 245

Stalin, Joseph, 131, 132, 134

Stanley, August Owsley, III, 220

Stanley, Kim, 167

Stein, Gertrude, 77, 85, 130

Steinbeck, John, 175

Steinem, Gloria, 178

Stella, Frank, 229

Stern, Jane, 250–251

Stern, Michael, 250–251

Stewart, James, 108

Stieglitz, Alfred, 84

Stone, Oliver, 68, 183, 205, 242; *Born on the Fourth of July*, 205; *Doors, The*, 68, 242; *JFK*, 183; *Natural Born Killers*, 109, 151; *Platoon*, 205; *U Turn*, 109; *U-Turn*, 241

Stone, Sharon, 172

Stracynski, J. Michael, 253–254; *Babylon 5*, 254; *Daredevil*, 254; *Rising Stars*, 254

Strasberg, Lee, 166–167

Strauss, William, 274; *Fourth Turning, The*, 274

Stravinsky, Igor, 79–80; *Firebird, The*, 79–80; *Rite of Spring*, 80

Student protests, 188–194

Sullivan, Ed, 167, 171, 215

Surrealism, 101–109

Symbolism, 55–56

T

Talese, Gay, 238; *Thy Neighbor's Wife*, 238

Tarantino, Quentin, 151, 164, 241; *Pulp Fiction*, 151, 164; *Reservoir Dogs*, 241

Tatlin, Vladimir, 135; *Model for the Monument to the Third International*, 135

Taylor, Kenneth, 237; *Living Bible, The*, 237

Television, 157–159, 251, 254–255

Temptations, 216

Thomson, Virgil, 125

Titian, 115; *Venus of Urbino*, 115

Townshend, Pete, 246

Tracy, Spencer, 95

Travel, Ronald, 151

Trotsky, Leon, 102

Truffaut, Francois, 203

Trump, Donald, 237

Tse-tung, Mao, 86

Tubb, Ernest, 128

Turner, Joseph, 50; *Rain, Stem, Speed*, 50

Turner, Steve, 165; *Angelheaded Hipster*, 165

Tzara, Tristan, 89, 91

U

U2, 247

V

Van Doren, Charles, 159; *Twenty-One*, 159

van Gogh, Vincent, 55

van Rijn, Rembrandt, 16; *Adoration of the Shepherds*, 16; *Landscape With an Obelisk*, 208

Verhaeren, Emile, 80

Verlaine, Paul, 43, 55–56

Vicious, Sid, 44, 245

Vining, Margaret, 266

Voltaire, François, 17, 18–19, 21, 57

von Hoddis, Jakob, 92

320

W

Wachowski, Andy, 253; *Bound*, 253; *Matrix, The*, 253
Wachowski, Larry, 253; *Bound*, 253; *Matrix, The*, 253
Wagner, Richard, 60, 61–63; *Parsifal*, 63; *Ring of the Nibelungen*, 61; *Tristan und Isolde*, 62–63
Walker, Alice, 238; *Color Purple, The*, 238
Wallace, Alfred Russel, 48
Walpole, Horace, 34; *Castle of Otranto, The*, 34
Warhol, Andy, 109, 151, 212, 242, 248; *Blow Job*, 109; *Haircut*, 109; *Sleep*, 109; *Two Hundred Campbell's Soup Cans*, 212
Waterman, Robert, 237; *In Search of Excellence*, 237
Watson, James, 265
Watson, John, 116–117
Wayne, John, 167, 204–205; *Green Berets, The*, 204
Weaver, Sigourney, 35
Wedekind, Frand, 89
Welles, Orson, 95, 141–143, 205; *Citizen Kane*, 141–143; *Macbeth*, 141; *Trial, The*, 114; *War of the Worlds*, 141
Wells, H. G., 141, 207; *War of the Worlds*, 141
West, Mae, 172, 218
Westwood, Vivienne, 245
Wexler, Haskell, 205, 254; *Medium Cool*, 205, 254
Whitman, Walt, 92
Wilde, Oscar, 32–33; *Decay of Living, The*, 32; *Importance of Being Earnest, The*, 32; *Picture of Dorian Gray, The*, 32

Williams, Hank, 128
Williams, William Carlos, 111
Wilson, Edmund, 111
Wilson, Sloan, 144; *Man in the Gray Flannel Suit, The*, 144
Wilson, Tom, 243
Wilson, Woodrow, 86
Winkler, Irwin, 154; *Guilty by Suspicion*, 154
Winters, Shelley, 167
Wojnarowicz, David, 234; *Untitled*, 234
Wolfe, Tom, 227
Women's movement: . *see* Feminism
Wordsworth, William, 37

Y

Yasgur, Max, 224
Yeats, William Butler, 31
Yogi, Maharishi Mahesh, 221
Young, La Monte, 221; *Piano Piece for David Tudor #1*, 221
Young, Marilyn, 191

Z

Zappa, Frank, 243; *Freak Out!*, 243; *We're Only In It For The Money*, 243
Zemeckis, Roger, 269–270; *Forrest Gump*, 269–270